INTERNATIONAL ORGANIZATIONS

A GUIDE TO INFORMATION SOURCES

Volume 1 in the International Relations Information Guide Series

Alexine L. Atherton

*Associate Professor of Political Science
Lincoln University*

Gale Research Company
Book Tower, Detroit, Michigan 48226

Library of Congress Cataloging in Publication Data

Atherton, Alexine L
    International organizations.

    (International relations information guide series; v. 1) (Gale information guide library)
    Includes indexes.
    1. International organization--Bibliography. I. Title.
Z6464.I6A74   016.06   73-17502
ISBN 0-8103-1324-3

Copyright © 1976 by
Alexine L. Atherton

No part of this book may be reproduced in any form without permission in writing from the publisher, except by a reviewer who wishes to quote brief passages or entries in connection with a review written for inclusion in a magazine or newspaper. Manufactured in the United States of America.

INTERNATIONAL ORGANIZATIONS

INTERNATIONAL RELATIONS INFORMATION GUIDE SERIES

Series Editor: Garold W. Thumm, Professor of Government and Chairman of the Department, Bates College, Lewiston, Maine

Also in the International Relations Series:

EASTERN EUROPE—*Edited by Robin Remington***

ECONOMICS AND FOREIGN POLICY—*Edited by Mark A. Amstutz**

THE EUROPEAN COMMUNITY—*Edited by J. Bryan Collester***

INTELLIGENCE, ESPIONAGE, COUNTERESPIONAGE, AND COVERT OPERATIONS—*Edited by Paul W. Blackstock and Frank Schaf, Jr.**

INTERNATIONAL AND REGIONAL POLITICS IN THE MIDDLE EAST AND NORTH AFRICA—*Edited by Ann Schulz**

THE MULTINATIONAL CORPORATION—*Edited by Helga Hernes**

SOUTH ASIA—*Edited by Richard J. Kozicki***

THE STUDY OF INTERNATIONAL RELATIONS—*Edited by Robert L. Pfaltzgraff, Jr. and Diane Pfaltzgraff**

SUB-SAHARAN AFRICA—*Edited by W.A.E. Skurnik**

*in press
**in preparation

The above series is part of the
GALE INFORMATION GUIDE LIBRARY

The Library consists of a number of separate series of guides covering major areas in the social sciences, humanities, and current affairs.

General Editor: Paul Wasserman, Professor and former Dean, School of Library and Information Services, University of Maryland

VITA

Alexine L. Atherton is presently an associate professor of political science at Lincoln University. She received her A.B. from Bryn Mawr in German literature and her Ph.D. from the University of Pennsylvania in political science. Atherton is the co-author of DYNAMICS OF INTERNATIONAL ORGANIZATION.

CONTENTS

Introduction xv

Abbreviations xvii

Bibliographical Essay xix

Part I: Sources of Information 3

Chapter 1: General Information 7
  A. Handbooks 7
  B. Chronologies and Registries of Events 8
  C. Dictionaries and Encyclopedias 9

Chapter 2: Bibliographies 13
  A. Bibliographies of Bibliographies 13
    1. Books 13
    2. Periodicals 13
  B. National Bibliographies 14
  C. Guides to the Literature and Subject Bibliographies 15
    1. Bibliographies of Social Science, Political Science, and International Relations 15
      a. Bibliographies of the Literature 15
      b. Guides to Literature and Resources 16
    2. International Organization: General 17
      a. Bibliographies of the Literature 17
      b. Catalogs and Guides to Publications 18
    3. The League of Nations 18
      a. Bibliographies of the Literature 18
      b. Catalogs and Guides to Publications 18
    4. The United Nations and Specialized Agencies 19
      a. Bibliographies of the Literature 19
      b. Catalogs and Guides to Publications 21
      c. United Nations Bibliographic Series 24
    5. The World Court 24
    6. Topical Bibliographies 25
      a. International Cooperation 25

Contents

	b.	International Administration	25
	c.	Security and Peacekeeping	25
	d.	Human Rights	25
	e.	International Space	26
	f.	Non-Self-Governing Territories	26
	g.	Disarmament and Arms Control	26
	h.	International Organization and Africa	27
	7.	Peace Studies	27
D.	Abstracts and Dissertations		28
	1.	Abstracts	28
	2.	Lists of Dissertations	28
E.	Periodicals		29
F.	Guides to Microforms		29

Chapter 3: Periodicals ... 33
- A. Lists of and Guides to Periodicals and Serials ... 33
- B. Indexes to Periodical Articles ... 34
- C. Selected Periodicals ... 35
  1. Periodicals Primarily Concerned with International Organizations ... 35
  2. Periodicals of the United Nations and Specialized Agencies ... 36
     - a. United Nations ... 36
     - b. Specialized Agencies ... 37
  3. Periodicals Frequently Containing Material on International Organizations ... 38
  4. Future and Peace-Oriented Journals ... 39
- D. Yearbooks ... 40
  1. General ... 40
  2. Yearbooks of International Organizations and Their Activities ... 41
  3. Yearbooks and Proceedings of International Law Associations ... 43
     - a. International Associations ... 43
     - b. National International Law Associations with Yearbooks in English ... 43
- E. Newspapers ... 44
  1. Directories ... 44
  2. Indexes to Articles in English ... 45
  3. Newspapers on Microfilm ... 45
  4. Newspapers Devoted to International Organizations ... 46

Chapter 4: Documents ... 49
- A. Indexes, Bibliographies, and Guides to Documents ... 49
  1. Government: United States and Foreign ... 49
  2. International Organizations ... 50
     - a. General ... 50
     - b. The League of Nations ... 51
     - c. The United Nations ... 52
     - d. The World Court ... 54

Contents

   B. Collected Documents and Records 54
       1. The League of Nations 54
       2. The United Nations 54
       3. The World Court 56
       4. Other International Organizations 57
       5. General Collections and Case Books 58
          a. Published 58
          b. In Microform 59
   C. Treaty Collections 60

Chapter 5: Miscellaneous Information 65
   A. Libraries and Their Resources 65
       1. General Information 65
       2. United States Library of Congress 66
       3. Libraries of the United Nations and Specialized Agencies 67
   B. Research Institutions and Projects 67
       1. Registries 67
       2. Institutions Concerned with International Organizations 69
   C. Personnel in International Organizations 71
   D. Lists of International Organizations 71
   E. Addresses of International Governmental Organizations 72
   F. Syllabi and Teaching Aids 73
   G. Opportunities for Publishing 75
   H. Grant Support: Where to Apply 75
   I. How to Cite Sources 77

Part II: Bibliography 81

Chapter 6: History and General Treatises 85
   A. History 85
       1. General 85
       2. The Hague Peace Conferences of 1899 and 1907 86
   B. General Treatises on International Organizations ... 86
       1. Books: General Accounts 86
       2. Readers and Collections of Essays 90
   C. The League of Nations: General Treatises 91
   D. From League to United Nations 95
   E. General Works on the United Nations 95
       1. Origins 95
       2. How It Works: Books Primarily Concerned with Structure, Organization, and Basic Facts 96
       3. Basic Texts 98
       4. Analyses and Assessments 99
       5. Personal Accounts 101
       6. Miscellaneous Works 102
       7. Collections of Essays and Readers 103
   F. New Methodologies and the Study of International Organizations .. 105
       1. Assessments 105
       2. New Methodologies Applied 106

Contents

Chapter 7: International Institutions: Powers, Structures,
   Organizations, and Issues 111
   A. Constitutions and Their Development 111
      1. The League of Nations Covenant 111
      2. The Making of the Charter of the United Nations 112
      3. Commentaries 113
   B. International Law and International Organizations 114
      1. General 115
         a. The Right of Access and Status 116
         b. Privileges and Immunities 117
         c. Other Legal Issues 117
      2. The Law Covering International Organizations 118
      3. Legislative Power and Legal Effects of Action by the United
         Nations and Related Agencies 119
   C. Organs of International Organizations: Structures and
         Activities 122
      1. League of Nations Organs 122
      2. The General Assembly (GA) 123
      3. The Security Council (SC) 123
      4. The Economic and Social Council (ECOSOC) 125
      5. Presiding Officers in the United Nations 125
      6. The International Law Commission (ILC) 126
      7. Other Institutions 126
      8. International Legislative Bodies and Conferences ... 126
   D. Organizational Issues and Problems 127
      1. Representation and Membership 127
         a. General Issues 127
         b. China 128
      2. Voting: Procedures and Problems 129
      3. Studies of the Decision-Making Process 130
      4. Financial Issues 131
   E. Secretariats and Their Problems 131
      1. General 131
      2. The International Civil Service 133
      3. International Administrative Tribunals and Their
         Jurisdiction 133
      4. Staffing and Personnel Policy 134
      5. Other Issues and Problems 134
   F. The Secretaries-General 135
      1. General Studies 135
      2. Joseph Avenol 137
      3. Trygve Lie 137
      4. Dag Hammarskjold 137
      5. U Thant 139
   G. International Courts and Tribunals 140
      1. General 140
      2. The Permanent Court of International Justice (PCIJ) 140
      3. The International Court of Justice (ICJ) 141

Chapter 8: Politics and International Organizations 145
   A. The United Nations in World Politics 145

Contents

- B. Politics in International Organizations 146
  1. The Process 146
  2. The Actors: Diplomats 148
- C. Nations and International Organizations 148
  1. General 148
  2. New Nations--Small Nations 148
  3. Blocs and Groups 149
     a. Afro-Asia as a Group 149
     b. Africa 149
     c. The Arabs 150
     d. Latin America 151
     e. Western Europe 151
     f. Scandinavia 151
     g. The Commonwealth 151
     h. Others: Asia, Europe, Pacific Islands 152
  4. Individual Nations 152
     a. Algeria 152
     b. Australia 152
     c. Austria 153
     d. Belgium 153
     e. Burma 153
     f. Canada 154
     g. China 154
     h. Denmark 155
     i. Egypt 155
     j. Greece 155
     k. India 156
     l. Israel (Palestine) 157
     m. Italy 157
     n. Japan 158
     o. Mexico 158
     p. Pakistan 158
     q. Spain 159
     r. Sweden 159
     s. Switzerland 159
     t. Turkey 160
     u. United Kingdom 160
     v. The USSR 161
     w. The United States 162
     x. The United States, the Soviet Union, and the United Nations 167
     y. Uruguay 168
     z. West Germany 168
     aa. Other Nations 168

Chapter 9: The Struggle for Peace and Security 173
- A. General 173
- B. Collective Security 174
  1. General Treatises 174
  2. Korea: A Case Study in Collective Security Action 176
  3. Sanctions 177

Contents

    C. International Organizations and the Search for Arms Control
and Disarmament............................... 178
    D. Conflict Resolution: Mediation and Conciliation.............. 180
        1. General 180
        2. The League Experience 183
        3. United Nations Experience 184
        4. Border Disputes and Territorial Change.................. 185
        5. Internal Wars 186
        6. The United Nations and Vietnam 186
        7. Techniques 187
    E. Peacekeeping: Preventive Diplomacy 187
        1. General 187
        2. International Forces 189
        3. Case Studies 193
            a. Peacekeeping in the Arab World.................. 193
            b. Kashmir 196
            c. The Congo 196
            d. Cyprus 199
    F. Arbitration and Adjudication 199

Chapter 10: Promoting Cross-National Transactions 205
    A. Regulating Communications............................ 205
        1. General 205
        2. International Telecommunications: The International Tele-
communications Union (ITU) 206
        3. International Civil Aviation: The International Civil
Aviation Organization (ICAO) 207
        4. The Sea and Waterways.......................... 209
        5. Space 210
        6. Postal Relations: The Universal Postal Union (UPU)........ 213
        7. Rail Transport 213
    B. Regulating International Trade.......................... 213
        1. General 213
        2. General Agreement on Tariffs and Trade (GATT) 214
        3. International Commodity Agreements and Cartels 215
    C. The International Monetary System: Policies and Regulation 216
        1. General 216
        2. The International Monetary Fund (IMF) 218

Chapter 11: Promoting Economic Cooperation and Welfare 223
    A. General 223
        1. Economic Organization and the League 223
            a. General 223
            b. Bank for International Settlements 223
        2. Economic Organization in the Modern World 224
    B. Aid Through Universal Organizations 226
        1. United Nations Relief and Rehabilitation Administration
(UNRRA)..................................... 226
        2. Development: Problems and International Strategies 227
        3. Aid Through Universal Multilateral Channels............. 228

Contents

    4. United Nations Conference on Trade and Development
       (UNCTAD) 231
    5. Development Decades: How Useful are They? 232
    6. Coordination 233
    7. Case Studies 233
    8. Technical Cooperation 234
    9. Fighting Hunger: Food and Agriculture Organization (FAO) .. 235
  C. The World Bank Group 236

Chapter 12: Promoting World Welfare 241
  A. Social Welfare and Development 241
  B. Safeguarding the World's Health: The World Health
     Organization (WHO) 242
    1. General 242
    2. A World System to Control Narcotics 244
  C. Internationalizing Labor Standards 244
    1. The Evolution of a System: The League and Before 244
    2. The International Labor Organization (ILO) Today 246
    3. Standard-Setting Internationally 247
    4. Development and the ILO 248
    5. Albert Thomas: A Prototype 248
    6. Nations and the ILO 249
  D. The Minds of Men: UNESCO's Mission 250
  E. Scientists Cooperate 252
    1. Restricting the Atom to Peaceful Purposes: The International
       Atomic Energy Agency (IAEA) 252
    2. Ecological Crises: Cooperative Responses 254
    3. The International Geophysical Year 255
    4. Population and International Organizations 256
  F. The World's Children: An International Responsibility? United
     Nations International Children's Emergency Fund
     (UNICEF) 256
  G. Nongovernmental Organizations 257

Chapter 13: International Organizations and People 263
  A. International Involvement in the Process of Decolonization 263
    1. General Studies 263
    2. The League Experience 263
      a. The Mandate System 263
      b. Individual Mandates Examined 264
      c. Specially Administered Areas 265
      d. Plebiscites 266
    3. The UN and Dependent Peoples 266
      a. The Trusteeship System 266
      b. Non-Self-Governing Territories 267
      c. The United Nations and Self-Determination 268
    4. Case Studies 268
      a. Cameroon 268
      b. Indonesia 269
      c. Italian Colonies 269
      d. New Guinea 270

Contents

        e. Portuguese Territories 270
        f. Pacific Trusts of the United States 271
        g. Rhodesia 271
        h. South West Africa 271
        i. Tanganyika 272
  B. Protecting the Rights of Minorities 273
  C. The Refugee: An International Responsibility? 274
  D. Protecting Individuals 276
    1. Human Rights and International Organizations 276
    2. Human Rights as Legal Rights: Documents and
       Commentaries 281
    3. The UN Tries to Intervene: South Africa 282

Chapter 14: Creating a New World 285
  A. Shaping Post-War Worlds 285
    1. World War I Proposals 285
    2. World War II Proposals 286
  B. The Ineffective League: New Approaches 287
  C. Proposals for Tomorrow 287
    1. Changing the United Nations System 288
      a. Charter Revision 288
      b. Improving the System 290
    2. New Ways 291
      a. The Federalist Way 295
      b. World Government 295
      c. Other Alternatives 296

Indexes
  Author Index 299
  Title Index 313
  Subject Index 341

INTRODUCTION

This volume was compiled to be a guide for the beginner as well as the more advanced student interested in exploring the field or delving into some facet of international organization. Part I contains information on bibliographies, guides, indexes, abstracts, and other materials. In most sections, works of a general nature, along with works specifically relating to international organizations, are included as the former often provide valuable information, sometimes of a background nature, for the researcher.

Part II is a bibliography of the field, covering past as well as present experiences and information. Annotations are provided for more recent books, especially significant ones from the end of the last century and in the early 1900's. Within sections an attempt has been made to group books with a similar objective or area of concentration; further, the order reflects this compiler's own evaluation of the usefulness to the user of the items.

In compiling this guide, use has been made of book reviews in the following journals: INTERNATIONAL AFFAIRS, FOREIGN AFFAIRS, INTERNATIONAL ORGANIZATION, THE AMERICAN JOURNAL OF INTERNATIONAL LAW, BRITISH YEARBOOK OF INTERNATIONAL LAW, and from PERSPECTIVE. Especially valuable was J. Zawodny's GUIDE TO THE STUDY OF INTERNATIONAL RELATIONS, which served as a preliminary guide to this compiler as she started her journey through the literature. Very close to the time of completion, Michael Haas's INTERNATIONAL ORGANIZATION: AN INTERDISCIPLINARY BIBLIOGRAPHY became available to this compiler. This is the most complete work of its kind to date and proved an invaluable asset in finishing this volume.

The Table of Contents is a detailed outline of the work and should serve as a starting point for the researcher. As a further aid works are cross-referenced. Author and title indexes are included.

ABBREVIATIONS

BIS	Bank for International Settlements
ECOSOC	Economic and Social Council (UN)
FAO	Food and Agriculture Organization
GA	General Assembly (UN)
GATT	General Agreement on Tariffs and Trade
IAEA	International Atomic Energy Agency
IBRD	International Bank for Reconstruction and Development
ICAO	International Civil Aviation Organization
ICJ	International Court of Justice
IDA	International Development Association (IBRD)
IFC	International Finance Corporation (IBRD)
ILC	International Law Commission (UN)
ILO	International Labor Organization
IMCO	Intergovernmental Maritime Consultative Organization
IMF	International Monetary Fund
INTERPOL	International Police
IRO	International Refugee Organization
ITO	International Trade Organization
ITU	International Telecommunication Union
OECD	Organization for Economic Cooperation and Development
ONUC	United Nations Operations in the Congo
PCA	Permanent Court of Arbitration
PCIJ	Permanent Court of International Justice
SC	Security Council (UN)
SIPRI	Stockholm International Peace Research Institute
UAR	United Arab Republic
UK	United Kingdom
UN	United Nations
UNCTAD	United Nations Conference on Trade and Development
UNEF	United Nations Emergency Force
UNESCO	United Nations Educational, Scientific and Cultural Organization
UNFCYP	United Nations Forces on Cyprus
UNHCR	United Nations High Commissioner for Refugees
UNICEF	United Nations International Children's Emergency Fund
UNIDO	United Nations Industrial Development Organization
UNIDROIT	International Institute for the Unification of Private International Law

Abbreviations

UNITAR	United Nations Institute for Training and Development
UNRRA	United Nations Relief and Rehabilitation Administration
UPU	Universal Postal Union
U.S.	United States
USSR	Union of Soviet Socialist Republics
WHO	World Health Organization
WMO	World Meteorological Organization

BIBLIOGRAPHICAL ESSAY

AN OVERVIEW OF THE LITERATURE ON THE LEAGUE

An international organization bibliography is a relatively new phenomenon, which had to wait for the creation and flourishing of international organizations themselves before it could occur. The development of these agencies of international interaction first began toward the end of the nineteenth century, when a few regulatory agencies were set up to facilitate the implementation of international regulations spelled out in treaties.

The smooth and successful functioning of these agencies gave rise to speculation about the possibility of more far-reaching institutions to facilitate transnational relations. Such speculations were based on actual experiences, not only the experiences of the "permanent" regulatory agencies but also those resulting from the multilateral treaty-making process. This international legislative process had, by the end of the nineteenth century, proved effective for resolving some aspects of the problems besetting states in their relations with one another. Especially successful were conferences drafting laws covering behavior in war, communications, and health.

The early writers on international organization were primarily concerned with the future--a better future. Their objective was to draw on analyses of international cooperative processes to propose increased cooperation and, in particular, a world organization dedicated to promoting and preserving peace. The onslaught of the First World War, disrupting the peace which had prevailed in Europe for almost one hundred years, heightened the desire to see progress towards resolving tensions and preventing war through the creation of a world organization. Thus, early works (for example, 1443, 1445, 1449-51) tended to be optimistic and prescriptive. They viewed the world's problems as arising out of the existence of separate, independent, and self-seeking nations pursuing narrow national objectives which could and did become conflictive at times. The resolution proposed was the creation of organizations based on the principles which were evolving out of the experiences of the multilateral conferences and regulatory agencies. These were the works of individuals concerned about the tragedies resulting from nationalist approaches to the resolution of problems and of those desiring peace and security.

Bibliographical Essay

The creation of the League of Nations was attended by great optimism on the part of many--statesmen, scholars, citizens--and the organization was carefully scrutinized. Accounts tended to be descriptive rather than analytic (411, 412, 416, 419, 422, 423, 425, 426, 429); they were primarily works of observers concerned and hopeful.

Increasing conflict in the world, rising tensions, and political maneuvering began to undermine the League's ability to play a significant and meaningful role in the world. The question which now plagued many authors in the field was, why? (418, 424, 427, 428, 430, 431). Hope and optimism gave way to disillusionment and discouragement as the world progressed towards full-scale war.

A final League action was the commission of an "authoritative" account (409) of the total experience of the organization. Walter's two volumes are straightforward and lucid. This precedent was followed when two other agencies, the United Nations Relief and Rehabilitation Administration (1125) and the International Refugee Organization (1404) dissolved themselves. All three works make extensive use of the documents available and are useful reference works.

The inability of the League to meet the challenges of the times led men to suggest ways to improve, modify, or replace the organization (1463-70). Prescriptive in intent, these works analyze the shortcomings of the League--organizational and political--to discern reasons for failure and suggest remedies.

Primary focus was on the League's structure, operation, and activities in the peace and security field. Few works appeared concerning the nonpolitical areas in which the League and related agencies were active. This is not surprising as it was only after the Second World War that the nonpolitical cooperative endeavors became a significant part of the work of international agencies. The League period was one of cautious and limited initiatives in such areas as communications (1016) and narcotics control (1223-25) where beginnings had already been made. The League's activities on behalf of colonial peoples (Chapter 13.A.2), minorities (1386-88, 1390, 1391), and refugees (1407, 1408) were described and analyzed as were the efforts at financial and economic corporation (1104-8). The International Labor Organization was created at the same time as the League and its activities and accomplishments were regarded by many observers as significant indicators of the potential of international agencies for promoting changes in national policies and actions (1226, 1229-36).

After the creation of the UN and specialized agencies, the League and its activities became background and bases for comparison. Basic texts, works on social, economic, and humanitarian cooperation usually start out with some form of historical survey of the League's accomplishments and failures and comparisons reappear throughout many of these works.

For some fifty years little original research was done on the League. Only when time had passed and more documentation became available did scholars turn again to the study of the shortlived organization (415, 417, 421, 665, 894-96). Studies which now could be labeled historical began to be published. It is to be expected that more will appear as the League becomes of interest to historians as well as to political scientists and international lawyers. The analysis and focus will change, new insights will emerge, and new perspectives be revealed.

THE UNITED NATIONS, 1946-61

World War II was again a period of speculation and suggestion. Although the League had failed, the idea that there should be a world organization was very much alive (436, 437, 527) diplomatically and in the literature. The major thrust was for more "teeth" in such an organization, giving it a capability for action more powerful than that of its predecessor.

Optimism again was the theme of most writers on the UN during its first years of operation (442, 444). International lawyers as well as some political scientists undertook careful, scholarly analyses of the Charter (526, 529-31, 534-36, 542), many article by article. As interesting as these are, especially to the legal mind, many appear to the reader of the seventies as intellectual exercises rather than realistic appraisals of the capabilities of the organization. Some few (529, 531) have been brought up to date as the Charter has been given new meaning and direction during the first quarter century of the functioning of the UN.

There was optimism in the late forties and an expanding interest in international organizations as evidenced by the increase in courses taught and the number of articles not only in journals specifically directed to the study of international agencies but in other periodicals. There were similar increases in the number of books published and organizations founded. The UN was working. There were problems, to be sure; there were weaknesses. But, on the whole, the literature of the period reflects satisfaction, hope, and a feeling of moving towards a safer, more secure world characterized by increasing international cooperation to promote welfare and resolve transnational problems of communications, health, trade, etc. Dag Hammarskjold was leading the organization. The Secretary-General, in a very meaningful way, represented the UN and symbolized its strength and determination to succeed. Under his direction a new technique for containing conflict, the United Nations Emergency Force, was devised and put into operation. All seemed to be moving forward towards a better and stronger organization in a more peaceful and cooperative world (for example, 448, 449, 453, 456, 469, 472, 669, 672, 946).

Much analysis during this period emphasized the flexibility of the organization. The fact that the veto was being used, and the inability of the great powers to agree on arrangements to set up military forces for collective security action as directed by the Charter were seen as fortunate in light of the political realities of the cold war. The use of preventive diplomacy as a technique for containing conflict was seen as a proper adaptation of the organization to the realities of the world situation.

Whereas legalistic analyses of the Charter predominated during the early part of

Bibliographical Essay

this period, legal studies now were directed more to the impact of the organization on the development of international law (540, 541, 543) and legal issues raised by the existence and functioning of international organizations (547, 548, 552-54, 556-58, 560, 563).

This period was also one of increasing concern with the politics of the organization. Early descriptions of the powers and functions of the organs of the UN were succeeded by studies, many rigorous and quantitative, of the actual functioning of the UN (703, 705, 706, 708). The scientific movement within the discipline of political science was being slowly picked by some scholars concerned with international organizations (Chapter 6.C), who applied more systematic techniques to voting statistics, and used controlled observations and content analysis to study organizations. The periodical literature in particular has reflected these developments.

More descriptive and journalistic were the works dealing with the UN in the world (694-96, 700). Observers attempted to assess the impact of the UN on world politics to discover whether the existence of the organization was having an effect, especially on the ever-intensifying cold war. These works are generally not very satisfactory as there is no easy or reliable way to determine how important the actions or the existence of the UN has been on the development and implementation of broad national policies. More successful have been the case studies (955, 980, 1360, 1361, 1366, 1385), especially those analyzing specific conflicts or the process of decolonization in individual countries. Even these, however, must to a large extent draw conclusions based on inferences as the "actors" are often inaccessible to the observer or unwilling or unable to relate directly to the role of the international agency.

In preparation for the tenth anniversary of the organization and the possibility of Charter revision, the Carnegie Endowment for International Peace commissioned research organizations in a number of countries to undertake studies of the interaction of the country with the organizations (712, 736, 739, 741, 744, 749-51, 753, 763-65, 767, 768, 771, 773, 774, 776, 779, 791, 812, 822, 823). Many of these used a number of techniques to assess the role of the state in the organization and the impact of the UN on state behavior (see Chapter 7.C for other attempts to assess the effects of the organization in individual states and vice versa).

The tenth anniversary also occasioned books assessing the experiences of the UN (472, 473) and a number of works proposing changes in the system (1471, 1472, 1474, 1477, 1481), and in particular revisions of the Charter. Especially comprehensive was the careful study undertaken by Clark and Sohn (1472) which has been revised and updated and has served as the basis of much discussion and criticism concerning the possibility of moving the UN towards world government and to an agency for assuring peace and promoting world welfare.

The primary hope for the UN has been for peace in the world. It is therefore natural that much attention has been given to assessing its ability or inability to promote security and resolve conflicts. Early works concentrated on the potential and constitutional provisions for collective security, peaceful settlement

Bibliographical Essay

of disputes, and disarmament. They tended to be legalistic and/or theoretical (for example, 828, 839, 841, 883) and drew heavily on League experiences as a point of departure and basis for comparison. As the years passed and the UN became active in the field of peace and security, it was possible for scholars to analyze and evaluate accomplishments and failures and to base projections on these rather than on constitutional provisions and speculation. Among the insightful and scholarly works appearing during this period were those of Claude (376, 832, 837), with his acute theoretical models of power, and the more legalistic work of Stone (893).

Although studies of the UN in its political aspects have tended to dominate the bibliography, attention has also been focused on the "nonpolitical" aspects of international cooperation through agencies and organizations. Textbooks and basic books (Chapter 6.B and E.2, 3, 4, 7) deal with the totality of experiences of international organizations, although the nonpolitical sections are generally considerably shorter than those dealing with organizational issues and actions relating to political matters.

Much of the work in this area is descriptive and journalistic in character, cataloging the experiences of agencies in their attempts to resolve world economic, social, and humanitarian problems (1017, 1058, 1061, 1064, 1204, 1205, 1213, 1214, 1238, 1265, 1269, 1397, 1398). A considerable number of these books have been written by individuals active in the work of the agencies covered. The intent is usually to publicize the successes of these agencies, and, often, to encourage increased financial commitments from states in order to expand in their respective areas of concern.

A portion of the literature covering these areas is functional in orientation (see the relevant parts of 378 and 377), a bias which appears throughout a significant portion of the literature on international organization. Underlying these works is the assumption that cooperation breeds further cooperation not only in the area of concern but also in other areas of international behavior. During this period the first major attempt to test the theory of functionalism was undertaken by Ernst Haas (1242) in a rigorous manner. Successful as a beginning of theory-building in the field, it has, unfortunately, not been followed up to any significant extent.

During the early years of the UN, the western powers were to a large extent successful in keeping colonial questions from becoming major agenda items. Decolonization became important as a political issue only when the membership in the organization became increasingly open to ex-colonials. There was little analysis of the UN in the process except for some very effective works on the role of the UN in Indonesia's struggle to free herself from Dutch control (1361, 1363-65). Some attention was paid to the trusteeship system, to analyzing its evolution from the League mandate system and its workings (1347, 1349, 1351, 1367, 1369, 1372, 1385).

With the independence of Ghana, membership of ex-colonials began to increase and pressure for more UN action in the process of decolonization mounted. Works appearing toward the end of this period attempted to analyze the impact of the organization on the process (1322, 1347, 1349, 1351).

As outlined above, the bibliography of the first fifteen years of the UN is varied. Predominately descriptive, in part analytic, it has only shown minor attempts at adopting the more rigorous methodologies being pursued by many political scientists. Legal and legalistic approaches have been a significant element as international organization has been taught in the law schools and studied by international lawyers.

To a great extent the writers in the field are biased in favor of increasing the range of activities engaged in by organizations and their ability--financial and political--to deal with these. Many works are prescriptive in character, suggesting general and specific ways to strengthen and improve the agencies. During the period covered above, most authors appeared to be hopeful about the prospects for the UN and related agencies, although some disillusionment was felt, especially towards the end of the period. The usual approach to failures was to suggest better ways or alternative strategies. Throughout these works was a conviction that the organizations will continue to serve worthwhile purposes, albeit perhaps not those for which they were originally established.

THE UNITED NATIONS, 1962-75

The year 1961 was a year of tragedy for the UN. Dag Hammarskjold's death in Africa, the continuing deterioration of the Congo operation, and the escalating tensions and conflicts in the organization over finances led to a change in the tone of some of the literature. The hope and optimism of the middle and late fifties gave way to discouragements and even pessimism. The UN, which had so successfully aided in the Middle East, was now torn assunder in its efforts to assist in the Congo. Some authors saw this as necessitating more realism in looking at the organization than had characterized much of the work of the previous period (for example, 440, 457, 697, 700). However, in spite of the difficulties felt by some, hope and optimism continued to characterize a large portion of the literature (for example, 378, 379, 386, 439, 441, 455, 475, 476, 696).

The earlier concentration on legal interpretations of constitutions almost disappears from the bibliography, replaced by a substantial literature analyzing the legal effects of the activities of organizations (Chapter 7.B.3). A number of these works also try to show in what ways international organizations have been able to affect national policies.

Politics in the organization became increasingly stressed in the literature (Chapter 7.C.2, 3: 629, 630). Questions about the "how" were raised and attempts made to discover just what influences the output of the organization. Voting studies and observation continued to be the primary means for collecting and analyzing the data in both books and journal articles.

Bibliographical Essay

The rapidly increasing membership from the nonwestern world became the object of analysis and speculation about the future of the organization (713, 714, 718-23, 726). An issue of importance in the organization was that of the representation of the People's Republic of China. The legal and political aspects were thoroughly discussed in the literature (616-21) with the preponderance supporting either the representation of the People's Republic, replacing Nationalist China, or the so-called "two China" solution.

Trygvie Lie and Dag Hammarskjold saw their roles as very different from the Secretaries-General of the League. The League had had administrators, men whose primary responsibility was to follow the bidding of member states. It was a passive role. The drafters of the Charter wanted a new kind of Secretary-General, one who would have some political as well as administrative responsibilities. Trygvie Lie tried to pressure governments into adopting more cooperative policies and ended his career disliked by most members. Dag Hammarskjold's approach was a complex one. He was able to gain the confidence of states, to persuade them to cooperate with him and the organization, until "Leave it to Dag" became an accepted approach of many organs. The Secretary-General was given powers and responsibilities far beyond those envisaged by the drafters and yet Hammarskjold was meticulously careful to frame all his moves to fit the Charter--as he interpreted it. The deterioration in the Congo situation brought with it criticism of the Secretary-General from many members. Had Hammarskjold exceeded his authority? Had he favored some states over others? Had he acted without proper constitutional support? These were some of the questions raised, not only by members but also by students of the office. A substantial number of works on the office (659, 660, 662-64) appeared during this period as well as some penetrating analyses of Dag Hammarskjold--the man and his work (668-76).

Conflict resolution continued to be the focus of much scholarly activity during this period. The growing sophistication in studying conflict in the social sciences was reflected in the analysis of international conflict and the role--actual and potential--of the UN and other agencies in resolving and containing conflicts (877, 882, 884-92, 901-4). The studies tend to be more comprehensive and analytical than those of the previous period. A few have singled out particular aspects of the process, such as fact-finding and third party roles, to study in depth (916-18a).

Dag Hammarskjold's use of "preventive diplomacy" and his clear analysis of the possibilities and potential of this unique technique prompted a number of studies of its theory, legality, and practice (919, 920). The bias in most of these works is pro-UN and pro-expansion; the conviction that the organization, in spite of the crisis occasioned by its involvement in the Congo, had the potential and ability to use this technique successfully. The object of many of these works appears to be to show under what circumstances--within the UN and outside-- the use of preventive diplomacy is appropriate and possible.

Closely related to these studies are those concentrating on the actual use of force by international organization (Chapter 9.E.2, 3). The orientation of these works is varied--the legality of such operations, factors influencing efficiency,

Bibliographical Essay

appropriateness, and assessments of success or failure in dealing with the problems for which forces have been created. The general conclusion is that international forces can be useful when interposed between fighting factions or nations to <u>contain</u> violence, but have not been useful in assisting in the resolution of the actual conflict.

While most of the literature has concentrated on the political techniques and processes for resolving international conflicts, attention has also been directed to the legal process: adjudication (1008-10). Works have tended to analyze the actual record of international courts and tribunals as well as to suggest possibilities for expansion of the role of adjudication in international relations. The works included here are ones which focus on adjudication as one technique for conflict resolution and, thus, represent but a small portion of the literature on international courts and tribunals. In the general literature, the potential for expansion of adjudication is viewed pessimistically. The disillusionment of many with the International Court's decision on South West Africa (Chapter 13. D.3) intensified the negative attitude, especially on the part of nonwestern nations, which have often tended to regard the "law" used by the Court as "western" and, therefore, as not appropriate for a world increasingly nonwestern in composition.

The most significant shifts in the literature of the sixties and seventies paralleled developments in the organizations themselves. By the mid-sixties it was clear that the UN would no longer be an organization of developed states but would soon consist of a majority of developing and ex-colonial nations. The issues of interest and deep concern to these "new" nations became increasingly prominent on the agendas of the UN and other agencies. Foremost were the issues of economic development and decolonization. The new members were disenchanted with the gradualist approach of the older members and began to pressure for more resolute action. All agencies began to have to deal with these developments and the literature has reflected these shifts in concern.

Analyses of the role of the organization in the process of decolonization in general (1357-59) and in individual areas (Chapter 13.A.4) appeared. The task was clearly not a simple one as the process seemed inevitable. The UN's role on the whole was not crucial, although at times it was significant. Studies showed the extent to which weaker nations--now in the majority--were able to affect changes in the organization itself, especially as regards the interpretation and implementation of Chapter VII of the Charter and to what extent the organization has been able to influence the policy of the colonial powers.

While the fate of the unliberated areas arouses the emotions of new members, closer to their real concerns are the issues of economic development. International agencies have become the forum for pressuring the wealthy to assume more responsibility for assisting the poor. While the process is by its nature an internal one and while the rich have preferred bilateral to multilateral programs, the UN and all agencies have become involved in the process and have been objects of scholarly and polemic analysis. The body of literature devoted to this area is an ever-growing one (1114-17, 1119-22, 1128-30, 1140, 1144-47, 1151, 1160-69), which explores all aspects of development, as this has become

Bibliographical Essay

a part of the concern of international agencies. Special attention has been focused on the United Nations Conference on Trade and Development (1156-59), on international technical assistance (Chapter 11.B.8), and on the World Bank and affiliates (1188-91, 1197-1200, 1202, 1203).

The last years have seen a growing concern in the UN and agencies with "new" problems of the modern, technological world. The peaceful uses of atomic energy (1278-83), ecological balance (1287-94), outer space (1046-51, 1053-55), and population control (1295, 1296, 1298) have been among the issues discussed in the organization and the literature. Authors concerned with these areas generally analyze the international aspects of the problem and suggest appropriate actions for the agencies to take towards resolving these.

Over the past years the field of international organization has been firmly established as a discrete area of study with its own bibliography. Political scientists, international relations specialists, international lawyers and, to a lesser extent, historians have applied the methodologies of their disciplines to the area. Practitioners have written their assessments and personal experiences. The result is a literature of numerous perspectives. Generally the authors tend to look favorably on the agencies; their criticism is sympathetic and friendly. The intent is often to show how the agencies can become more effective as promoters of peace, security, and the world's welfare.

The literature has been descriptive and analytic. The more rigorous methodologies of many of today's social scientists have been adopted by but a few and have been more prominent in the journal literature than in books. There does not appear to be any substantial pressure within the discipline to adopt these newer methodologies extensively.

While the bibliography concentrates on books, the importance of journal articles to any student of the field must not be overlooked. The field has, since 1947, had its own journal, INTERNATIONAL ORGANIZATION (146), and an excellent and unique periodical, INTERNATIONAL CONCILIATION (147), was published by the Carnegie Endowment for International Peace from 1907 until 1972. International lawyers, as well as some political scientists, have contributed numerous articles to international law journals and yearbooks (Chapter 3.D.3) and to many periodicals in allied fields (Chapter 3.C.3). A good source of specific information about the agencies and their activities can be found in the numerous yearbooks (Chapter 3.D.2) and periodicals (Chapter 3.C.2) published by the organizations themselves. This body of literature has been made more accessible by the indexes and guides (Chapter 3.A, B.) which have been published and are kept up to date. These, along with the numerous bibliographies covering the field (Chapter 2), provide the student with excellent and usable overviews of the literature and can guide him in his research.

One body of literature which has not been discussed thus far, but of which a representative sample has been included in the last chapter, is the futures and peace-oriented journals (Chapter 3.C.4 and Chapter 14). Man has always speculated about his world and, finding it deficient in so many ways, has constructed in his mind new and better ones. The instabilities and insecurities of

Bibliographical Essay

the international state system as it has been functioning have led many minds to search for better ways--federal arrangements, world governments, strengthened international agencies for cooperation and concerted effort. Many of these works are not merely outlines of fanciful utopias but are based on careful and, at times, keenly insightful analyses of the functioning state system and the role of existing international organizations. At a time when many political scientists are severely criticizing value-laden and prescriptive works, authors on international organization have not been intimidated. They have continued to combine the roles of scholar and philosopher, student and apologist, researcher and prescriber. Many are unwilling to accept the world as it is, unwilling to deny man the ability to change his world and create a better one. Man's longing for peace, security, and a good life continue, and many authors continue to search for and suggest ways to reach these goals, fulfilling man's fundamental needs and desires.

Part I

SOURCES OF INFORMATION

Part I
SOURCES OF INFORMATION

Part I is primarily concerned with providing information on how to get information. Bibliographies, guides, indexes, and catalogs are cited to help the student and researcher locate those works and documents pertinent to his topic. The wealth of material available today is overwhelming and time spent with these aids will help reduce aimless wandering. In many instances a number of works covering the same material are included in the hope that at least one will be available in the researcher's library.

Chapter 1
GENERAL INFORMATION

Chapter 1
GENERAL INFORMATION

Information in this section is of a factual nature. Basic handbooks and chronologies are useful to place information and to provide an overview in time perspective.

A. HANDBOOKS

1. League of Nations. HANDBOOK OF INTERNATIONAL ORGANIZATIONS. Geneva, Switzerland, 1939. 491 p.

    Source of information on headquarters, objectives, members, governing body, officers, activities, and official publications of international organizations.

2. Myers, Denys Peter. HANDBOOK OF THE LEAGUE OF NATIONS. A COMPREHENSIVE ACCOUNT OF ITS STRUCTURE, OPERATION AND ACTIVITIES. Boston, Mass.: World Peace Foundation, 1935. 424 p.

    Comprehensive account of structure, operation, and activities.

3. Vincent, Jack E. A HANDBOOK OF THE UNITED NATIONS. Woodbury, N.J.: Barron's, 1969. 211 p.

    A brief description of evolution, organs.

4. Masters, Ruth D. HANDBOOK OF INTERNATIONAL ORGANIZATIONS IN THE AMERICAS. Washington, D.C.: Carnegie Endowment, 1945. 453 p.

5. United Nations Office of Public Information. BASIC FACTS ABOUT THE UNITED NATIONS. New York, 1972- . Periodically.

    Outline of the structure and functions of the UN and the specialized agencies. Membership lists included.

6. League of Nations. Secretariat. Information Section. ESSENTIAL

General Information

FACTS ABOUT THE LEAGUE OF NATIONS. 10th ed. Geneva, Switzerland, 1939. 359 p.

Gives a brief description of the League and its activities.

B. CHRONOLOGIES AND REGISTRIES OF EVENTS

7. United Nations. Secretariat. Department of Public Information. Research Section. UNITED NATIONS CHRONOLOGY AUGUST 1941-SEPTEMBER 1953. New York, 1954. 34 p. Rev. ed., 1964. 139 p.

8. Chamberlin, Waldo, et al. A CHRONOLOGY AND FACT BOOK OF THE UNITED NATIONS, 1941-1969. 3rd ed. Dobbs Ferry, N.Y.: Oceana, 1970. 236 p.

   Lists major problems and actions, members with dates of admission, officers and members of the four major bodies, and information on the annual budget.

9. Mezerik, A.G., ed. INTERNATIONAL REVIEW SERVICE. New York: International Review Service, 1958- . Bimonthly.

   Each publication centers on a major international problem and includes comprehensive analysis, chronology, texts, tables, maps, and bibliography. Yearly: "Chronology of the UN."

10. THE ANNUAL REGISTER OF WORLD EVENTS. London: Longmans, Green, 1759- . (Title and publishers have varied.)

    Events are surveyed according to political and geographical areas followed by subjects.

11. CHRONOLOGY OF INTERNATIONAL EVENTS. 11 vols. London: Royal Institute of International Affairs, 1945-55.

    Was published semimonthly. Record of events and official documents each described in a brief paragraph. Arranged by country and international group.

12. FACTS ON FILE: A WEEKLY DIGEST WITH CUMULATIVE INDEX. New York: Pearson's Index, Facts on File, Inc., 1940- . Weekly.

13. KEESING'S CONTEMPORARY ARCHIVES: WEEKLY DIARY OF WORLD EVENTS WITH INDEX CONTINUALLY KEPT UP-TO-DATE. London: Keesing's, 1931- .

    Weekly survey of reports, statistics, and data summarized and translated from British and foreign news sources and international organizations. Subject indexes.

General Information

14. League of Nations. Secretariat. Information Section. MONTHLY SUMMARY OF THE LEAGUE OF NATIONS. Geneva, Switzerland, 1921-40. Monthly.

    Popular survey of the League's work during the preceding month; published in five languages. Included a calendar of events, listing of conferences, committees, and meetings.

15. THE CHRONICLE OF UNITED NATIONS ACTIVITIES: WEEKLY REPORT. New York: Hasid, 1956-61.

    No longer published, this was an independent publication having no official connection with the UN. Contains voting in the General Assembly with brief summaries of debates, main committee reports, and short reports on items on the agenda.

16. THE UNITED NATIONS NEWS: A MONTHLY REPORT ON THE UNITED NATIONS AND ITS RELATED AGENCIES. New York: Woodrow Wilson Foundation, 1946- .

17. United States Congress. Senate (84th, 2nd session). Committee on Foreign Relations. Subcommittee on Disarmament. DISARMAMENT: A SELECTED CHRONOLOGY, JANUARY 1, 1918 - MARCH 19, 1956. Staff Study, no. 2. Washington, D.C.: Government Printing Office, 1956. 33 p.

C. DICTIONARIES AND ENCYCLOPEDIAS

18. Plano, Jack C., and Olton, Roy. THE INTERNATIONAL RELATIONS DICTIONARY. New York: Holt, Rinehart & Winston, 1969. 351 p.

19. Dunner, Joseph, ed. DICTIONARY OF POLITICAL SCIENCE. Totowa, N.J.: Littlefield, Adams, 1970. 607 p.

20. White, Wilbur W. WHITE'S POLITICAL DICTIONARY. New York: World Publishing Co., 1947. 378 p.

21. Theimer, Walter. AN ENCYCLOPEDIA OF MODERN WORLD POLITICS. Edited, revised, and enlarged by Peter Campbell. London: Faber, 1950. 471 p.

    Expansion of this author's PENGUIN POLITICAL DICTIONARY which was first published in England in 1939 and has gone through a number of editions.

22. Sills, David L., ed. INTERNATIONAL ENCYCLOPEDIA OF THE SOCIAL SCIENCES. 17 vols. New York: Macmillan and the Free Press, 1968.

General Information

23. WORLDMARK ENCYCLOPEDIA OF THE NATIONS: A PRACTICAL GUIDE TO THE GEOGRAPHIC, HISTORICAL, POLITICAL, SOCIAL, AND ECONOMIC STATUS OF ALL NATIONS, THEIR INTERNATIONAL RELATIONSHIPS, AND THE UNITED NATIONS SYSTEM. New York: Worldmark Press, Harper, 1960. 4156 p.

Chapter 2
BIBLIOGRAPHIES

Chapter 2
BIBLIOGRAPHIES

A. BIBLIOGRAPHIES OF BIBLIOGRAPHIES

1. Books

24. Besterman, T[heodore]. A. A WORLD BIBLIOGRAPHY OF BIBLIOGRAPHIES AND OF BIBLIOGRAPHICAL CALENDARS, ABSTRACTS, DIGESTS, INDEXES, AND THE LIKE. 3rd ed. 4 vols. Geneva, Switzerland: Societas Bibliographica, 1955-56.

    Records 84,403 separately published bibliographies. No annotations. Includes a high proportion of foreign material.

25. THE BIBLIOGRAPHIC INDEX, A CUMULATIVE BIBLIOGRAPHY OF BIBLIOGRAPHIES. New York: Wilson, 1938- . Biannual.

    Appears twice a year and covers material published in books, pamphlets, and periodicals since 1937; mostly in English.

26. Besterman, T[heodore]. A., comp. INDEX BIBLIOGRAPHICUS. 3rd ed. 2 vols. Paris, France: United Nations Educational, Scientific and Cultural Organization, 1952.

    Volume 2 covers the social sciences, education, and humanistic studies. A directory of current periodical abstracts and bibliographies. An international selection.

2. Periodicals

27. United Nations Educational, Scientific and Cultural Organization. UNESCO BULLETIN FOR LIBRARIES. Paris, France, 1947- . Monthly.

    Announces new bibliographical tools and reference works in all fields. Annual index.

Bibliographies

B. NATIONAL BIBLIOGRAPHIES

General bibliographies indicating holdings in foreign libraries are included along with information on the United States Library of Congress.

28. THE CUMULATIVE BOOK INDEX: WORLD LIST OF BOOKS IN THE ENGLISH LANGUAGE. New York: Wilson, 1898- . Monthly (except August).

    Alphabetical arrangement of authors, titles, subjects, editors, translators, illustrators, and series. Gives full bibliographic information. Frequent cumulations.

29. THE PUBLISHERS' TRADE LIST ANNUAL. BOOKS IN PRINT: AN AUTHOR-TITLE SERIES INDEX TO THE PUBLISHERS' TRADE LIST ANNUAL. New York: Bowker, 1948- .

    Contains author and title indexes.

30. THE PUBLISHERS' TRADE LIST ANNUAL. SUBJECT GUIDE TO BOOKS IN PRINT: AN INDEX TO THE PUBLISHERS' TRADE LIST ANNUAL. New York: Bowker, 1957- .

    Lists according to Library of Congress headings all of the books appearing in the annual volume of BOOKS IN PRINT.

31. United States Library of Congress. A CATALOG OF BOOKS REPRESENTED BY LIBRARY OF CONGRESS PRINTED CARDS ISSUED TO JULY 31, 1942. 167 vols. Ann Arbor, Mich.: Edwards, 1942-46.

    Author and main entry catalog of books for which Library of Congress cards have been printed.

    _____. SUPPLEMENT: CARDS ISSUED AUGUST 1, 1942 - DECEMBER 31, 1947. 42 vols. 1948.

    This five-year cumulation replaced the monthly and quarterly issues and annual cumulations.

32. _____. THE NATIONAL UNION CATALOG: A CUMULATIVE AUTHOR LIST REPRESENTING LIBRARY OF CONGRESS PRINTED CARDS AND TITLES REPORTED BY OTHER AMERICAN LIBRARIES, 1953-57. 28 volumes. Washington, D.C.: Library of Congress, 1958. Cumulation for 1958-62, 54 vols.; Cumulation for 1963-67, 72 vols.; Cumulation for 1968-72 in publication.

    The title changed to NATIONAL UNION CATALOG in 1956.

    _____. THE NATIONAL UNION CATALOG: A CUMULATIVE AU-

Bibliographies

THOR LIST REPRESENTING LIBRARY OF CONGRESS PRINTED CARDS AND TITLES REPORTED BY OTHER AMERICAN LIBRARIES, 1963- .

> Monthly issues, quarterly, and annual cumulations as well as the five-year cumulations which are listed above.

33. _____. LIBRARY OF CONGRESS CATALOG: A CUMULATIVE LIST OF WORKS REPRESENTED BY LIBRARY OF CONGRESS PRINTED CARDS: BOOKS - SUBJECTS, 1950-1954. 20 vols. Ann Arbor, Mich.: Edwards, 1955. Cumulation for 1950-54, 20 vols.; Cumulation for 1955-59, 22 vols.; Cumulation for 1960-64, 25 vols.; Cumulation for 1965-69, 42 vols.

> A complement to the author catalog. Three current quarterly issues and annual cumulation.

34. _____. General Reference and Bibliography Division. CURRENT NATIONAL BIBLIOGRAPHIES. Helen F. Conover, comp. Washington, D.C.: Government Printing Office, 1955. 132 p.

C. GUIDES TO THE LITERATURE AND SUBJECT BIBLIOGRAPHIES

1. Bibliographies of Social Science, Political Science, and International Relations

The works in the first section are primarily annotated lists of books; in the second section are works which also cover reference material and documents.

a. BIBLIOGRAPHIES OF THE LITERATURE

35. The Council on Foreign Relations. FOREIGN AFFAIRS BIBLIOGRAPHY: A SELECTED AND ANNOTATED LIST OF BOOKS ON INTERNATIONAL RELATIONS, 1952-62. By Henry L. Roberts, assisted by Jean Gunther. New York: Bowker, 1964. 773 p.

> Earlier editions were published for 1919-32 (William L. Langer and Hamilton Fish Armstrong, eds.); 1932-42 (Robert G. Woolbert, ed.); 1942-52 (Henry L. Roberts and associates, eds.). Covers books and collections of documents. Brief, critical annotations; many cross-references; author and title indexes.

36. Dexter, Byron [V.], ed. THE FOREIGN AFFAIRS 50-YEAR BIBLIOGRAPHY: NEW EVALUATION OF SIGNIFICANT BOOKS ON INTERNATIONAL RELATIONS, 1920-70. New York: Bowker, 1972. 936 p.

Bibliographies

37. INTERNATIONAL BIBLIOGRAPHY OF POLITICAL SCIENCE. Paris, France: United Nations Educational, Scientific and Cultural Organization, Annual.

    Prepared by the International Committee for Social Science Documentation under the auspices of the International Political Science Association. In English and French.

38. Headicar, B. M., and Fuller, C., comps. A LONDON BIBLIOGRAPHY OF THE SOCIAL SCIENCES. 11 vols. London: London School of Economics, 1931-55.

    Arranged chronologically under subjects and their subdivisions.

39. de Grazia, Alfred, gen. ed. INTERNATIONAL AFFAIRS. Universal Reference System: Political Science, Government and Public Policy Series, vol. 3. New York: Universal Reference Service, 1965- . Annual.

    Contains annotated entries on books and articles. Excellent indexes and classifications. First publication covered material before 1965; subsequent volumes annually.

40. Gould, Wesley L., and Barkun, Michael, eds. SOCIAL SCIENCE LITERATURE: A BIBLIOGRAPHY FOR INTERNATIONAL LAW. Princeton, N.J.: Princeton University Press, 1973. 641 p.

b. GUIDES TO LITERATURE AND RESOURCES

41. Walford, Arthur J., ed. GUIDE TO REFERENCE MATERIAL. 3rd ed. 3 vols. London: The Library Association, 1973. 3 supplements: 1965-66; 1967-68; 1969-70 (1973).

    Lists and describes reference books and bibliographies.

42. Lewis, Peter R. THE LITERATURE OF THE SOCIAL SCIENCES: AN INTRODUCTORY SURVEY AND GUIDE. London: The Library Association, 1960. 222 p.

    Covers sources in the social sciences from 1800. No subject indexes.

43. White, Carl M., et al. SOURCES OF INFORMATION IN THE SOCIAL SCIENCES: A GUIDE TO THE LITERATURE. Totowa, N.J.: Bedeminster, 1964. 511 p.

    Divided by subjects. Bibliographic review of basic monographic works with annotations, lists of guides, sources of reviews, bibliographies, abstracts, and sources of unpublished information.

Bibliographies

44. Winchell, Constance M. GUIDE TO REFERENCE WORKS. 7th ed. Chicago, Ill.: American Library Association, 1951. 662 p. 4 supplements: 1950-52; 1953-55; 1956-58; 1959-62.

    Arrangement by disciplines. Covers periodicals and newspapers, government documents, and dissertations; annotated.

45. Wynar, L.R. GUIDE TO REFERENCE MATERIALS IN POLITICAL SCIENCE AND SELECTIVE BIBLIOGRAPHY. Denver, Colo.: Colorado Bibliographic Institute, 1966. 318 p.

46. Harmon, R.B. POLITICAL SCIENCE: A BIBLIOGRAPHIC GUIDE TO THE LITERATURE. New York: Scarecrow, 1965. 388 p.

2. International Organization: General

In this and the following sections the works are of two types: the works in the first part are <u>about</u> organizations; the works in the second part are <u>of</u> organizations.

a. BIBLIOGRAPHIES OF THE LITERATURE

47. Haas, Michael, comp. INTERNATIONAL ORGANIZATION: AN INTERDISCIPLINARY BIBLIOGRAPHY. Hoover Institute Bibliographic Series XLI. Stanford, Calif.: Hoover Institute Press, 1971. 944 p.

    Comprehensive coverage of the literature, books, and periodicals. Entries included under multiple headings; not annotated.

48. Jacobson, Harold K[aron]., comp. INTERNATIONAL ORGANIZATION: A CLASSIFIED BIBLIOGRAPHY. East Lansing, Mich.: Michigan State University Press, 1969. 261 p. (For Asian Studies Center.)

48a. Holler, Frederick L. INTERNATIONAL RELATIONS AND ORGANIZATIONS, COMPARATIVE AND AREA STUDIES. Information Sources of Political Science, vol. 4. Santa Barbara, Calif.: American Biographical Center-Clio Press, 1975.

    Comprehensive and annotated.

49. Robinson, Jacob, comp. INTERNATIONAL LAW AND ORGANIZATION: GENERAL SOURCES OF INFORMATION. Leiden, Netherland: Sijthoff, 1967. 560 p.

    Annotated list of general books, register of periodicals and yearbooks. Comments on gaps in the literature. Only incidentally concerned with international organizations.

50. Speeckaert, G.P., comp. INTERNATIONAL ORGANIZATION: A SELECT BIBLIOGRAPHY, 1885-1974. Brussels, Belgium: Union of International Associations (with assistance from United Nations Educational, Scientific and Cultural Organization and in collaboration with International Federation of Documentation), 1965. 148 p.

Bibliographies

> Titles by subject and organization without annotations. Books, periodicals, and pamphlets in western languages. Covers public and private organizations.

51. Rudzinski, A. SELECTED BIBLIOGRAPHY ON INTERNATIONAL ORGANIZATION. New York: Carnegie Endowment, 1953. 36 p.

52. Aufricht, Hans, comp. GENERAL BIBLIOGRAPHY OF INTERNATIONAL ORGANIZATION AND POST-WAR RECONSTRUCTION. New York: Commission to Study the Organization of Peace, 1942. 28 p.

b. CATALOGS AND GUIDES TO PUBLICATIONS

53. Union of International Associations. DIRECTORY OF PERIODICALS PUBLISHED BY INTERNATIONAL ORGANIZATIONS. 2nd ed. Brussels, Belgium, 1959. 251 p.

   > Lists periodical publications of supranational and intergovernmental institutions, and of international nongovernmental organizations.

3. The League of Nations

a. BIBLIOGRAPHIES OF THE LITERATURE

54. League of Nations. Library. BOOKS ON THE WORK OF THE LEAGUE OF NATIONS CATALOGUED IN THE LIBRARY OF THE SECRETARIAT. Geneva, Switzerland, 1928. 274 p.

55. League of Nations. Health Organization. BIBLIOGRAPHY OF THE TECHNICAL WORK OF THE HEALTH ORGANIZATION OF THE LEAGUE, 1920-45. London: Allen & Unwin, 1946. 235 p.

   > Comprehensive coverage of published and unpublished documents.

b. CATALOGS AND GUIDES TO PUBLICATIONS

56. Aufricht, Hans. GUIDE TO LEAGUE OF NATIONS PUBLICATIONS: A BIBLIOGRAPHICAL SURVEY OF THE WORK OF THE LEAGUE, 1920-1947. New York: Columbia University Press, 1951. 701 p.

   > Covers the entire period of the League and includes all types of documents, both those on sale and those not included in the sales catalogs. Documents of the principal

autonomous organs of the League, i.e., the Permanent Court, the International Labor Organization, etc., are included. Publications of the principal organs as well as the organization of the League and its main activities are covered.

57. Breycha-Vauthier, Arthur Carl von. SOURCES OF INFORMATION: A HANDBOOK ON THE PUBLICATIONS OF THE LEAGUE OF NATIONS. London: Allen & Unwin; New York: Columbia University Press, 1939. 118 p.

> Intended to provide a selective guide to materials available in League publications for students and researchers. Materials concerning problems in the field of international relations, economics, law, and social problems are listed and described.

58. Carroll, Marie Juliette. KEY TO LEAGUE OF NATIONS DOCUMENTS PLACED ON PUBLIC SALE, 1920-1929. Boston, Mass.: World Peace Foundation, 1930. 340 p. 4 supplements 1930-36.

> Lists of documents are arranged chronologically. Subject indexes.

59. League of Nations. CATALOGUE OF PUBLICATIONS, 1920-1935. Geneva, Switzerland, 1935. 5 supplements 1936-45.

> Lists publications offered for sale. Contains explanatory notes for each division.

60. League of Nations. Library. BRIEF GUIDE TO THE LEAGUE OF NATIONS PUBLICATIONS. Rev. ed. Geneva, Switzerland, 1930. 32 p.

> Excellent brief description of publications. Explanation of classification system by subjects.

4. The United Nations and Specialized Agencies

a. BIBLIOGRAPHIES OF THE LITERATURE

61. United Nations Association of the United States of America. READ YOUR WAY TO WORLD UNDERSTANDING: A SELECTED ANNOTATED READING GUIDE OF BOOKS ABOUT THE UNITED NATIONS AND THE WORLD IN WHICH IT WORKS FOR PEACE AND HUMAN WELFARE. Rev. ed. New York: Scarecrow, 1963. 320 p.

> Annotated bibliography by subject and author chiefly for use in schools. Gives reading level of entries.

62. Flynn, Alice H., comp. WORLD UNDERSTANDING: A SELECTED

Bibliographies

BIBLIOGRAPHY. Dobbs Ferry, N.Y.: Oceana, 1965. 278 p. (For United Nations Association of the United States of America.)

63. Shepard, M. INTERNATIONAL ADMINISTRATION: THE UNITED NATIONS AND SPECIALIZED AGENCIES: A SUGGESTED LIST OF REFERENCES DATING FROM 1945. Washington, D.C.: United States Library of Congress, Legislative Reference Service, 1952. 28 p. Paperbound.

64. Cormack, M., ed. SELECTED PAMPHLETS ON THE UNITED NATIONS AND INTERNATIONAL RELATIONS. New York: Carnegie Endowment, 1951. 33 p. Pamphlet.

    Annotated guide to international organizations, politics, and programs with emphasis on the organization and work of the UN and specialized agencies.

65. Collart, Yves. DISARMAMENT; A STUDY GUIDE AND BIBLIOGRAPHY ON THE EFFORTS OF THE UNITED NATIONS. The Hague, Netherlands: Nijhoff, 1958. 110 p. (For World Federation of UN Associations and United Nations Educational, Scientific, and Cultural Organization.)

66. United Nations. Library. A BIBLIOGRAPHY OF THE CHARTER OF THE UNITED NATIONS. New York, 1955. 136 p. Pamphlet. (ST/LIB/Ser. B/3.)

    Extensive bibliography of books, pamphlets, documents, and periodicals covering the charter article by article.

67. United Nations. Dag Hammarskjold Library. CURRENT ISSUES: A SELECTED BIBLIOGRAPHY ON SUBJECTS OF CONCERN TO THE UNITED NATIONS. New York, December 1965- . Pamphlet. (ST/LIB/Ser. B/2.)

    Appears irregularly and succeeds LIST OF SELECTED ARTICLES.

68. United Nations. Headquarters Library. SELECTED BIBLIOGRAPHY OF SPECIALIZED AGENCIES RELATED TO THE UNITED NATIONS. New York, 1949. 28 p. Pamphlet. (ST/LIB/Ser. B/1.)

    Contains material on documents, publications of member governments, books and pamphlets about the structure, history, activities, and programs of the various agencies.

69. United States. Office of Education. THE UNITED NATIONS AND RELATED ORGANIZATIONS: A BIBLIOGRAPHY. Washington, D.C.: Government Printing Office, 1960. 17 p.

70. United Nations Educational, Scientific and Cultural Organization. INTERNATIONAL SOCIAL SCIENCE BULLETIN. Paris, France, 1941- . Quarterly.

    First section lists and describes or abstracts documents and publications of member governments. It also lists books and pamphlets about the structure, history, activities, and programs of the agencies.

Bibliographies

71. International Labour Office. Library. BIBLIOGRAPHY ON THE INTERNATIONAL LABOUR ORGANIZATION. Geneva, Switzerland, 1959. 143 p.

    Covers the period 1929-53 continuing the BIBLIOGRAPHY OF THE INTERNATIONAL LABOUR ORGANIZATION which was published until 1929. Contains bibliographies on the ILO, reports and monographs prepared by the ILO, books, theses, and official reports and articles.

72. Jones, H. D. UNESCO: A SELECTED LIST OF REFERENCES. Washington, D.C.: United States Library of Congress, 1948. 56 p.

    Annotated entries on books, official documents, pamphlets, and articles. Covers background, history, purpose, functions, and programs.

73. General Agreement on Tariffs and Trade. GATT BIBLIOGRAPHY, 1947-1953. Geneva, Switzerland, 1954. Ninth supplement, 1963. 41 p.

    Contains text of GATT, selected GATT publications, and a chronological list of references on the organization.

74. Loftus, Martin L. THE INTERNATIONAL MONETARY FUND: A SELECTED BIBLIOGRAPHY, 1946-1950; 1951-1952; 1953-1954; 1955-1958; 1959-1962. Washington, D.C.: International Monetary Fund. Seratim.

    Comprehensive bibliography containing materials put out by the IMF, as well as works on the organization.

75. World Health Organization. ARTICLES AND STUDIES ON THE WORLD HEALTH ORGANIZATION, 1946-1957. Geneva, Switzerland, 1959. 11 p.

b. CATALOGS AND GUIDES TO PUBLICATIONS

76. Winton, Harry N. PUBLICATIONS OF THE UNITED NATIONS SYSTEM: A REFERENCE GUIDE. 2nd ed. New York: Bowker, 1972. 213 p.

    Guide to the agencies and their publications. Covers purposes, goals, and activities of twenty UN agencies.

77. United Nations. Secretariat. Department of Public Information. UNITED NATIONS PUBLICATIONS. New York, 1945- . Annual.

    Volume for 1954 contains a cumulation and complete catalog. Entries are arranged by subject under the issuing bodies. General descriptions of UN audiovisual materials.

78. United Nations. Economic and Social Council. BIBLIOGRAPHY OF

Bibliographies

PUBLICATIONS OF THE UNITED NATIONS AND SPECIALIZED AGENCIES IN THE SOCIAL WELFARE FIELD, 1946-52. New York, 1955. 270 p.

> Annotated entries concerned with international programs, bibliographies, directories of organizations. Subject classification outline and cumulative index.

79. UNITED NATIONS PUBLICATIONS: CHECK LIST. 1973. BOOKS IN PRINT: ENGLISH. New York: Unipub, n.d. Irregularly.

> Periodically published list covering all UN publications which are available in categories denoted by a sales number.

80. United Nations. Secretariat. Office of Public Information for Human Welfare. A STUDY GUIDE ON THE WORK OF THE ECONOMIC AND SOCIAL COUNCIL. New York, 1962. 52 p.

81. International Atomic Energy Agency. INTERNATIONAL ATOMIC ENERGY AGENCY PUBLICATIONS. CATALOGUE 1972. Vienna, Austria, 1972. 165 p.

> Lists all publications of the IAEA issued since 1958 and still available. Listed by subject in alphabetical order. Contains a section on periodicals issued by the agency. Supplements are issued periodically under the title: NEW INTERNATIONAL ATOMIC ENERGY AGENCY PUBLICATIONS... SUPPLEMENT TO THE 1972 CATALOGUE.

82. Food and Agriculture Organization. CATALOGUE OF PUBLICATIONS, 1945-1972. Rome, Italy, 1974.

> Complete catalog listing both FAO and FAO-associated publications, including those out of print.

83. _____. FAO BOOKS IN PRINT, 1973. Rome, Italy, 1973. 96 p.

> Includes titles available in English, whether published directly by FAO or by other publishers by arrangement with the organization. Arranged by subject; contains basic documents, bibliographies, and catalogs. Indexed by author, title, and subject.

84. General Agreement on Tariffs and Trade. GATT: PUBLICATIONS OF THE GENERAL AGREEMENT ON TARIFFS AND TRADE, 1973-1974. Geneva, Switzerland, 1974. 10 p.

> Contains entries on GATT's organization and activities.

85. International Labour Office. CATALOGUE OF PUBLICATIONS IN ENGLISH OF THE INTERNATIONAL LABOUR OFFICE, 1919-1950. Biblio-

graphical Contributions, no. 5. Geneva, Switzerland, 1951. 379 p.

> Comprehensive indexed catalog covering the work of the organization.

86. International Labour Office Library. SUBJECT GUIDE TO PUBLICATIONS OF THE INTERNATIONAL LABOUR OFFICE, 1919-1964. Geneva, Switzerland, 1967. 478 p.

> Subject headings with cross-references. Includes sales publications and important series produced by offset processes.

87. International Labour Office. ILO PUBLICATIONS: NEW PUBLICATIONS. Geneva, Switzerland, 1968- . Bimonthly.

> Annotated listing of publications in English, French, Spanish, and German.

88. United Nations Educational, Scientific and Cultural Organization. UNESCO PUBLICATIONS: CATALOGUE, 1973. Paris, France, 1973. 208 p.

> Contains books and periodicals published directly by UNESCO. Has alphabetical and subject lists.

89. _____. GENERAL CATALOGUE OF UNESCO PUBLICATIONS AND UNESCO SPONSORED PUBLICATIONS, 1946-59. Paris, France, 1962. 217 p.

> Complete catalog. Supplements were issued for the periods 1960-63 and 1964-67.

90. World Health Organization. PUBLICATIONS OF THE WORLD HEALTH ORGANIZATION, 1947-57; A BIBLIOGRAPHY. Geneva, Switzerland, 1958. 128 p.

91. _____. PUBLICATIONS OF THE WORLD HEALTH ORGANIZATION, 1968-1972. Geneva, Switzerland, 1974. 158 p.

> Contains books and materials published by the WHO.

92. World Meteorological Organization. Secretariat. CATALOGUE OF PUBLICATIONS: METEOROLOGY AND RELATED FIELDS SUCH AS HYDROLOGY, MARINE SCIENCES AND HUMAN ENVIRONMENT. Geneva, Switzerland, 1973. 106 p.

> Contains publications issued by the WMO itself or jointly with other organizations. Publications for sale and out of print included.

93. United Nations Institute for Training and Research. UNITAR PUBLICATIONS, SPRING 1973. New York, 1973. 14 p.

Bibliographies

Lists materials available and those in process. Arranged by subject topics.

c. UNITED NATIONS BIBLIOGRAPHIC SERIES

94. UNITED NATIONS BIBLIOGRAPHICAL SERIES: (ST/LIB/Ser. B/-)
    1. SELECTED BIBLIOGRAPHY OF SPECIALIZED AGENCIES RELATED TO THE UNITED NATIONS (no. 68).
    2. CURRENT ISSUES: A SELECTED BIBLIOGRAPHY ON SUBJECTS OF CONCERN TO THE UNITED NATIONS (no. 67).
    3. A BIBLIOGRAPHY OF THE CHARTER OF THE UNITED NATIONS (no. 66).
    4. INDEX TO MICROFILM OF UN DOCUMENTS IN ENGLISH, 1946-50.
    5/rev.1. LIST OF UNITED NATIONS DOCUMENTS SERIES SYMBOLS (no. 356).
    7. LIST OF PERIODICALS AND NEWSPAPERS CURRENTLY RECEIVED.
    8. BIBLIOGRAPHICAL STYLE MANUAL (no. 364).
    12. DISARMAMENT: A SELECT BIBLIOGRAPHY, 1962-67 (no. 107).

5. The World Court

95. Douma, J., comp. BIBLIOGRAPHY OF THE INTERNATIONAL COURT OF JUSTICE, INCLUDING THE PERMANENT COURT, 1918-64. Leiden, Netherlands: Sijthoff, 1965. 387 p.

    Annotated and comprehensive coverage of organization and work of the court.

96. International Court of Justice. BIBLIOGRAPHY OF THE INTERNATIONAL COURT OF JUSTICE. The Hague, Netherlands, 1946- . Annual.

97. _____. CATALOGUE OF THE PUBLICATIONS OF THE INTERNATIONAL COURT OF JUSTICE. The Hague, Netherlands: International Court of Justice, Registry, 1963. 22 p.

    Covers all the materials of the court available for sale.

98. Permanent Court of International Justice. BIBLIOGRAPHICAL LIST OF OFFICIAL AND UNOFFICIAL PUBLICATIONS CONCERNING THE PERMANENT COURT OF INTERNATIONAL JUSTICE. 2nd ed. Compiled by J. Douma. The Hague, Netherlands, 1926. 159 p. Supplement: 1927-40/45.

    Indexed by authors and subjects, cumulative.

Bibliographies

6. Topical Bibliographies

The following bibliographies are topically arranged and cover specified areas.

a. INTERNATIONAL COOPERATION

99. Hicks, Frederick Charles. "The Literature of International Cooperation." In PAPERS AND PROCEEDINGS, pp. 41-159. Chicago: American Library Institute, 1919.

100. Viet, J. INTERNATIONAL COOPERATION AND PROGRAMMES OF ECONOMIC AND SOCIAL DEVELOPMENT. Paris, France: United Nations Educational, Scientific and Cultural Organization, 1962. 107 p.

> Annotated, covering books, articles, and papers. Divided into bilateral, multilateral, and regional programs. Covers the period from 1944-60.

b. INTERNATIONAL ADMINISTRATION

101. Rogers, W. C., comp. INTERNATIONAL ADMINISTRATION: A BIBLIOGRAPHY. Chicago, Ill.: Public Administration Service, 1945. 32 p. Pamphlet.

> Covers administration and management of varied activities undertaken internationally.

c. SECURITY AND PEACEKEEPING

102. Legault, Albert, comp. PEACE-KEEPING OPERATIONS: A BIBLIOGRAPHY. Paris, France: International Information Center on Peace-Keeping Operations, 1967. 203 p.

103. Williams, Stillman P., comp. TOWARD A GENUINE WORLD SECURITY SYSTEM: AN ANNOTATED BIBLIOGRAPHY FOR LAYMAN AND SCHOLAR. Washington, D.C.: United World Federalists, 1964. 65 p.

> Annotated bibliography of sources for areas of world law, order, and peace.

d. HUMAN RIGHTS

104. United Nations. Economic and Social Council. BIBLIOGRAPHY ON THE PROTECTION OF HUMAN RIGHTS OF WORKS PUBLISHED AFTER DECEMBER, 1939. Prepared by the Secretariat. New York, 1951.

Bibliographies

248 p. (E/CN. 4/540.)

Comprehensive, annotated bibliography.

e. INTERNATIONAL SPACE

105. United Nations. INTERNATIONAL SPACE BIBLIOGRAPHY. New York, 1966. 166 p. (Sales E. 66. I. 21.)

Lists books, reports, bulletins, government documents, and periodicals from thirty-four major countries. Arranged by type of material under country; subdivided by subject.

f. NON-SELF-GOVERNING TERRITORIES

106. Conover, Helen F., comp. NON-SELF-GOVERNING AREAS WITH SPECIAL EMPHASIS ON MANDATES AND TRUSTEESHIPS: A SELECTED LIST OF REFERENCES. 2 vols. Washington, D.C.: United States Library of Congress, 1947. ix, 467 p.

An annotated bibliography of 3603 books and articles in English, French, German, and Spanish. The work is divided into three sections: policies and practices of colonial governments; mandates and trusteeships; and regions. Entries cover information relating to economic, social, and educational conditions in the areas.

g. DISARMAMENT AND ARMS CONTROL

The 1960's saw a large upsurge in interest in disarmament, reflecting itself in the appearance of a number of bibliographies on the subject. The following are a selection. Many of the entries in Section 7, "Peace Studies," also cover disarmament. (See also 127.)

107. United Nations. Secretariat. DISARMAMENT: A SELECT BIBLIOGRAPHY, 1962-67. New York, 1968. (ST/LIB/Ser. B/12.)

108. Collart, Yves. DISARMAMENT; A STUDY GUIDE AND BIBLIOGRAPHY ON THE EFFORTS OF THE UNITED NATIONS. The Hague, Netherlands: Nijhoff, 1958. 110 p. (For World Federation of UN Associations and United Nations Educational, Scientific and Cultural Organization.)

Summary of the work done under the auspices of the UN from 1945-67.

109. United States. Department of the Army. DISARMAMENT: A BIBLIOGRAPHICAL RECORD: 1916-1960. Washington, D.C.: Government

Bibliographies

Printing Office, 1960. 122 p.

> Arranged by subject. Covers books, articles, documents, dissertations. Contains a chronology on disarmament. (See also 110.)

110. Moscowitz, Harry, and Roberts, Jack. UNITED STATES SECURITY, ARMS CONTROL AND DISARMAMENT, 1960-61. Washington, D.C.: United States Department of Defense, 1961. 105 p.

    > Detailed and annotated companion to DISARMAMENT: A BIBLIOGRAPHIC RECORD, 1916-60 (see 109).

111. Friends Committee on National Legislation. BIBLIOGRAPHY ON THE ECONOMICS OF DISARMAMENT. Philadelphia, 1961. 5 p. Mimeo.

    > Series of comprehensive listings covering official and other sources, pamphlets, articles, books.

112. League of Nations. ANNOTATED BIBLIOGRAPHY ON DISARMAMENT AND MILITARY QUESTIONS. Geneva, Switzerland, 1931. 163 p.

h. INTERNATIONAL ORGANIZATION AND AFRICA

113. Johnson, Carol A., and Russell, Sara S. "Selected Bibliography: Africa and International Organizations." INTERNATIONAL ORGANIZATION (Boston) 16(Spring 1962): 449-64.

7. Peace Studies

(See also Section 6g, "Disarmament and Arms Control," above.)

114. Pickus, Robert, and Woito, Robert, comps. TO END WAR: AN INTRODUCTION TO THE IDEAS, BOOKS, ORGANIZATIONS AND WORK. 3rd ed. New York: Harper, 1971. 261 p. Paperbound.

    > Covers all aspects of peace studies. Good introductory essay on war/peace field. Includes books, organizations, and periodicals.

115. United World Federalists. UNITED WORLD FEDERALISM: PANORAMA OF RECENT BOOKS, FILMS AND JOURNALS ON WORLD FEDERATION, THE UNITED NATIONS AND WORLD PEACE. Boston, 1960. 26 p.

    > Annotated and topically arranged.

116. Conover, Helen F., comp. WORLD GOVERNMENT: A LIST OF SELECTED REFERENCES. Washington, D.C.: Library of Congress, 1947. 11 p. Pamphlet.

Bibliographies

>Annotated; covering books, newspapers, and magazines.

117. Keohane, Robert O[wen]., and Nye, Joseph S., Jr. "Bibliography on Transnationalism." INTERNATIONAL ORGANIZATION (Boston) 25(Summer 1971): 749-58.

118. Cook, Blanche W., ed. BIBLIOGRAPHY ON PEACE RESEARCH IN HISTORY. Santa Barbara, Calif.: American Bibliographical Center-Clio Press, 1969. 74 p.

    >Covers books, dissertations, and works in progress. Also lists many of the organizations engaged in peace research.

D. ABSTRACTS AND DISSERTATIONS

1. Abstracts

Abstracts permit the student to survey and select relevant information from a large amount of material from articles, books, and other sources.

119. CURRENT THOUGHT ON PEACE AND WAR: A SEMI-ANNUAL DIGEST OF LITERATURE AND RESEARCH IN PROGRESS ON THE PROBLEMS OF WORLD ORDER AND CONFLICT. Oshkosh, Wis.: Wisconsin State University, Department of Political Science, 1960- .

120. INTERNATIONAL POLITICAL SCIENCE ABSTRACTS. Oxford, England: Basil Blackwell, 1951- . Quarterly.

    >Prepared by the International Political Science Association and the International Studies Conference. Approximately 150 journals are abstracted.

121. PEACE RESEARCH ABSTRACTS JOURNAL. Clarkson, Ontario, Canada: Canadian Peace Research Association, 1964- . Monthly.

    >Extremely comprehensive coverage of the literature. Cross-referenced.

2. Lists of Dissertations

122. DISSERTATION ABSTRACTS: ABSTRACTS OF DISSERTATIONS AND MONOGRAPHS IN MICROFILM. Ann Arbor, Mich.: University Microfilm, 1938- . Monthly.

    >Includes approximately 140 universities. Indexed yearly.

Bibliographies

123. DOCTORAL DISSERTATIONS ACCEPTED BY AMERICAN UNIVERSITIES. New York: Wilson, 1934- . Yearly. (For Association of Research Libraries.)

> Listing arrangement by fields, then by institution, and then author's name.

124. "Doctoral Dissertations in Political Science in Universities in the United States and Canada." THE AMERICAN POLITICAL SCIENCE REVIEW. September issue, 1911- . Annual.

> Lists and amends the titles in progress and completed.

125. "Doctoral Dissertations in American Universities Concerning the United Nations, 1943-61." INTERNATIONAL ORGANIZATION (Boston) 16 (Summer 1962): 668-75.

> Arranged by topic and organization of dissertations, their authors and universities.

E. PERIODICALS

126. PERSPECTIVE: MONTHLY REVIEWS OF NEW BOOKS ON GOVERNMENT/POLITICS/INTERNATIONAL AFFAIRS. Washington, D.C.: Perspective, 1971- .

> A selection of books, reviewed monthly.

127. ARMS CONTROL AND DISARMAMENT, QUARTERLY BIBLIOGRAPHY WITH ABSTRACTS AND ANNOTATIONS. Washington, D.C.: Government Printing Office, 1964-73. Quarterly.

> Compiled by the Arms Control and Disarmament Bibliographic Division, Reference Department, Library of Congress. Guide to source material, books, monographs, and publications of governments and international organizations.

F. GUIDES TO MICROFORMS

(See also 222, 223, 230, 244.)

128. Diaz, Albert James, ed. GUIDE TO MICROFORMS IN PRINT. Washington, D.C.: National Cash Register, Microcard Editions, 1961- . Annual.

> Arranged by author. Journals are listed by title and newspapers by city.

129. SUBJECT GUIDE TO MICROFORMS IN PRINT. Washington, D.C.: National Cash Register, Microcard Editions, 1962- . Annual.

Bibliographies

130. Campion, Eleanor Este, ed. UNION LIST OF MICROFILMS, CUMULATION, 1949-59. 2 vols. Ann Arbor, Mich.: Edwards, 1961.

    Arranged alphabetically. Includes location of negative, postive, and of originals when available.

Chapter 3
PERIODICALS

Chapter 3
PERIODICALS

Periodicals are a valuable source of information, as they cover many topics not lending themselves to book-length treatment. This chapter covers guides and indexes, as well as lists of important periodicals.

A. LISTS OF AND GUIDES TO PERIODICALS AND SERIALS

131. ULRICH'S PERIODICALS DIRECTORY: A CLASSIFIED GUIDE TO A SELECTED LIST OF CURRENT PERIODICALS, FOREIGN AND DOMESTIC. 10th ed. Edited by E. C. Graves. New York: Bowker, 1963. 667 p.

   Lists several thousand titles. Includes date of foundation, frequency, price, size, and address. Indicates features of each, such as illustrations, book reviews, and bibliographies. Classified arrangement with title index.

132. Gregory, W[inifred]., ed. UNION LIST OF SERIALS IN LIBRARIES OF THE UNITED STATES AND CANADA. 2nd ed. New York: Wilson, 1943. 3065 p. Supplements: 1941-43 (1945); 1944-49 (1953).

   Lists more than 120,000 titles in about 650 libraries. Gives bibliographic details as well as holdings.

133. United States Library of Congress. NEW SERIAL TITLES: A UNION LIST OF SERIALS COMMENCING PUBLICATION AFTER DECEMBER 31, 1949. Washington, D.C., 1953- . Annual.

   Replaces SERIAL TITLES NEWLY RECEIVED (1951-52). Annual volume gives place of publication, dates, class, location, frequency, address, and subscription price.

134. United Nations Educational, Scientific and Cultural Organization. A SELECTED INVENTORY OF PERIODICAL PUBLICATIONS. Paris, France, 1959. 129 p.

   An inventory of fifty-nine leading abstracting, indexing, and allied services in the field.

Periodicals

135. INTERNATIONAL RELATIONS DIGEST OF PERIODICAL LITERATURE. Berkeley, Calif.: University of California, Bureau of International Relations, 1950- . Monthly.

136. Androit, John L., ed. GUIDE TO UNITED STATES GOVERNMENT SERIALS AND PERIODICALS. 2 vols. McLean, Va.: Documents Index, 1972- . Annual.

> Lists all current serials, periodicals, releases, and reports. From 1959-72, approved as GUIDE TO UNITED STATES PUBLICATIONS.

137. United Nations Educational, Scientific and Cultural Organization. WORLD LIST OF SOCIAL SCIENCE PERIODICALS. Paris, France, 1953. 161 p.

> Lists titles of about 600 specialized periodicals published in more than fifty countries. Each periodical is explained fully. Four indexes list titles, scientific institutions publishing periodicals, specific subjects, and disciplines.

138. Davis, Edward P., comp. PERIODICALS OF INTERNATIONAL ORGANIZATIONS. Washington, D.C.: Pan American Union, 1950. 21 p.

> Part one deals with the UN and specialized agencies. General index and listing of periodicals of governments and international organizations.

139. DIRECTORY OF PERIODICALS PUBLISHED BY INTERNATIONAL ORGANIZATIONS. 2nd ed. Brussels, Belgium: Union of International Associations, 1959. 251 p.

B. INDEXES TO PERIODICAL ARTICLES

140. INTERNATIONAL INDEX TO PERIODICALS: A GUIDE TO PERIODICAL LITERATURE IN THE SOCIAL SCIENCES AND HUMANITIES. New York: Wilson, 1913- . Quarterly.

> Listed are periodicals indexed, their abbreviations, and a key. Contains author and subject indexes. Cumulated in annual volumes which are in turn cumulated into permanent volumes appearing approximately every three years.

141. Public Affairs Information Service. BULLETIN OF THE PUBLIC AFFAIRS INFORMATION SERVICE, ANNUAL CUMULATIONS. New York, 1915- .

> Lists alphabetically by subject, current books, government documents, periodical articles, and pamphlets. Listed at the beginning of the annual volume are a key to periodical references, a directory of publishers and organizations, and a list of publications analyzed.

Periodicals

142. READERS' GUIDE TO PERIODICAL LITERATURE. 1900- . New York: Wilson, 1905- . Semimonthly, September-June; monthly, July-August.

    Includes scientific and scholarly publications. Author, subject, and title indexes. Indexing is cumulative and includes permanent cumulated volumes.

143. United States. Department of State. Library. INTERNATIONAL POLITICS: A SELECTIVE MONTHLY. Washington, D.C., 1956- .

    Entries are chiefly from unofficial material, most of it in English. Included are monographs and articles found in a selected list of periodicals, which are analyzed regularly in the library.

144. Field, Norman S., ed. LEAGUE OF NATIONS AND UNITED NATIONS MONTHLY LIST OF SELECTED ARTICLES. POLITICAL QUESTIONS. 6 vols. Dobbs Ferry, N.Y.: Oceana, 1971- .

    Reproduction of card file begun by the League covering some 3,000 periodicals from all over the world. Eventually to cover legal questions, political questions, economics, and population. Six volumes of political questions, cumulative 1920-70, are completed.

145. ABC POL SCI. ADVANCE BIBLIOGRAPHY OF CONTENTS: POLITICAL SCIENCE AND GOVERNMENT. Santa Barbara, Calif.: American Bibliographical Center-Clio Press, March 1969- .

    Eight issues with indexes are published annually. Cumulated into an annual index. Covers 250 journals in political science and government. Contains list of the serial publications covered in that issue; tables of contents of these serials; and subject, law, and author indexes. A cumulative five-year index will be published in spring 1974.

C. SELECTED PERIODICALS

1. Periodicals Primarily Concerned with International Organizations

146. INTERNATIONAL ORGANIZATION. Madison, Wis. (until 1972, Boston): World Peace Foundation, 1947- . Quarterly.

    Articles on the UN and specialized agencies, as well as regional organizations. Periodically issues are devoted to a single topic and are published separately. Contains list of works published arranged by topic and organization.

147. INTERNATIONAL CONCILIATION. New York: Carnegie Endowment for International Peace, 1907-72. Frequency varied. From 1955-72, 5 times a year.

Periodicals

Each issue is an extended essay on a topic related to the work of international organizations. Particularly valuable were the "Issues Before the (number) General Assembly," a summary of the backgrounds and previous international action on agenda items.

148. VISTA. New York: United Nations Association of the United States of America, 1965- . Bimonthly.

    Covers the work of the organization and analytic articles. Has a section once a year on "Issues Before the (number) General Assembly." Covers U.S. policy and action. Succeeds CHANGING WORLD.

149. Institute for Annual Review of United Nations Affairs. ANNUAL REVIEW OF UNITED NATIONS AFFAIRS. New York: New York University Press, 1949- . Annual.

    Papers presented by Secretariat members and academic observers on wide range of UN activities and decisions in political, social, and legal areas.

150. ASSOCIATIONS. Brussels, Belgium: Union of International Associations, October 1955- . Monthly.

    Supersedes INTERNATIONAL ASSOCIATIONS (January 1949-55). Gives news of intergovernmental and nongovernmental organizations and a table of forthcoming meetings.

2. Periodicals of the United Nations and Specialized Agencies

a. UNITED NATIONS

151. UN MONTHLY CHRONICLE. New York: United Nations, Office of Public Information, May 1964- . Monthly except August.

    Supersedes: UNITED NATIONS BULLETIN (August 3, 1946 - June 15, 1954, semimonthly) and UNITED NATIONS REVIEW (July 1954 - April 1964, monthly). Designed to advance public understanding of the UN and specialized agencies. Comprehensive, documented accounts of activities and information on related agencies. Indexed yearly.

152. UNITED NATIONS REPORTER. New York: United Nations, Office of of Public Information, April 1950- . Monthly.

    Supersedes UNITED NATIONS NEWSLETTER (May 1948 - April 1950). Short, illustrated monthly resume of highlights of activities of the UN and specialized agencies.

153. UNITED NATIONS WEEKLY BULLETIN. New York: United Nations, August 1946 - December 1947.

    Weekly summaries of activities of the organization.

b. SPECIALIZED AGENCIES

154. CERES: FAO REVIEW. Rome, Italy: Food and Agricultural Organization, 1968- . Bimonthly.

    Summarizes work of the organization.

155. INTERNATIONAL LABOUR REVIEW. Geneva, Switzerland: International Labour Office, 1921- . Monthly.

    International medium for discussion of labor questions, carrying authoritative articles, reports, and inquiries of conditions of labor and employment throughout the world. Bibliography of official and unofficial books and pamphlets on social and economic questions with special implications for labor.

156. GATT ACTIVITIES IN (year). Geneva, Switzerland, 1950- . Irregular.

    Previously THE ACTIVITIES OF GATT (year), describes the trade policy issues and other work before the contracting parties and Secretariat during the period covered.

157. TELECOMMUNICATIONS JOURNAL. Geneva, Switzerland: International Telecommunications Union, 1962- . Monthly.

    Describes the work of the union and problems of international telecommunications.

158. UNESCO CHRONICLE. Paris, France: United Nations Educational, Scientific and Cultural Organization, July 1955- . Monthly.

    Combines UNESCO BULLETIN and UNESCO NEWSLETTER. Reviews UNESCO action throughout the world and gives timetables of conferences and meetings.

159. UNESCO COURIER. New York, 1948- . Monthly.

    Describes the work of the organization and the problems and situations with which UNESCO is concerned. Popular style with many photographs.

160. UNION POSTALE. Bern, Switzerland: Universal Postal Union, 1875- . Monthly.

    Reviews work of the organization and provides information

of interest to postal administrations.

161. WHO CHRONICLE. Rome, Italy, 1947- . Monthly.

    Covers health work of the World Health Organization and health problems throughout the world.

162. WMO BULLETIN. Geneva, Switzerland, 1952- . Quarterly.

    A summary of the work of the World Meteorological Organization. Covers developments in international meteorology of interest to members and others concerned with the application of meteorology to human activity.

3. Periodicals Frequently Containing Material on International Organizations

163. THE AMERICAN JOURNAL OF INTERNATIONAL LAW. Washington, D.C.: The American Society of International Law, 1907- . With supplements. Quarterly.

164. Indian Society of International Law. INDIAN JOURNAL OF INTERNATIONAL LAW. Delhi, India, 1960- . Quarterly.

165. DISARMAMENT AND ARMS CONTROL: AN INTERNATIONAL QUARTERLY JOURNAL. Oxford, England: Pergamon Press, 1963- . Quarterly.

    International forum for discussion of disarmament and arms control.

166. THE AMERICAN POLITICAL SCIENCE REVIEW. Washington, D.C.: American Political Science Association, 1906- . Quarterly.

167. BACKGROUND: JOURNAL OF THE INTERNATIONAL STUDIES ASSOCIATION. San Francisco, Calif.: San Francisco State College, Institute for Research on International Behavior, 1957- . Quarterly.

168. NEW YORK UNIVERSITY JOURNAL OF INTERNATIONAL LAW AND POLITICS. New York: New York University Law Society, 1968- . Semiannual.

169. COLUMBIA JOURNAL OF TRANSNATIONAL LAW. Buffalo, N.Y.: William S. Hein, 1961- . Triannually.

Periodicals

170. FOREIGN AFFAIRS: AN AMERICAN QUARTERLY REVIEW. New York: Council on Foreign Relations, 1922- . Quarterly.

171. INTERNATIONAL AFFAIRS. London: The Royal Institute of International Affairs, 1922- . Quarterly.

172. THE INTERNATIONAL AND COMPARATIVE LAW QUARTERLY. London: British Institute of International and Comparative Law, 1952- . Quarterly.

173. INTERNATIONAL JOURNAL. Toronto, Canada: Canadian Institute of International Affairs, 1946- . Quarterly.

174. THE JOURNAL OF CONFLICT RESOLUTION: A QUARTERLY FOR RESEARCH RELATED TO WAR AND PEACE. Beverly Hills, Calif.: Sage Publications, 1957- . Quarterly.

> Prior to September 1972, published by University of Michigan, The Center for Conflict Resolution, Ann Arbor, Michigan.

175. JOURNAL OF INTERNATIONAL AFFAIRS. Edited by graduate students of the School of International Affairs, Columbia University. New York: Columbia University, 1947- . Semiannual.

176. THE JOURNAL OF POLITICS. Gainesville, Fla.: University of Florida, Southern Political Science Association, 1939- . Quarterly.

177. WORLD POLITICS. A QUARTERLY JOURNAL OF INTERNATIONAL RELATIONS. Princeton, N.J.: Princeton University, Center of International Studies, 1948- . Quarterly.

4. Future and Peace-Oriented Journals

The mushrooming interest in future and peace research in the last decade has led to the publication of a large number of periodicals, many of which carry articles on international organizations. A selection follows.

178. BULLETIN OF PEACE PROPOSALS. Oslo, Norway: International Peace Research Institute, 1970- . Quarterly.

179. COOPERATION AND CONFLICT: NORDIC STUDIES IN INTERNATIONAL CONFLICT. Stockholm, Sweden: Nordic Committee for the Study of International Politics, 1965- . Semiannual.

180. INTERNATIONAL PEACE RESEARCH NEWSLETTER. Oslo, Norway: International Peace Research Association, International Peace Research Institute, 1963- . Three times a year.

Periodicals

181. JOURNAL OF PEACE RESEARCH. Oslo, Norway: International Peace Research Institute, 1964- . Quarterly.

182. PEACE RESEARCH. Oakville, Ontario, Canada: Canadian Peace Research Institute, 1969- . Monthly.

183. PEACE RESEARCH REVIEWS. Oakville, Ontario, Canada: Canadian Peace Research Institute, 1970- . Irregular.

184. QUAKER SERVICE BULLETIN. Philadelphia: American Friends Service Committee, 1919- . Three times a year.

185. THE FUTURIST. Washington, D.C.: World Future Society, 1966- . Irregular.

186. TRANSACTION (SOCIAL SCIENCE AND MODERN SOCIETY). New Brunswick, N.J.: Rutgers - The State University, November 1963- . Bimonthly.

187. WAR/PEACE REPORT. New York: Center for War/Peace Studies, 1961- . Bimonthly.

188. WORLD FEDERALIST. The Hague, Netherlands: World Association of World Federalists, 1954- . Quarterly.

189. WORLD JUSTICE. Louvain, Belgium: Research Center for International Social Justice, 1959- . Quarterly.

D. YEARBOOKS

1. General

190. THE INTERNATIONAL YEARBOOK AND STATEMEN'S WHO'S WHO. London: Burke's Peerage, 1953- .

    Includes information on international organizations.

191. STATESMAN'S YEAR BOOK: STATISTICAL AND HISTORICAL ANNUAL OF THE WORLD. London and New York: Macmillian, 1864- .

    Gives descriptions and statistical information concerning international organizations.

Periodicals

2. Yearbooks of International Organizations and Their Activities

192. YEARBOOK OF INTERNATIONAL ORGANIZATIONS. Brussels, Belgium: Union of International Associations, 1948- .

    Useful international reference manual with full descriptions of some 1500 associations whose membership and purposes cross national boundaries. Covers both intergovernmental and nongovernmental organizations.

193. WORLD POLITY: A YEARBOOK OF STUDIES IN INTERNATIONAL LAW AND ORGANIZATION. Washington, D.C.: Institute of World Polity, 1957- .

    Information concerning important developments in international organizations, especially as these relate to the development of international law.

194. YEARBOOK OF INTERNATIONAL CONGRESS PROCEEDINGS. Brussels, Belgium: Union of International Associations, 1969- .

    Listing and description of the proceedings of intergovernmental and nongovernmental organizations.

195. THE LEAGUE FROM YEAR TO YEAR. Geneva, Switzerland: League of Nations, Information Section, 1927/28-1938.

    Covers major events of organs and related agencies. Contains charts of membership, lists of sales agents and information centers, and other information.

196. YEARBOOK OF THE LEAGUE OF NATIONS. Brooklyn, N.Y.: Brooklyn Daily Eagle, 1921-25.

    Nonofficial coverage of each year's activities.

197. YEARBOOK OF THE UNITED NATIONS. New York: United Nations, Department of Public Information, United Nations Publications, 1946/47- .

    Record of activities of the UN and specialized agencies. Subjects are treated in detailed essays with documentary references. Tables and lists of informational data and a comprehensive index of persons, countries, and subjects are included. Usually appears a couple of years after the year covered (1972 volume appeared spring 1975).

198. YEARBOOK OF THE INTERNATIONAL LAW COMMISSION. New York: United Nations, 1963- .

    Contains studies, reports, and discussions of the ILC. Valuable in tracing the development of conventions with which that body has been charged.

199. UNITED NATIONS JURIDICAL YEARBOOK. New York: United Nations, 1963- .

> Information on legal status of organizations, reports of legal activities, and decisions of international tribunals.

200. ANNUAL REPORT OF THE PERMANENT COURT OF INTERNATIONAL JUSTICE. Leiden, Netherlands: Sijthoff, 1925- .

> Contains basic documents of the court and a summary of its action. (Series E of PUBLICATIONS OF THE PERMANENT COURT OF INTERNATIONAL JUSTICE.)

201. YEARBOOK OF THE INTERNATIONAL COURT OF JUSTICE. The Hague, Netherlands: International Court of Justice. Registry, 1947- .

> Contains the court's basic texts, description of the organization of the court, and its jurisdiction in contentious and advisory proceedings. Covers the work for the year. A continuation of the ANNUAL REPORT OF THE PERMANENT COURT OF INTERNATIONAL JUSTICE (see 200).

202. INTERNATIONAL LABOUR ORGANIZATION YEARBOOK. Geneva, Switzerland, 1930- .

> Covers the structure, organization, and yearly activities of the organization.

203. YEARBOOK ON HUMAN RIGHTS. New York: United Nations, Secretariat, 1946- .

> Covers constitutional and judicial material relevant to the promotion of human rights nationally and internationally.

204. ISRAEL YEARBOOK ON HUMAN RIGHTS. Tel Aviv, Israel: Tel Aviv University, Faculty of Law, 1971- .

> Treats general human rights problems and situations in specific countries as well as reviewing international standards and actions.

205. SIPRI YEARBOOK OF WORLD ARMAMENTS AND DISARMAMENT. Stockholm, Sweden: International Peace Research Institute; New York: Humanities Press, 1968/69- .

> Unique reference book covering current trends in world military expenditures, technology of the arms race, and the quest for arms control and disarmament. Valuable chronology of proposals. Also covers peacekeeping forces.

Periodicals

206. YEARBOOK OF AIR AND SPACE LAW. Montreal, Canada: Queen's University Press, 1967- .

    Covers national and international laws and discusses the work of the International Civil Aviation Organization for the year covered.

3. Yearbooks and Proceedings of International Law Associations

a. INTERNATIONAL ASSOCIATIONS

207. Academie de Droit International de la Hage. RECUEIL DES COURS. Leiden, Netherlands: Sijthoff, 1923- .

    The general course is described and each of the other public international law courses is summarized in a paragraph or two. Outstanding authorities on international law and organization are invited to give the courses.

208. Dupuy, R. J., ed. THE HAGUE ACADEMY OF INTERNATIONAL LAW. JUBILEE BOOK (1923-1973). Leiden, Netherlands: Sijthoff, 1973.

    Gives origins of the academy, description of history, appraisal of activities, and analysis of programs, as well as summaries of lectures given.

209. Institut de Droit International. ANNUAIRE, INSTITUT DE DROIT INTERNATIONAL. Basel, Switzerland: Editions juridiques et sociologiques, 1873- .

    Distinguished contributions on the development of international law and organization since the inception of the institute.

210. Grotius Society. TRANSACTIONS (PROBLEMS OF WAR). London, 1915-58.

    Republished as GROTIUS SOCIETY TRANSACTIONS by Oceana (Dobbs Ferry, N.Y.). Vols. 1-45 (1915-58) completed.

b. NATIONAL INTERNATIONAL LAW ASSOCIATIONS WITH YEARBOOKS IN ENGLISH

211. American Society of International Law. PROCEEDINGS. Washington, D.C., 1907- .

Periodicals

212. Australian Association of International Law. AUSTRALIAN YEARBOOK OF INTERNATIONAL LAW. Sydney, Australia: Butterworths, 1955- . Irregular.

213. Royal Institute of International Affairs. BRITISH YEARBOOK OF INTERNATIONAL LAW. Oxford, England: Geoffrey Cumberlege, 1920- .

214. International Law Association, Canadian Branch. THE CANADIAN YEARBOOK OF INTERNATIONAL LAW. Vancouver, Canada: University of British Columbia Publications Centre, 1962- .

215. Chinese Society of International Law. THE ANNALS OF THE CHINESE SOCIETY OF INTERNATIONAL LAW. Taipai, China, 1964- .

216. Nigerian Society of International Law. PROCEEDINGS. Lagos, Nigeria, 1972- .

217. Netherlands International Law Review and Dutch Inter-University Institute for International Law. NETHERLANDS YEARBOOK OF INTERNATIONAL LAW. Leiden, Netherlands: Sijthoff, 1969- .

218. Soviet Association of International Law. SOVIET YEARBOOK OF INTERNATIONAL LAW. Moscow, USSR: Navka Publishing House, 1958- .

219. Tokyo Japan Branch of the International Law Association. THE JAPANESE ANNUAL OF INTERNATIONAL LAW. Tokyo, Japan, 1957- .

E. NEWSPAPERS

1. Directories

220. Gregory, Winifred, ed. AMERICAN NEWSPAPERS 1821-1936: A UNION LIST OF FILES AVAILABLE IN THE UNITED STATES AND CANADA. New York: Wilson, 1937. 791 p.

> Compiled under the auspices of the Bibliographical Society of America. Lists depositories of files of newspapers for the dates given in libraries in the United States and Canada. Contains notes on newspapers published in foreign countries.

221. Merrill, John C., et al, eds. THE FOREIGN PRESS. Baton Rouge, La: Louisiana State University Press, 1964. 277 p.

> Deals primarily with newspapers and magazines.

222. Schwegmann, George A., Jr., comp. NEWSPAPERS ON MICROFILM FOR THE UNITED STATES, 1948-72. Washington, D.C.: United States Library of Congress, Microfilming Clearing House, 1973. 1079 p.

> Contains approximately 16,000 entries representing about 4,000 foreign and 12,000 domestic newspapers.

223. _____. NEWSPAPERS ON MICROFILM FOR FOREIGN COUNTRIES, 1948-72. Washington, D.C.: United States Library of Congress, Microfilming Clearing House, 1973. 288 p.

224. WILLING'S PRESS GUIDE. London: James Willing, 1871- . Annual.

> Covers press of the United Kingdom, Commonwealth, and some foreign publications. Lists times of publication, price, publisher, and address. Previously published as Frederick May's London Press Dictionary.

225. NEWSPAPERS RECEIVED CURRENTLY IN THE LIBRARY OF CONGRESS. 3rd ed. Washington, D.C.: United States Library of Congress, 1972. 23 p.

> Formerly NEWSPAPERS CURRENTLY RECEIVED AND PERMANENTLY RETAINED IN THE LIBRARY OF CONGRESS.

2. Indexes to Articles in English

226. THE CHRISTIAN SCIENCE MONITOR INDEX. Corvallis, Oreg.: Helen M. Cropsey, 1900- . Monthly, with semiannual and annual cumulations.

227. THE NEW YORK TIMES INDEX. New York: THE NEW YORK TIMES, 1913- . Monthly with quarterly and annual cumulations.

> Entries are under names and subjects, cross-referenced to persons and related events in addition to date, page, and column. Also brief abstracts compiled chronologically and arranged alphabetically under subject headings.

228. INDEX TO THE TIMES. London: THE TIMES, 1906- . Monthly with annual cumulations.

> References to date, page, and column.

229. THE WALL STREET JOURNAL INDEX. New York: Dow Jones, 1958- . Monthly with annual cumulations.

3. Newspapers on Microfilm

230. NEWSPAPERS IN MICROFORM: UNITED STATES, 1948-72. Washington,

Periodicals

D.C.: United States Library of Congress, 1973.

Supersedes NEWSPAPERS ON MICROFILM. 6th ed. 1967.

4. Newspapers Devoted to International Organizations

231.   THE INTERDEPENDENT. New York: United Nations Association, United States of America, April 1974- . Monthly.

   Reports on what international organizations are doing to advance the world toward a more unified and peaceful planet. Shows how U.S. government is responding to the need to cooperate. Journalistic in style.

Chapter 4
DOCUMENTS

Chapter 4

DOCUMENTS

A. INDEXES, BIBLIOGRAPHIES, AND GUIDES TO DOCUMENTS

Materials coming from international organizations have become so voluminous as to frighten the neophyte. However, researchers sooner or later will need to search these out. Fortunately, many guides and indexes have already been compiled and are of invaluable assistance.

1. Government: United States and Foreign

232. Boyd, Anne Morris. UNITED STATES PUBLICATIONS. 3rd ed. (Revised by Rae Elizabeth Rips.) New York: Wilson, 1949. xx, 647 p.

    Comprehensive treatment of the publications of the U.S. government. Indexes and bibliographic guides to foreign relations are listed with annotations.

233. Leidy, W. Phillip. A POPULAR GUIDE TO GOVERNMENT PUBLICATIONS. 2nd ed. New York and London: Columbia University Press, 1963. 291 p.

    The table of contents is arranged in alphabetical and topical order.

234. OFFICIAL PUBLICATIONS OF EUROPEAN GOVERNMENTS. Paris, France: American Library of Paris, Reference Service on International Affairs, 1926. 259 p.

    Bibliography of official material published by European governments.

235. Schmeckebier, Laurence F[rederick]., and Eastin, Roy B. GOVERNMENT PUBLICATIONS AND THEIR USE. 2nd rev. ed. Washington, D.C.: Brookings, 1969. 510 p.

    Covers catalogs, indexes, bibliographies, and reports. Lists depository libraries for government publications.

236. Meyriat, Jean, ed. A STUDY OF CURRENT BIBLIOGRAPHIES OF NATIONAL OFFICIAL PUBLICATIONS: SHORT GUIDE AND INVENTORY. Paris, France: United Nations Scientific, Educational and Cultural Organization, International Committee for Social Sciences Documentation, 1958. 260 p.

> Systematic inventory of lists and catalogs of official documents and official publications categories of ninety-seven countries. Contains a narrative guide to the bibliographic control and identification of official material.

237. Childs, James Bennett, ed. GOVERNMENT DOCUMENT BIBLIOGRAPHY IN THE UNITED STATES AND ELSEWHERE. 3rd ed. Washington, D.C.: Government Printing Office, 1942. 96 p. (For the United States Library of Congress, Division of Documents.)

> Contains check lists and catalogs of government documents of the United States and approximately fifty foreign countries.

2. International Organizations

a. GENERAL

238. Dimitrov, Th. D., ed. DOCUMENTS OF INTERNATIONAL ORGANIZATIONS: A BIBLIOGRAPHIC HANDBOOK COVERING THE UNITED NATIONS AND OTHER INTER-GOVERNMENTAL ORGANIZATIONS. Chicago, Ill.: American Library Association, 1973. 301 p.

> Examines cumulative experience of the use of international documents in the dissemination of information.

239. Turner, Robert K., and Alexander, Patricia S., comps. DOCUMENTS OF INTERNATIONAL ORGANIZATIONS: A SELECTED BIBLIOGRAPHY. 3 vols. Boston, Mass.: World Peace Foundation, 1947-50.

> Planned as a quarterly, it was published for three years. Covered official documentation of the UN, specialized agencies, the League, and regional organizations.

240. Levi, Werner, comp. DOCUMENTS RELATING TO INTERNATIONAL ORGANIZATIONS. Minneapolis, Minn.: Burgess, n.d. 89 p. Mimeographed.

241. Gregory, Winifred, ed. INTERNATIONAL CONGRESSES AND CONFERENCES, 1840-1937: A UNION LIST OF THEIR PUBLICATIONS AVAILABLE IN THE LIBRARIES OF THE UNITED STATES AND CANADA. New York: Wilson, 1938. 229 p.

242. Schaaf, R. W. DOCUMENTS OF INTERNATIONAL MEETINGS. Washington, D.C.: United States Library of Congress, 1953. 210 p.

 Annotated bibliography of documents and official records.

b. THE LEAGUE OF NATIONS

(See also 56, 58.)

243. Ghebali, Victor Yves, and Ghebali, Catherine, eds. A REPERTOIRE OF SERIAL DOCUMENTS, 1919-47. 2 vols. Dobbs Ferry, N.Y.: Oceana, 1973. 787 p. (For Carnegie Endowment for International Peace.)

 A comprehensive compilation of serial documents, many listed for the first time. Includes correspondence; minutes; and reports of League committees, conferences, and the Secretariat. Detailed explanation of the numbering and symbol systems of League documents. Functionally structured: Part I, League Institutional Structure; Part II, the League Activities in Connection with the Implementation of Peace Treaties; Part III, the League Activities in Connection with the Maintenance of International Peace and Security; and Part IV, the League Activities in Connection with the Promotion of Functional Cooperation.

244. Reno, Edward A., Jr., ed. LEAGUE OF NATIONS DOCUMENTS, 1919-46: A DESCRIPTIVE GUIDE AND KEY TO THE MICROFILM COLLECTIONS. 3 vols. New Haven, Conn.: Research Publications, vol. 1, 1973. 282 p.; vol. 2, 1974. 539 p.; vol. 3 in prep.

 Over 25,000 documents are abstracted, calendared, controlled, categorized, and indexed. Organized by original League subject categories, by year and type of document. Abstracts of the documents have been made (see 270).

245. LIST OF CONVENTIONS WITH INDICATION OF THE RELEVANT ARTICLES CONFERRING POWERS ON THE ORGANS OF THE LEAGUE OF NATIONS. London: Allen & Unwin, 1945. 160 p.

 Comprehensive listing.

246. Kluyver, Mrs. C. A., ed. DOCUMENTS OF THE LEAGUE OF NATIONS. Leiden, Netherlands: Sijthoff, 1920. 367 p.

 An early guide to the contents, symbol systems, and series of the League.

Documents

c. THE UNITED NATIONS

The most complete collection of UN documents is in the Dag Hammarskjold Library in New York and in the UN Library in Geneva, Switzerland. A number of libraries in the United States and other countries have been designated as depositories and receive certain categories of material.

247. Brimmer, Brenda, et al. A GUIDE TO THE USE OF UNITED NATIONS DOCUMENTS, INCLUDING REFERENCE TO THE SPECIALIZED AGENCIES AND SPECIAL U.N. BODIES. Rev. ed. Dobbs Ferry, N.Y.: Oceana, 1962. 287 p.

> A description of the documentation system of the UN and suggestions on techniques of research.

248. Moor, Carol Carter, and Chamberlin, Waldo. HOW TO USE UNITED NATIONS DOCUMENTS. New York: New York University Press, 1952. 26 p.

> Explains and lists the many tools and guides to the documentation and publications. Has a selected guide by subject. Contains guide to symbol system and symbols used in press releases.

249. McConaughy, John Bothwell, and Blanks, Hazel Janet. A STUDENT'S GUIDE TO UNITED NATIONS DOCUMENTS AND THEIR USE. New York: Council on International Relations and United Nations Affairs, 1969. 17 p.

> Directory of reference sources of documents. Explains symbols.

250. Patch, William. THE USE OF UNITED NATIONS DOCUMENTS. Urbana, Ill.: Illinois University Library School, n.d. 29 p.

251. United Nations. UNITED NATIONS OFFICIAL RECORDS, 1948-62: A REFERENCE CATALOGUE. New York, 1963. 107 p. (ST/CS/Ser.J/2.)

252. United Nations. Library. UNDEX: UNITED NATIONS DOCUMENTS INDEX. New York, 1970- . Irregular.

> Supersedes: UNITED NATIONS DOCUMENTS INDEX (1950-70, monthly) and CHECKLIST OF UNITED NATIONS DOCUMENTS (1949, covering the period 1946-49). Less comprehensive than the previous indexes, UNDEX is limited to selected portions of documents and publications mostly in the economic, social, and human rights fields. Cumulations annually.

Documents

253. _____. INDEX TO PROCEEDINGS OF THE GENERAL ASSEMBLY. New York, 1952- . Annual. (ST/LIB/Ser. B/A.)

   Started with the fifth session (1950-51) with the twentieth and twenty-first sessions omitted.

254. _____. INDEX TO PROCEEDINGS OF THE SECURITY COUNCIL. New York, 1964- . Annual. (ST/LIB/Ser. B/S.)

   Started with nineteenth year (1964). Omitted twenty-first year (1966).

255. Deardoff, John. UNITED NATIONS SECURITY COUNCIL: INDEX TO MATTERS IN THE OFFICIAL RECORDS, 1946-64. Columbus, Ohio: Ohio State University Libraries, United Nations Collection, 1969. 106 p.

256. United Nations. Library. INDEX TO PROCEEDINGS OF THE ECONOMIC AND SOCIAL COUNCIL. New York, 1952- . Annual. (ST/LIB/Ser. B/E.)

   First index covered the fifth to fourteenth sessions. Omitted are forty-fourth, forty-sixth, and fifty-first sessions.

257. Deardoff, John. UNITED NATIONS ECONOMIC AND SOCIAL COUNCIL: INDEX TO DOCUMENTS, 1946-65. Columbus, Ohio: Ohio State University, United Nations Collection, 1969. 177 p.

258. United Nations. Library. INDEX TO DOCUMENTS OF THE TRUSTEESHIP COUNCIL. New York, 1952- . Annual. (ST/LIB/Ser. B/T.)

   Started with coverage of the eleventh session. Omitted are the thirty-third, thirty-fourth, and thirty-eighth sessions.

259. _____. LIST OF UNITED NATIONS DOCUMENTS SERIES SYMBOLS. Rev. ed. New York, 1970. 180 p. (ST/LIB/Ser. B/5/rev.1.)

260. Royal Institute of International Affairs. UNITED NATIONS DOCUMENTS, 1941-45. London, 1946. 271 p.

261. Schnapper, M. D., ed. UNITED NATIONS AGREEMENTS. Washington, D.C.: American Council on Public Affairs, 1944. 376 p.

262. United Nations. Office of Legal Affairs. LIST OF TREATY COLLECTIONS. New York, 1956. 189 p. (ST/LEG/5.)

   Part I contains general collections and includes indexes, chronologies, bibliographies, and handbooks. Part II lists collections by subject matter. Part III lists collections by country. Indexed.

Documents

d. THE WORLD COURT

(See also 96, 97, 279, 280.)

263.   Permanent Court of International Justice. GENERAL INDEXES. Leiden, Netherlands: Sijthoff, 1927-35. (Series F.)
      Covers the series publications of the court.

B. COLLECTED DOCUMENTS AND RECORDS

Included here are only frequently consulted documents. Consult materials in the first part of this chapter for information on how to locate other documents.

1. The League of Nations

264.   LEAGUE OF NATIONS DOCUMENTS AND PUBLICATIONS. ? vols. New Haven, Conn.: Research Publications, 1973- .
      A complete microfilm collection containing documents, serial publications, and miscellaneous publications. Over 25,000 official League subject categories are used. See 248 for indexes to the total collection.

265.   League of Nations. OFFICIAL JOURNAL. Geneva, Switzerland, 1920-46. Monthly.
      Verbatim records of Council meetings, texts of reports and resolutions, and official documents received by the Council.

266.   _____. RECORDS. Geneva, Switzerland, 1920-46. Annual.
      Verbatim records of the League Assembly.

2. The United Nations

(See also 260, 667, 966, 970.)

267.   UNITED NATIONS CONFERENCE ON INTERNATIONAL ORGANIZATION, SAN FRANCISCO, 1945. 22 vols. London and New York: United Nations, Information Organization, 1945-55.
      Complete documentation of the Conference with historical background. Indexed.

Documents

268. United States Department of State. THE UNITED NATIONS CONFERENCE ON INTERNATIONAL ORGANIZATION: SELECTED DOCUMENTS WITH HISTORICAL BACKGROUND. U.S. Department of State Publication 2490; Conference Series 83. Washington, D.C.: Government Printing Office, 1946. 992 p.

269. THE UNITED NATIONS IN THE MAKING: BASIC DOCUMENTS. Boston, Mass.: World Peace Foundation, 1946. 136 p.

    Covers the origins and creation of the organization; selective and indexed.

270. Djonovich, Susan J., comp. and ed. RESOLUTIONS OF THE GENERAL ASSEMBLY. Ser. 1, 1946-1948. United Nations Resolutions, vol. 1. Dobbs, Ferry, N.Y.: Oceana, 1973- .

    There are 15 volumes projected for this series. Basic arrangement will consist of four series of resolutions, supplementary documents, and voting records of the four major organs of the UN. To be chronological with subject indexes for each series. Resolutions and clarifying documents upon which the resolutions were formulated will be photographically reproduced with the documents in the appendices at the end of the appropriate volumes. System of cross-referencing.

271. United Nations. General Assembly. OFFICIAL RECORDS. New York, 1946- . Annual.

    Verbatim proceedings. Supplement 1: "Report of the Secretary-General on the Work of the Organization." Supplement 2: "Report of the Security Council to the General Assembly." Supplement 3: "Report of the Economic and Social Council to the General Assembly." Supplement 4: "Report of the Trusteeship Council to the General Assembly."

272. United Nations. Security Council. OFFICIAL RECORDS. New York, 1946- . Annual.

    Verbatim proceedings.

273. United Nations. Economic and Social Council. OFFICIAL RECORDS. New York, 1946- . Annual.

    Verbatim proceedings. Contains annual reports of committees, commissions, and other related bodies.

274. United Nations. Trusteeship Council. OFFICIAL RECORDS. New York, 1946- . Annual.

    Verbatim proceedings. Contains reports from the administering powers and various investigatory bodies.

Documents

3. The World Court

275. Scott, James Brown, ed. THE HAGUE COURT REPORTS. 2 vols. New York: Oxford University Press, 1916 (vol. 1) and 1932 (vol. 2).

    Covers the work of the Permanent Court of Arbitration.

276. Hudson, Manley O[ttmer]., ed. WORLD COURT REPORTS: A COLLECTION OF JUDGMENTS, ORDERS AND OPINIONS OF THE PERMANENT COURT OF INTERNATIONAL JUSTICE. 4 vols. Washington, D.C.: Carnegie, 1934-43. Reprint. Dobbs Ferry, N.Y.: Oceana, 1960.

277. Hambro, Eduard, ed. THE CASE LAW OF THE INTERNATIONAL COURT: A REPERTOIRE OF THE JUDGMENTS, ADVISORY OPINIONS AND ORDERS OF THE PERMANENT COURT OF INTERNATIONAL JUSTICE AND OF THE INTERNATIONAL COURT OF JUSTICE. 2 vols. Leiden, Netherlands: Sijthoff, 1952 (vol. 1), 706 p.; 1960 (vol. 2), 376 p.

    A valuable collection of the cases of the court with good indexing and cross-references.

278. Syatauw, J. J. G. DECISIONS OF THE INTERNATIONAL COURT OF JUSTICE: A DIGEST. Leiden, Netherlands: Sijthoff, 1969. 288 p.

    A useful digest in a useful form.

279. PUBLICATIONS OF THE PERMANENT COURT OF INTERNATIONAL JUSTICE. Leiden, Netherlands: Sijthoff, 1922-46.

    These publications were published in the following series:

    Series A. COLLECTION OF JUDGMENTS

    Series B. COLLECTION OF ADVISORY OPINIONS

    Series A/B. COLLECTION OF JUDGMENTS, ORDERS AND ADVISORY OPINIONS (In 1931 the Court adopted a new version of its rules and combined Series A and Series B.)

    Series C. PLEADINGS, ORAL STATEMENTS AND DOCUMENTS

    Series D. ACTS AND DOCUMENTS CONCERNING THE ORGANIZATION OF THE COURT

    Series E. ANNUAL REPORTS

    Series F. GENERAL INDEXES

280. PUBLICATIONS OF THE INTERNATIONAL COURT OF JUSTICE. The Hague, Netherlands: International Court of Justice, Registry, 1947- .

    Published in the following series:

    Series A: REPORTS OF JUDGMENTS, ADVISORY OPINIONS

Documents

	AND OTHERS (Decisions published unbound separately as rendered and bound yearly.)
Series B:	PLEADINGS, ORAL ARGUMENTS, DOCUMENTS (Contains all documents on each case; published after disposition of case.)
Series C:	ACTS AND DOCUMENTS CONCERNING THE ORGANIZATION OF THE COURT
Series D:	YEARBOOK

281. COLLECTION OF TEXTS GOVERNING THE JURISDICTION OF THE COURT. The Hague, Netherlands: The International Court of Justice, Registry, 1967- . Annual.

   Material previously contained in Chapter X of the YEARBOOK: now published separately.

282. United States Department of State. THE INTERNATIONAL COURT OF JUSTICE: SELECTED DOCUMENTS RELATING TO THE DRAFTING OF THE STATUTE. Department of State Publication 2491; Conference Series 841. Washington, D.C.: Government Printing Office, 1946. 167 p.

4. Other International Organizations

283. United Nations. Office of Legal Affairs. LEGISLATIVE TEXTS AND TREATY PROVISIONS CONCERNING THE LEGAL STATUS, PRIVILEGES AND IMMUNITIES OF INTERNATIONAL ORGANIZATIONS. 2 vols. New York, 1959. 392 p.

284. General Agreement on Tariffs and Trade. BASIC INSTRUMENTS AND SELECTED DOCUMENTS SERIES. Geneva, Switzerland, 1952- . Irregular.

   Contains important decisions, resolutions, recommendations, and reports adopted by the contracting parties. Supplements appear periodically.

285. International Bank and Monetary Fund. UNITED NATIONS MONETARY AND FINANCIAL CONFERENCE, BRETTON WOODS, NEW HAMPSHIRE, JULY 1-22 1944. FINAL ACT AND RELATED DOCUMENTS. Department of State Publication 2187; Conference Series 55. Washington, D.C.: Government Printing Office, 1944. 122 p.

286. World Health Organization. HANDBOOK OF RESOLUTIONS AND DECISIONS OF THE WORLD HEALTH ASSEMBLY AND THE EXECUTIVE BOARD, June 1948-May 1961. 11th ed. Geneva, Switzerland, 1971. 582 p.

Documents

287. _____. BASIC DOCUMENTS. Geneva, Switzerland, 1949- . Annual.

5. General Collections and Case Books

a. PUBLISHED

The collections which follow are more useful as supplementary texts than for research purposes. (See also 275-82, 1410, 1438.)

288. van Panhuys, H. F., et al, eds. INTERNATIONAL ORGANIZATION AND INTEGRATION: A COLLECTION OF TEXTS AND DOCUMENTS RELATING TO THE UNITED NATIONS, ITS RELATED AGENCIES AND REGIONAL INTERNATIONAL ORGANIZATIONS WITH ANNOTATIONS. Leiden, Netherlands, 1969. 1172 p. (For Cornelis van Vollenhaven Foundation.)

289. Sohn, Louis B., ed. BASIC DOCUMENTS OF THE UNITED NATIONS. University Casebook Series. Brooklyn, N.Y.: The Foundation Press, 1968. 329 p.

290. _____. THE UNITED NATIONS IN ACTION: TEN CASES FROM UNITED NATIONS PRACTICE. 2nd ed. University Casebook Series. Brooklyn, N.Y.: The Foundation Press, 1968. 459 p.

  Presents for teaching purposes original, condensed materials from official records describing procedures for action when peace is threatened.

291. _____. CASES ON UNITED NATIONS LAW. 2nd ed. University Casebook Series. Brooklyn, N.Y.: The Foundation Press, 1967. 1108 p.

  Extensive casebook on problems which have arisen in the work of the UN.

292. Chen, Samuel Shih-Tsai, ed. BASIC DOCUMENTS OF INTERNATIONAL ORGANIZATIONS. New York: MSS Publishing, 1972. 300 p.

293. Harley, John Eugene. DOCUMENTARY TEXTBOOK ON THE UNITED NATIONS: HUMANITY'S MARCH TOWARD PEACE. 2nd ed. Los Angeles, Calif.: Center for International Understanding, 1950. 1497 p.

294. Leyden. Rijksuniversiteit UNITED NATIONS TEXTBOOK: TEXTS OF IMPORTANT U.N. DOCUMENTS WITH ANNOTATIONS. 3rd ed. Leiden, Netherlands: Leiden University Press, 1958. 442 p.

295. Watkins, James T., and Robinson, J. William. GENERAL INTERNA-

TIONAL ORGANIZATION: A SOURCE BOOK. Princeton, N.J.: Van Nostrand, 1956. 259 p.

> Well selected collection including documents from the nineteenth century, as well as ones related to the evolution and development of the League and UN.

b. IN MICROFORM

An increasing amount of material is appearing in microform and the researcher should be on the lookout for more recent materials. (See Chapter 2.F.)

296. Leonard, L[eonard]. Larry, ed. AREA AND INTERNATIONAL DOCUMENT SERVICES. New York: Microform Aids Company, 1973- .

> Offers publications in microform of complete and authoritative documentation of international issues. Each publication includes limited circulation documents unavailable even to depository libraries. Documents are organized in logical sequence with cross-referenced tables of contents, and are supplemented with background notes, annexes, and indexes.

The following have already been published and are available in microfiche, microfilm, or (on special order) in hardcopy printout:

297. Moss, Alfred G., ed. CONSTITUTIONALISM OF THE UNITED NATIONS SYSTEM. New York: Microform Aids, 1973- .

> Comprehensive source for constitutional documents of principle and subsidiary organs. Includes the treaties and resolutions establishing UN organs and their terms of reference. Cumulative updating preiodically. Already published as of spring 1974:
>
> a. "Outer Space: The Committee on the Peaceful Uses of Outer Space, 1961 to date."
> b. "The Sea Bed: The Committee on the Peaceful Uses of the Sea Bed and Ocean Floor Beyond the Limits of National Jurisdiction, 1968 to date."
> c. "The Limits of National Jurisdiction, 1968 to date."
> d. "The Special Committee on the Question of Defining Aggression, 1953 to date."

298. Leonard, L[eonard]. Larry, et al, eds. SKYJACKING AND TERRORISM. New York: Microform Aids, 1973.

> a. "The Issue Before the U.N. 27th General Assembly, 1972." (1078 p.) Complete record of UN consideration of the issue. Includes select bibliographies, spe-

cial UN studies, and records of committee and General Assembly deliberations. Indexed.

b. "Sanctions Considered by ICAO Against Skyjacking, 1973." (514 p.) Complete documentation of deliberations with background documentation of ICAO resolutions and conventions on skyjacking.

c. "The U.N. Security Council Debate on Terrorism in Lebanon, April 1973." (490 p.) Complete documentation with background on the terrorism issue in the Middle East.

299. Leonard, L. Larry, ed. ISSUES BEFORE THE U.N. 27th GENERAL ASSEMBLY: THE TEXTS OF RESOLUTION ADOPTED AND THE VOTES BY GOVERNMENTS. New York: Microform Aids, 1973. 612 p.

A complete file on the decisions including background notes on the agenda items leading to its resolutions. Index.

C. TREATY COLLECTIONS

(See also 266.)

300. Parry, Clive, ed. THE CONSOLIDATED TREATY SERIES: 1648-1918. 100 vols. Dobbs Ferry, N.Y.: Oceana, 1969- .

Annotated with translations of summaries where necessary; 120 volumes planned.

301. League of Nations. TREATY SERIES: PUBLICATION OF TREATIES AND INTERNATIONAL ENGAGEMENTS REGISTERED WITH THE SECRETARIAT OF THE LEAGUE. 205 vols. Geneva, Switzerland, 1920-46.

Includes treaties between the members and also between members and nonmembers. Indexed in 9 volumes.

302. United Nations. TREATY SERIES: TREATIES AND INTERNATIONAL AGREEMENTS REGISTERED OR FILED AND RECORDED WITH THE SECRETARIAT OF THE UNITED NATIONS. New York, 1946- .

Texts of every treaty and international agreement entered into by any member of the UN. Indexed once a year.

303. Hudson, Manley O[ttmer]., ed. INTERNATIONAL LEGISLATION: 1919-1940. 9 vols. Washington, D.C.: Carnegie Endowment for International Peace, 1931. 1,180 p. Reprint. Dobbs Ferry, N.Y.: Oceana, 1971-73.

Collection of texts of multipartite international instruments of general interest.

Documents

303a. Rohn, Peter H. WORLD TREATY INDEX. 5 vols. Santa Barbara, Calif.: American Bibliographical Center—Clio Press, 1975. 3,126 p.

>   Covers 1920-70. Indexes United Nations Treaty Series, League of Nations Treaty Series, and more than three dozen national sources. Approximately 23,000 treaties cited. Supplements will update treaty information.

303b. _____. TREATY PROFILES. Santa Barbara, Calif.: American Bibliographical Center—Clio Press, 1975. 300 p.

>   Highlights significant trends in the formulation of treaties.

304. United Nations. MULTILATERAL TREATIES IN RESPECT OF WHICH THE SECRETARY-GENERAL PERFORMS DEPOSITORY FUNCTIONS AS OF DECEMBER 31, ... New York, 1946- . Annual.

>   Contains all the major multilateral treaties negotiated by international organizations and states. Contains also an Annex of the final clauses amended by states.

305. _____. MULTILATERAL TREATIES IN RESPECT OF WHICH THE SECRETARY-GENERAL PERFORMS DEPOSITORY FUNCTIONS. LIST OF SIGNATURES, RATIFICATIONS, ACCESSIONS, ETC. AS OF DECEMBER 31, ... New York, 1946- . Periodically.

>   Useful way to check on participants of treaty arrangements, as well as reservations made at the time of ratification or thereafter. Annex lists states which have made special amendments.

Chapter 5
MISCELLANEOUS INFORMATION

Chapter 5

MISCELLANEOUS INFORMATION

A. LIBRARIES AND THEIR RESOURCES

The following information is included to help the researcher locate where he can most effectively pursue his work.

1. General Information

306. United Nations Educational, Scientific and Cultural Organization. GUIDE TO NATIONAL BIBLIOGRAPHICAL INFORMATION CENTERS. 3rd ed. Paris, France, 1970. 195 p.

    Lists the main national bibliographic centers of general scope, including those specializing in the social sciences.

307. Avicenne, Paul, comp. BIBLIOGRAPHICAL SERVICES THROUGHOUT THE WORLD, 1965-69. Paris, France, 1972. 303 p.

    Updates information contained in earlier editions. Provides information on bibliographical activities in sixty-two countries.

308. WORLD GUIDE TO LIBRARIES. 3rd ed. 4 vols. New York: Bowker, 1970. 2,281 p.

    Arranged by areas, countries, and subject fields.

309. United States Library of Congress. A DIRECTORY OF INFORMATION RESOURCES IN THE UNITED STATES: SOCIAL SCIENCES. Rev. ed. Washington, D.C., 1973. 700 p.

    Gives information about libraries, information centers, professional societies. Subject index.

310. Young, Margaret Labash; Kruzas, Anthony T; and Young, Harold C., eds. DIRECTORY OF SPECIAL LIBRARIES AND INFORMATION CENTERS. 3rd ed. 3 vols. Detroit, Mich.: Gale Research, vol. 1, 1974, 1,450 p.; vol. 2, 1974, 682 p.; vol. 3, periodic supplements.

Miscellaneous Information

        More than 10,000 special libraries and information centers listed with information on principal subjects, addresses, special collections, services, and publications.

311.   International Committee for Social Sciences Documentation. INTERNATIONAL REPERTORY OF SOCIAL SCIENCE DOCUMENTATION CENTERS. Paris, France: United Nations Educational, Scientific and Cultural Organization, Department of Social Sciences, 1952. 42 p.

        Concise and precise data about research institutions in many countries.

312.   INTERNATIONAL LIBRARY DIRECTORY: A WORLD DIRECTORY OF LIBRARIES. London: The A. P. Wales Organization, Publishing Division, 1963. 1083 p.

        Type of library and its character. Books and periodical collections are indicated.

313.   Ash, Lee, and Lorenz, Denis, comps. SUBJECT COLLECTIONS: A GUIDE TO SPECIAL BOOK COLLECTIONS AND SUBJECT EMPHASES AS REPORTED BY UNIVERSITY, COLLEGE, PUBLIC AND SPECIAL LIBRARIES IN THE UNITED STATES AND CANADA. 2nd ed. New York: Bowker, 1967. 1230 p.

        Collections listed by subject headings and type of institution.

314.   Downs, Robert B. AMERICAN LIBRARY RESOURCES: A BIBLIOGRAPHICAL GUIDE. Chicago, Ill.: American Library Association, 1951. 428 p. Supplements, 1950-61 (1962), 226 p.; 1961-70 (1972), 244 p.

        Guide to published accounts of library collections. Includes government publications, catalogs, periodicals, manuscripts. Indexes of names, subjects, and libraries.

315.   _____. RESOURCES OF CANADIAN ACADEMIC AND RESEARCH LIBRARIES. Ottawa, Canada: Association of Universities and Colleges of Canada, 1967. 312 p.

        Emphasizes library procedures and facilities.

2. United States Library of Congress

A number of catalogs of the holdings of the Library have been cited. (See 31-34.)

316.   United States Library of Congress. THE NATIONAL UNION CATALOG OF MANUSCRIPT COLLECTIONS. Ann Arbor, Mich.: Edwards, 1962- . Periodically.

Miscellaneous Information

Lists bibliographically the manuscript resources of American repositories. About 12,000 from approximately 400 repositories have so far been described and indexed.

3. Libraries of the United Nations and Specialized Agencies

The UN (Geneva and New York) and specialized agencies all maintain libraries containing their own documentation and publications, as well as publications from many countries relating to the work of the particular organization.

317. United Nations. Library. CONSOLIDATED LIST OF DEPOSITORY LIBRARIES AND SALES AGENTS AND OFFICES OF THE UNITED NATIONS AND SPECIALIZED AGENCIES. 5th ed. New York, 1958. 44 p.

318. United Nations. Library. Geneva. MONTHLY LIST OF BOOKS CATALOGED IN THE LIBRARY OF THE UNITED NATIONS. Geneva, Switzerland: League of Nations, 1928-45; United Nations, 1946- . Monthly.

   Works relating to questions of every kind studied by the UN (and the League before it) are listed.

319. United Nations. Library. New York. NEW PUBLICATIONS IN THE UNITED NATIONS HEADQUARTERS LIBRARY. New York, 1949- . Monthly.

   List of recent books, periodicals, and newspapers. Publications of the UN and specialized agencies are not included.

B. RESEARCH INSTITUTIONS AND PROJECTS

(See also Chapter 3.D.3 and 118, 119, 174.)

1. Registries

320. Carnegie Endowment for International Peace. INSTITUTE OF INTERNATIONAL AFFAIRS. New York, 1953. 131 p.

   Handbook listing and describing institutions of world affairs. Contains descriptions, policies, programs, and problems. In most cases publications of the institutes are mentioned.

321. _____. CURRENT RESEARCH IN INTERNATIONAL AFFAIRS. New York, 1948-52. Annual.

Miscellaneous Information

Appeared as December issue of INTERNATIONAL CONCILIA-
TION. Major research, much of it long-term, reported on.
Indexes of persons and subjects.

322. International Committee for Social Sciences Documentation. INTERNA-
TIONAL REPERTORY OF SOCIAL SCIENCE DOCUMENTATION CENTERS.
Paris, France: United Nations Educational, Scientific and Cultural Or-
ganization, Department of Social Sciences, 1952. 42 p.

> Concise and precise data about leading research institutions
> in countries. Data given for direction, organization, sub-
> jects covered, publications, and services.

323. United Nations Educational, Scientific and Cultural Organization. THE
INTERNATIONAL REGISTER OF CURRENT TEAM RESEARCH IN THE
SOCIAL SCIENCES, 1950-52: A TENTATIVE SURVEY. Paris, France,
1955. 312 p.

> Entries are under the name of the institution and consecu-
> tively numbered.

324. INTERNATIONAL REPERTORY OF INSTITUTIONS FOR PEACE AND
CONFLICT RESEARCH. Reports and Papers in the Social Sciences
Series, no. 28. Paris, France: United Nations Educational, Scientific
and Cultural Organization, 1973. 91 p.

325. Savord, Ruth, and Wasson, Donald, comps. AMERICAN AGENCIES
INTERESTED IN INTERNATIONAL AFFAIRS. New York: Praeger,
1955. 296 p. (For the Council on Foreign Relations.)

> Gives information on action groups and organizations engaged
> in research.

326. Walton, Ann D., and Lewis, Marianna O., eds. THE FOUNDATION
DIRECTORY. 3rd ed. New York: Russell Sage Foundation, 1967.
1198 p. (For the Foundation Library Center.)

> Selected list of foundations: general research, special pur-
> pose, community, company-sponsored, and family. Includes
> data on donor, purpose, and activity.

327. Association of the Bar of the City of New York. HAMMARSKJOLD
FORUMS: CASE STUDIES ON THE ROLE OF LAW IN THE SETTLE-
MENT OF INTERNATIONAL DISPUTES. Dobbs Ferry, N.Y.: Oceana,
1962-72. Irregular.

> Distinguished series of forums resulting in the publication
> of volumes containing working papers, condensation of dis-
> cussion, and extensive bibliography. To date sixteen vol-
> umes have been published.

Miscellaneous Information

2. Institutions Concerned with International Organizations

There are a number of organizations concerned with peace and the future; only a few have been included here.

328. The Carnegie Endowment for International Peace. 345 East Forty-sixth Street, New York, N.Y. 10017.

   Publication: INTERNATIONAL CONCILIATION (ceased publication) (see 147). The Carnegie Endowment has been the most active promoter of research and publication in the field. In recent years it has sponsored the reprinting of much valuable material on and documentation of the League.

329. Center for War/Peace Studies. 218 East Eighteenth Street, New York, N.Y. 10003.

   Publication: WAR/PEACE REPORT (see 187). "Aims to bring independent specialists with skill and knowledge on the problems of war and peace into a working relationship with the leadership of American nongovernmental organizations."

330. Consortium on Peace Research, Education and Development. 11 West Forty-second Street, Room 780, New York, N.Y. 10036.

   Involved in peace research and peace education. Promotes peace studies programs in schools and colleges, aids in developing curriculum materials.

331. Council on Foreign Relations. 58 East Sixty-eighth Street, New York, N.Y. 10021.

   Publication: FOREIGN AFFAIRS (see 170).

332. Foreign Policy Association. 345 East Forty-sixth Street, New York, N.Y. 10017.

   Publication: HEADLINE SERIES. Bimonthly. "Its objective is to stimulate wider interest, greater understanding and more effective participation by the American citizens in world affairs."

333. The Peace Research Society. Department of Regional Sciences, Wharton School, University of Pennsylvania, Philadelphia, Pa. 19104.

   Publication: PEACE RESEARCH SOCIETY (International) PAPERS, 1974- . Twice a year. Sponsors conferences on peace research.

334. The Stanley Foundation. Stanley Building, Muscatine, Iowa 52671.

Miscellaneous Information

Publications: (a) THE STRATEGY FOR PEACE: CONFERENCE REPORT, 1959- . Annual. (b) CONFERENCE ON THE UNITED NATIONS OF THE NEXT DECADE REPORTS, 1965- . Annual. (c) VANTAGE CONFERENCE REPORTS. Irregular. (d) OCCASIONAL PAPERS. Irregular.

"The Stanley Foundation encourages study, research and education in the field of foreign relations, contributing to secure peace with freedom and justice. Emphasis is given to activities related to world organization."

335. United Nations Association of the United States of America. 833 United Nations Plaza, New York, N.Y. 10017.

Publications: VISTA and the INTERDEPENDENT (see 148 and 231). "A national membership organization working for increased understanding of and support for, effective US participation in the UN and other international organizations. Sponsors studies on major political problems facing the US in its participation in international commissions."

336. Commission to Study the Organization of Peace. American Association for the United Nations. 866 United Nations Plaza, New York, N.Y. 10017.

Publication: REPORT OF THE COMMISSION. 1939- . Annual. The Commission is the research affiliate of the American Association for the United Nations and has devoted itself to studying the basis of international organization and suggesting ways to improve on the system.

337. National Policy Panel. United Nations Association of the United States of America. 833 United Nations Plaza, New York, N.Y. 10017.

Publication: POLICY PANEL REPORTS. Irregular. Set up to study the UN potential and to suggest ways to influence policy-makers in the United States.

338. Stockholm International Peace Research Institute (SIPRI). Stockholm, Sweden.

Publication: SIPRI YEARBOOK (see 205). Supports research on all aspects of disarmament, arms control, and peacekeeping forces.

339. World Law Fund. 11 West Forty-second Street, New York, N.Y. 10036.

Publication: WORLD ORDER BOOK SERIES. Develops and publishes teaching materials for secondary school and college use in the field of peace and world order studies. Sponsors World Order Models Project, a transnational research effort aimed at producing designs for a new world order.

Miscellaneous Information

340. World Peace Foundation. 40 Mt. Vernon Street, Boston, Mass. 02108.

    Publication: INTERNATIONAL ORGANIZATION (see 146).
    "The World Peace Foundation is a non-profit organization which was founded in 1910...for the purpose of promoting peace, justice, and goodwill among nations. For many years the foundation has sought to increase public understanding of international problems by an objective presentation of the facts of international relations." Has sponsored publication of documents and secondary sources in the field.

C. PERSONNEL IN INTERNATIONAL ORGANIZATIONS

341. United Nations. Secretariat. Protocol and Liason Section. DELEGATIONS TO THE UNITED NATIONS. New York, 1946- . Annual.

    Gives the membership in the general committee of the General Assembly, main committees, and delegations to the General Assembly by country. Before March/April 1952 issued as DELEGATIONS TO THE UNITED NATIONS. From 1952 to August 1954 this was issued as PERMANENT MISSIONS AND DELEGATIONS TO THE UNITED NATIONS. Issued each session of the General Assembly.

342. WHO'S WHO IN THE UNITED NATIONS. Yonkers-on-Hudson, N.Y.: Burchel, 1951. 580 p.

    Sketches of significant personalities gathered during the Fifth General Assembly. Many pictures included. Outdated.

D. LISTS OF INTERNATIONAL ORGANIZATIONS

343. Union of International Associations. THE 1,978 INTERNATIONAL ORGANIZATIONS FOUNDED SINCE THE CONGRESS OF VIENNA. Brussels, Belgium, 1957. 232 p.

    Chronological listing.

344. League of Nations. LIST OF INTERNATIONAL UNIONS, ASSOCIATIONS, INSTITUTIONS, COMMISSIONS, BUREAUS, ETC. London: H.M. Stationery Office, 1919. 16 p.

345. United States Citizens in World Affairs. A DIRECTORY OF NON-GOVERNMENTAL ORGANIZATIONS. Compiled by Katherine C. Carrigue. New York: Foreign Policy Association, 1953. 392 p.

    A directory of nongovernmental organizations in the United States concerned wholly or in part with the field of inter-

Miscellaneous Information

national relations

346. Wilkie, Lloyd, comp. INTERNATIONAL PEACE/DISARMAMENT DIRECTORY, 1962-67. 3rd ed. York, Pa., 1967.

   Lists organizations and periodicals with addresses in more than eighty countries.

347. United States Department of State. Bureau of United Nations Affairs. INTERNATIONAL ORGANIZATIONS IN WHICH THE UNITED STATES PARTICIPATES, 1949. Washington, D.C.: Government Printing Office, 1950. 343 p.

   Contains basic data related to origin and development of the organizations: membership, purposes, powers and functions, finances, structure, and U.S. relations.

E. ADDRESSES OF INTERNATIONAL GOVERNMENTAL ORGANIZATIONS

The UN and specialized agencies are listed below. Consult entries in previous section for other governmental and nongovernmental organizations.

Food and Agriculture Organization. Viale delle Terme di Caracella, 00100 Rome, Italy.

General Agreement on Tariffs and Trade. Villa la Booage, Palais des Nations, 1211 Geneva 10, Switzerland.

Intergovernmental Maritime Consultative Organization. 101-104 Piccadilly, London W 1, United Kingdom.

International Atomic Energy Agency. Kaertner Ring 11, A-1010 Vienna 1, Austria.

International Bank for Reconstruction and Development, International Development Association, International Finance Corporation. 1818 H. Street N.W., Washington, D.C. 20433.

International Civil Aviation Organization. 1080 University Street, Montreal 101, Canada.

International Court of Justice. Palais de la Paix, The Hague, Netherlands.

International Labor Organization. 154 rue de Lausanne, 1211 Geneva 22, Switzerland.

International Monetary Fund. Nineteenth & H Streets N.W., Washington, D.C. 20431.

Miscellaneous Information

International Telecommunications Union. 2 rue de Varembe, 1211 Geneva 20, Switzerland.

Permanent Court of Arbitration. Palais de la Paix, The Hague, Netherlands.

United Nations Secretariat. United Nations Plaza, New York, N.Y. 10017.

United Nations Information Center. 1028 Conner Avenue N.W., Washington, D.C. 20006.

United Nations Educational, Scientific and Cultural Organization. 9 Place de Fontenay, 75 Paris 7e, France.

United Nations Industrial Development Organization. Felderhaus, Rathausplatz 2, A 91010 Vienna, Austria.

UNIPUB, Inc. 650 First Avenue, P.O. Box 433, New York, N.Y. 10016. (Sales agent for: United Nations, Food and Agriculture Organization, International Atomic Energy Agency, World Health Organization, World Meteorological Organization.)

United Nations Institute for Training and Research. 801 United Nations Plaza, New York, N.Y. 10017.

Universal Postal Union. Weltpoststrasse 4, CH 3000 Berne 15, Switzerland.

World Health Organization. 20 Avenue Appia, 1211 Geneva 27, Switzerland.

World Meteorological Organization. 41 Avenue Guiseppe Motta, 1211 Geneva 20, Switzerland.

F. SYLLABI AND TEACHING AIDS

(For possible texts, see Chapter 6B and E.) A number of materials have appeared as aids to teachers, some of which are listed below.

348. Rohn, Peter H., et al. BASIC COURSES IN INTERNATIONAL ORGANIZATION: AN ANTHOLOGY OF SYLLABI. Beverly Hills, Calif.: Sage Publications, 1970. 128 p. (For International Studies Association.)

> Thirteen syllabi from professors teaching at different types of institutions.

349. Thompson, Elizabeth M. RESOURCES FOR TEACHING ABOUT THE UNITED NATIONS WITH ANNOTATED BIBLIOGRAPHY. Washington, D.C.: National Educational Association, 1962. 90 p.

Miscellaneous Information

350. Kenworth, Leonard S. TELLING THE UN STORY: NEW APPROACHES TO TEACHING ABOUT THE UN AND ITS RELATED AGENCIES. Paris, France: United Nations Educational, Scientific and Cultural Organization, 1963. 106 p.

351. United Nations. Office of Public Information. TEACHING HUMAN RIGHTS: A HANDBOOK FOR TEACHERS. 2nd ed. New York, 1963. 79 p.

352. Beitz, Charles R., et al. PEACE STUDIES: COLLEGE COURSES ON PEACE AND WORLD ORDER. New York: Institute for World Order, University Program, 1973. 145 p. Mimeographed.

    A response to the proliferation of peace studies being taught. Course outlines are divided into categories (conflict, revolution and peace, world order, world politics, and others). The institute intends to continue to collect and disseminate syllabi.

353. Miller, David C., and Hunt, Ronald. A GRADUATE LEVEL SURVEY OF FUTURE STUDIES: A CURRICULUM DEVELOPMENT PROJECT. San Francisco, Calif., 1972.

    Massive report of an experimental project at California State, San Jose. Good teaching ideas and bibliography.

354. TEACHING POLITICAL SCIENCE. Beverly Hills, Calif.: Sage Publications, 1973- . Biannual.

    Scheduled to appear biannually, the journal contains primarily articles on technique.

355. DEA NEWS: FOR TEACHERS OF POLITICAL SCIENCE. Washington, D.C.: American Political Science Association, Division of Educational Affairs, 1974- . Biannual.

    To be published biannually, the paper contains articles on teaching and from teachers. Will report on educational issues and on questions about public awareness of government affairs.

356. United Nations in cooperation with United Nations Educational, Scientific and Cultural Organization. HOW TO PLAN AND CONDUCT MODEL UN MEETINGS. Dobbs Ferry, N.Y.: Oceana, 1961. 127 p.

357. EDUCATIONAL FILM GUIDE. New York: Wilson, 1936- . Annual.

    Annual with cumulative monthly supplements. Supersedes EDUCATIONAL FILM CATALOG. Lists films alphabetically and by subject; gives brief descriptions.

Miscellaneous Information

358. United States Library of Congress. LIBRARY OF CONGRESS CATALOG: MOTION PICTURES AND FILMSTRIPS: A CUMULATIVE LIST OF WORKS REPRESENTED BY LIBRARY OF CONGRESS PRINTED CARDS. Washington, D.C., 1953- . Quarterly.

   Includes entries on all motion pictures and filmstrips currently cataloged in the library.

G. OPPORTUNITIES FOR PUBLISHING

359. Ross, Mary Bucher, ed. DIRECTORY OF PUBLISHING OPPORTUNITIES: A GUIDE TO ACADEMIC, BUSINESS, RESEARCH, SCIENTIFIC AND TECHNICAL PUBLISHING OPPORTUNITIES. 2nd ed. Orange, N.J.: Academic Media, 1973. 732 p.

   Contains information on address, frequency of issue, payment, style requirements, length, acknowledgement of receipt of manuscript. Divided by disciplines.

H. GRANT SUPPORT: WHERE TO APPLY

360. Sclar, Deanna, ed. ANNUAL REGISTER OF GRANT SUPPORT. Orange, N.J.: Academic Media, 1969- . Annual.

   Contains information on eligibility, financial support, number of applicants, and information on application. The following are from the ANNUAL REGISTER:

   American Association of University Women Educational Foundation. 2401 Virginia Avenue, N.W., Washington, D.C. 20037. -- "Dissertation and postdoctoral fellowships for the support of scholarly research in all fields of knowledge."

   American Philosophical Society. 104 South Fifth Street, Philadelphia, Pa. 19106. -- "Grants-in-aid, in all fields of learning, to aid research....Grants for postdoctoral research in all fields of knowledge."

   Business and Professional Women's Foundation. 2012 Massachusetts Avenue, N.W., Washington, D.C. 20036. -- "Scholarships to assist women who need further education or training in order to enter a career field or to improve their chances for professional advancement....These scholarships are designed primarily to assist mature women who wish to return to school...."

   The Danforth Foundation. 222 South Central Avenue, St. Louis, Mo. 63105. -- Fellowships for study toward the Ph.D., intended to assist prospective college teachers in any field common to the undergraduate liberal arts curriculum in the United States. "Graduate Fellowships for Women: grants for women to undertake full or part-time graduate

Miscellaneous Information

study leading to the M.A. or Ph.D. degree and a subsequent career as a full-time teacher...."

Department of State. Bureau of Educational and Cultural Affairs. Washington, D.C. 20520. -- Fulbright-Hayes Grants: "Grants for predoctoral study or research in most fields of endeavor....Grants for scholars and specialists in the entire range of academic and professional fields to conduct postdoctoral research...."

John Simon Guggenheim Memorial Foundation. 90 Park Avenue, New York, N.Y. 10016. -- "Fellowships for Scholars...in any field of knowledge...to engage in research under the freest possible conditions."

International Research and Exchanges Board. 110 E. Fifty-ninth Street, New York, N.Y. 10022. -- "Grants to individuals and institutions wishing to arrange new forms of scholarly contact and exchange in the social sciences...to provide for brief visits for purposes of consultation and discussion. ...Grants for collaborative projects in the social sciences ...involving scholars from the United States and from one or more of the exchange countries...."

National Education Association. 1201 Sixteenth Street, N.W., Washington, D.C. 20036. -- "Scholarship award for advanced study or research in any country....Past subjects have included international education and international professional organizations."

National Fellowships Fund. Suite 484, 795 Peachtree Street, N.E., Atlanta, Ga. 30308. -- "Awards to promote development of Black Americans for academic careers in the United States."

Office of Education. 400 Maryland Avenue, S.W., Washington, D.C. 20202. -- Fellowships to students accepted for study in approved graduate programs at schools affiliated with the National Defense Fellowship Program. "Awards for Research and study abroad in world affairs."

Rockefeller Brothers Fund. 30 Rockefeller Plaza, New York, N.Y. 10020. -- "Special program support for...direct operations of, experimental or new undertakings in the fields of international relations and understanding....Fellowships and scholarships for study or research in...social sciences...."

The Rotary Foundation. 1600 Ridge Avenue, Evanston, Ill. 60201. -- "Fellowships for graduate study abroad in any field...support is not available...for independent or unsupervised research."

The Southern Fellowship Fund. Suite 484, 795 Peachtree Street, N.E., Atlanta, Ga. 30308. -- "Predoctoral and postdoctoral fellowships to support prospective college teachers for predominantly Black institutions...."

Miscellaneous Information

Woodrow Wilson International Center for Scholars. Smithsonian Institution Building, Washington, D.C. 20007. -- "Fellowships at the advanced studies level. Fellowships are tenable in residence at the Woodrow Wilson International Center for Scholars."

American Political Science Association. 1527 New Hampshire Avenue, N.W., Washington, D.C. 20007. -- "Fellowships to aid prospective Black political science graduate students."

Carnegie Endowment for International Peace. 345 East Forty-sixth Street, New York, N.Y. 10017. -- "Travel and Main-enance Assistance in the Field of International Organization."

Center for Advanced Study in Behavioral Sciences. 202 Junipero Serra Boulevard, Stanford, Calif. 94305. -- Post-doctoral fellowships in all fields of knowledge contributing to an understanding of human behavior.

The Fund for Peace. 12th floor, 1855 Broadway, New York, N.Y. 10023. -- "Fellowships for pre- and post-doctoral graduate study related to international peace and justice, law, political science and economics."

National Science Foundation. 1800 G Street, N.W., Washington, D.C. 20550. -- "Grants to support dissertation research in various disciplines of the social sciences...."

Social Science Research Council. 230 Park Avenue, New York, N.Y. 10017. -- "Predoctoral and postdoctoral fellowships for research training in the social sciences with special consideration given to unorthodox projects unlikely to command support from other sources.

University Consortium for World Order Studies. 1855 Broadway, New York, N.Y. 10023. -- "Fellowships for graduate and postgraduate study in fields appropriate to the study of world order."

Society for the Psychological Study of Social Issues. P.O. Box 1248, Ann Arbor, Mich. 48106. -- "Grants for scientific research in social problem areas of interest to behavioral science and human welfare...international relations (including disarmament and the prevention of wars).

I. HOW TO CITE SOURCES

361. Turabian, Kate L. A MANUAL FOR WRITERS OF TERM PAPERS, THESES AND DISSERTATIONS. 3rd ed. Chicago, Ill.: The University of Chicago Press, 1967. 164 p.

362. A UNIFORM SYSTEM OF CITATION: FORMS OF CITATION AND ABBREVIATION. 10th ed. Cambridge, Mass.: The Harvard Law Review Association, 1964. 130 p.

Miscellaneous Information

> Source for citing judicial, statutory, quasi-statutory, and secondary materials. Also has sections on foreign citations, general rules of citations, and general rules of style.

363. Rothman, Marie H. CITATION RULES AND FORMS OF UNITED NATIONS DOCUMENTS AND PUBLICATIONS. Brooklyn, N.Y.: Long Island University Press, 1971. 64 p.

364. United Nations. Dag Hammarskjold Library. BIBLIOGRAPHICAL STYLE MANUAL. New York, 1963. 68 p. (ST/LIB/Ser. B/8.)

    > Covers books, pamphlets, periodicals, newspapers, governmental publications, as well as UN and League documents. Suggests appropriate abbreviations.

PART II
BIBLIOGRAPHY

Part II
BIBLIOGRAPHY

The majority of works in this section are books: Chapter 3 should be consulted for guides and indexes to periodical literature. Works are arranged functionally and are extensively cross-referenced. The works in Chapter 6 often contain material relevant to the other chapters and should be consulted especially for brief, introductory accounts of the topic being investigated.

Chapter 6

HISTORY AND GENERAL TREATISES

Chapter 6

HISTORY AND GENERAL TREATISES

A. HISTORY

1. General

Most of the basic books on international organization, the League, and UN contain historical materials.

(See below sections B, C, D. 1-3. See also 47, 48, 49, 50, 51, 52.)

365. Mangone, Gerard J. A SHORT HISTORY OF INTERNATIONAL ORGANIZATION. New York: McGraw-Hill, 1954. 326 p.

> A short, highly readable history of international organizations and law from early times in Europe. Good documentary references.

366. Morley, Felix. THE SOCIETY OF NATIONS: ITS ORGANIZATION AND CONSTITUTIONAL DEVELOPMENT. Washington, D.C.: Brookings, 1932. 700 p.

> Early history of the development of international institutions and cooperative techniques.

367. Schiffer, Walter. THE LEGAL COMMUNITY OF MANKIND: A CRITICAL ANALYSIS OF THE MODERN CONCEPT OF WORLD ORGANIZATION. New York: Columbia University Press, 1954. 367 p.

> Critical examination of the historical bases of the concept of world organization based on extensive historical material. Examination of the concepts which underlay the development of the League and the UN. Tries to clarify modern concepts of international organization.

368. Reinsch, Paul Samuel. PUBLIC INTERNATIONAL UNIONS, THEIR WORK AND ORGANIZATION: A STUDY OF INTERNATIONAL

History and General Treatises

ADMINISTRATIVE LAW. Boston, Mass.: Ginn, 1911. 197 p.

> A dated but useful historical account of the development of international agencies up to the beginning of the century.

369. Dunn, Frederick S. THE PRACTICE AND PROCEDURE OF INTERNATIONAL CONFERENCES. Baltimore, Md.: The Johns Hopkins University Press, 1929. 232 p.

> An early account of the evolution of the procedures, activities, and accomplishments of international conferences.

370. Hill, Norman L[lewellyn]. THE PUBLIC INTERNATIONAL CONFERENCE. Stanford, Calif.: Stanford University Press, 1929. 267 p.

> A scholarly examination of the history, organization, and procedures of international conferences.

2. The Hague Peace Conferences of 1899 and 1907

371. Scott, James Brown. THE REPORTS OF THE HAGUE CONFERENCES OF 1899 and 1907. London: Oxford University Press, 1917. 972 p.

> Collection of proposals and results of these important conferences.

372. Choate, J. H. THE TWO HAGUE CONFERENCES. Princeton, N.J.: Princeton University Press, 1913. 123 p.

> A good contemporary report of the occurrences of the conferences.

373. Davis, Calvin de A. THE UNITED STATES AND THE FIRST HAGUE PEACE CONFERENCE OF 1899. Ithaca, N.Y.: Cornell University Press, 1962. 236 p.

B. GENERAL TREATISES ON INTERNATIONAL ORGANIZATIONS

1. Books: General Accounts

(See also 47-52, 146, 147, 192, 231, 238-42, 288, 292, 295, 348, 1483, 1488, 1493. For Bibliographies, see Chapter 2.C.2.)

374. Goodspeed, Stephen S. THE NATURE AND FUNCTION OF INTERNATIONAL ORGANIZATIONS. 2nd ed. New York: Oxford University Press, 1967. 744 p.

> Comprehensive study of the UN family and other intergovern-

mental organizations. Concerned more with organizational aspects than with political. Surveys successes and failures.

375. Cheever, Daniel S., and Haviland, H. Field, Jr. ORGANIZING FOR PEACE: INTERNATIONAL ORGANIZATION IN WORLD AFFAIRS. Cambridge, Mass.: Riverside, 1954. 927 p.

> Well-organized, comprehensive study and overview of international organizations. Compares and contrasts organization and experiences of League and UN as to structure, functions, and constitutions.

376. Claude, Inis L., Jr. SWORDS INTO PLOWSHARES. 4th ed. New York: Random House, 1971. 526 p.

> An acute analysis of problems, progress, and prospects of significant international agencies. Presents theoretical bases, evolving trends, and constitutional problems. An unusually readable text.

377. Jacob, Philip E.; Atherton, Alexine L.; and Wallenstein, Arthur. THE DYNAMICS OF INTERNATIONAL ORGANIZATION. Rev. ed. Homewood, Ill.: Dorsey, 1972. 772 p.

> Functional analysis of evolution, operations, and problems of world and regional organizations. Many case studies woven into analysis.

378. Plano, Jack C., and Riggs, Robert E. FORGING WORLD ORDER: THE POLITICS OF INTERNATIONAL ORGANIZATION. New York: Macmillan, 1967. 606 p.

> Investigation of contemporary international organizations: political setting, problems, and processes. Emphasis on the interaction of political institutions and the individuals who shape them.

379. Blaisdell, Donald C. INTERNATIONAL ORGANIZATION. New York: Ronald, 1966. 535 p.

> Well-organized text setting forth the evolution of modern international organizations--world and regional--analyzing their functioning, problems, and prospects. Each chapter ends with a set of questions for study aid.

380. Chamberlain, Joseph P., et al. INTERNATIONAL ORGANIZATION. New York: Carnegie Endowment, 1955. 173 p.

> A factual study showing origins, purpose, membership, and powers of international organizations. Especially concerned with the role of nongovernmental agencies in this development.

History and General Treatises

381. Leonard, Leonard Larry. INTERNATIONAL ORGANIZATION. New York: McGraw-Hill, 1951. 630 p.

    Survey of the development, structure, and functioning of international organizations, with emphasis on the UN. More attention given to activities than to procedures and techniques. Descriptive with some analysis.

382. Levi, Werner. FUNDAMENTALS OF WORLD ORGANIZATION. Minneapolis, Minn.: University of Minnesota Press, 1950. 244 p.

    Consideration of nature, objectives, and problems of international organizations, with a focus on the human element. Attempts to construct a viable framework for world organization which will avoid many of the problems of the League and UN. Sees need for more "politics" in the UN.

383. Vandenbosch, Amry, and Hogan, Willard N. TOWARD WORLD ORDER. New York: McGraw-Hill, 1963. 399 p.

    Analysis of world organizations pointing to usefulness in creating world order.

384. Potter, Pitman B. AN INTRODUCTION TO THE STUDY OF INTERNATIONAL ORGANIZATIONS. 3rd ed. New York: Appleton-Century-Crofts, 1948. 493 p.

    Early text on range of international organizations including history, powers, and functioning. The first edition was published in 1922.

385. Reuter, Paul. INTERNATIONAL INSTITUTIONS. New York: Rinehart, 1958. 316 p.

    Analysis of the range of international organizations, with emphasis on constitutional arrangements and problems.

386. Miller, Lynn. ORGANIZING MANKIND: AN ANALYSIS OF CONTEMPORARY ORGANIZATION. Boston, Mass.: Holbrook, 1972. 378 p.

    An introductory text on international and regional organization with a world order orientation.

387. Luard, Evan, ed. THE EVOLUTION OF INTERNATIONAL ORGANIZATIONS. New York: Praeger, 1966. 342 p.

    Case studies done by experts in the field emphasizing changes which have taken place in some of the more important international organizations. Factors inhibiting and influencing change are analyzed. Uneven quality of contributions.

History and General Treatises

388. Eagleton, Clyde. INTERNATIONAL GOVERNMENT. 3rd ed. New York: Ronald, 1957. 583 p.

    Analysis and critique of international organizations. Sees these as expressions of an emerging world government, pointing out the direction of change necessary to accomplish this.

389. Mangone, Gerard J. THE IDEA AND PRACTICE OF WORLD GOVERNMENT. New York: Columbia University Press, 1951. 278 p.

    Brief introduction to international organizations, their development, practices, and problems.

390. Hill, Norman L[lewellyn]. INTERNATIONAL ORGANIZATION. New York: Harper and Row, 1963. 458 p.

    A fairly well-organized, shallow account of the organization and work of the agencies. Not always reliable.

391. Chadwick, Gerald W. St. J. INTERNATIONAL ORGANIZATIONS. London: Meuthen Educational, 1969. 117 p.

    In a book designed primarily for students, the author examines the aims and functions of various international organizations, reviews the history of the League and the UN, and surveys regional agencies.

392. Mander, Linden A. FOUNDATIONS OF MODERN SOCIETY. 2nd ed. Stanford, Calif.: Stanford University Press, 1948. 942 p.

    A comprehensive text covering all phases of international cooperation: evolution, organization, and activities.

393. Singh, Nagendra. RECENT TRENDS IN THE DEVELOPMENT OF INTERNATIONAL LAW AND INTERNATIONAL ORGANIZATION PROMOTING INTERSTATE COOPERATION AND WORLD PEACE. Delhi, India: Chaud, 1969. 259 p.

394. Woolf, Leonard Sidney. INTERNATIONAL GOVERNMENT. New York: Brentano's, 1916. 435 p.

    An early analysis of international organizations as manifestations of evolution toward world government.

395. Morozov, G. I. INTERNATIONAL ORGANIZATIONS: SOME THEORETICAL PROBLEMS. Moscow, Union of Soviet Socialist Republics: Mysl, 1969. 231 p.

    Comprehensive Marxist analysis of past and present international organizations by a leading Soviet scholar.

History and General Treatises

396. Carlston, Kenneth S. LAW AND ORGANIZATION IN WORLD SOCIETY. Urbana, Ill.: University of Illinois Press, 1962. 356 p.

    Integrates detailed examination of a sociopolitical legal problem with a general theory of law and organization. Starting from an in-depth study of the relationship of nationalization to the present nature of society, the author extends his inquiry to a more general consideration of the premises of international order and organization.

397. Chen, Samuel Shih-Tsai. THE THEORY AND PRACTICE OF INTERNATIONAL ORGANIZATION. New York: MSS Publishing, 1971. 200 p.

2. Readers and Collections of Essays

398. Falk, Richard A., and Hanreider, Wolfram P., eds. INTERNATIONAL LAW AND ORGANIZATION: AN INTRODUCTORY READER. Philadelphia, Pa.: Lippincott, 1968. 346 p.

    Half the book deals with international organizations. Selections are from outstanding scholars and many are classics. A reader which can be used in a general course on international relations, as well as in a more specific course.

399. Larus, Joel, ed. FROM COLLECTIVE SECURITY TO PREVENTIVE DIPLOMACY. READINGS IN INTERNATIONAL ORGANIZATION AND THE MAINTENANCE OF PEACE. New York: Wiley, 1965. 567 p.

    Contains source materials as well as commentaries from leading scholars relating primarily to the practice of peacekeeping through international organizations and pointing to future prospects.

400. Mendlovitz, Saul H., ed. LEGAL AND POLITICAL PROBLEMS OF WORLD ORDER. New York: The Fund for Education Concerning World Peace Through World Law, 1962. 867 p.

    A selection of readings and source materials coordinated with Clark and Sohn's WORLD PEACE THROUGH WORLD LAW (see 1472).

401. Cordier, Andrew W., and Foote, Wilder, eds. THE QUEST FOR PEACE: THE DAG HAMMARSKJOLD MEMORIAL LECTURES. New York: Columbia University Press, 1965. 414 p.

    Collection of twenty-four lectures given in various world centers--none comunist--in memory of the Secretary-General. Covers a wide range of UN responsibilities relating to the search for and the maintenance of international peace, world economic cooperation, and regard for human rights.

402. Wood, Robert S., ed. THE PROCESS OF INTERNATIONAL ORGANIZATIONS. New York: Random House, 1971. 534 p.

> A good general collection of readings.

403. Goodrich, Leland M., and Kay, David A., eds. THE POLITICS OF INTERNATIONAL ORGANIZATION. Madison, Wis.: University of Wisconsin Press, 1973. 477 p.

> A selection of articles from the journal INTERNATIONAL ORGANIZATION. Covers many aspects of international organizations. Many of excellent quality from leading scholars.

404. James, Alan, ed. THE BASES OF INTERNATIONAL ORDER: ESSAYS IN HONOUR OF C. A. W. MANNING. New York: Oxford University Press, 1973. 218 p.

> Good collection of articles explicating Manning's concept of "order" and applying it.

405. Bunting, G. R., and Lee, Marc J., eds. THE EVOLUTION OF THE UNITED NATIONS. New York: Pergamon, 1965. 86 p.

> Seminar papers emphasizing the UN and the problems of the developing countries.

406. Bryson, Lyman, et al. FOUNDATIONS OF WORLD ORGANIZATION: A POLITICAL AND CULTURAL APPRAISAL. New York: Harper, 1962. 512 p.

> Over forty scholarly papers, primarily reactions of observers, many casual and anecdotal.

407. Laves, Walter H. C., ed. THE FOUNDATIONS OF A MORE STABLE WORLD ORDER: SYMPOSIUM. Chicago, Ill.: University of Chicago Press, 1941. 193 p.

408. Fawcett, James E.S., and Higgins, Rosalyn, eds. INTERNATIONAL ORGANIZATION: LAW IN MOVEMENT, ESSAYS IN HONOR OF JOHN McMAHON. London: Oxford University Press, 1974. 192 p.

> A reader covering many aspects of international organization. Especially emphasized is the development and furtherance of international law.

C. THE LEAGUE OF NATIONS: GENERAL TREATISES

Covenant, see Chapter 7.A.1; International Law, see 538, 539, 550, 551, 553; Organs, see Chapter 7.C.1; Organizations Questions, see 609, 610, 622, 623;

History and General Treatises

Secretariat, see 634-38, 653; Secretaries-General, see Chapter 7.F.2 and 659; Nations, see 727, 730, 733, 736, 747, 748, 754, 761, 762, 766, 816, 817, 819; Arms Control, see 862, 871-76; Conflict Resolution, see Chapter 9.D.2; International Forces, see 942-44; Economic Cooperation, see Chapter 11.A.1; Social Development, see 1211, 1212; Drug Control, see 1222-24; Labor, see 1226-36; Intellectual Cooperation, see 1263; Mandates, Plebiscites, etc. see Chapter 13.A.2 and 1313, 1321, 1322; Minorities, see 1386-94, 1413; Refugees, see 1389, 1398, 1399, 1403, 1407, 1408; Human Rights, see 1409-14, 1427, 1439; Improving the System, see Chapter 14.B.

For Bibliographies, see 54, 55-60; Periodicals, see 195, 196; Documents, see 243-46, 264-66. For Basic Information, see 2, 6, 14.

In the past few years there has been renewed interest in the League and the appearance of studies making use of materials not previously available to scholars.

409. Walters, F. P. A HISTORY OF THE LEAGUE OF NATIONS. 2 vols. London: Oxford University Press, 1952. 953 p.

   Definitive history of all phases of the League's work. Documents available at the time extensively used and cited.

410. Knudson, J. I. A HISTORY OF THE LEAGUE OF NATIONS. Atlanta, Ga.: Turner E. Smith, 1938. 451 p.

   History, including preliminary work leading up to the creation of the League.

411. Marburg, T. THE DEVELOPMENT OF THE LEAGUE OF NATIONS IDEA. 2 vols. New York: Macmillan, 1932. 852 p.

   A history and analysis of the development and functioning of the League.

412. Howard-Ellis, C. THE ORIGIN, STRUCTURE AND WORKING OF THE LEAGUE OF NATIONS. London: Allen & Unwin, 1928. 528 p.

   An analysis of the procedures and early experiences of the League in its effort to eliminate war and create a world society. Also focuses attention on the International Labor Organization and the Permanent Court of International Justice.

413. Fosdick, Raymond B., et al. THE LEAGUE OF NATIONS STARTS: AN OUTLINE BY ITS ORGANIZERS. London: Macmillan, 1920. 282 p.

   Informative and interesting views by those who were there.

History and General Treatises

414. Schwarzenberger, George. THE LEAGUE OF NATIONS AND THE WORLD ORDER. London: Constable, 1936. 191 p.

    A short appraisal of the League as an agency for the promotion of peace and community.

415. Dexter, Byron V. THE YEARS OF OPPORTUNITY: THE LEAGUE 1920-1926. New York: Viking, 1967. 264 p.

    Analysis of collective security as practiced during the first seven years of the League. Concludes that the organization in the end advanced the objectives of the most warlike powers.

416. Hudson, Manley O[ttmer]. PROGRESS IN INTERNATIONAL ORGANIZATION. Oxford, England: Oxford University Press, 1932. 162 p.

    An assessment of the progress made in international cooperation and the promotion of international law and adjudication.

417. Zimmern, A. E. THE LEAGUE OF NATIONS RULE OF LAW, 1918-1935. New York: Russell and Russell, 1969. 542 p. (Reprint from the 2nd rev. ed. of 1939.)

    The author regards the League as a particular method for carrying on relations between states. Sees the common purpose of the establishers as one of remedying the defects and shortcomings in the European state system which contributed to the outbreak of World War I. Studies the Covenant and working of the League.

418. Jacks, Lawrence P. CO-OPERATION OR COERCION? New York: Dutton, 1938. 153 p.

    A critical look at the League's action, concluding that the League's failure was primarily due to trying to enforce through coercion rather than soliciting cooperation.

419. League of Nations. Secretariat. TEN YEARS OF WORLD CO-OPERATION. Geneva, Switzerland, 1930. 467 p.

    Description of the organization and outline of achievements.

420. League of Nations. REPORT ON THE WORK OF THE LEAGUE DURING THE WAR. Geneva, Switzerland, 1945. 167 p.

    Deals with the last years of the League and the turnover of responsibilities. Gives an account of the amazing amount of important work which went on in nonpolitical areas.

421. Stone, Ralph. THE IRRECONCILABLES: THE FIGHT AGAINST THE LEAGUE OF NATIONS. Lexington, Ky.: University of Kentucky Press,

History and General Treatises

1970. 208 p.
Definitive analysis of the role of sixteen senators who, during the fight between Wilson and the U.S. Senate over the League, became known as the "irreconcilables."

422. Wells, Herbert G. THE IDEA OF A LEAGUE OF NATIONS IN THE FOURTH YEAR: ANTICIPATIONS OF A WORLD PEACE. New York: Macmillan, 1918. 154 p.

423. Beer, Max. THE LEAGUE ON TRIAL: A JOURNEY TO GENEVA. Translated by H. Johnston. London: Allen & Unwin, 1933. 415 p.

424. Butler, Harold B. THE LOST PEACE: A PERSONAL INTERPRETATION. London: Faber, 1942. 246 p.

425. Duggan, Stephen P., ed. THE LEAGUE OF NATIONS. Boston, Mass.: Atlantic Monthly Press, 1919. 357 p.

426. Pollock, Frederick. THE LEAGUE OF NATIONS. 2nd ed. London: Stevens, 1922. 266 p.

427. Rappard, William E. THE QUEST FOR PEACE SINCE THE WORLD WAR. Cambridge, Mass.: Harvard University Press, 1940. 516 p.

428. Reynolds, Ernest E. THE LEAGUE EXPERIMENT. London: Nelson, 1939. 163 p.

429. Sweetser, Arthur. THE LEAGUE OF NATIONS AT WORK. New York: Macmillan, 1920. 215 p.

430. Davis, Harriet Ide (Eager), ed. PIONEERS IN WORLD ORDER: AN AMERICAN APPRAISAL OF THE LEAGUE OF NATIONS. New York: Columbia University Press, 1944. 272 p.

Sixteen essays by Americans who, in one capacity or another, were associated with the work of the League.

431. Fosdick, Raymond B., ed. LETTERS ON THE LEAGUE OF NATIONS: FROM THE FILES OF RAYMOND B. FOSDICK. Princeton, N.J.: Princeton University Press, 1966. 184 p.

The letters of a man who for twenty years was associated with the League. Shows the frustrations of a believer as the League proved inadequate in handling the major problems of the day.

History and General Treatises

D. FROM LEAGUE TO UNITED NATIONS

(See also 267-69.)

432. League of Nations. THE LEAGUE HANDS OVER. Geneva, Switzerland, 1946. 126 p.

    Brief account of the closing of the League and disposition of its responsibilities and assets.

433. Murray, Gilbert. FROM THE LEAGUE TO U.N. London and New York: Oxford University Press, 1948. 217 p.

    Lectures and articles presented from 1933 to 1946. Clear, concise, thoughtful look at problems of the League pointing out what lessons could be learned.

434. Bentwick, Norman. FROM GENEVA TO SAN FRANCISCO. AN ACCOUNT OF THE INTERNATIONAL ORGANIZATION OF THE NEW ORDER. London: Victor Gollancz, 1946. 111 p.

    Short account of problems of the transition and transfer from League to UN.

E. GENERAL WORKS ON THE UNITED NATIONS

Charter, see Chapter 7.A.2.3; Chapter 14.C.1; Organs, see Chapter 7.C.2-7; Organizational Questions, see Chapter 7.D; Secretariats, see Chapter 7.E; Secretaries-General, see Chapter 7.F; Politics, see Chapter 8.A and B; Nations, see Chapter 8.C; Peace, see Chapter 9.A; Collective Security, see Chapter 9.B; Arms Control, see Chapter 9.C; Conflict Resolution, see Chapter 9.E; Oceans, see 1042; Space, see Chapter 10.A.5; Commodity Agreements, see 1064; Economic Cooperation, see Chapter 11.A.2 and B.2-8; Social Development, see Chapter 12.A and F; Drug Control, see 1223-25; Trusteeships and Non-Self-Governing Peoples, see Chapter 12.A.3 and 4, 1321-23; Minorities, see 1389, 1392-96, 1413; Refugees, see 1397-1406; Human Rights, see Chapter 13.D; Improvements of the System, see Chapter 14.C.

For Bibliographies, see 61-65, 76-79, 94; Periodicals, see 149, 151-53, 197; Documents, see 247-52, 259, 260, 267-70, 289-91, 293, 294, 296-99, 302, 304, 305, 311, 312; Teaching aids, see 348-51.

1. Origins

(See also 779, 789, 791.)

History and General Treatises

435. Arne, Sigrid. UNITED NATIONS PRIMER. 2nd ed. New York: Rinehart, 1948. 267 p.

    A useful guide to the major conferences leading up to the establishment of the UN. Emphasis on the developments taking place between the Atlantic Charter in 1941 and the 1945 Conference in San Francisco.

436. United States Department of State. ORGANIZING THE UNITED NATIONS. A SERIES OF ARTICLES FROM THE DEPARTMENT OF STATE BULLETIN. Washington, D.C., 1946. 57 p.

    Brief description of origins of the UN with emphasis on the role of the United States.

437. American Association for the United Nations. WE, THE PEOPLE: A BRIEF HISTORY OF THE UNITED NATIONS. New York, 1946. 84 p.

    Brief outline of the origins and beginnings of the UN.

2. How It Works: Books Primarily Concerned with Structure, Organization, and Basic Facts

(See also 3, 5, 7, 8, 15, 16, 67, 69.)

438. Coyle, Benjamin V. THE UNITED NATIONS AND HOW IT WORKS. New York: Columbia University Press, 1961. 268 p.

    General survey of the operations of the UN covering its functions in international disputes, trade, education, disarmament, technical services, regulatory arrangements, and space. Also discusses related agencies.

439. Bailey, Sydney D. THE UNITED NATIONS: A SHORT POLITICAL GUIDE. New York: Praeger, 1963. 136 p.

    Introductory guide to the organization showing how it developed and functions. Brief but complete, with good tables.

440. Nicholas, H. G. THE UNITED NATIONS AS A POLITICAL INSTITUTION. 5th ed. London: Oxford University Press, 1975. 270 p.

    Description of the UN as a political institution which must be understood through its politics as well as through its formal constitution. Brief, lively, and very readable. Shows the dominating role of the United States in the process.

441. Gross, Ernest A. THE UNITED NATIONS: STRUCTURE FOR PEACE. New York: Harper & Row, 1962. 141 p. (For the Council on Foreign

History and General Treatises

Relations.)

A concise, analytical treatment by a former U.S. representative to the UN. Concerned in large part with how the United States can advance its own security and the cause of peace through the UN.

442. Evatt, Herbert V. THE UNITED NATIONS. Cambridge, Mass.: Harvard University Press, 1948. 154 p.

Short and descriptive treatment.

443. Lyon, Peter. THE U.N. IN ACTION. New York: Avon Books, 1963. 127 p.

Brief and rather superficial treatment; includes description of specialized agencies and commissions.

444. Galt, T. F. HOW THE UNITED NATIONS WORKS. New York: Crowell, 1947. 218 p.

Early, brief, descriptive treatment of the organization and its agencies.

445. Meigs, Cornelia. THE GREAT DESIGN: MEN AND EVENTS IN THE UNITED NATIONS FROM 1945-1963. Boston, Mass.: Little, Brown, 1965. 319 p.

Designed for young audiences, the author puts forth an American viewpoint on many of the principal conflicts within the organization.

446. Savage, Katharine. THE STORY OF THE UNITED NATIONS. London: Bodley Head, 1962. 176 p.

Emphasizes the political side of the UN with special concern for its role during the period of the Berlin airlift.

447. Hertzberg, Sidney, and Hazel W. THE UN IN THE AGE OF CHANGE. New York: United Nations Association of the United States of America, 1967. 52 p.

Brief analysis of the organization as it faces problems of the changing world of the mid-sixties.

448. Cohen, Benjamin. THE UNITED NATIONS: CONSTITUTIONAL DEVELOPMENTS, GROWTH AND POSSIBILITIES. Cambridge, Mass.: Harvard University Press, 1961. 136 p.

Lectures primarily concerned with the powers of the UN Charter and the responsibilities of states. Examines problems which may arise in interpreting the document. The author had long, practical experience with the UN and related agencies.

History and General Treatises

449. Boyd, Andrew. UNITED NATIONS: PIETY, MYTH AND TRUTH. Harmondsworth, England: Penguin, 1962. 185 p.

    A popularly written book by a World Federalist telling the story of the UN from its early days.

'450. United Nations. Office of Public Information. EVERYMAN'S UNITED NATIONS: A COMPLETE HANDBOOK OF THE ACTIVITIES AND EVOLUTION OF THE UNITED NATIONS DURING ITS FIRST TWENTY YEARS, 1945-1965. 8th ed. New York, 1968. 646 p. Paperbound and clothbound. (Sales E.67.1.2 and E.67.1.5.)

    A useful reference book on the organization and its activities. Events are chronologically entered according to topic. Covers the UN and related agencies.

451. _____. EVERYMAN'S UNITED NATIONS: A SUMMARY OF THE ACTIVITIES OF THE UNITED NATIONS DURING THE PERIOD 1966-1970. New York, 1971. 254 p. Paperbound and clothbound. (Sales E.71.1.10 and E.71.1.13)

    A summary of the UN's activities from 1966 to 1970.

452. United Nations. Secretariat. Department of Public Information. Research Section. STRUCTURE OF THE UNITED NATIONS. 7th ed. New York, 1954. 90 p. (ST/DPI/7.)

    Handy reference work on the structure and organization of the UN.

3. Basic Texts

453. Goodrich, Leland M. THE UNITED NATIONS. New York: Crowell, 1959. 419 p.

    Basic survey text for the major issues and activities of the UN. Brief history, exposition of structure, and analysis of phases in its history. Clear and convincing in style.

454. Vandenbosch, Amry, and Hogan, Willard N. THE UNITED NATIONS: BACKGROUND, ORGANIZATION, FUNCTIONS, ACTIVITIES. New York: McGraw-Hill, 1952. 456 p.

    A good general text which blends accurate information and critical analysis.

455. Tung, William L. INTERNATIONAL ORGANIZATION UNDER THE UNITED NATIONS SYSTEM. New York: Crowell, 1969. 431 p.

    A survey of international organizations centering on the UN system. Strong legal and structural emphasis. Extensively footnoted with good bibliography. Dry.

456. Chase, Eugene Parker. THE UNITED NATIONS IN ACTION. New York: McGraw-Hill, 1950. 464 p.

> History of growth and work of the organization in simple, at times superficial, nontechnical language. Sees UN as an emerging world government.

4. Analyses and Assessments

(See also Chapter 14.C.1.)

457. Claude, Inis L., Jr. THE CHANGING UNITED NATIONS. New York: Random House, 1967. 159 p.

> An excellent, brief analysis of the changes in the structure, procedures, and approach of the UN with prognosis for future developments.

458. Gutteridge, Joyce A. C. THE UNITED NATIONS IN A CHANGING WORLD. Dobbs Ferry, N.Y.: Oceana, 1970. 118 p.

> An examination of the changes in the organization from a strictly legal point of view and how these relate to the Charter. Considers new procedures which have been devised to meet the needs of the times and how far these are consistent with the purposes and principles set forth in the Charter. The author was legal adviser to the United Kingdom Permanent Delegation to the UN.

459. McClelland, Charles A. THE UNITED NATIONS: THE CONTINUING DEBATE. San Francisco: Chandler, 1960. 198 p.

> Analysis and assessment of the organization. Balanced and convincing.

460. Fehrenbach, T. R. THE UNITED NATIONS IN WAR AND PEACE. New York: Random House, 1968. 179 p.

> A consideration of the effectiveness of the UN in promoting cooperation among states.

461. Joyce, James Avery. REVOLUTION ON EAST RIVER. New York: Abelard, 1956. 244 p.

> An analysis of the world's hope in the UN and the increasing power of the third world countries in developing the policies of the organization.

462. O'Brien, Conor Cruise, and Topolski, Felix. UNITED NATIONS: SACRED DRAMA. London: Hutchinson, 1968. 320 p.

History and General Treatises

Challenging essay attempting to lay out what the UN in essence is, and showing the extensive gaps between ideal and practice. Calls for the organization to become more realistic.

463. Becker, Benjamin M. IS THE UNITED NATIONS DEAD? Philadelphia, Pa.: Whitmore, 1970. 163 p.

    Shrewd comments on the difficulties and achievements of the organization. Asserts the need for extensive amendment and implementation of the Charter.

464. Hazzard, Shirley. DEFEAT OF AN IDEAL: A STUDY OF THE SELF-DESTRUCTION OF THE UNITED NATIONS. Boston, Mass.: Atlantic-Little, Brown, 1973. 286 p.

    A former member of the Secretariat shows the corruption of structure and competence arising from neglect by the great powers and the organization's tendency to yield to American pressures.

465. Griffin, G. Edward. THE FEARFUL MASTER: A SECOND LOOK AT THE UNITED NATIONS. Boston, Mass.: Western Islands Publishers, 1964. 244 p.

    A critical evaluation of the organization.

466. Elmandrjra, M. THE UNITED NATIONS SYSTEM: AN ANALYSIS. Studies in International Politics. Hamden, Conn.: Shoe String, 1973. 368 p. Illus.

    Descriptive analysis of the UN and related agencies.

467. Pearson, Lester B., ed. A CRITICAL EVALUATION OF THE UN. Vancouver, Canada: University of British Columbia Press, 1961. 55 p.

    Three lectures by a sympathetic and concerned participant in the development of the organization.

468. Atlee, Clement R. THE FUTURE OF THE UNITED NATIONS. New Delphi, India: Indian Council for Cultural Relations, 1961. 29 p.

469. Roosevelt, Eleanor, and De Witt, William. U.N.: TODAY AND TOMORROW. New York: Harper, 1953. 250 p.

470. Watts, V. Orva. THE UNITED NATIONS: PLANNED TYRANNY. New York: Devin-Adair, 1955. 149 p.

471. Moore, Bernard. THE SECOND LESSON: SEVEN YEARS AT THE UNITED NATIONS. London: Macmillan, 1957. 229 p.

First-hand account of the early years of the organization by a British Broadcasting Corporation correspondent. Sharp insights into personalities of leading delegates. Looks at accomplishments of the various organs, pointing out potential problems.

472. Wortley, B. A. THE UNITED NATIONS: THE FIRST TEN YEARS. New York: Oceana, 1957. 250 p.

    A stimulating and readable series of lectures assessing accomplishments and failures, and including the specialized agencies.

473. Manly, Chesley. THE UN RECORD: TEN FATEFUL YEARS FOR AMERICA. Chicago, Ill.: Regency, 1955. 256 p.

    A highly critical evaluation whose primary objective is to see the United States out of the organization.

474. Bloomfield, Lincoln P. THE UNITED NATIONS AT TWENTY AND AFTER. New York: Foreign Policy Association, 1965. 63 p.

    Brief, readable analysis of the progress and potential of the organization.

475. Eichelberger, Clark M., Chairman. THE UNITED NATIONS: THE FIRST TWENTY-FIVE YEARS. New York: Harper and Row, 1970. 178 p. (For the Commission to Study the Organization of Peace.)

    Published every five years since the tenth year, gives general introduction to the UN as a peacekeeping organization and discusses its operation in the settlement of conflicts, disarmament, safeguarding human rights, and economic development. Emphasis on examining ways to strengthen and expand the role of the UN.

476. Tetlow, Edwin. THE UNITED NATIONS: THE FIRST TWENTY-FIVE YEARS. London: Peter Owen, 1970. 208 p.

    A curious mixture of wisdom, humor, and popular gossip. Entertaining if not really a serious attempt at analysis.

5. Personal Accounts

(See also 710, 950, 951, 954, 957, 958, 977, 983, 1070.)

477. Wadsworth, James J. THE GLASS HOUSE: THE UNITED NATIONS IN ACTION. New York: Praeger, 1965. 224 p.

    A tolerant and humane evaluation of the organization by a U.S. representative. Presents his own personal experience as well as descriptive analysis of what the UN and Specialized Agencies are and do. Shows how the U.S. mission functions.

478. Tavaras de Sa, Hernane. THE PLAY WITHIN THE PLAY: THE INSIDE STORY OF THE UN. New York: Knopf, 1966. 316 p.

> A disgruntled Brazilian journalist who spent five years as Undersecretary for Public Information assesses the organization. The author shows a good deal of contempt for Afro-Asians.

479. Townley, Ralph. THE UNITED NATIONS: A VIEW FROM WITHIN. New York: Scribner's, 1968. 365 p.

> With twenty years experience in the Secretariat, the author describes the origins, structure, theory, and practice of the UN and its affiliated agencies. The account is lively, comprehensive, and hopeful.

480. Stevenson, Adlai E. LOOKING OUTWARD: YEARS OF CRISIS AT THE UNITED NATIONS. New York: Harper and Row, 1963. 295 p.

> The speeches and writings of a former U.S. Ambassador to the UN. Evaluates many of the policies set forth by the United States at the organization. Shows the need for minimum institutions for order if world security is to be attained.

6. Miscellaneous Works

(See also 342.)

481. Munves, James. A DAY IN THE LIFE OF THE UNITED NATIONS: THE HUNDRED FACES OF PEACE. New York: Washington Square Press, 1970. 285 p.

482. de Guinzbourg, V[ictor]. THE ETERNAL MACHIAVELLI IN THE UNITED NATIONS WORLD. New York: United Nations, 1969. 899 p.

> A collection of salient UN documents and proverbs assembled by a former member of the UN Military Staff Committee.

483. Prosser, Michael H., ed. SOW THE WIND, REAP THE WHIRLWIND: HEADS OF STATE ADDRESS THE UNITED NATIONS. 2 vols. New York: William Morrow, 1970. 1485 p.

> Collection of 150 speeches by heads of state made during the first twenty-five years. The introduction is an interesting essay on symbolic and metamorphic rhetoric of various national leaders. Approximately eighty countries are represented.

History and General Treatises

484. Brody, H. U.N. DIARY: SEARCH FOR PEACE. New York: Classics, 1957. 286 p.

    The author records the proceedings of the UN from January 1956 to July 1957, a period which covered major debate on Suez and Hungary.

485. Szapiro, Jerry. THE NEWSPAPER MAN'S UNITED NATIONS: A GUIDE FOR JOURNALISTS ABOUT THE UNITED NATIONS AND SPECIALIZED AGENCIES. New York: International Documents Service, 1961. 229 p.

486. Szalai, Alexander, et al. THE UNITED NATIONS AND THE NEWS MEDIA. New York: United Nations Institute for Training and Research, 1972. 323 p. Reprint, 1974.

    A thoughtful inquiry into the coverage given the UN by major news media throughout the world. Contains a wealth of statistical tables.

7. Collections of Essays and Readers

487. Kay, David A., ed. THE UNITED NATIONS POLITICAL SYSTEM. New York: Wiley, 1967. 419 p.

    A reader, traditionally organized and dealing with origins, evolution, diplomatic role, contribution to peacekeeping, decolonization, and economic aid and development.

488. Waters, Maurice, ed. THE UNITED NATIONS: INTERNATIONAL ORGANIZATION AND ADMINISTRATION. New York: Macmillan, 1967. 596 p.

    A collection of readings, speeches, and documents on every phase of UN organization and operation. Selections show differing national points of view although predominately western. Goes into most of the affiliated agencies.

489. Barros, James, ed. THE UNITED NATIONS: PAST, PRESENT, AND FUTURE. New York: The Free Press, 1972. 279 p.

    A broad-scale, short survey of the organization. Deals with major organs and agents of the UN. Concerned with the continuity between the League and UN, deals with the past and present activities of the organs and projects and speculates on future roles.

490. Gordenker, Leon, ed. THE UNITED NATIONS IN INTERNATIONAL POLITICS. Princeton, N.J.: Princeton University Press, 1971. 246 p.

    An innovative theoretical framework is used to bring together six essays using the behavioral approach. The essays focus

History and General Treatises

on the UN as a subsystem within the larger system of the world political environment, and examine standards to be used in determining the degree of the UN's influence and value.

491. Falk, Richard A., and Mendlovitz, Saul H., eds. THE UNITED NATIONS. The Strategy of World Order Series, vol. 3. New York: World Law Fund, 1966. 863 p.

   A set of readings covering most aspects of the organization's structure and functioning. Includes suggestions for changes and revisions.

492. Padelford, Norman J., and Goodrich, Leland M., eds. THE UNITED NATIONS IN THE BALANCE: ACCOMPLISHMENTS AND PROSPECTS. New York: Praeger, 1965. 494 p.

   A good collection of essays by recognized academic scholars concentrating primarily on peace and security questions.

493. Gregg, Robert W., and Barkun, Michael, eds. THE UNITED NATIONS SYSTEM AND ITS FUNCTIONS: SELECTED READINGS. Princeton, N.J.: Van Nostrand, 1968. 469 p.

   Using a functional systems approach, the authors arrange selections which include works of many leading scholars. The functions analyzed are: articulation and aggregation of interests, communication, socialization and recruitment, conflict management, and integration.

494. Twitchett, Kenneth J., ed. THE EVOLVING UNITED NATIONS: A PROSPECT FOR PEACE? London: Europa Publications, 1970. 239 p. (For David Davies Memorial Institute of International Studies.)

   Survey of UN expectations and experience. The author examines the gap between the voting power in the General Assembly and real power. Sees the organization as one which can agitate but is incapable of action.

495. Paxman, John M., and Boggs, George T., eds. THE UNITED NATIONS: A REASSESSMENT, SANCTIONS, PEACEKEEPING AND HUMANITARIAN ASSISTANCE. Virginia Legal Studies. Charlottesville, Va.: University Press of Virginia, 1973. 167 p.

   A selection of articles covering a wide variety of issues and cases.

496. Tompkins, E. B., ed. THE UNITED NATIONS IN PERSPECTIVE. Stanford, Calif.: The Hoover Institute, 1972. 155 p.

   Selection of papers presented at a conference held under the auspices of the Hoover Institute. From a political perspective, the participants analyze and assess the UN's performance and prospects. Suggestions for revisions and reorganization of Charter and structure are made.

497. Moore, Raymond A., ed. THE UNITED NATIONS RECONSIDERED. 2nd ed. Studies in International Affairs, no. 2. Columbia, S.C.: University of South Carolina Press, 1963. 170 p.

> A collection of articles drawn mainly from U.S. senators and statesmen who are negative towards the UN. Mostly propaganda rather than political analysis.

F. NEW METHODOLOGIES AND THE STUDY OF INTERNATIONAL ORGANIZATIONS

The growing interest in more systematic empirical and innovative research into political phenomena has also been evident in the field of international organization.

(See also 119, 174, 882, 906, 917, 918.)

1. Assessments

498. Alger, Chadwick F. "Methodological Innovation in Research on International Organizations." In POLITICAL SCIENCE ANNUAL, 1969-1970, vol. 2, edited by James A. Robinson, pp. 209-40. Indianapolis, Ind.: Bobbs-Merrill, 1969.

> A study of the degree to which changes in research methods in political science have affected research on international organization and suggestions for extending the use of more rigorous empirical methods in the field.

499. _____. "Research on Research: A Decade of Quantitative and Field Research on International Organizations." INTERNATIONAL ORGANIZATION 24(Summer 1970): 414-50.

> An excellent and well-organized overview of quantitative research in the field.

500. Goodwin, Geoffrey L., and Strange, Susan, eds. RESEARCH ON INTERNATIONAL ORGANIZATION. London: Heinemann Education, 1968. 71 p. (For Social Science Research Council--Great Britain.)

> An evaluation of research completed.

501. Van Wagenen, Richard W. RESEARCH IN THE INTERNATIONAL ORGANIZATION FIELD. Princeton, N.J.: Princeton University, Center for Research on World Political Institutions, 1952. 78 p.

History and General Treatises

   An overview of the work undertaken and in progress at the time of writing.

502. Weitz, Harold, et al. AN APPROACH TO THE ANALYSIS OF RESOLUTIONS OF THE ECONOMIC AND SOCIAL COUNCIL. UNITAR Research Reports, no. 16. New York: United Nations Institute for Training and Research, 1972. 113 p.

503. Thompson, Margaret C., et al. POLITICAL INTERGRATION: A SURVEY OF THEORIES. Amsterdam, Netherlands: Europa Institute, University of Amsterdam, 1968. 152 p.

   An overview of the theories of economic integration, relating these to the current status of international agencies and co-operation.

2. New Methodologies Applied

(See also 493, 702, 922, 1242, 1428, 1486.)

For the last few years, most studies using newer methodologies have appeared in periodicals. INTERNATIONAL ORGANIZATION contains a section which includes both reports of original research and critical essays.

504. Brinton, Clarence Crane. FROM MANY, ONE: THE PROCESS OF POLITICAL INTEGRATION, THE PROBLEM OF WORLD GOVERNMENT. Cambridge, Mass.: Harvard University Press, 1948. vi, 126 p.

   An analysis of the prerequisites of integrating the world and an assessment of the progress made to date.

505. Deutsch, Karl. NATIONALISM AND SOCIAL COMMUNICATIONS: AN INQUIRY INTO THE FOUNDATIONS OF NATIONALITY. New York: Wiley, 1953. 302 p.

   Study of the conditions and bases of nationalism and the possibilities for moving to international integration.

506. _____. POLITICAL COMMUNITY AT THE INTERNATIONAL LEVEL: PROBLEMS OF DEFINITION AND MEASUREMENT. Garden City, N.Y.: Doubleday, 1954. 80 p.

   An early statement of Deutsch's approach to the study of international integration.

507. _____, et al. POLITICAL COMMUNITY AND THE NORTH ATLANTIC AREA: INTERNATIONAL ORGANIZATION IN THE LIGHT OF HISTORICAL EXPERIENCE. Princeton, N.J.: Princeton University Press, 1957. 244 p.

Integration theory outlined and applied.

508. Etzioni, Amitai. POLITICAL UNIFICATION: A COMPARATIVE STUDY OF LEADERS AND FORCES. New York: Holt, Rinehart and Winston, 1965. 366 p.

   Etzioni approaches integration by studying leaders and their problems.

509. Liska, George. INTERNATIONAL EQUILIBRIUM: A THEORETICAL ESSAY ON THE POLITICS AND ORGANIZATION OF SECURITY. Cambridge, Mass.: Harvard University Press, 1957. 223 p.

   Using systems analysis, the author fits international security agencies into a wider world perspective.

510. Buchanan, William, et al. AN INTERNATIONAL PEACE FORCE AND PUBLIC OPINION: POLLED OPINION IN THE U.S., 1939-53. Princeton, N.J.: Princeton University, Center for Research on Political Institutions, n.d. 39 p.

511. Congalton, A. A., and Kitton, M. PUBLIC OPINION AND THE UNITED NATIONS. Wellington, Australia: Victoria University College, Department of Psychology, 1965. 84 p.

512. Roepke, Wilhelm. INTERNATIONAL ORDER AND ECONOMIC INTEGRATION. Dordrecht, Netherlands: Reidel, 1960. 284 p.

   Overview of the problems and progress towards international economic integration.

513. Balassa, Bela. THE THEORY OF ECONOMIC INTEGRATION. Homewood, Ill.: Irwin, 1961. 304 p.

   A systematic analysis of the characteristics of integration, the problems it poses, and the criteria by which it would be judged. The author draws together a large amount of the literature in systematic form.

514. de Vree, Johan K. POLITICAL INTEGRATION: THE FORMATION OF THEORY AND ITS PROBLEMS. The Hague, Netherlands: Mouton, 1972. 408 p.

   An analysis of the various theories of integration in the literature. Development of the instruments and criteria for the reconstruction and assessment of theories. Historical review, synthesis, and analysis of thought and writing on international political integration.

515. Plischke, E. SYSTEMS OF INTEGRATING THE INTERNATIONAL COMMUNITY. Princeton, N.J.: Van Nostrand, 1964. 198 p.

An overview of the main contemporary types of interstate cooperation including confederations, supranational associations, federal unions, and political associations found within the Communist bloc.

516. Kramer, John Francis. A COMPUTER SIMULATION OF AUDIENCE EXPOSURE IN A MASS MEDIA SYSTEM: THE UNITED NATIONS INFORMATION CAMPAIGN IN CINCINNATI, 1947-48. Cambridge, Mass.: Massachusetts Institute of Technology, Center for International Studies, 1969. 558 p.

An extensive piece of research reported in complete form.

Chapter 7
INTERNATIONAL INSTITUTIONS: POWERS, STRUCTURES, ORGANIZATIONS, AND ISSUES

Chapter 7
INTERNATIONAL INSTITUTIONS:
POWERS, STRUCTURES, ORGANIZATIONS, AND ISSUES

A. CONSTITUTIONS AND THEIR DEVELOPMENT

(See also 297, 385, 448.)

517. Peaslee, Amos J., ed. INTERNATIONAL GOVERNMENTAL ORGANIZATIONS: CONSTITUTIONAL DOCUMENTS. 3rd ed. 2 vols. New York: Macmillan, 1974.

   An invaluable collection for the researcher. The first volume covers from the African Postal Union to the Intergovernmental Maritime Consultative Organization; the second from the International Atomic Energy Agency to the World Metereological Organization.

1. The League of Nations Covenant

(See also 538.)

518. Miller, David Hunter. THE DRAFTING OF THE COVENANT. 2 vols. New York: Putnam, 1928. 1412 p.

   A comprehensive history of the development of the Covenant by a legal adviser of the American Commission. Includes consideration of all official documents leading to the final draft. Presents the Covenant as the result of collective efforts in several countries.

519. Williams, Sir John Fischer. SOME ASPECTS OF THE COVENANT OF THE LEAGUE OF NATIONS. London: Oxford, 1934. 322 p.

   An acute analysis of some of the major problems of the Covenant.

International Institutions

520. Wilson, Florence. THE ORIGINS OF THE LEAGUE COVENANT. London: Hogarth, 1928. 268 p.

521. Engel, Salo. LEAGUE REFORM. New York: Columbia University Press, 1940. 282 p.

522. Keen, Frank N. A BETTER LEAGUE OF NATIONS. New York: Smith, 1934. 160 p.
    > In 1924 an attempt was made to close the "gaps" in the Covenant by the adoption of the Geneva Protocol.

523. Miller, David H[unter]. THE GENEVA PROTOCOL. New York: Macmillan, 1925. 279 p.

524. Noel-Baker, P[hilip]. J. THE GENEVA PROTOCOL FOR THE PACIFIC SETTLEMENT OF INTERNATIONAL DISPUTES. London: King, 1925. 238 p.

525. Williams, Sir John Fischer. THE GENEVA PROTOCOL OF 1924. London: Allen & Unwin, 1925. 18 p.

2. The Making of the Charter of the United Nations

(See also 66.)

526. Brierly, James L. THE COVENANT AND THE CHARTER. Cambridge: Cambridge University Press, 1947. 37 p.
    > Contrasts the cooperative character of the Covenant with the quasi-organic character of the Charter. Sees the most important innovation as the power given the Secretary-General to act for the organization.

527. Russell, Ruth B., assisted by Muther, Jeanette E. A HISTORY OF THE UNITED NATIONS CHARTER: THE ROLE OF THE UNITED STATES 1940-1945. Washington, D.C.: Brookings, 1958. 966 p.
    > An excellent reference tool on negotiations leading to the final act. A detailed and thorough study, in good part based on unpublished State Department materials. Well-organized.

528. United Nations. Office of Public Information. GUIDE TO THE CHARTER OF THE UNITED NATIONS. New York, 1947-
    > Brief account of the development and meaning of the Charter.

3. Commentaries

(See also Chapter 14.C.1 and 542, 555-57, 591, 1351, 1355-59, 1415, 1418, 1434, 1436.)

529. Goodrich, Leland M., et al. THE CHARTER OF THE UNITED NATIONS: COMMENTARY AND DOCUMENTS. 3rd ed. New York: Columbia University Press, 1969. 756 p.

> Includes discussion of its history and origins. Article-by-article commentary showing what drafters intended and how articles have been interpreted over time. Extensive list of documents and bibliography.

530. Bentwick, Norman, and Martin, Andrew. A COMMENTARY OF THE CHARTER OF THE UNITED NATIONS. New York: Macmillan, 1950. 239 p.

> Written for the layman, the book lacks references and is superficial in parts. Article-by-article analysis showing the Charter's relationship to traditional international law and its evolution during the first five years.

531. Kelsen, Hans. THE LAW OF THE UNITED NATIONS: A CRITICAL ANALYSIS OF ITS FUNDAMENTAL PROBLEMS. Rev. ed. New York: Praeger, 1966. 994 p. (For London Institute of World Affairs.)

> Useful, scholarly, and stimulating analysis, although very formal and legalistic. The author's emphasis is on the flaws in the Charter and how these can be remedied. Also discussed are those parts of the Charter which impose obligations and confer rights.

532. _____. RECENT TRENDS IN THE LAW OF THE UNITED NATIONS: SUPPLEMENT TO THE LAW OF THE UNITED NATIONS. New York: Praeger, 1951. 86 p.

> Examines four major issues: organization of collective defense through NATO, Korea, the increased responsibilities of the Secretary-General, and the Uniting for Peace Resolution. These are examined to show how they have affected the Charter and to suggest that a new law of the UN seems to be emerging.

533. United Nations. Secretariat. REPERTORY OF PRACTICE OF UNITED NATIONS ORGANS. 5 vols. with supplements. New York, 1955- . Seratim.

> A comprehensive analysis of the provisions of the Charter as these have been applied by the various organs of the UN. Includes Advisory Opinions of the Court and decisions taken

by the Secretariat.

534. Halderman, J. W. THE UNITED NATIONS AND THE RULE OF LAW: CHARTER DEVELOPMENT THROUGH THE HANDLING OF INTERNATIONAL DISPUTES. Dobbs Ferry, N.Y.: Oceana, 1967. 326 p.

> An investigation of the world constitutional system showing how this has been affected by the actions taken in the handling of disputes. Well-documented.

535. Martin, Andrew, and Edwards, John B. S. THE CHANGING CHARTER: A STUDY IN THE REFORM OF THE UNITED NATIONS. London: Sylvan Press, 1955. 128 p.

> Shows how the Charter has been changed during the early years of the organization and indicates that many problems which people are concerned about can be handled by this process of informal change.

536. Ross, Alf. CONSTITUTIONS OF THE UNITED NATIONS: ANALYSIS OF STRUCTURE AND FUNCTION. Copenhagen, Denmark: Ejnar Munksgaard, 1950. 236 p.

> Juridical analysis of the structure and functions of the Charter with inquiry into its legal character. Analyzes constitutional developments during the first five years.

537. United States Delegation to the United Nations Conference on International Organization. CHARTER OF THE UNITED NATIONS: REPORT TO THE PRESIDENT ON THE RESULTS OF THE SAN FRANCISCO CONFERENCE. United States Department of State Publication 2349, Conference Series 71. Westport, Conn.: Greenwood Press, 1946. 266 p. Reprint.

B. INTERNATIONAL LAW AND INTERNATIONAL ORGANIZATIONS

General, see 393, 396, 398, 408, 416, 1489; World Court, see Chapter 7.G and 9.F; Constitutions, see Chapter 7.A; the League, see 458, 582; the UN, see 458, 592, 698, 777, 893, 901, 911, 983; Forces, see 921, 927-29, 930, 933, 939-41; Communications, see 1009, 1013-15, 1020, 1021; Aviation, see 1014, 1021, 1024, 1025, 1026, 1031, 1033, 1034, 1036; Seas, 1028, 1031-33, 1037, 1039, 1040, 1043-45; Space, see 1044, 1046-51, 1056, 1057; Trade, see 1061, 1068; the Monetary system, see 1078, 1099-1103; Aid, see 1151; Labor Standards, see Chapter 12.C.3; Atomic Energy, see 1280; the Environment, see 1280, 1289, 1291; Population, see 1295; South West Africa, see 1384; Minorities, see 1393-96; Refugees, see 1397, 1398; Human Rights, see Chapter 13.D.

For Periodicals, see Chapter 3.D.3 and 163, 164, 168, 169.

1. General

538. Walp, Paul K. CONSTITUTIONAL DEVELOPMENTS OF THE LEAGUE OF NATIONS. Lexington, Ky.: University of Kentucky Press, 1931. 183 p.

    Study of the ways the Covenant was used and interpreted.

539. Williams, Sir John Fischer. CHAPTERS ON CURRENT INTERNATIONAL LAW AND THE LEAGUE OF NATIONS. London: Longmans, Green, 1929. 521 p.

    The impact of the League directly and indirectly on the development of international law.

540. Wright, Quincy. INTERNATIONAL LAW AND THE UNITED NATIONS. New York: Asia Publishing House, 1960. 134 p.

    Emphasizes the importance of the UN as a symbol of unity in the world. Examines important legal issues such as domestic jurisdiction and the prevention of aggression.

541. Michigan. University of. Law School. INTERNATIONAL LAW AND THE UNITED NATIONS. Eighth Summer Institute on International and Comparative Law. Ann Arbor, Mich.: University of Michigan Press, 1957. 578 p.

    Papers investigating a number of important issues relating to the UN.

542. Freeman, Harrop A. THE UNITED NATIONS ORGANIZATION AND INTERNATIONAL LAW. World Organization Series IV. Philadelphia, Pa.: Pacifist Research Bureau, 1946. 284 p.

    An early commentary on the relationship between the Charter and general international law.

543. Van der Molen, Gezina Hermina, et al. THE UNITED NATIONS: TEN YEARS' LEGAL PROGRESS. The Hague, Netherlands: Nederlandse Studentenvereniging voor Wereldrechtsorder, 1956. 192 p.

    A collection of nine essays by outstanding authorities on international law and organization dealing with such areas as the law covering UN sovereignty, the International Law Commission, the International Court, and the development of criminal law.

544. Unidroit (International Institute for the Unification of Private International

Law). DIGEST OF LEGAL ACTIVITIES OF INTERNATIONAL ORGANIZATIONS AND OTHER INSTITUTIONS. Vol. 1. Rev. ed. Dobbs Ferry, N.Y.: Oceana, 1974. 329 p. (First volume with binder.)

> Loose-leaf publication covering the different phases of the development of all legal activities undertaken by international organizations and institutions on private and public law. To be updated annually.

545. Jessup, Philip C. PARLIAMENTARY DIPLOMACY: AN EXAMINATION OF THE LEGAL QUALITY OF THE RULES OF PROCEDURE OF THE ORGANS OF THE UNITED NATIONS. Leiden, Netherlands: Sijthoff, 1957. 140 p.

> Shows how the rules of procedure have been used to hinder and assist organs in carrying out their functions.

a. THE RIGHT OF ACCESS AND STATUS

(See also 655, 656.)

546. Tobiassen, L. K. THE RELUCTANT DOOR: THE RIGHT OF ACCESS TO THE UNITED NATIONS. Washington, D.C.: Public Affairs Press, 1969. 421 p.

> A useful and detailed study of the legal and administrative problems for organizations and host countries. Traces the genesis and development of access practices with a minute investigation of prominent cases in which access has been restricted. Especially concerned with the situation existing for the UN and United States.

547. Weissberg, Guenter. THE INTERNATIONAL STATUS OF THE UNITED NATIONS. Dobbs Ferry, N.Y.: Oceana, 1961. 240 p. (For the Parker School of Foreign and Comparative Law.)

> Investigation of an impressive number and variety of agreements the UN has made with states and other entities. Suggests the independent nature of the organization and its international personality. An exhaustive review of the literature.

548. Crosswell, C. M. PROTECTION OF INTERNATIONAL PERSONNEL ABROAD: LAW AND PRACTICE AFFECTING PRIVILEGES AND IMMUNITIES OF INTERNATIONAL ORGANIZATIONS. Dobbs Ferry, N.Y.: Oceana, 1952. 208 p.

> Comprehensive analysis of practices affecting personnel connected with various international organizations.

549. Ahluwalia, Kuljit. THE LEGAL STATUS, PRIVILEGES AND IMMUNITIES

OF THE SPECIALIZED AGENCIES OF THE UNITED NATIONS AND CERTAIN OTHER INTERNATIONAL ORGANIZATIONS. The Hague, Netherlands: Nijhoff, 1964. 230 p.

>Discusses the development and changing trends in the legal status and judicial capacity of organizations, and laws applicable to transactions within headquarters. Covers both world and regional organizations.

550. Jenks, Clarence Wilfred. THE HEADQUARTERS OF INTERNATIONAL INSTITUTIONS: A STUDY OF THEIR LOCATION AND STATUS. London: Royal Institute of International Affairs, 1945. 102 p.

>Study made for use during consideration of locations for the UN and related agencies.

b. PRIVILEGES AND IMMUNITIES

551. Michaels, David B. INTERNATIONAL PRIVILEGES AND IMMUNITIES. The Hague, Netherlands: Nijhoff, 1971. 249 p.

>Studies the provisions and practices in sixty organizations going back to 1804. Proposes a design for a universal statute.

552. Jenks, Clarence Wilfred. INTERNATIONAL IMMUNITIES. Dobbs Ferry, N.Y.: Oceana, 1961. 214 p.

>A concise compendium of international agreements and judicial decisions with Jenk's usual perceptive observations. Relates principal immunities to their functions and practical applications. An excellent and authoritative work.

553. Hill, Martin. IMMUNITIES AND PRIVILEGES OF INTERNATIONAL OFFICIALS: THE EXPERIENCE OF THE LEAGUE OF NATIONS. Washington, D.C.: Carnegie Endowment, 1947. 295 p.

>A scholarly treatment of the practices and problems during the League period. Written to assist the UN in its working out of similar problems.

554. King, John Kerry. THE PRIVILEGES AND IMMUNITIES OF THE PERSONNEL OF INTERNATIONAL ORGANIZATIONS. Odense, Denmark: Strandberg Bogtryk, 1949. 296 p.

c. OTHER LEGAL ISSUES

555. Rahmatullah, K. IMPLIED POWERS OF THE UNITED NATIONS. Delhi, India: Vikas Publications, 1970. 236 p.

Shows how the organization has in many places loosely interpreted the Charter and thereby permitted itself a wider area for action. Relates the way organizations handle implied powers to their effectiveness.

556. Rajan, M. S. UNITED NATIONS AND DOMESTIC JURISDICTION. Rev. ed. New York: Longmans, Green, 1959. 692 p.

An extensive study of Article 2.7. Discusses problems of interpretation by examining arguments made in a number of cases. Argues for a narrow interpretation of the provision.

557. Broms, Bengt. THE DOCTRINE OF EQUALITY OF STATES AS APPLIED IN INTERNATIONAL ORGANIZATIONS. Vammala, Finland: Vammalan Kirjapaino Oy., 1959. 379 p.

Examines legal opinions and practices in the League, UN, and other organizations going back to medieval times.

558. Fakher, Hassein. THE RELATIONSHIP AMONG THE PRINCIPAL ORGANS OF THE UNITED NATIONS. London: Staples, 1951. 200 p.

A very careful analysis of the six principal organs with a detailed examination of the Charter as it developed from Dumbarton Oaks to San Francisco.

2. The Law Covering International Organizations

(See also 650.)

559. Bowett, D. W. THE LAW OF INTERNATIONAL INSTITUTIONS. New York: Praeger, 1963. 365 p.

A comprehensive survey of the structures, functions, and procedures of a large number of organizations, stressing the legal aspects. Primarily descriptive. Includes regional organizations as well as global.

560. Jenks, Clarence Wilfred. THE PROPER LAW OF INTERNATIONAL ORGANIZATIONS. Dobbs Ferry, N.Y.: Oceana, 1962. 323 p.

Discusses aspects of international law applicable to international organizations from a perspective which sees international law as having outgrown the limitations of a system based on the relations of states. Part one covers problems of the personal law of international corporate bodies and the choice of laws; part two, internal administrative law; and part three, the legal transactions of international bodies and third parties.

561. Schermers, Henry G. STRUCTURE. International Institutional Law, vol. 1. Leiden, Netherlands: Sijthoff, 1972. 327 p.

> Careful examination of law covering international institutions. Other volumes to follow.

562. Seyersted, Finn. INTERNATIONAL PERSONALITY OF INTERGOVERNMENTAL ORGANIZATIONS: ITS SCOPE AND ITS VALIDITY VIS-A-VIS NON-MEMBERS: DO THE CAPACITIES REALLY DEPEND UPON THE CONSTITUTIONS? Copenhagen, Denmark: Krohns Bogtrykkeri, 1966. 104 p.

> Based on an examination of constitutions and decisions of court. The author discusses the personality of agencies, giving also the major positions of leading scholars on the topic.

563. Zeydel, Walter H., and Chamberlin, Waldo, comps. ENABLING INSTRUMENTS OF MEMBERS OF THE UNITED NATIONS: A COMPILATION OF THE LEGISLATION AND EXECUTIVE ORDERS AND OTHER INSTRUMENTS WHICH DETERMINE THE LEGAL POSITION OF MEMBERS OF THE UNITED NATIONS AND SPECIALIZED AGENCIES. New York: Carnegie Endowment, 1951. 142 p.

> A useful reference tool.

3. Legislative Power and Legal Effects of Action by the United Nations and Related Agencies

564. Higgins, Rosalyn. THE DEVELOPMENT OF INTERNATIONAL LAW THROUGH THE POLITICAL ORGANS OF THE UNITED NATIONS. New York: Oxford University Press, 1963. 423 p.

> An excellent study of UN practice, systematic and lucid, evidencing a keen sense of how the organization works. The author demonstrates that state practice, in the end, is the real determining factor in establishing the existence of international law. Practice may be evidenced by votes and views expressed in collective international bodies. The author warns against using the notion of "legal" correctness. She points out the necessity, at times, to decide on the basis of political preference. Only thus will the law expand and become relevant to state behavior.

565. Castaneda, Jorge. LEGAL EFFECTS OF UNITED NATIONS RESOLUTIONS. New York: Columbia University Press, 1970. 255 p.

> A careful legal analysis of six types of General Assembly resolutions which, in the author's opinion, "produce true juridical effects against which members have no legal recourse." Shows that some resolutions take on a quality which puts them in a category separate from mere recommendations.

Examines the effect of these resolutions on state behavior.

566. Schwebel, Stephen M., ed. THE EFFECTIVENESS OF INTERNATIONAL DECISIONS. Papers of a Conference of the American Society of International Law and the Proceedings of the Conference. Dobbs Ferry, N.Y.: Oceana, 1971. 538 p.

   Good collection of analytic papers showing the extent to which international decisions of various organizations are carried out and how these may be rendered more effective. Participants were official legal advisers.

567. Kelsen, Hans, et al. THE UNITED NATIONS: TEN YEARS' LEGAL PROGRESS. The Hague, Netherlands: Nederlandse Studentenvereiniging voor Wereldrechtsorde, 1956. 200 p.

   A collection of essays reflecting on the progress made by the UN towards the development of international law.

568. Schachter, Oscar, et al. TOWARD WIDER ACCEPTANCE OF UN TREATIES. New York: Arno, 1971. 194 p.

   Concerned with causes and factors influencing delay on the part of states in ratifying international agreements. A useful statistical analysis of the ratifications of multilateral conventions. Organized for easy reference.

569. Yemin, Edward. LEGISLATIVE POWERS IN THE UNITED NATIONS AND SPECIALIZED AGENCIES. Leiden, Netherlands: Sijthoff, 1969. 244 p.

   Examines functions of international organizations and the extent to which these have taken on legislative powers. Largely concerned with the process of revision of constituent instruments. The author indicates that many states are bound by revisions to which they have not given their consent. Concentrates on specialized agencies in which he sees growing regulatory powers which he equates with legislative power.

570. Han, Henry H. INTERNATIONAL LEGISLATION BY THE UNITED NATIONS: LEGAL PROVISIONS, PRACTICE AND PROSPECTS. New York: Exposition Press, 1971. 221 p.

   An analysis of UN involvement in the initiation, drafting, and enforcing of multilateral treaties.

571. Detter, Ingrid. LAW MAKING BY INTERNATIONAL INSTITUTIONS. Stockholm, Sweden: Norstedt, 1965. 353 p.

   Deals primarily with the development of norms directly related to the competence of international organizations, indicating the techniques used to bind members. Shows how

International Institutions

organizations, once they have original consent, tend to proceed without reference to individual member consent. An impressive wealth of acts and decisions included.

572. Schneider, J. W. TREATY-MAKING POWER OF INTERNATIONAL ORGANIZATIONS. Geneva, Switzerland: Droz, 1963. 154 p.

    An empirical and well-organized analysis of the legal significance of acts of international organizations.

573. Chiu, Hungdah. THE CAPACITY OF INTERNATIONAL ORGANIZATIONS TO CONCLUDE TREATIES, AND THE SPECIAL LEGAL ASPECTS OF THE TREATIES SO CONCLUDED. The Hague, Netherlands: Nijhoff, 1966. 242 p.

    An excellent survey incorporating extensive legal analysis.

574. Falk, Richard A. THE AUTHORITY OF THE UNITED NATIONS OVER NON-MEMBERS. Princeton, N.J.: Princeton University Press, 1965. 101 p. (For the Center of International Studies.)

    An historical analysis of the development of the use of Article 2.6 showing factors related to decisions relevant to nonmembers.

575. Weitz, Harold, et al. AN APPROACH TO THE ANALYSIS OF RESOLUTIONS OF THE SECURITY COUNCIL. UNITAR (United Nations Institute for Training and Research) Research Reports, no. 16. New York: UNITAR, 1972. 113 p.

    An analysis of the effects of various types of Security Council resolutions.

576. Asamoah, O. V. THE LEGAL SIGNIFICANCE OF THE DECISIONS OF THE GENERAL ASSEMBLY OF THE UNITED NATIONS. The Hague, Netherlands: Nijhoff, 1966. 274 p.

    Categorizes various types of decisions, showing the legal significance of each. Relies heavily on intention of the General Assembly; whether it intended to bind or obligate members or merely to declare. Shows how international law is evolving due to actions of the UN.

577. Hingorani, R. C., ed. INTERNATIONAL LAW THROUGH THE UNITED NATIONS. Bombay, India: Tripathi, 1972. 214 p.

C. ORGANS OF INTERNATIONAL ORGANIZATIONS: STRUCTURES AND ACTIVITIES

(See also 558.)

1. League of Nations Organs

(See also 245.)

578. Burton, Margaret Ernestine. THE ASSEMBLY OF THE LEAGUE OF NATIONS. Chicago, Ill.: University of Chicago Press, 1941. 441 p.

    Description of the origin, history, and characteristics of the Assembly. Outlines and evaluates the committees, rules of procedures, and handling of disputes. Scholarly.

579. Brett, Oliver, ed. THE FIRST ASSEMBLY: A STUDY OF THE PROCEEDINGS OF THE FIRST ASSEMBLY OF THE LEAGUE OF NATIONS. London: Macmillan, 1921. 285 p.

580. Conwell-Evans, Thomas P. THE LEAGUE COUNCIL IN ACTION: A STUDY OF THE METHODS EMPLOYED BY THE COUNCIL OF THE LEAGUE OF NATIONS TO PREVENT WAR AND TO SETTLE INTERNATIONAL DISPUTES. New York: Oxford University Press, 1929. 300 p.

    An analytic and scholarly study of twenty-three disputes handled by the Council. Shows how a jurisprudence developed based on new principles of international law.

581. Greaves, Harold Richard Goring. THE LEAGUE COMMITTEES AND WORLD ORDER. London: Oxford University Press, 1943. 217 p.

    Good analysis of the functioning of the committees and rules procedure, with an evaluation of their effectiveness.

582. Rosenne, Shabtai. LEAGUE OF NATIONS COMMITTEE OF EXPERTS FOR THE PROGRESSIVE CODIFICATION OF INTERNATIONAL LAW 1925-1928. 2 vols. Dobbs Ferry, N.Y.: Oceana, 1972. 1,000 p.

    Using the reports, minutes, and other documents, the author shows how the Committee worked and why the group failed to produce a standard code. Introduction contains a lengthy discussion of the history of various attempts at codification.

583. Langer, Elisabeth M., and Turbull, Laura S. LEAGUE OF NATIONS LIST OF COMMISSIONS AND COMMITTEES, ECONOMIC AND FINANCIAL SECTION. New York: Woodrow Wilson Memorial Library of the Woodrow Wilson Foundation, n.d. 120 p. Mimeographed.

International Institutions

Cross-referenced catalog of 120 committees working under the League.

584. League of Nations. THE COMMITTEES OF THE LEAGUE OF NATIONS: CLASSIFIED LIST AND ESSENTIAL FACTS. League of Nations Series 1945, vol. 2. Geneva, Switzerland, 1945. 73 p.

    Gives origin, character, purposes, and demise.

2. The General Assembly (GA)

(See also 253, 270, 271, 565, 576, 628, 704, 706-9, 754, 1034, 1046.)

585. Russell, Ruth B. with the assistance of Clausen, Peter. THE GENERAL ASSEMBLY: PATTERNS, PROBLEMS, PROSPECTS. New York: Carnegie Endowment, 1970. 81 p. Pamphlet.

    Appraises flaws in the institutional arrangements and procedures of the Assembly. Traces its evolution over twenty-five years and discusses specific proposals for reform.

586. Bailey, Sydney D. THE GENERAL ASSEMBLY OF THE UNITED NATIONS: A STUDY OF PROCEDURE AND PRACTICE. Rev. ed. New York: Praeger, 1964. 400 p.

    Defines functions and purposes of the organ and describes its workings, with details on bloc voting patterns. Gives his projections for the future effectiveness of the General Assembly and the UN as a whole.

587. United Nations. General Assembly. RULES OF PROCEDURE OF THE GENERAL ASSEMBLY. New York, 1972. 84 p. (Sales E. 72.I. 13.)

3. The Security Council (SC)

(See also 254, 255, 272, 575, 625, 626.)

588. Boyd, Andrew. FIFTEEN MEN ON A POWDER KEG. New York: Stein and Day, 1971. 383 p.

    A history of the Security Council focusing on its origins, actions, and possibilities. A good guide showing the importance of personalities in the functioning of the organ. Goes into some cases (Cuba, Czechoslovakia, and the Middle East of 1967) in detail.

589. Lall, Arthur. THE SECURITY COUNCIL IN A UNIVERSAL UN. New

York: Carnegie Endowment, 1972. 42 p.

> Shows the structure and process of decision making. Examines the inability to convene timely meetings on crises, along with an inability to create a firm and common conclusion on issues. Thesis is that the Council sabotages the effectiveness of the UN and needs to be reconstituted.

590. Chai, F. Y. CONSULTATION AND CONSENSUS IN THE SECURITY COUNCIL. New York: United Nations Institute for Training and Research, 1972. 56 p.

> Study of the procedures whereby the Security Council has found it possible to reach consensus. Concludes that this enhances the effectiveness of the organ.

591. Hiscocks, Richard. THE SECURITY COUNCIL: STUDY IN ADOLESCENCE. New York: The Free Press, 1974. 352 p.

> The author surveys the historical background of the UN's creation, examining the Council's constitution and functions as envisaged in the Charter and as demonstrated in practice. He also deals extensively with the main international crises and problems since World War II. The author concludes with a chapter on the Council's future prospects in light of recent changes in the world situation.

592. Kahng, Tae Sin. LAW, POLITICS AND THE SECURITY COUNCIL: AN INQUIRY INTO THE HANDLING OF LEGAL QUESTIONS INVOLVED IN INTERNATIONAL DISPUTES AND SITUATIONS. The Hague, Netherlands: Nijhoff, 1964. 252 p.

> The author attempts to clarify the practice of the Security Council in handling legal questions. Shows how the Council has handled "legal" as opposed to "political" issues and concludes that the practice of the Council has been quasi-judicial, preferring not to rely on legal opinions of the Secretary-General or to utilize advisory opinions of the Court.

593. Kasluck, Paul. WORKSHOP OF SECURITY. Melbourne, Australia: Cheshire, 1948. 181 p.

594. United Nations. Security Council. PROVISIONAL RULES OF PROCEDURE OF THE SECURITY COUNCIL. New York, 1969. 23 p. (Sales E.69.I.9.)

International Institutions

4. The Economic and Social Council (ECOSOC)

(See also 80, 256, 257, 273, 502.)

595. Sharp, Walter R. THE UNITED NATIONS ECONOMIC AND SOCIAL COUNCIL. New York: Columbia University Press, 1969. 322 p.

    A wide-ranging and systematic examination of ECOSOC since its inception in 1946. Evaluates its work and considers its future in light of the rapid expansion of the UN system in the area of social and economic affairs. Concerned with composition, staffing, and decision-making patterns, not much attention given to the political context in which the organ functions.

596. Padelford, Norman J. POLITICS AND THE FUTURE OF ECOSOC. Cambridge, Mass.: The M.I.T. Press, 1961. 32 p.

    Neither a very equitable nor a complete account.

597. Finer, Herman. THE UNITED NATIONS ECONOMIC AND SOCIAL COUNCIL. Boston, Mass.: World Peace Foundation, 1946. 121 p.

    A descriptive account of the international machinery soon after it began to operate. Emphasis on structural and procedural devices. Examines problem of coordinating activities of the specialized agencies and the UN.

598. Stinebower, Leroy D. THE ECONOMIC AND SOCIAL COUNCIL: AN INSTRUMENT OF INTERNATIONAL COOPERATION. New York: Commission to Study International Peace, 1946. 39 p.

    Early look at purposes, organization, and potential.

599. United Nations Economic and Social Council. RULES OF PROCEDURE OF THE FUNCTIONAL COMMISSIONS OF THE ECONOMIC AND SOCIAL COUNCIL. Rev. ed. New York, 1970. 17 p. (Sales E.70.I.21.)

5. Presiding Officers in the United Nations

600. Werners, S. E. THE PRESIDING OFFICERS IN THE UNITED NATIONS. Haarlem, Netherlands: De Erven F. Bohn, 1967. 209 p.

    A meticulous and cautious analysis of the powers, duties, and responsibilities of presiding officers of the principal deliberative organs. Comparison with the League of Nations. Well-organized and readable account containing much useful information.

6. The International Law Commission (ILC)

(See also 198.)

601. Briggs, Herbert W. THE INTERNATIONAL LAW COMMISSION. London: Oxford University Press, 1966. 380 p.

   A scholarly exposition of the origins, statute, procedures, and methods of the Commission. Gives history of the drafting of the statute, and the relationship of the ILC to the General Assembly and member states. Although Briggs was a member of the ILC, there are few personal references included.

602. United Nations. THE WORK OF THE INTERNATIONAL LAW COMMISSION. Rev. ed. New York, 1972. 243 p. (Sales E.72.I.17.)

   Good outline of the structure, procedures, and accomplishments of the ILC.

7. Other Institutions

(See also 258, 274.)

603. Merillat, H. C. L., ed. LEGAL ADVISERS AND INTERNATIONAL ORGANIZATIONS. Dobbs Ferry, N.Y.: Oceana, 1966. 142 p.

   Discussion of the problems which arise in practice for legal advisers showing how these have been approached and resolved.

604. Dale, Doris C. THE UNITED NATIONS LIBRARY: ITS ORIGINS AND DEVELOPMENT. Chicago, Ill.: American Library Association, 1970. 250 p.

605. United Nations. THE UNITED NATIONS INTERNATIONAL SCHOOL: ITS HISTORY AND DEVELOPMENT. New York, 1973. 184 p.

8. International Legislative Bodies and Conferences

606. Hovey, J. A. THE SUPERPARLIAMENTS. New York: Praeger, 1967. 202 p.

   Examines the history and structure of several international consultative assemblies discussing function, capabilities, and potential. Examines reactions to, possibilities of, and limitations of these bodies.

607. Union of International Associations. INTERNATIONAL CONGRESS ORGANIZATION: THEORY AND PRACTICE. Brussels, Belgium, 1961. 128 p.

> Drawing on experience, the authors present very practical and pragmatic suggestions on the organization of large multinational meetings.

608. Pastuhov, Vladimir D. A GUIDE TO THE PRACTICE OF INTERNATIONAL CONFERENCES. Washington, D.C.: Carnegie Endowment, 1945. 274 p.

> A former member of the League Secretariat provides information on all aspects of conference management, including planning, staffing, budgeting, organizing, directing, and the actual holding of conferences and committee meetings. He gives special attention to follow-up work and links technical processes with theory and representative literature of the field.

D. ORGANIZATIONAL ISSUES AND PROBLEMS

1. Representation and Membership

(See also 654, 770, 807, 1310, 1311.)

a. GENERAL ISSUES

609. Graham, Malbone W. THE LEAGUE OF NATIONS AND THE RECOGNITION OF STATES. Berkeley, Calif.: University of California Press, 1933. 79 p.

610. Stein, E. SOME IMPLICATIONS OF EXPANDING UN MEMBERSHIP. New York: Carnegie Endowment, 1956. 77 p.

> Looks into problems, prospects, and possible consequences of continued expansion of membership to include numerous mini-states.

611. Blair, Patricia W. THE MINISTATE DILEMMA. Rev. ed. Occasional Paper, no. 6. New York: Carnegie Endowment, 1968. 98 p.

> Concerned with areas containing less than 300,000 persons. Discusses criteria for membership, the rights of nonmembers, and the status of intermediate membership in the League, UN, and other international organizations.

612. Singh, Nagendra. TERMINATION OF MEMBERSHIP IN INTERNATIONAL ORGANIZATIONS. New York: Praeger, 1958. 226 p.

A thorough, scholarly, and juridical study. Primarily concerned with China, arguing the legitimacy of her claim to membership. Careful legal analysis of the provisions of the Charter and other constituent instruments on the right of withdrawal.

613. Green, Leslie C. "Representation in the Security Council." INDIAN YEARBOOK OF INTERNATIONAL AFFAIRS II (1962): 48-75.

An analysis of the members of the Security Council and explanation of the politics involved in determining their selection.

614. Olynyk, Stephen D. MEMBERSHIP OF THE SOVIET UKRAINE IN THE UNITED NATIONS: BACKGROUND, STATUS AND LEGAL IMPLICATIONS. Washington, D.C., 1959. 276 p.

A study of the negotiations resulting in the Ukraine's membership.

b. CHINA

(See also 722, 746.)

615. Brock, David. THE U.N. AND CHINA DILEMMA. New York: Vintage, 1956. 87 p.

Surveys arguments in the UN and the criteria used in matters of recognition. Pleads for a judicial resolution rather than a political one.

616. Reynolds, C. V., Jr. WHY NOT ADMIT RED CHINA TO THE UNITED NATIONS? Berkeley, Calif.: McCutchen, 1970. 103 p.

Rests case for admission on the importance of China in world affairs and traditional Chinese-American relations.

617. Chen, Lung-Chu, and Lasswell, Harold C. FORMOSA, CHINA AND THE UNITED NATIONS. New York: St. Martin's, 1967. 443 p.

Thesis: situation should be resolved by the UN's recognition of the Peoples Government while Formosa should become an independent state. Good summary of arguments for and against admission.

618. Appleton, Sheldon. THE ETERNAL TRIANGLE? COMMUNIST CHINA, THE UNITED STATES AND THE UNITED NATIONS. East Lansing, Mich.: Michigan State University Press, 1961. 288 p.

A well-organized and well-written analysis of the problems of seating Communist China. The voting up until 1961 in the General Assembly is analyzed.

619. Bailey, Sydney D. CHINESE REPRESENTATION IN THE SECURITY COUNCIL AND THE GENERAL ASSEMBLY OF THE UNITED NATIONS. Brighton, England: University of Sussex, Institute for the Study of International Organization, 1970. 33 p.

620. Mezerik, A. G., ed. CHINA REPRESENTATION IN THE U.N. New York: International Review Service, 1965. 116 p.

621. Brown, Benjamin H., and Greene, Fred. CHINESE REPRESENTATION: A CASE STUDY IN UNITED NATIONS POLITICAL AFFAIRS. New York: Woodrow Wilson Foundation, 1955. 52 p.

2. Voting: Procedures and Problems

(See also 704, 705, 720, 1096.)

622. Koo, Wellington, Jr. VOTING PROCEDURES IN INTERNATIONAL POLITICAL ORGANIZATIONS. New York: Columbia University Press, 1947. 320 p.

> A penetrating and well-documented study using a functional theory of voting procedures. Especially concerned with the League and UN. Gives history of collective political action prior to the League.

623. Riches, Cromwell Adams. THE UNANIMITY RULE AND THE LEAGUE OF NATIONS. Baltimore, Md.: The Johns Hopkins University Press, 1933. 224 p.

> A careful analysis of the ways the unanimity rule shaped the politics of the organization.

624. _____. MAJORITY RULE IN INTERNATIONAL ORGANIZATIONS. Baltimore, Md.: The Johns Hopkins University Press, 1940. 322 p.

> A scholarly study of the trend from unanimity to majority decision in organizations.

625. Jimenez de Arechage, Eduardo. VOTING AND HANDLING OF DISPUTES IN THE SECURITY COUNCIL. New York: Carnegie Endowment, 1950. 189 p.

> A thorough study by a member of the Council of the problems during the first five years. Goes into the evolution, legality, and functions of the Council. Shows how the organ interpreted and adapted the bare bones of its legal mandate and how it

adjusted to new circumstances. In analyzing a controversy, the author shows how the vote ran at various stages.

626. Bailey, Sydney D. VOTING IN THE SECURITY COUNCIL. Bloomington, Ind.: University of Indiana Press, 1970. 287 p.

> A careful and informative analysis of voting from 1946 to 1967. Discusses the origins of voting arrangements and of the double veto; shows ins-and-outs of the use of the veto. Concludes that the veto has not hampered the UN, and that there is a growing use of consensus techniques to a large extent, resulting from the incentive to negotiate encouraged by the existence of the veto.

627. ———. "The Veto in the Security Council." INTERNATIONAL CONCILIATION 566(January 1968): 1-60.

> A well-informed, meticulously accurate study of the veto intended to dispel popular misconceptions. Contains useful tables.

628. Padleford, Norman J. ELECTIONS IN THE UNITED NATIONS GENERAL ASSEMBLY: A STUDY IN POLITICAL BEHAVIOR. Cambridge, Mass.: Massachusetts Institute of Technology, Center for International Studies, 1959. 72 p.

> A brief discussion of how elections are conducted and what influences decision makers.

3. Studies of the Decision-Making Process

(See also 632, 1046.)

629. Hadwen, John G., and Kaufmann, Johan. HOW UNITED NATIONS DECISIONS ARE MADE. Leiden, Netherlands: Sijthoff, 1960. 150 p.

> Two delegates (from the Netherlands and Canada) discuss how UN business is carried on by national delegations. They give much inside information, taking the reader behind the scenes to show that personal relations and informal discussion are more important than the formal exchanges and debates. Consideration is given to the type of people who are assigned to delegations and to how resolutions are initiated and sponsored.

630. Cox, Robert W., and Jacobson, Harold K[aron]., eds. THE ANATOMY OF INFLUENCE: DECISION-MAKING IN INTERNATIONAL ORGANIZATIONS. New Haven, Conn.: Yale University Press, 1973. 497 p.

> Consists of substantial case studies of the decision-making process in eight economic and social agencies having a world-

wide scope: ITU, ILO, UNESCO, WHO, IAEA, IMF, GATT. Individual contributors use a similar framework which makes the work truly comparative.

4. Financial Issues

631. Stoessinger, John G., et al. FINANCING THE UNITED NATIONS SYSTEM. Washington, D.C.: Brookings, 1964. 348 p.

   In collaboration with ten experts, the author goes into many ramifications of the financial plight of the UN and outlines possible solutions. Shows financing techniques of other international organizations in a cursory way.

632. Singer, David J. FINANCING INTERNATIONAL ORGANIZATIONS: THE UNITED NATIONS BUDGET PROCESS. The Hague, Netherlands: Nijhoff, 1961. 201 p.

   An excellent study of the process by which the UN sets its budget and appropriates funds. Shows how the process came into being and the role of the Advisory Committee on Administration and Budgetary Questions vis-a-vis the Secretariat. Clear and objective in analysis and presentation.

633. Nichols, Calvin J. FINANCING THE UN: PROBLEMS AND PROPOSALS. Cambridge, Mass.: Massachusetts Institute of Technology, Center for International Studies, 1961. 36 p.

E. SECRETARIATS AND THEIR PROBLEMS

1. General

(See also 101, 779, 1213, 1272.)

634. Loveday, A. REFLECTION ON INTERNATIONAL ADMINISTRATION. Oxford, England: Clarendon, 1956. 334 p.

   The author, many years in the front ranks of international administrators, draws on his own experiences to study the problems confronting the heads of international agencies. Looks into methods of recruitment, maintenance of morale and discipline, functioning of committees, conducting of research, and handling finances. His study is well-considered, his conclusions sober and valuable.

635. Ranshofen-Wertheimer, Egan Ferdinand. THE INTERNATIONAL SECRETARIAT: A GREAT EXPERIMENT IN INTERNATIONAL ADMINISTRATION.

International Institutions

Washington, D.C.: Carnegie Endowment, 1945. 527 p.

A former member of the League shows the importance of the Secretariat to the functioning of the League. Gives experience and problems of creating and running the Secretariat, and draws lessons for the new UN.

636. Hill, Norman Llewellyn. INTERNATIONAL ADMINISTRATION. New York: McGraw-Hill, 1931. 292 p.

An early examination of the various types of international agency organizations, personnel policies, and methods of financing.

637. Jordan, Robert S., ed. INTERNATIONAL ADMINISTRATION: ITS EVOLUTION AND CONTEMPORARY APPLICATION. London: Oxford University Press, 1971. 308 p.

Investigates origins and evolving concept of an international administration and international civil service. Shows the influence of British and French concepts and practices on their development. Study of current uses of international administrations, including their role in peacekeeping operations.

638. Royal Institute of International Affairs. THE INTERNATIONAL SECRETARIAT OF THE FUTURE. London, 1944.

Looking back for lessons to be learned, the authors study the League experience to make concrete proposals for future policies to be used in establishing the UN Secretariat.

639. Egger, Rowland. THE ADMINISTRATION OF INTERNATIONAL ORGANIZATIONS. New York: Carnegie Endowment, 1942. 103 p.

640. Sayre, Francis B. EXPERIMENTS IN INTERNATIONAL ADMINISTRATION. New York: Harper, 1919. 200 p.

Pre-League experiences described and analyzed.

641. Bailey, Sydney D. THE SECRETARIAT OF THE UNITED NATIONS. Rev. ed. United Nations Study, no. 11. New York: Praeger, 1964. 140 p.

Study of the evolution, organization, and growing strength of the Secretariat. Analysis of the conflict between the idea of an independent civil service for the UN and recurrent demands for political representation in the Secretariat. Good statement of conflicting views of the proper functions and composition.

International Institutions

2. The International Civil Service

642. Langrod, Georges. THE INTERNATIONAL CIVIL SERVICE. Dobbs Ferry, N.Y.: Oceana, 1963. 358 p.

   Concentrates on administrative as well as political aspects of the civil service as it has developed from the early international unions. Shows how Hammarskjold conceived of its role and his ideas for reforms. Analyzes mistakes and achievements.

643. Young, Tien-Chen. THE INTERNATIONAL CIVIL SERVICE. Brussels, Belgium: International Institute of Administrative Sciences, 1958. 268 p.

   An elementary book on personnel problems which relies heavily on others for its conclusions.

644. Bedjaoui, Mohammed. INTERNATIONAL CIVIL SERVICE. London: Stevens, 1958. 692 p.

   A well-documented presentation of the duties, privileges, security, and guarantees of independence of international officials. Concentrates on legal and judicial issues of all the major international secretariats from a strictly French legalistic tradition.

645. Hammarskjold, Dag. THE INTERNATIONAL CIVIL SERVANT IN LAW AND IN FACT. London: Oxford University Press, 1961. 28 p.

   A lecture given by the late Secretary-General at Oxford on the nature of the international secretariat and the political powers and duties of the Secretary-General. A reply to the savage attacks made on him during the 1960 Assembly.

3. International Administrative Tribunals and Their Jurisdiction

646. Koh, Byung Charles. THE UNITED NATIONS ADMINISTRATIVE TRIBUNAL. Baton Rouge, La.: Louisiana State University Press, 1966. 176 p.

   A brisk and comparative survey of the structure and function of the tribunal, showing how its powers have been consistently limited. Reviews its jurisdiction.

647. Schechter, Alan H. INTERPRETATION OF AMBIGUOUS DOCUMENTS BY INTERNATIONAL ADMINISTRATIVE TRIBUNALS. London: Stevens, 1964. 183 p. (Under the auspices of the London Institute of World Affairs.)

   The author traces the interesting legal developments since

World War II. He analyzes the actions of the UN Administrative Tribunal, the ILO Tribunal, and the European Court of Justice, indicating how these have interpreted international rules and regulations. Looks at employment contracts, staff rules and regulations, and treaty provisions.

648. King, John K[erry]. INTERNATIONAL ADMINISTRATIVE JURISDICTION WITH SPECIAL REFERENCE TO THE DOMESTIC LAWS OF THE UNITED STATES OF AMERICA. Brussels, Belgium: International Institute of Administration, 1952. 288 p.

4. Staffing and Personnel Policy

(See also 935, 936, 1166, 1172, 1178.)

649. Torre, Mottram, ed. THE SELECTION OF PERSONNEL FOR INTERNATIONAL SERVICE. Geneva, Switzerland: World Federation for Mental Health, 1964. 161 p.

>   An interesting and imaginary exchange of office minutes on recruitment of a fictitious international secretariat.

650. Akehurst, Michael Barton. THE LAW GOVERNING EMPLOYMENT IN INTERNATIONAL ORGANIZATIONS. Cambridge Studies in International and Comparative Law. Cambridge, England: Cambridge University Press, 1967. 322 p.

>   Special attention is given to three topics: the source of applicable law, judicial review of administrative decisions, and unilateral amendment of conditions of service. These are used to show how law serves to facilitate the growth of an individual career service.

651. Rhodes, James Robert. STAFFING THE UNITED NATIONS SECRETARIAT. Brighton, England: University of Sussex, Institute for the Study of International Organizations, 1970. 30 p.

652. Behanon, Kavoor Thomas. REALITIES AND MAKE-BELIEVE: PERSONNEL POLICY IN THE UNITED NATIONS SECRETARIAT. New York: William-Frederick, 1952. 70 p.

5. Other Issues and Problems

653. Purves, Chester. THE INTERNATIONAL ADMINISTRATION OF AN INTERNATIONAL SECRATARIAT. London: The Royal Institute of International Affairs, 1945. 78 p.

An interesting and practical discussion of some of the major issues and problems of an international secretariat.

654. Sharp, Walter R. IMPLICATIONS OF EXPANDING MEMBERSHIP FOR UNITED NATIONS ADMINISTRATION AND BUDGET. New York: Carnegie Endowment, 1956. 34 p. Mimeographed.

Discussion of the problems, prospects, and possible consequences for the organization if the membership continues to increase.

655. Wriggins, Howard. THE STATUS OF THE UNITED NATIONS SECRETARIAT. New York: Woodrow Wilson Foundation, 1954. 29 p. Pamphlet.

Account of the legal status of those in the Secretariat and the Secretariat as an entity.

656. Michaels, David B. PRIVILEGES AND IMMUNITIES OF THE INTERNATIONAL CIVIL SERVANT. Falls Church, Va., 1970. 439 p.

657. Guetzkow, Harold. MULTIPLE LOYALTIES: THEORETICAL APPROACH TO A PROBLEM OF INTERNATIONAL ORGANIZATION. Publication 4, Center for Research on World Political Institutions. Princeton, N.J.: Princeton University Press, 1955. 62 p.

658. Huss, P. J., and Carpozi, George J., Jr. RED SPIES IN THE UN. New York: Coward McCann, 1965. 287 p.

Examination to call United States attention to espionage incidents and specific cases which the authors claim threaten the cause of international peace. Concerned primarily with Soviet and Cuban cases.

F. THE SECRETARIES-GENERAL

1. General Studies

(See also 1242, 1252, 1253.)

659. Rovine, Arthur. THE FIRST FIFTY YEARS: THE SECRETARY-GENERAL IN WORLD POLITICS, 1920-1970. Leiden, Netherlands: Sijthoff, 1970. 480 p.

A thorough, conscientiously researched, well-documented study of the evolution of the office. Compares the careers and achievements of the incumbents, showing the unique background of each in fulfilling his office. Emphasis put on role of the office in political disputes and how these have affected its character.

660. Gordenker, Leon. THE UN SECRETARY-GENERAL AND THE MAINTENANCE OF PEACE. New York: Columbia University Press, 1967. 380 p.

   A thoughtful and clear study of the first three Secretaries-General and how each of these viewed the political functions of the office. The author assesses the influence of the three men on the functioning of the organization. Shows how each conceived of his task and his actual involvement as a mediator and negotiator.

661. Schwebel, Stephen M. THE SECRETARY-GENERAL OF THE UNITED NATIONS: HIS POLITICAL POWERS AND PRACTICE. Cambridge, Mass.: Harvard University Press, 1952. 299 p.

   Shows the historical evolution of the office, comparing the League and UN experiences, concentrating on political aspects. Traces the developments of the powers of the Secretaries-General, and discusses their relations with the Security Council, General Assembly, nonpolitical UN organs, and national governments.

662. Pechota, Vratislav. THE QUIET APPROACH: A STUDY OF THE GOOD OFFICES EXERCISED BY THE UNITED NATIONS SECRETARY GENERAL IN THE CAUSE OF PEACE. New York: United Nations Institute for Training and Research, 1972. 68 p.

   An analysis of the role of the Secretary-General and examination of those activities included under the term "Good Offices." Concerned with the factors important in the procedure: the relationship between the Secretary-General and the other organs, types of techniques used, and methods which seem most appropriate.

663. Srivastava, Padma. U.N. AND PEACEFUL CO-EXISTENCE: THE ROLE OF THE UNITED NATIONS IN PEACEFUL CO-EXISTENCE AS CONCEIVED AND PROMOTED BY ITS SECRETARIES-GENERAL. Delhi, India: Universal Book and Stationery, 1969. 89 p.

664. Clifford, J. M. THE THIRTY-EIGHTH FLOOR. New York: McGraw-Hill, 1965. 65 p.

   Brief account of the role of the Secretary-General in the development of the organization.

International Institutions

2. Joseph Avenol

665. Barros, James. BETRAYAL FROM WITHIN: JOSEPH AVENOL, SECRETARY-GENERAL OF THE LEAGUE OF NATIONS, 1933-1940. New Haven, Conn.: Yale University Press, 1969. 305 p.

   A well-written, superbly researched political biography. Sees Avenol as an unprincipled reactionary who used his talents against the League's interests by collaborating with the Axis powers behind the scenes. Uses many hitherto unpublished and unworked sources.

3. Trygve Lie

666. Lie, Trygve. IN THE CAUSE OF PEACE: SEVEN YEARS WITH THE UNITED NATIONS. New York: Macmillan, 1954. 490 p.

   Lie's recollections covering his seven years in office. Gives his own view of the office and how he set about to implement it. Discusses how he worked to establish the organization in its permanent headquarters, including the problem of the selection of large numbers of personnel. The author gives his philosophy of the role of the organization in furthering the cause of peace and how he, as Secretary-General, was to share in the responsibility.

667. Cordier, Andrew W., et al, eds. TRYGVE LIE, 1946-1953. Public Papers of the Secretaries-General of the United Nations, vol. 1. New York: Columbia University Press, 1973. 549 p.

   Reports, statements, speeches, diplomatic correspondence, and press conferences, with commentaries by men who worked closely with Lie.

4. Dag Hammarskjold

668. Zacher, Mark W. DAG HAMMARSKJOLD'S UNITED NATIONS. Columbia Studies in International Organizations, no. 7. New York: Columbia University Press, 1970. 295 p.

   Relies heavily on public documents and Hammerskjold's writings and actions, supplemented by interviews. Gives a brief description of his background and political attitudes when he came to the office. Shows how the Secretary-General's views on the goals of the UN developed and what strategies and tactics he used to further these goals.

669. Lash, Joseph D. DAG HAMMARSKJOLD: CUSTODIAN OF THE BRUSH-

FIRE PEACE. Garden City, N.Y.: Doubleday, 1961. 304 p.

> An in-depth study of the man and his work by a man who was a correspondent at headquarters. Based in large part on extensive interviews with Hammarskjold, his collaborators, and friends. Perceptive understanding not only of his conception of his office but of the man himself. A skillful weaving together of the man's life and his life's work.

670. Urquhart, Brian. HAMMARSKJOLD. New York: Knopf, 1972. 630 p.

> A good account of the man and his work by a long-time UN official. Unpublished material from Hammarskjold's private papers is used throughout. Shows his personal development along with a perceptive analysis of Hammarskjold's influence on international affairs.

671. Van Dusen, Henry P. DAG HAMMARSKJOLD: A BIOGRAPHICAL INTERPRETATION OF "MARKINGS." London: Faber and Faber, 1967. 240 p.

> An insightful look at the relationship between Hammarskjold's inner life and outer life. The author correlates diary entries and contemporary events in the Secretary-General's public life and career, and shows the religious, intellectual, and political developments in his life.

672. Miller, Richard Irwin. DAG HAMMARSKJOLD AND CRISIS DIPLOMACY. Rev. ed. New York: Oceana, 1962. 344 p.

> A compact story of Hammarskjold's activities as Secretary-General by an educator who was a UN observer for two-and-a-half years. Shows his growing stature and influence as he handled the major crises of the organization.

673. Kelen, Emery. HAMMARSKJOLD. New York: Putnam, 1966. 316 p.

> A journalistic treatment which ends up being less than satisfactory.

674. Henderson, James L. HAMMARSKJOLD: SERVANT OF A WORLD UNBORN. London: Methuen, 1969. 150 p.

> Designed to introduce teenagers to one of the outstanding figures of the twentieth century, the author blends a narrative of the Secretary-General's public life with evidence from MARKINGS (see 677) and elsewhere of his inner and spiritual life.

675. Cordier, Andrew W., and Foote, Wilder, eds. DAG HAMMARSKJOLD, 1953-56; DAG HAMMARSKJOLD, 1956-57; DAG HAMMARSKJOLD, 1957-58; DAG HAMMARSKJOLD, 1958-60; and DAG HAMMARSKJOLD, 1960-61. Public Papers of the Secretaries-General of the United Nations, vols. 1-5. New York: Columbia University Press, 1972-75.

Contain selected reports, statements, speeches, diplomatic correspondence, and press conferences. Edited with commentaries by men who knew Hammarskjold. The introduction contains a valuable account of the nomination background in the Swedish government and the qualities which led to his success at the UN.

676. Foote, Wilder, ed. SERVANT OF PEACE: A SELECTION OF THE SPEECHES AND STATEMENTS OF DAG HAMMARSKJOLD, SECRETARY-GENERAL OF THE UNITED NATIONS 1953-1961. New York: Harper, 1963. 388 p.

Includes both political and philosophical materials showing his role in the UN and relationship to main currents in international life.

677. Hammarskjold, Dag. MARKINGS. New York: Knopf, 1964. 247 p.

A remarkable collection of jottings and entries which contain virtually nothing about his public activity but a great deal about his inner state of mind. The impact is of the whole man, at times baffling and perplexing.

678. Aulen, Gustaf. DAG HAMMARSKJOLD'S WHITE BOOK. Philadelphia, Pa.: Fortress, 1969. 154 p.

A profound interpretation of MARKINGS (see 677) by a leading Swedish theologian.

5. U Thant

679. Bingham, June. U THANT OF BURMA: THE SEARCH FOR PEACE. New York: Knopf, 1966. 300 p.

An "interim" biography by the wife of a former ambassador to the UN. Good presentation of his personal qualities showing his transformation from a schoolmaster to a cosmopolitan statesman. Little information is given of U Thant as an administrator.

680. Thant, U. TOWARD WORLD PEACE. New York: Yoseloff, 1964. 404 p.

A selection of speeches and public statements by U Thant as Permanent Representative from Burma and as Secretary-General.

International Institutions

G. INTERNATIONAL COURTS AND TRIBUNALS

(See also Chapter 9.F and 817.)

The works included here are primarily concerned with the operation and organization of international courts. See Chapter 9 for a discussion of the work of the courts.

1. General

(See also 95, 98, 275.)

681. Hudson, Manley O[ttmer]. INTERNATIONAL TRIBUNALS PAST AND FUTURE. Washington, D.C.: Carnegie Endowment, 1944. 287 p.

   A study of the evolution of international tribunals from 1794 through the League experience, discussing organization, structure, administration, financing, jurisdiction, procedure, and applications of the law. Analyzes the differences in the types of materials international tribunals have to deal with and those handled in municipal systems.

2. The Permanent Court of International Justice (PCIJ)

(See also 200, 263, 276, 279.)

682. Hudson, Manley O[ttmer]. THE WORLD COURT: 1921-1938. Boston, Mass.: World Peace Foundation, 1938. 345 p.

   The standard reference work on the organization and decisions of the Permanent Court of International Justice giving judgments, orders, and opinions.

683. _____. THE PERMANENT COURT OF INTERNATIONAL JUSTICE. Rev. ed. New York: Macmillan, 1943. 831 p.

   An exhaustive and scholarly study of the organization, procedures, and the law applied by the Permanent Court.

684. Fachiri, Alexander P. THE PERMANENT COURT OF INTERNATIONAL JUSTICE: ITS CONSTITUTION, PROCEDURE AND WORK. 2nd ed. New York: Oxford University Press, 1932. 416 p.

International Institutions

3. The International Court of Justice (ICJ)

(See also 96, 97, 201, 277, 278, 280-83, 285, 287-90, 533.)

685. Rosenne, Shabtai. THE WORLD COURT: WHAT IT IS AND HOW IT WORKS. 3rd ed. Dobbs Ferry, N.Y.: Oceana, 1973. 230 p.

    A solid guide and introduction to the court's organs and operations by the Israeli ambassador to the UN. Describes how judges are appointed, what law is applied, how a case is tried, and assesses the record of the court.

686. _____. THE INTERNATIONAL COURT OF JUSTICE: AN ESSAY IN POLITICAL AND LEGAL THEORY. New York: Central Book Co., 1957. 620 p.

    A comprehensive study of the court rather than its jurisprudence. Shows the interplay of political and legal factors bearing on the court, and the role it has been called upon to perform. Discusses the relationship between the court and the UN and specialized agencies. Large amount of statistical material included.

687. Liacouras, Peter J. THE INTERNATIONAL COURT OF JUSTICE. 2 vols. Durham, N.C.: Duke University Press, World Rule of Law Center, 1962.

    Record and role of the court in international relations. The author is especially concerned with the position taken by national judges in contentious cases.

688. Basak, Adam. DECISIONS OF THE UNITED NATIONS ORGANS IN THE JUDGEMENTS AND OPINION OF THE INTERNATIONAL COURT OF JUSTICE. Wroclaw, Poland: Societe des Sciences et des Lettres, 1969. 223 p.

    Interesting account of the court's role as an authoritative interpreter of the constitutions of organizations and judge of the legality of their activities.

689. Anand, Ram Prakash. THE INTERNATIONAL COURT OF JUSTICE AND IMPARTIALITY BETWEEN NATIONS. World Rule of Law Booklet Series, no. 26. Durham, N.C.: Duke University Press, World Rule Law Center, 1955. 45 p.

    Short study of the political role of the court.

690. Lauterpacht, Hersch. THE DEVELOPMENT OF INTERNATIONAL LAW BY THE INTERNATIONAL COURT. Rev. ed. London: Stevens, 1958. 428 p.

    A perceptive and enlightening comment on the jurisdiction of the court.

International Institutions

691. Stone, Julius, and Woetzel, Robert K., eds. TOWARD A FEASIBLE INTERNATIONAL COURT. Geneva, Switzerland: World Peace Through Law Center, 1970. 352 p.

   A collection of various approaches showing how the court should and could be changed to make it a more effective agency for resolving international disputes.

692. Pomerance, Michla. THE ADVISORY FUNCTION OF THE INTERNATIONAL COURT IN THE LEAGUE AND UN ERAS. Baltimore, Md.: The Johns Hopkins University Press, 1973. 456 p. (For American Society of International Law.)

   Good survey of the role and effectiveness of advisory opinions. Jurisdiction thoroughly analyzed. Critically examines course of advisory opinions and contrasts experience of League and UN in use, non-use, and abuse of courts' advisory functions.

693. White, Gilliam N. THE USE OF EXPERTS BY INTERNATIONAL TRIBUNALS. Syracuse, N.Y.: Syracuse University Press, 1965. 274 p.

Chapter 8

POLITICS AND INTERNATIONAL ORGANIZATIONS

Chapter 8

POLITICS AND INTERNATIONAL ORGANIZATIONS

A. THE UNITED NATIONS IN WORLD POLITICS

The works in this section focus on the interaction of the UN and the world. Many of the more general treaties (Chapter 6.E) also relate to this topic.

694. Courlander, Harold M. SHAPING OUR TIMES: WHAT THE UNITED NATIONS IS AND DOES. Dobbs Ferry, N.Y.: Oceana, 1960. 240 p.

> Presents the role of the UN within world politics.

695. Feller, A. H. UNITED NATIONS AND WORLD COMMUNITY. Boston, Mass.: Little, Brown, 1952. 166 p.

> A first class discussion of the UN and its interaction with world affairs. Optimistic in assessing prospects for the future.

696. Munro, Sir Leslie. UNITED NATIONS: HOPE FOR A DIVIDED WORLD. New York: Holt, 1962. 185 p.

> A former president of the General Assembly outlines the UN system as to organization and function. Assesses possibility of world peace through international cooperation funnelled through the organizations. Shows UN influence on world situations.

697. Lee, Marc J. THE UNITED NATIONS AND WORLD REALITIES. London: Pergamon, 1965. 258 p.

> Assesses the UN in relation to political, social, and economic problems, with special emphasis on the Congo. Analyzes national attitudes and suggests future prospects.

698. Ross, Alf. THE UNITED NATIONS: PEACE AND PROGRESS. Totowa, N.J.: Bedminster, 1966. 454 p.

Penetrating legal insights by a legal realist. An examination of the UN as a political phenomenon for creating a basis for free-world policy towards that world body. Extensive coverage results in some problems being dealt with too briefly.

699. Forgac, A. NEW DIPLOMACY AND THE UNITED NATIONS. New York: Pageant, 1965. 173 p.

Shows the impact of the UN on modern diplomacy through an examination of the functions of diplomats and foreign offices. Goes into ceremonies, titles, and precedents set by the organization.

700. MacLaurin, John (pseud.). THE UNITED NATIONS AND POWER POLITICS. New York: Harper, 1951. 491 p.

A study of the machinery and organic structure and functions of the organization and its relations with national governments. Traces the course of specific world problems through the UN. The entire work of the organization is covered thoroughly, simply, and clearly.

701. Cosgrove, C. A., and Twitchett, Kenneth J., eds. THE NEW INTERNATIONAL ACTORS: THE UNITED NATIONS AND THE EUROPEAN ECONOMIC COMMUNITY. New York: St. Martin's, 1970. 272 p.

An attempt by twelve scholars to assess the extent to which organizations play significant roles on various levels of international affairs, and to show the qualities which make international institutions "actors." There is no common analytical framework to hold the contributions together.

B. POLITICS IN INTERNATIONAL ORGANIZATIONS

1. The Process

(See also Chapter 6.E. and Chapter 7.D.2 and 3 and 928.)

702. Alker, Hayward R., Jr., and Russett, Bruce M. WORLD POLITICS IN THE GENERAL ASSEMBLY. New Haven, Conn.: Yale University Press, 1965. 352 p.

A factor analysis of voting statistics to discern which kinds of issues produce similar voting patterns. The authors use 231 roll call votes from four sessions (2nd, 7th, 12th, 16th) in this highly sophisticated work.

Politics and International Organizations

703. Best, Gary. "Diplomacy in the United Nations." Doctoral dissertation, Northwestern University Press, 1960.

   Primarily concerned with the permanent missions, based on interviews. Explores beliefs and attitudes.

704. Keohane, Robert Owen. "Political Influence in the General Assembly." INTERNATIONAL CONCILIATION: 557 (March 1966): 1-64.

   A study of voting supplemented by interviews showing the way in which influence is exercised in the General Assembly.

705. Hovet, Thomas, Jr. BLOC POLITICS IN THE UNITED NATIONS. Cambridge, Mass.: Massachusetts Institute of Technology, Center for International Studies, 1958. 252 p.

   Comprehensive collection of statistics on UN voting. Alliances, regulatory associations, common markets, and emerging federations and their role within the UN are analyzed. Examines blocs and groups acting separately and in coalition discussing the policy implications of their existence and action.

706. Haviland, Henry Field, Jr. THE POLITICAL ROLE OF THE GENERAL ASSEMBLY. United Nations Studies, no. 7. New York: Carnegie Endowment, 1951. 190 p.

   A penetrating analysis of General Assembly practice showing how the Assembly came to assume the role of the Security Council. Outlines twenty-two issues involving about 105 resolutions of the first five years.

707. Silverstein, Harvey B. THE 22nd UNITED NATIONS GENERAL ASSEMBLY: ISSUES AND ALIGNMENTS. Tucson, Ariz.: University of Arizona, Institute of Government Research, 1971. 39 p.

   A study of the politics of one General Assembly showing how states lined up on votes and why.

708. Riggs, Robert E. POLITICS IN THE UNITED NATIONS: A STUDY OF UNITED STATES INFLUENCE IN THE GENERAL ASSEMBLY. Illinois Studies in the Social Sciences, vol. 41. Urbana, Ill.: University of Illinois Press, 1958. 200 p.

   A study of the extent to which U.S. policy influences the General Assembly. Concludes that the United States is most successful on political questions involving security but ineffectual when it comes to colonial issues. Shows what methods have been used by the United States to attain its ends.

709. "Issues Before the (number) General Assembly." Published as the fall edition of INTERNATIONAL CONCILIATION until 1972 and now in VISTA, THE MAGAZINE OF THE UNITED NATIONS ASSOCIATION.

A good handy reference to the issues to be raised in forthcoming Assembly with background of the issue and prior UN action.

2. The Actors: Diplomats

710. Baehr, Peter R. THE ROLE OF A NATIONAL DELEGATION IN THE GENERAL ASSEMBLY. New York: Carnegie Endowment, 1970. 90 p.

>   Based on his experience as a delegate from the Netherlands during the 23rd General Assembly in 1968, the author examines activities which take place within national delegations and analyzes their composition. Studies the relationships between members and the decision-making process.

711. Cardozo, Michael H. DIPLOMATS IN INTERNATIONAL COOPERATION: STEP-CHILDREN OF THE FOREIGN SERVICE. Ithaca, N.Y.: Cornell University Press, 1962. 163 p.

C. NATIONS AND INTERNATIONAL ORGANIZATIONS

1. General

712. MacIver, Robert M. THE NATIONS AND THE UNITED NATIONS. New York: Manhattan, 1959. 171 p. (For Carnegie Endowment for International Peace.)

>   The concluding volume in a series commissioned by Carnegie which deals with individual nations and their relations, policy, and activities vis-a-vis the UN. The author gives summaries of those studies which were finished without drawing any general conclusions. Major objective was to gather material on the attitudes of individual nations toward the possibility of Charter revision.

2. New Nations--Small Nations

713. Kay, David A. THE NEW NATIONS IN THE UNITED NATIONS 1960-1967. New York: Columbia University Press, 1970. 269 p.

>   In his analysis of the impact of new states on the organization the author shows where demands have been made, outlines patterns of interaction in the exercise of political influence, and analyzes the successes and general nature of the UN political process as it has evolved under the impact of these new states. Shows the major trend as that of a shift in

concern from preoccupation with peace and peacekeeping to decolonization and development. Makes use of voting behavior studies.

714. Akzin, Benjamin. NEW STATES AND INTERNATIONAL ORGANIZATIONS: A REPORT PREPARED ON BEHALF OF THE INTERNATIONAL POLITICAL SCIENCE ASSOCIATION. Paris, France: United Nations Educational, Scientific and Cultural Organization, 1955. 200 p.

   A fair and forthright analysis of the problems confronting newly independent states in their relations with international organizations. Shows how the emergence of these is affecting the character of the organizations.

715. Rapoport, Jacques, et al. SMALL STATES AND TERRITORIES: STATUS AND PROBLEMS. New York: Arno Press, 1971. 216 p.

716. Wilcox, Francis O. UN AND NONALIGNED NATIONS. New York: Foreign Policy Association, 1962. 55 p.

3. Blocs and Groups

717. Vincent, Jack E. THE CAUCUSING GROUPS OF THE UNITED NATIONS: AN EXAMINATION OF THEIR ATTITUDES TOWARD THE ORGANIZATION. Stillwater, Okla.: Oklahoma State University, 1964. 152 p.

a. AFRO-ASIA AS A GROUP

(See also 921, 1354.)

718. Sharma, D. N. AFRO-ASIAN GROUP IN THE U.N. Allahabad, India: Chaitanya, 1969. 411 p.

   A survey of the major questions of concern to the Afro-Asian group from an anticolonial perspective. A tendency to regard the group as monolithic.

b. AFRICA

(See also 113, 734, 800, 905, 1323, 1331, 1332.)

719. Barros, James. AFRICAN STATES AND THE UNITED NATIONS VERSUS APARTHEID. New York: Carlton, 1967. 132 p.

The author gives the political side of the problem of apartheid from the point of view of the African states as UN members. He traces their growing influence and numerical development in attempting to influence racial policies within a nation by means of an international organization.

720. Hovet, Thomas, Jr. AFRICA AND THE UNITED NATIONS. Evanston, Ill.: Northwestern University Press, 1963. 336 p.

> A detailed analysis and interpretation of the voting record of African states in the UN and of voting records on African issues. Suggests a number of measures of cohesion of the African caucusing group as a whole and of its subgroups.

721. United Nations. Office of Public Information. THE UNITED NATIONS AND AFRICA. New York, 1962. 262 p.

> A collection of basic information on the economic and social activities of the UN and related agencies in Africa.

722. Hippolyte, Mirlande. LES ETATS DU GROUP DE BRAZZAVILLE AUX NATIONS UNIES. Paris, France: Colin, 1970. 333 p.

> A thoughtful analysis of the political impact of the Brazzaville group at the UN. Votes, speeches, and sponsorship of resolutions are examined focusing on three issues: the Algerian "problem," the Congo, and Chinese membership.

c. THE ARABS

(See also Chapter 9.E.3 and 921, 930-32, 950, 951, 1405.)

723. El-Hadi Affi, Mohamed. THE ARABS AND THE UNITED NATIONS. London: Longmans, Green, 1964. 235 p.

> A propagandistic account which is very selective and avoids any indication of controversies in Arab relations.

724. Dib, George Moussa. THE ARAB BLOC IN THE UNITED NATIONS. Amsterdam, Netherlands: Djambatan, 1956. 128 p.

> An Arab scholar, the author seeks to fit the Arab states into the wider framework of the UN and the power situation in which the UN operates. Shows on which issues the Arab states vote as a bloc. Generally incomplete and not always impartial.

Politics and International Organizations

d. LATIN AMERICA

(See also 900, 906, 1977, 1156.)

725. Houston, John A. LATIN AMERICA IN THE UNITED NATIONS. New York: Carnegie Endowment, 1957. 346 p.

    Shows the role of the Latin American republics in laying the foundations for the functioning of the UN. Indicates the amount of agreement and divergence among the states on particular issues.

726. United Nations. Office of Public Information. THE UNITED NATIONS AND LATIN AMERICA. New York, 1962. 233 p.

    A collection of basic information about the work of the UN and related agencies in Latin America.

727. Kelchner, Warren H. LATIN AMERICAN RELATIONS WITH THE LEAGUE OF NATIONS. Boston, Mass.: World Peace Foundation, 1930. 207 p.

e. WESTERN EUROPE

728. Bloomfield, Lincoln P. WESTERN EUROPE AND THE UNITED NATIONS: TRENDS AND PROSPECTS. Cambridge, Mass.: Massachusetts Institute of Technology, Center for International Studies, 1959. 110 p.

    A study of the attitudes of Western Europeans, taken country by country, towards the UN. Includes a study of the UN as it relates to each one's national interests, domestic politics, and special historical relationship with the organization.

729. Robertson, A. H. THE RELATIONS BETWEEN THE COUNCIL OF EUROPE AND THE UNITED NATIONS. New York: United Nations Institute for Training and Research Publications, 1973. 72 p.

f. SCANDINAVIA

730. Jones, Samuel S. SCANDANAVIAN STATES AND THE LEAGUE OF NATIONS. Princeton, N.J.: Princeton University Press, 1939. 298 p.

g. THE COMMONWEALTH

731. Miller, T. B. THE COMMONWEALTH AND THE UNITED NATIONS. Sydney, Australia: Sydney University Press, 1967. 237 p.

Analyzes positions of Commonwealth states at the UN, showing the breakdown of any uniform policy on most issues. Sees the UN often overstepping its powers.

732. Price, Peter. POWER AND LAW: A STUDY IN PEACEFUL CHANGE, WITH SPECIAL REFERENCE TO THE BRITISH COMMONWEALTH AND THE UNITED NATIONS. Geneva, Switzerland: Droz, 1954. 155 p.

   Shows the role of the UN vis-a-vis the Commonwealth as the latter became a group of independent states.

733. Manning, C. A. THE POLICIES OF THE BRITISH DOMINIONS IN THE LEAGUE OF NATIONS. Geneva, Switzerland: Kundig, 1932. 159 p.

h. OTHERS: ASIA, EUROPE, PACIFIC ISLANDS

Asia, see 921, 1169, 1203; Europe, see 701, 1123, 1124, 1392, 1407, 1416; Pacific Islands, see 1328, 1331, 1337, 1338, 1375-77.

734. Baker, William Gedney. "The United States and Africa in the United Nations." Doctoral dissertation, Universite de Geneve, 1968. 241 p. 241 p. Dissertation.

   Study concentrates on the fifteenth General Assembly in 1960-61 and on the dissension there.

4. Individual Nations

a. ALGERIA

(See also 722.)

735. Alwan, Mohamed. ALGERIA BEFORE THE UNITED NATIONS. New York: Robert Speller, 1959. 133 p.

   A study of the Algerian case as it progressed through the UN, with analysis of the votes.

b. AUSTRALIA

(See 1339, 1363, 1371, 1372.)

736. Harper, Norman, and Sissons, David. AUSTRALIA AND THE UNITED NATIONS. New York: Manhattan Publishing, 1959. 400 p. (For

Carnegie Endowment for International Peace.)

> An able assessment of Australian attitudes towards the organization, contrasting the optimum approval at the time of San Francisco and shortly afterwards with the growing cautiousness thereafter. Good discussion of the attitudes of the people of New Guinea and Papua.

737. Hudson, W. J. AUSTRALIA AND THE COLONIAL QUESTION AT THE UNITED NATIONS. Honolulu, Hawaii: East West Center Press, 1970. 214 p.

> Analyzes Australia's actions in the UN on matters arising from her own and other countries' administration of Non-Self-Governing territories and trusteeships under the Charter. Examines Australia's first policy of strict legalism to hold international supervision at bay and then her gradual relaxation of that policy in the 1960's.

c. AUSTRIA

738. Strasser, Wolfgang. OESTERREICH UND DIE VEREINTEN NATIONEN. Vienna, Austria: Baumueller, 1967. 439 p.

> A record of Austria's contribution to the UN noting the special problems of a neutral country.

d. BELGIUM

(See also Chapter 9.E.3.b. and 930, 932, 935.)

739. Study Group of the Institut Royal des Relations Internationales of Brussels. LA BELGIQUE ET LES NATIONS UNIES. New York: Manhattan Publishing, 1958. 372 p. (For Carnegie Endowment for International Peace.)

> Study of the attitudes of Belgians towards the UN and the role that country has played in the organization with special emphasis on the colonial question as it has affected Belgium. Explains Belgium's strong stand on domestic jurisdiction (Article 2.7).

e. BURMA

740. Trager, Frank N., et al. BURMA'S ROLE IN THE UNITED NATIONS 1948-1955. New York: Institute of Pacific Relations, 1956. 100 p. Mimeographed.

> A study of Burma's voting record and sponsorship of resolutions.

Also attention to the publications of the UN as they impinge on Burma.

f. CANADA

(See also 926, 1413, 1490.)

741. Soward, F. H., and McInnis, Edgar. CANADA AND THE UNITED NATIONS. New York: Manhattan Publishing, 1956. 296 p. (For Carnegie Endowment for International Peace.)

> Gives historical background showing Canada's role in matters of personnel and policy. Special emphasis on her role as a mediator.

742. Taylor, Alastair, et al. PEACEKEEPING: INTERNATIONAL CHALLENGE AND CANADIAN RESPONSE. Toronto, Canada: Canadian Institute of International Affairs, 1968. 211 p. Paperbound.

> A valuable account of Canada's contribution to peacekeeping activities--from the planning stage to execution.

743. Eastman, Samuel Mack. CANADA AT GENEVA. Toronto, Canada: Ryerson, 1946. 117 p.

g. CHINA

(See also 615-21, 885, 87, 897-99.)

744. China Institute of International Affairs. CHINA AND THE UNITED NATIONS. New York: Manhattan Publishing, 1959. 296 p. (For Carnegie Endowment for International Peace.)

> From the standpoint of the Chinese Nationalists, the book assesses the contribution of China to the founding and work of the organization.

745. Weng, Byron, S. J. PEKING'S UN POLICY: CONTINUITY AND CHANGE. New York: Praeger, 1970. 248 p.

> The first comprehensive study of the attitude of the People's Republic of China towards the UN prior to her admission. Empirical, well-documented, and clearly written. The author has used all published statements and actions from the People's Republic of China relating to the UN down to her 1971 admission. Probes for assumptions and political dynamics that explain continuities and changes in her position towards the organization.

746. Finke, Blythe F. CHINA JOINS THE U.N. Charlottesville, N.Y.: Sam-Har, 1973. 31 p.

747. Hsia, Chi-Feng. CHINA AND THE LEAGUE: AND MY EXPERIENCES IN THE SECRETARIAT. Shanghai, China: Commercial, 1928. 171 p.

748. Quan, Lau King. CHINA'S ROLE WITH THE LEAGUE OF NATIONS, 1919-36. Hong Kong, China: Asiatic, 1939. 432 p.

h. DENMARK

749. Sorensen, Max, and Haagerup, Niels J. DENMARK AND THE UNITED NATIONS. New York: Manhattan Publishing, 1956. 133 p. (For Carnegie Endowment for International Peace.)

> Brief historical survey of Denmark's relations with the League and straightforward account of her UN policy and actions based on parliamentary debates, newspaper reports, and other sources. Gives Denmark's stand on major issues.

i. EGYPT

(See also Chapter 9.E.3 and 934.)

750. Study Group of the Egyptian Society of International Law. EGYPT AND THE UNITED NATIONS. New York: Manhattan Publishing, 1958. 197 p. (For Carnegie Endowment for International Peace.)

> Gives Egyptian attitudes toward the UN and its policies and Egypt's actions in the organization.

j. GREECE

(See also 896, 983, 995.)

751. Calogeropoulos-Stratis, S., et al. LA GRECE ET LES NATIONS UNIES. New York: Manhattan Publishing, 1957. 175 p. (For Carnegie Endowment for International Peace.)

> Major portions devoted to the role of the UN in the defense of Greek independence from 1946-49 and the Cyprus case. Shows Greece's stand on major issues not only of the UN but in international relations generally.

Politics and International Organizations

k. INDIA

(See also Chapter 9.E.3.b and 1261.)

752. Reddy, T. Ramakrishna. INDIA'S ROLE IN THE UNITED NATIONS. Cranbury, N.J.: Farleigh Dickinson University Press, 1968. 164 p.

> India's conception of the UN and her attitude toward such issues as amending the Charter, peacekeeping forces, financing, and colonialism. Feels India has used the organization to try to enhance her prestige and to seek a recognized place in world affairs. Studies the slow rate of economic development. Shows influence of political idealism in shaping India's policy.

753. Indian Council on World Affairs. INDIA AND THE UNITED NATIONS. New York: Manhattan Publishing, 1957. 213 p. (For Carnegie Endowment for International Peace.)

> One of the national studies in which the authors assess the role of India in the UN and Indian attitudes towards the organization.

754. Boland, Gertrude C., and Goodall, Merrill R. SOLIDARITY IN THE GENERAL ASSEMBLY: THE INDIAN ROLE 1946-47. Claremont, Calif.: Claremont Asian Studies, 1962. 25 p. Pamphlet.

> Short case study of the activities of India in her attempt to bring about harmony in the Assembly.

755. Dayal, Shiv. INDIA'S ROLE IN THE KOREAN QUESTION: A STUDY IN THE SETTLEMENT OF INTERNATIONAL DISPUTES UNDER THE UNITED NATIONS. Delhi, India: Chand, 1959. 360 p.

756. Bilgrami, Jafar R. INDIA'S ROLE IN THE U.N. WITH SPECIAL REFERENCE TO TRUST AND NON-SELF-GOVERNING TERRITORIES. New Delhi, India: Jamia Millia, 1969. 269 p.

757. Menon, V. K. Krishna. KASHMIR: V. K. KRISHNA MENON'S SPEECHES IN THE SECURITY COUNCIL. Delhi, India: Ministry of Information and Broadcasting, Publication Division, 1958. 223 p.

> Gives Menon's--and official Indian--position during the Kahmir crisis.

758. Berkes, Ross N., and Bedi, Mohinder S. THE DIPLOMACY OF INDIAN FOREIGN POLICY IN THE UNITED NATIONS. Stanford, Calif.: Stanford University Press, 1958. 256 p.

> Shows how India has used the UN to further aims on her

foreign policy.

759. Schleicher, Charles P. and Bains, J. S. THE ADMINISTRATION OF INDIA'S FOREIGN POLICY THROUGH THE UNITED NATIONS. Dobbs Ferry, N.Y.: Oceana, 1969. 140 p.

760. Singh, Nagendra. INDIA AND INTERNATIONAL LAW. Mystic, Conn.: Verry Lawrence, 1969. 90 p. Paperbound.

> Parts of this study are relevant to India's participation in the League and the UN.

761. Verma, D. N. INDIA AND THE LEAGUE OF NATIONS. Patna, India: Baharati Bhawon, 1968. 350 p.

> A study of how India, having no power to control her own affairs independently, influenced international behavior of truly sovereign states through her membership in the League. A detailed account of the process by which India first participated at Paris and got international status by being in the League.

762. Ram, V. Shiva, and Shama, Brij Mohan. INDIA AND THE LEAGUE OF NATIONS. Lucknow, India: Upper India Publishing House, 1932. 239 p.

l. ISRAEL (PALESTINE)

(See also Chapter 10.E.3 and 930-32, 950, 951, 1333-36, 1405.)

763. Study Group Set Up by the Hebrew University of Jerusalem. ISRAEL AND THE UNITED NATIONS. New York: Manhattan Publishing, 1956. 322 p. (For Carnegie Endowment for International Peace.)

> This study of Israeli public opinion vis-a-vis the UN finds a general frustration with the organization and belief that Israel must rely on her own resources as the UN is too heavily pro-Arab.

m. ITALY

(See also 894, 1366-70.)

764. Study Group of the Italian Society for International Organization. ITALY AND THE UNITED NATIONS. New York: Manhattan Publishing, 1959. 208 p. (For Carnegie Endowment for International Peace.)

Study of attitudes of Italians gathered through press and other media along with general evaluation of relationship between Italy and the UN.

n. JAPAN

(See also 987-99, 1337.)

765. Study Group of the Japanese Association of International Law. JAPAN AND THE UNITED NATIONS. New York: Manhattan Publishing, 1958. 246 p. (For Carnegie Endowment for International Peace.)

> A study of attitudes in Japan using press, statements of leaders, and other sources, soon after her admission to the organization. Focuses primarily on structure and the Charter.

766. Matsushita, Masatos. JAPAN AND THE LEAGUE OF NATIONS. New York: Columbia University Press, 1929. 177 p.

o. MEXICO

767. Castaneda, Jorge. MEXICO AND THE UNITED NATIONS. Prepared under the auspices of El Colegio de Mexico. New York: Manhattan Publishing, 1958. 232 p. (For Carnegie Endowment for International Peace.)

> Studies of public opinion showing the impact the UN has had on national policies.

p. PAKISTAN

(See also Chapter 9.E.3.b.)

768. Hasan, K. Sarwar. PAKISTAN AND THE UNITED NATIONS. New York: Manhattan Publishing, 1960. 302 p. (For Carnegie Endowment for International Peace.)

> A defense of Pakistan's position as regards Kashmir. Shows public opinion of the country towards the organization and illustrates well the psychology of anticolonialism.

769. Ahmad, Mushtaq. THE UNITED NATIONS AND PAKISTAN. Karachi, Pakistan: Pakistan Institute of International Affairs, 1955. 168 p.

> A very biased account of Pakistan's role in the UN and interpretation of the Kashmir case.

q. SPAIN

770. Sanders, R. F. SPAIN AND THE UNITED NATIONS. New York: Vantage, 1966. 114 p.

    Primarily concerned with the UN resolution which ostracized her and the changes in 1950 which led to her membership in 1955.

r. SWEDEN

(See also 895, 945.)

771. Study Group of the Swedish Institute of International Affairs. SWEDEN AND THE UNITED NATIONS. New York: Manhattan Publishing, 1956. 315 p. (For Carnegie Endowment for International Peace.)

    A study of the attitude and policy of Sweden. Analysis of Sweden's major contribution to the organization: trained manpower.

s. SWITZERLAND

772. Ehni, Reinhart. DIE SCHWEIZ UND DIE VEREINTEN NATIONEN VON 1944-47. Tuebingen, Germany: Mohr, 1967. 147 p.

    The story of Switzerland's experiences with the League and how these influenced her decision not to join the UN unless the organization made special provisions for her.

773. Belin, Jacqueline, and Guggenheim, Paul. LA SUISSE ET LES NATIONS UNIES. New York: Manhattan Publishing, 1956. 140 p. (For Carnegie Endowment for International Peace.)

    Almost entirely concerned with Switzerland's interpretation of the requirements of the law of neutrality, and how these have affected her decisions on policy towards international organizations. Clearly shows Switzerland's objections to the Charter, but also her willingness to cooperate with the organization by, for example, participating in the Korean Armistice Commission.

774. Zehnder, Alfred. DIE SCHWEIZ UND DIE VEREINTEN NATIONEN. Bern, Switzerland: Herbert Long, 1970. 95 p. (For the Schweizerische Gesellschaft fuer die Vereinten Nationen.)

Politics and International Organizations

t. TURKEY

775. Gonlubol, Mehmet. TURKISH PARTICIPATION IN THE UNITED NATIONS 1945-54. Ankara, Turkey: Ankara Universities Basimeui, 1963. 187 p.

> A synopsis of official Turkish behavior and the positions taken and votes cast by the Turkish UN delegation. Shows Turkey to be a rather silent participant.

776. Institute of International Relations of the Faculty of Political Science, University of Ankara. TURKEY AND THE UNITED NATIONS. New York: Manhattan Publishing, 1961. 235 p. (For Carnegie Endowment for International Peace.)

> Shows Turkish positions on a number of issues. Indicates that her attitude was one of basic distrust towards the League but became more positive towards the UN.

777. Ataov, Turkkaya, and Gonlubol, Mehmet. TURKEY IN THE UNITED NATIONS: A LEGAL AND POLITICAL APPRAISAL. Ankara, Turkey: Ajans Turkish Press, 1960. 46 p.

> A brief survey of Turkey's role and the impact of UN's actions on the country.

u. UNITED KINGDOM

(See also 637, 964, 1067, 1254, 1255, 1332-35, 1352, 1385.)

778. Higgins, Rosalyn. THE ADMINISTRATION OF THE UNITED KINGDOM'S FOREIGN POLICY THROUGH THE UNITED NATIONS. Syracuse, N.Y.: Syracuse University Press, 1966. 63 p.

> Studies the impact of the UN on the administration of British foreign policy and on traditional diplomacy, including the adjustments within the government.

779. Goodwin, Geoffrey L. BRITAIN AND THE UNITED NATIONS. New York: Manhattan Publishing, 1957. 491 p. (For Carnegie Endowment for International Peace.)

> Assessment of the impact of the organization on Britain and the role played by the United Kingdom in the UN and specialized agencies, including their secretariats.

780. Institute of Public Administration. UNITED KINGDOM ADMINISTRATION AND INTERNATIONAL ORGANIZATIONS. London: Royal Institute of International Affairs, 1951. 55 p. Pamphlet.

A brief factual survey of the administrative arrangements developed by the United Kingdom to deal with the activities of the UN and agencies. Britain has made extensive use of interdepartmental committees. Contains a useful section on conference briefing, procedures, and training.

v. THE USSR

(See also 1056, 1248, 1258, 1259.)

781. Dallin, Alexander. THE SOVIET UNION AT THE UNITED NATIONS: AN INQUIRY INTO SOVIET MOTIVES AND OBJECTIVES. New York: Praeger, 1962. 250 p.

    Goes into general Soviet attitudes toward international law, the League, and the UN with details on a number of issues. Shows that there has been a general pattern of emphasizing national sovereignty.

782. Jacobson, Harold Karan. THE USSR AND THE UN'S ECONOMIC AND SOCIAL ACTIVITIES. Notre Dame, Ind.: University of Notre Dame Press, 1963. 309 p.

    A scholarly and painstaking record of the facts. Shows not only Soviet positions but also the reactions of other states to them. Studies the impact of the interaction of the Soviet Union and other states on the UN's institutions and functions.

783. Rubinstein, Alvin Z. THE SOVIETS IN INTERNATIONAL ORGANIZATIONS: CHANGING POLICY TOWARD DEVELOPING COUNTRIES, 1953-1963. Princeton, N.J.: Princeton University Press, 1964. 380 p.

    Case studies on the Soviet participation in the specialized agencies, showing the post-Stalin policies. Extensive use of records, documents of the UN, and Soviet writings on these organizations.

784. Grzybowski, Kazimierz. INTERNATIONAL ORGANIZATIONS FROM THE SOVIET POINT OF VIEW. World Rule of Law Booklet Series, no. 29. Durham, N.C.: Duke University Press, Rule of Law Research Center, 1965. 140 p. Pamphlet.

    A study of the development and evolution of the Soviet Union's policy in international organizations.

785. Dallin, Alexander. THE SOVIET VIEW OF THE UNITED NATIONS. Cambridge, Mass.: Massachusetts Institute of Technology, Center for International Studies, 1959. 104 p.

    Study of the changes which the Soviet view has gone through

since the beginning of the UN.

786. Osakwe, Chris. THE PARTICIPATION OF THE SOVIET UNION IN UNIVERSAL INTERNATIONAL ORGANIZATIONS: A POLITICAL AND LEGAL ANALYSIS OF SOVIET STRATEGIES AND ASPIRATIONS INSIDE ILO, UNESCO AND WHO. Leiden, Netherlands: Sijthoff, 1972. 210 p. Reprint. New York: Humanities, 1973.

 A detailed study of the Soviet Union's role in the three organizations with a full account of the ideological and political premises of Soviet policy.

787. Davis, Kathryn W. THE SOVIETS AT GENEVA. Geneva, Switzerland: Kundig, 1934. 315 p.

w. THE UNITED STATES

(See also 347, 373, 441, 473, 480, 527, 658, 708, 734, 914, 915, 926, 1050, 1056, 1070, 1072, 1154, 1155, 1201, 1256, 1257, 1267, 1268, 1375-77, 1427, 1435, 1438, 1444, 1446, 1471, 1477.)

788. Hyde, L. K., Jr. THE UNITED STATES AND THE UNITED NATIONS: PROMOTING THE PUBLIC WELFARE, EXAMPLES OF AMERICAN COOPERATION 1945-1955. New York: Manhattan Publishing, 1960. 242 p. (For Carnegie Endowment for International Peace.)

 Analysis of action taken by the United States from 1945 to 1955 to advance American foreign policy objectives in social and economic fields. Explores refugee problems, technical assistance, economic development, and human rights. Shows the United States going from idealistic, large-scale support to a more legalistic position as disillusionment in the United States towards international agencies grew.

789. Tiwari, S. C. GENESIS OF THE UNITED NATIONS: A STUDY OF THE DEVELOPMENT OF THE POLICY OF THE UNITED STATES OF AMERICA IN RESPECT OF THE ESTABLISHMENT OF A GENERAL INTERNATIONAL ORGANIZATION FOR THE MAINTENANCE OF INTERNATIONAL PEACE AND SECURITY 1941-1945. Varanasi, India: Nivedya Niketan, 1968. 457 p.

 A study of the American role in the creation of the UN. Investigates political parties and nongovernmental organizations and the effects of these on the White House and State Department.

790. United States Department of State. GENERAL: THE UNITED NATIONS. Foreign Relations of the United States, 1946, vol. 1. Washington, D.C.: Government Printing Office, 1972. 1557 p.

Politics and International Organizations

Complete record of the United States' early participation in the organization, with documents.

791. Weiler, Lawrence D., and Simons, Anne Patricia. THE UNITED STATES AND THE UNITED NATIONS. New York: Manhattan Publishing, 1967. 589 p. (For Carnegie Endowment for International Peace.)

    The authors analyze the way in which American plans for an organization to maintain peace were developed and the factors which influenced American attitudes as to the kind of organization sought. Studies the impact of UN membership on U.S. foreign policy and the American position on various political issues, showing how these fit in with overall American policy and especially with security considerations.

792. Haas, Ernst B. TANGLE OF HOPES: AMERICAN COMMITMENTS AND WORLD ORDER. Englewood Cliffs, N.J.: Prentice Hall, 1969. 320 p.

    A review of what has happened to American objectives and expectations since joining the network of international organizations. The author seeks to provide a systematic framework for re-examining U.S. policies and problems. Shows how American policies in the organizations fit with more general foreign policy aims. Provides insights into the linkages between domestic politics, environmental developments, and international systems and organizations.

793. _____. THE WEB OF INTERDEPENDENCE: THE UNITED STATES AND INTERNATIONAL ORGANIZATIONS. Englewood Cliffs, N.J.: Prentice Hall, 1970. 115 p.

    An analysis of the grassroots support of Americans for the organization, which the author finds not as affected as official Washington by the misfortunes of the organizations. Shows that the United States is now so enmeshed in the thickening web of interdependence as to make withdrawal virtually impossible. Discusses how American groups and policymakers formulate specific policy demands in international organizations.

794. Bloomfield, Lincoln P. THE UNITED NATIONS AND U.S. FOREIGN POLICY. 3rd ed. Boston: Atlantic-Little, Brown, and Co., 1969. 584 p.

    The author first analyzes U.S. policy goals, and then studies the capabilities and limitations of the UN with respect to serving these goals. The evaluation of the potential usefulness of the organization is realistic.

795. Riggs, Robert E. U.S./U.N. FOREIGN POLICY AND INTERNATIONAL ORGANIZATION. New York: Appleton-Century-Crofts, 1971. 347 p.

Politics and International Organizations

Good analytic study of the pursuit of American objectives through the UN. U.S. behavior in main organs is analyzed and the effects of U.S. activities on the UN's internal politics is studied, showing the resulting impact on the attainment of American foreign policy goals. The analysis is based on a close evaluation of UN experience in dealing with certain major issues.

796. Higgins, Benjamin. UNITED NATIONS AND U.S. FOREIGN ECONOMIC POLICY. Homewood, Ill.: Irwin, 1962. 243 p.

> The author looks for the role of the UN in U.S. foreign economic policy. He supports the increased use of multilateral agencies. Good material on the UN Resident Representatives and the field relations of the United States and UN.

797. Gardner, Richard N. THE UNITED STATES AND THE UNITED NATIONS: CAN WE DO BETTER? New York: Columbia University Press, 1972. 38 p. (For the American Assembly.) Paperbound.

> Short defense of the UN as a useful organization. Calls for increased U.S. support.

798. _____. IN PURSUIT OF WORLD ORDER: U.S. FOREIGN POLICY AND INTERNATIONAL ORGANIZATIONS. Rev. ed. New York: Praeger, 1966. 296 p.

> A survey of American foreign policy and international organizations, covering both political and welfare areas, by a former Deputy Assistant Secretary of State for International Affairs.

799. _____. BLUEPRINT FOR PEACE: BEING THE PROPOSALS OF PROMINENT AMERICANS TO THE WHITE HOUSE CONFERENCE ON INTERNATIONAL COOPERATION. New York: McGraw-Hill, 1966. 410 p.

> The reports and proposals from the White House Conference held in 1965. A vast range of topics is covered.

800. Wilcox, Francis O., and Haviland, H[enry]. Field, eds. THE UNITED STATES AND THE UNITED NATIONS. Baltimore, Md.: The John Hopkins University Press, 1961. 188 p.

> A symposium centering on two major themes: the impact of the newly emergent African states and the extent to which the UN can serve to build a constructive, dignified relationship between these and the United States. Concerned with problems of economic and social development, and peaceful settlement of disputes.

801. Russell, Ruth B. AMERICAN SECURITY POLICY AND THE UNITED NATIONS. Washington, D.C.: Brookings, 1968. 510 p.

A study of what the Charter security system was and was not meant to be. A history of the efforts at arms control and disarmament and the development of the peacekeeping techniques. The work is primarily concerned with the UN, showing the role the United States has played in it. The author concludes that the UN could be strengthened and U.S. policy objectives furthered by consistent effort to develop the organizations's conciliatory possibilities.

802. Finkelstein, Lawrence S., ed. UNITED STATES AND INTERNATIONAL ORGANIZATION. Cambridge, Mass.: The M.I.T. Press, 1969. 223 p. [Published as INTERNATIONAL ORGANIZATION 23 (Summer 1969).]

Ten essays looking at postwar international patterns. Studies the implications of the changes in the patterns in order to explicate U.S. participation in multilateral organizations, arms control, and matters of international law. Discusses U.S. aims and interests relative to international agencies.

803. Uhl, Alexander. THE U.S. AND U.N.: PARTNERS FOR PEACE. Washington, D.C.: Public Affairs Institute, 1962. 81 p. Pamphlet.

Brief discussion of the worth of the UN to the United States.

804. Gross, Franz B. THE UNITED STATES AND THE UNITED NATIONS. Norman, Okla.: University of Oklahoma Press, 1964. 356 p.

A collection of essays prepared under the auspices of the Foreign Policy Research Institute, including a wide range of perspectives on the impact of the UN on American policy. Conservative and hardnosed.

805. Summers, Robert Edward. THE UNITED STATES AND INTERNATIONAL ORGANIZATIONS. The Reference Shelf, vol. 24, no. 5. New York: Wilson, 1952. 194 p.

Descriptive account of the involvement of the United States in various organizations.

806. McClure, Wallace [M]. WORLD LEGAL ORDER: POSSIBLE CONTRIBUTIONS BY THE PEOPLE OF THE UNITED STATES. Chapel Hill, N.C.: The University of North Carolina Press, 1960. 386 p.

An analysis of U.S. involvement and participation in the UN showing how this could be improved. Very critical of U.S. policy in the organization.

807. United States. Department of State. Division of International Conferences. PARTICIPATION OF THE UNITED STATES GOVERNMENT IN INTERNATIONAL CONFERENCES INCLUDING THE COMPOSITION OF UNITED STATES DELEGATIONS AND SUMMARIES OF THE PROCEEDINGS. Washington, D.C.: Government Printing Office, 1931/32– .

Politics and International Organizations

Annual. (Title varies.)

Includes for each conference the names of the delegation, the list of other countries participating, and a short statement of the agenda and recommendations.

808. United States. Department of State. UNITED STATES--UNITED NATIONS. INFORMATION SERIES. Washington, D.C.: Government Printing Office, 1945-47. Monthly.

Report of U.S. participation.

809. _____. UNITED STATES AND THE UNITED NATIONS: REPORT BY THE PRESIDENT...TO THE CONGRESS. Washington, D.C.: Government Printing Office, 1947- . Annual.

Assessment of activities, role of the United States, and value to the United States.

810. United States. Department of State. Division of International Organization Affairs. INTERNATIONAL AGENCIES IN WHICH THE UNITED STATES PARTICIPATES. Washington, D.C.: American Council on Public Affairs, Public Affairs Press, 1946. 328 p. 2nd. ed. Washington, D.C.: Government Printing Office, 1950. 343 p.

811. Beichman, Arnold. THE OTHER STATE DEPARTMENT: THE UNITED STATES MISSION TO THE UNITED NATIONS; ITS ROLE IN THE MAKING OF FOREIGN POLICY. New York: Basic Books, 1968. 221 p.

Primarily anecdotal in character. Gives revealing comments on Stevenson's uneasy relations with Kennedy and Goldberg's initial close ties with Johnson. The differences between Washington and New York are clearly delineated.

812. Scott, William A., and Withey, Stephen B. THE UNITED STATES AND THE UNITED NATIONS: THE PUBLIC VIEW. Prepared under the auspices of the University of Michigan Survey Research Center. New York: Manhattan Publishing, 1958. 324 p. (For Carnegie Endowment for International Peace.)

A study of U.S. attitudes and policies towards the UN concerning the level of information, expectations, opinions on UN operations, and interest in foreign affairs by the American people. Uses a number of survey research institutes.

813. Van Wagenen, Richard W. SOME VIEWS OF AMERICAN DEFENSE OFFICIALS ABOUT THE UNITED NATIONS. Cambridge, Mass.: Massachusetts Institute of Technology, Center for International Studies, 1959. 47 p. Paperbound.

Based on interviews with twenty-five Department of Defense officials covering three issues: U.S. survival in a nuclear war, possibility that world peace will never be achieved, and the UN as a vehicle to carry out U.S. policy or as a mechanism to narrow the gap between East and West.

814. Corwin, Edward S. THE CONSTITUTION AND WORLD ORGANIZA- TION. Princeton, N.J.: Princeton University Press, 1944. 64 p.

   An early study of the Constitutional obstacles to total U.S. participation.

815. Schmeckebier, Laurence Frederick. INTERNATIONAL ORGANIZATIONS IN WHICH THE UNITED STATES PARTICIPATES. Washington, D.C.: Brookings, 1935. 375 p.

816. Kuehl, Warren F. SEEKING WORLD ORDER: THE UNITED STATES AND INTERNATIONAL ORGANIZATIONS TO 1920. Nashville, Tenn.: Vanderbilt University Press, 1969. 391 p.

   A study of the origins, development, successes, and failures of the major peace groups in the United States from 1815 until 1920. Emphasis is put on the leadership and initiatives emanating from the United States. Focuses on attempts by groups to encourage the formation of a politically organized world.

817. Fleming, Denna Frank. THE UNITED STATES AND WORLD ORGANI- ZATIONS 1920-33. New York: Columbia University Press, 1938. 583 p. Reprint. New York: AMS Press, 1966.

   Deals with the relationships of the United States with world organizations and especially with attempts in this country to promote entry into the World Court.

818. _____. THE UNITED STATES AND THE WORLD COURT. Garden City, N.Y.: Doubleday, Doran, 1945. 206 p.

   Examines the vain fight for the entrance of this country into the permanent court.

819. Dickinson, Thomas H. THE UNITED STATES AND THE LEAGUE. New York: Dutton, 1923. 151 p.

x. THE UNITED STATES, THE SOVIET UNION, AND THE UNITED NATIONS

(See also 783, 863, 865, 923, 1052, 1503.)

820. Rubinstein, Alvin Z., and Ginsburg, G., eds. SOVIET AND AMERICAN POLICIES IN THE UNITED NATIONS; A TWENTY-FIVE YEAR PERSPEC- TIVE. New York: United Nations, 1971. 211 p.

Politics and International Organizations

Seven essays of the roles of the Soviet Union and the United States showing their attitudes towards UN interferences in situations affecting them. Decribes times when the two agree, noting that when they do they can force the organization to take action.

821. Stoessinger, John G. THE UNITED NATIONS AND THE SUPERPOWERS. 3rd ed. New York: Random House, 1973. 210 p.

   Ten analytical studies of various patterns of United States-Soviet interaction.

y. URUGUAY

822. Uruguayan Institute of International Law. URUGUAY AND THE UNITED NATIONS. New York: Manhattan Publishing, 1958. 140 p. (For Carnegie Endowment for International Peace.)

   A presentation of the country's official stand on a number of important issues. Studies public opinion and positions.

z. WEST GERMANY

823. Droege, Heinz, et al. THE FEDERAL REPUBLIC OF GERMANY AND THE UNITED NATIONS. New York: Carnegie Endowment, 1967. 226 p. (For the Deutsche Gesellschaft fuer Auswaertige Politik.)

824. Deutsche Gesellschaft fuer die Vereinten Nationen. ZEHN JAHRE VEREINTE NATIONEN VON 1945-1955: DEUTSCHLAND UND DIE VEREINTEN NATIONEN. Frankfurt am Main, Germany: Continentale, 1956. 296 p.

   Study of the relationship between the UN and West Germany during the first ten years, including an extensive treatment of the organization's handling of the problem of Germany within the framework of East-West relations.

825. Scheuner, Ulrich, and Lindemann, Beate, eds. DIE VEREINTEN NATIONEN UND DIE MITARBEIT DER BUNDESREPUBLIK DEUTSCHLAND. Munich, Germany: Oldenbourg, 1973. 338 p.

aa. OTHER NATIONS

Bulgaria, see 896; Cameroon, see 1360; Congo, see Chapter 9.E.3.b and 930, 932, 935; Cyprus, see Chapter 9.E.d and 932; Czechoslovakia, see 1262; Finland, see 895; France, see 1336, 1352, 1360; Germany, see 1340-43; Indonesia, see 1361-65; Ireland, see 1260; Korea, see 845-50, 1406; Lebanon, see 1336; Lybia, see 1366, 1369, 1370; Netherlands, see 1361-65; New Guinea, see 1339, 1371, 1372; Portugal, see 1373, 1374; Rhodesia, see 839, 841, 1378; Somalia, see 1367-70; South Africa, see 839, 851, 852, 1379-84, 1416, 1432-34; 1441-42; Syria, see 1336; Tanganyika, see 1385.

Chapter 9

THE STRUGGLE FOR PEACE AND SECURITY

Chapter 9

THE STRUGGLE FOR PEACE AND SECURITY

A. GENERAL

(See also 103, 114, 115, 1494, 1498, 1499, 1504.)

826. Falk, Richard A., and Mendlovitz, Saul H., eds. TOWARD A THEORY OF WAR PREVENTION. The Strategy of World Order, vol. 1. New York: World Law Fund, 1966. 414 p.

  A series of articles drawn from a broad range of disciplinary perspectives with the central focus on war prevention. The work is coordinated with Clark and Sohn's WORLD PEACE THROUGH WORLD LAW (see 1472).

827. Luard, Evan. CONFLICT AND PEACE IN THE MODERN INTERNATIONAL SYSTEM. 2nd ed. London: University of London Press, 1970. 343 p.

  An empirical study going into the causes of conflict and the measures the UN has developed to help restrain and contain this.

828. Morgenthau, Hans T., ed. PEACE, SECURITY AND THE UNITED NATIONS. Chicago, Ill.: University of Chicago Press, 1946. 133 p.

  Brief look at the potential of the new UN for promoting and maintaining peace.

829. Setalvad, Motilal C. THE ROLE OF THE UNITED NATIONS IN THE MAINTENANCE OF WORLD PEACE. London: Asia Publishing House, 1968. 79 p. (For the Indian School of International Studies.)

  An Indian member of the delegation to the UN outlines briefly the purposes, main developments, and difficulties of the UN as a peace-maintaining organization.

830. Goodrich, Leland M., and Simons, Anne Patricia. THE UNITED NATIONS

AND THE MAINTENANCE OF INTERNATIONAL PEACE AND SECURITY. Washington, D.C.: Brookings, 1955. 709 p.

> A painstaking analysis of the UN system with detailed accounts of the way the organization handled issued brought before it. An objective view of its successes and failures. Emphasis is on the roles of the General Assembly and Security Council and the UN plan for the regulation of armaments.

831. Teng, Catherine G. SYNOPSES OF UNITED NATIONS CASES IN THE FIELD OF PEACE AND SECURITY 1946-67. 2nd ed. New York: Carnegie Endowment, 1968. 87 p.

> A useful brief synopsis of all important cases which have come before the organization indicating actions taken.

832. Claude, Inis L., Jr. "The United Nations and the Use of Force." INTERNATIONAL CONCILIATION 532 (March 1961): 325-84.

> An excellent analysis within a theoretical framework of the potential of the UN in the control of the use of force.

833. Brownlie, Ian. INTERNATIONAL LAW AND THE USE OF FORCE BY STATES. New York: Oxford University Press, 1963. 532 p.

> A valuable historical account of the development of treaty and customary international law; shows the role international organizations have played in this development.

834. Salter, L. THE PATH FROM VIOLENCE TO INTERNATIONAL ORDER. Philadelphia, Pa.: Dorrance, 1970. 165 p.

> The role of international organizations in the search for more orderly international relations free of violent action.

B. COLLECTIVE SECURITY

1. General Treatises

(See also 297.)

835. Martin, Andrew. COLLECTIVE SECURITY. A PROGRESS REPORT. Paris, France: United Nations Educational, Scientific and Cultural Organization, 1952. 243 p.

> An historical outline of the development of the theory and practice of collective security in the League and the UN.

836. Finkelstein, Marina S., and Lawrence S., eds. COLLECTIVE SECURITY. San Francisco, Calif.: Chandler, 1966. 290 p.

>A good collection of selections well-chosen to show the development of idea and theory as well as experiences with collective security.

837. Claude, Inis L., Jr. POWER AND INTERNATIONAL RELATIONS. New York: Random House, 1962. 320 p.

>An excellent analysis of the assumptions, pre-conditions, and requirements for a viable system of the management of power in international relations, including an exhaustive treatment of collective security as one alternative.

838. Haas, Ernst B. COLLECTIVE SECURITY AND THE FUTURE INTERNATIONAL SYSTEM. Denver, Colo.: University of Denver, Social Science Foundation and Graduate School of International Studies, 1968. 117 p.

>An excellent critical analysis of the potential for developing a workable system of collective security within the framework of the UN.

839. Hogan, Willard N. INTERNATIONAL CONFLICT AND COLLECTIVE SECURITY: THE PRINCIPLE OF CONCERN IN INTERNATIONAL ORGANIZATIONS. Lexington, Ky.: University of Kentucky Press, 1955. 202 p.

>Discusses collective security theory and analyzes the relevant trends since World War I from the viewpoint of structure and function, expecially as applied to the League and UN.

840. Stromberg, R. N. COLLECTIVE SECURITY AND AMERICAN FOREIGN POLICY FROM THE LEAGUE OF NATIONS TO NATO. New York: Praeger, 1963. 301 p.

>Traces the inception, growth, and decline of the idea of collective security. Sees its failure in the reluctance of nations to commit themselves to action under a collective security system.

841. Ball, J. H. COLLECTIVE SECURITY: THE WHY AND HOW. Boston, Mass.: World Peace Foundation, 1943. 63 p. Pamphlet.

>An early and optimistic view of the potential for developing a workable collective security system.

842. Bourquin, Maurice, ed. COLLECTIVE SECURITY: A RECORD OF THE SEVENTH AND EIGHTH INTERNATIONAL STUDIES CONFERENCE, PARIS, FRANCE: 1934, LONDON, 1935. Paris, France: International Institute of Intellectual Cooperation, 1936. 514 p.

843. Wright, Quincy, ed. NEUTRALITY AND COLLECTIVE SECURITY. Chicago, Ill.: University of Chicago Press, 1936. 293 p.

844. Stone, Julius. AGGRESSION AND WORLD ORDER: A CRITIQUE OF UNITED NATIONS THEORIES OF AGGRESSION. Berkeley, Calif.: University of California Press, 1958. 240 p.

> Analysis of the concept of aggression and what role it might serve in peace enforcement. Studies the work of the League and the UN towards defining the concept.

2. Korea: A Case Study in Collective Security Action

(See also 755.)

845. Goodrich, Leland M. KOREA: A STUDY OF U.S. POLICY IN THE UNITED NATIONS. New York: Council on Foreign Relations, 1956. 235 p.

> An analysis and appraisal of the United States attempt to deal with Korea through the agency of the UN. Sees the United States as using the UN to try to shift responsibility from a problem it had failed to solve to an organization which was really too weak to solve it. Critical of much U.S. policy.

846. Gordenker, Leon. THE UNITED NATIONS AND THE PEACEFUL UNIFICATION OF KOREA. The Hague, Netherlands: Nijhoff, 1959. 319 p.

> An analysis of the functioning of the UN in Korea showing the composition and activities of the UN Temporary Commission and the UN Commission on Korea. Concludes that the two commissions had no way to bring about the unity of the two parts of the country.

847. Yoo, Tae-Ho. THE KOREAN WAR AND THE UNITED NATIONS: A LEGAL AND DIPLOMATIC HISTORICAL STUDY. Louvain, Belgium: Desbarox, 1965. 216 p.

> Clear and impartial chronological resume of the events in the involvement of the UN. Primarily descriptive.

848. Fehrenbach, T. R. THIS KIND OF PEACE. New York: McKay, 1966. 412 p.

> A well-researched study of the role of the UN in Korea, before, during, and after the war. Journalistic.

849. Lyons, Gene M. MILITARY POLICY AND ECONOMIC AID: THE KOREAN CASE, 1950-1953. Columbus, Ohio: Ohio State University Press, 1961. 311 p.

850 Vatcher, William H., Jr. PANMUNJOM: THE STORY OF THE KOREAN MILITARY ARMISTICE NEGOTIATIONS. New York: Praeger, 1958. 322 p.

3. Sanctions

851. Segal, Ronald, ed. SANCTIONS AGAINST SOUTH AFRICA. Baltimore, Md.: Penguin, 1964. 272 p. Paperbound.

   An illuminating collection of papers given in London in 1964 at the International Conference on Economic Sanctions against South Africa. Included are papers by experts on the economic, racial, political, legal, and strategic aspects of sanctions. General conclusion is that sanctions are legal, practical, and necessary.

852. Kapungu, Leonard T. THE UNITED NATIONS AND ECONOMIC SANCTIONS AGAINST RHODESIA. Lexington, Mass.: Heath, 1973. 160 p.

   Full account of the developments that led up to Ian Smith's unilateral declaration of independence and the ensuing sanctions declared by the UN. Compares these with previous efforts and experiences with sanctions. Examines why sanctions have not worked, supporting his conclusions with trade statistics.

853. Doxey, Margaret P. ECONOMIC SANCTIONS AND INTERNATIONAL ENFORCEMENT. New York: Oxford University Press, 1971. 171 p.

   A study of League and UN use of economic sanctions concluding that they have been of limited usefulness. In a number of case studies, the author analyzes the factors which bear on their effectiveness, surveying structure, application, and problems. Good examination of the methodological problems in measuring the apparent results of economic sanctions.

853a. Brown-John, C. Lloyd. MULTILATERAL SANCTIONS IN INTERNATIONAL LAW. New York: Praeger, 1975. 426 p.

   Examines the range of sanctions used in international relations. Detailed study of the League's sanctions imposed on Italy, Organization of American States on the Dominican Republic and the UN's on Southern Rhodesia.

854. United States Congress. House Committee on Foreign Affairs. Subcommittee on International Organizations and Movements. SANCTIONS AS AN INSTRUMENTALITY OF THE UNITED NATIONS: RHODESIA AS A CASE STUDY. Washington, D.C.: Government Printing Office, 1972. 184 p.

   A study of the effects of the sanctions against Rhodesia, concluding they have been of limited value in bringing about the changes desired by the UN.

855. Mitrany, David. THE PROBLEM OF INTERNATIONAL SANCTIONS. New York: Oxford University Press, 1925. 88 p.

856. Royal Institute of International Associations. THE CHARACTER OF INTERNATIONAL SANCTIONS AND THEIR APPLICATION. 2nd ed. London: Oxford University Press, 1938. 247 p.

857. Wild, Payson S. SANCTIONS AND TREATY ENFORCEMENT. Cambridge, Mass.: Harvard University Press, 1934. 246 p.

C. INTERNATIONAL ORGANIZATIONS AND THE SEARCH FOR ARMS CONTROL AND DISARMAMENT

(See also 107-12, 127, 165, 205, 346, 1498, 1500.)

858. Bechhoefer, Bernhard G. POSTWAR NEGOTIATIONS FOR ARMS CONTROL. Washington, D.C.: Brookings, 1961. 655 p.

   An analysis of the negotiations which have taken place since the end of the war inside and outside the UN.

859. Henkin, Louis. DISARMAMENT. The Hammarskjold Forum Series, no. 4. Dobbs Ferry, N.Y.: Oceana, 1963-64. 112 p. (For the Association of the Bar of the City of New York.) Pamphlet.

   Emphasis placed on the role of the UN in the process of negotiating for disarmament.

860. United Nations. Office of Public Information. THE UNITED NATIONS AND DISARMAMENT 1945- . Rev. ed. New York, 1970. 515 p. (Sales 70.IX. 1.)

   Gives the various proposals for general disarmament from the initial presentation to the General Assembly in 1945 through 1965. Summarizes deliberations and negotiations with details on the economic and social consequences. Complete documentation.

861. United Nations. BASIC PROBLEMS OF DISARMAMENT. New York, 1970. 265 p. (Sales E.70.I.14 and 17.)

   Good outline of the problems, proposals, and international action.

862. Dupuy, Trevor Nevitt, Associates. DOCUMENTARY HISTORY OF ARMS CONTROL AND DISARMAMENT. New York: Bowker, 1973. 643 p.

Covers proposals, negotiations, and agreements.

863. Quester, George H. NUCLEAR DIPLOMACY: THE FIRST TWENTY-FIVE YEARS. New York: Donnellow, 1971. 327 p. (For the Harvard University, Center of International Affairs.)

   One of the most objective historical analyses of Soviet-American nuclear relationships from the end of the war.

864. Dean, Arthur H. TEST BAN AND DISARMAMENT: THE PATH OF NEGOTIATION. New York: Harper and Row, 1966. 153 p.

   Shows the evolution of the 1963 Test Ban Treaty and how it fit in with the ongoing negotiations for disarmament.

865. McVitty, Marion H. A COMPARISON AND EVALUATION OF CURRENT DISARMAMENT PROPOSALS. New York: World Law Fund, 1964. 43 p. Paperbound.

   An excellent and usable comparison of the U.S. and Soviet disarmament treaties showing how they fit with the Clark and Sohn proposals (see 1472).

866. _____. PREFACE TO DISARMAMENT: AN APPRAISAL OF RECENT PROPOSALS. Chicago, Ill.: World Without War Publications, 1971. 72 p. Pamphlet.

   Description of where we are and steps now needed.

867. Shotwell, James T[hompson]., and Salvin, Marina. LESSONS ON SECURITY AND DISARMAMENT FROM THE HISTORY OF THE LEAGUE OF NATIONS. New York: King's Crown, 1949. 149 p. (For Carnegie Endowment for International Peace.)

   Brief description of the work of the League in the area of disarmament. A useful chronology of all security disputes before the League. Shows how League experience was used in establishing the UN and in moving ahead on disarmament.

868. Wainhouse, David W., et al. ARMS CONTROL AGREEMENTS: DESIGNS FOR VERIFICATION AND ORGANIZATION. Baltimore, Md.: The Johns Hopkins University Press, 1968. 179 p.

   Shows the role projected for international organizations in the proposals for disarmament, both for narrow and broad gauge measures.

869. Melman, Seymour, ed. INSPECTION FOR DISARMAMENT. New York: Columbia University Press, 1958. 303 p.

   Good study of the possibilities for effective inspection.

870. Bodnar, James S. REPORT ON THE DEBATE IN THE UNITED NATIONS DISARMAMENT COMMISSION, APRIL 21-JUNE 16, 1965. Washington, D.C.: United States Arms Control and Disarmament Agency, 1965. 132 p.

871. Buell, Raymond L. THE WASHINGTON CONFERENCE. New York: Appleton, 1922. 461 p.

872. Ichihashi, Yamato. THE WASHINGTON CONFERENCE AND AFTER: A HISTORICAL SURVEY. Stanford, Calif.: Stanford University Press, 1928. 443 p.

873. Myers, Denys P[eter]. WORLD DISARAMENT: ITS PROBLEMS AND PROSPECTS. Boston, Mass.: World Peace Foundation, 1932. 370 p.

874. Noel-Baker, Philip J. DISARMAMENT. New York: Harcourt, Brace, 1926. 352 p.

875. Wheeler-Bennett, John W. DISARMAMENT AND SECURITY SINCE LOCARNO, 1925-31: BEING A POLITICAL AND TECHNICAL BACKGROUND OF THE GENEVA DISARMAMENT CONFERENCE, 1932. New York: Macmillan, 1932. 383 p.

876. _____./ THE DISARMAMENT DEADLOCK. London: Routledge, 1934. 314 p.

D. CONFLICT RESOLUTION: MEDIATION AND CONCILIATION

1. General

(See also 522-25, 590, 662, 663, 955, 959, 960, 962-65, 1029, 1122, 1363.)

877. Black, Cyril E., and Falk, Richard A., eds. CONFLICT MANAGEMENT. The Future of the International Legal Order, vol 3. Princeton, N.J.: Princeton University Press, 1971. 427 p.

> Fifteen essays, cross-national, which make use of recent technological and scientific advances. Discusses the impact of the Charter on claimed rights to use force. Good analysis of UN role in conflict management.

878. Edmead, Frank. ANALYSIS AND PREDICTION IN INTERNATIONAL MEDIATION. New York: United Nations Institute for Training and Research, 1971. 58 p.

Insightful proposal for enhancing the effectiveness of the UN. The author suggests that a UN agency should continuously "monitor" conflict-laden situations by application of a working model of analysis which he describes in order to select the propitious moment and means of mediation.

879. Bloomfield, Lincoln P., ed. THE POWER TO KEEP PEACE: TODAY AND IN A WORLD WITHOUT WAR. Rev. ed. Berkeley, Calif.: World Without War Council, 1971. 249 p. Paperbound.

Discusses procedures for permanent peacekeeping and the incorporation of these into the UN. Includes documents.

880. Colt, Jean-Pierre. INTERNATIONAL CONCILIATION. London: Europa Publications, 1972. 367 p.

A definitive, descriptive and analytical treatment of bilateral and multilateral arrangements and experiences concentrating on the UN, ICAO, GATT, UNCTAD, and ILO.

881. Young, Oran R. TRENDS IN INTERNATIONAL PEACEMAKING. Princeton, N.J.: Princeton University, Woodrow Wilson School of Public and International Affairs, Center of International Studies, 1966. 45 p. Monograph.

A brief study of the theory and use of preventive diplomacy as a technique for promoting peace.

882. Bailey, Sydney D. PEACEFUL SETTLEMENT OF DISPUTES: IDEAS AND PROPOSALS FOR RESEARCH. New York: United Nations Institute for Training and Research, 1970. 67 p. Pamphlet.

Reviews studies undertaken by governments, international committees, political, social, behavioral, and natural scientists into the causes of disputes, their content, and means and terms of settlement. Presents a program of questions and ideas for further coordinated research.

883. Jackson, Elmore, ed. MEETING OF MINDS. New York: McGraw-Hill, 1952. 200 p.

Reviews with the assistance of some distinguished contributors the history of mediation in labor disputes in the United States, Sweden, and Britain in order to derive generalizations about peacemaking. Sees the personality of the mediator as a crucial factor.

884. Study Group on the Peaceful Settlement of International Disputes. REPORT OF A STUDY GROUP ON THE PEACEFUL SETTLEMENT OF INTERNATIONAL DISPUTES. London: David Davies Memorial Institute of International Studies, 1966. 289 p.

Able study of the history of the methods and techniques used in the peaceful settlement of disputes. Makes recommendations for improving techniques and promoting wider use.

885. Randolph, Lillian L. THIRD-PARTY SETTLEMENT OF DISPUTES IN THEORY AND PRACTICE. Dobbs Ferry, N.Y.: Oceana, 1973. 294 p.

   Analytic and descriptive.

886. Northedge, F. S., and Donelan, M. D. INTERNATIONAL DISPUTES: THE POLITICAL ASPECTS. London: Europa Publications, 1973. 326 p. (For the David Davies Memorial Institution of International Studies.)

887. Waldock, Humphry, ed. INTERNATIONAL DISPUTES: THE LEGAL ASPECTS. London: Europa Publications, 1973. 326 p. (For the David Davies Memorial Institute of International Studies.)

888. Donelan, M. D., and Grieve, M. J. INTERNATIONAL DISPUTES: CASE HISTORIES: 1945-1970. London: Europa Publications, 1973. 286 p. (For the David Davies Memorial Institute of International Studies.)

   Series of studies (see 886-88) of conflicts and their resolution. The first two are analytic; the last a series of case histories, and a factual, objective cataloging and chronology of major and minor disputes since World War II.

889. Pechota, Vratislav. COMPLEMENTARY STRUCTURES OF THIRD PARTY SETTLEMENT OF INTERNATIONAL DISPUTES. New York: United Nations Institute for Training and Research, 1972. 63 p.

   An exhaustive categorization of those elements in the international system which facilitate third-party interventions.

890. Kertesz, Stephen D. THE QUEST FOR PEACE THROUGH DIPLOMACY. Englewood Cliffs, N.J.: Prentice-Hall, 1967. 182 p.

   An analysis of past and present successes and failures of diplomacy in dealing with major international crises. Focuses on the use of large multinational organizations, including the UN, showing the nature of diplomacy and its limitations.

891. Edwards, David V. CREATING A NEW WORLD POLITICS: FROM CONFLICT TO COOPERATION. New York: McKay, 1973. 207 p.

   Study of procedures and experiences of international efforts to resolve conflicts.

892. Randle, Robert F. ORIGINS OF PEACE: A STUDY OF PEACEMAKING AND THE STRUCTURE OF PEACE SETTLEMENTS. New York: Free

Press, 1973. 568 p.

> Historical treatment of efforts to resolve the problems left by wars.

893. Stone, Julius. LEGAL CONTROLS OF INTERNATIONAL CONFLICT: A TREATISE ON THE DYNAMICS OF DISPUTES-AND WAR-LAW. Rev. ed. New York: Rinehart, 1959. 907 p.

> While most of the book is concerned with law, a good portion analyzes the provisions and techniques of international organizations for settling conflict. Legalistic, scholarly, and acute.

2. The League Experience

(See also 578, 580, 1011.)

894. Barros, James. THE CORFU INCIDENT OF 1923: MUSSOLINI AND THE LEAGUE OF NATIONS. Princeton, N.J.: Princeton University Press, 1965. 339 p.

> A thorough search of the Greek and Italian archives has resulted in a well-documented and lucid account of the incident showing the role of the League.

895. _____. THE ALAND ISLAND QUESTION: ITS SETTLEMENT BY THE LEAGUE OF NATIONS. New Haven, Conn.: Yale University Press, 1968. 339 p.

> The author gives a detailed and fully documented account of the dispute arising between Finland and Sweden after World War I and the role the League played in the settlement. Analysis of different ways international organizations can be used by members to pursue national interests.

896. _____. THE LEAGUE OF NATIONS AND THE GREAT POWERS: THE GREEK-BULGARIAN INCIDENT, 1925. London: Oxford University Press, 1970. 428 p.

> A detailed account of the role of the League in bringing about a settlement in this case with an analysis of why the League was successful in this case while failing in so many others.

897. Willoughby, W. W. THE SINO-JAPANESE CONTROVERSY AND THE LEAGUE OF NATIONS. Baltimore, Md.: The Johns Hopkins University Press, 1935. 758 p.

> An extensive treatment of the League's activity as the Sino-Japanese controversy intensified.

898. Thorne, Christopher. THE LIMITS OF FOREIGN POLICY: THE WEST, THE LEAGUE, AND THE FAR EASTERN CRISIS OF 1931-1933. New York: Putnam, 1973. 462 p.

 Examines in detail the setting and development of the Manchurian crisis. Well-written and carefully researched.

899. Johnson, Grace Allen, and Ames, Herbert B. THE CASE OF CHINA AND JAPAN BEFORE THE LEAGUE OF NATIONS: A DRAMATIZATION OF THE EVENTS, 1931-33. Boston, Mass.: Peabody Fund, 1933. 60 p.

900. La Foy, Margaret. THE CHACO DISPUTE AND THE LEAGUE OF NATIONS. Ann Arbor, Mich.: Edwards, 1946. 166 p.

 A well-researched account of the dispute and the efforts made to settle it. Particularly concerned with the jurisdictional problems arising between the Pan American Union and the League.

3. United Nations Experience

(See also 534.)

901. Bhutto, A. Z. PEACE-KEEPING BY THE UNITED NATIONS. Karachi, Pakistan: Pakistan Publishing House, 1967. 80 p. Pamphlet.

 A brief, clear account of the development of peacekeeping techniques in the UN, drawing broad legal and political implications.

902. Azud, Jan. THE PEACEFUL SETTLEMENT OF DISPUTES AND THE UNITED NATIONS. Bratislava, Yugoslavia: VSAV, 1971. 271 p.

 An analysis of the disputes which are brought to the organization and the types of techniques used to bring about settlement.

903. United Nations Association of the United States of America. MULTILATERAL ALTERNATIVES TO UNILATERAL INTERVENTION. CONTROLLING CONFLICTS IN THE 1970'S: A REPORT. New York, 1969. 62 p. Paperbound.

 A brief analysis of the ways multilateral agencies could be used more effectively by states.

904. Miller, Linda B. WORLD ORDER AND LOCAL DISORDER: THE UNITED NATIONS AND INTERNAL CONFLICTS. Princeton, N.J.: Princeton University Press, 1967. 244 p.

A good factual account of the role the UN has played in conflicts, using case studies. Shows the ways the organization has tried to contain conflicts with the limited means at its disposal.

905. Andemicael, Berhanykun. PEACEFUL SETTLEMENT AMONG AFRICAN STATES: ROLES OF THE UNITED NATIONS AND THE ORGANIZATION OF AFRICAN UNITY. New York: United Nations Institute for Training and Research, 1972. 80 p. Pamphlet.

Brief analysis of the way the two organizations have become involved in African situations, showing when their activities have been complimentary and when conflictual.

906. Etzioni, Minerva M. THE MAJORITY OF ONE: TOWARDS A THEORY OF REGIONAL COMPATIBILITY. Beverly Hills, Calif.: Sage, 1970. 230 p.

A study of the handling of political and security matters since 1950 showing the interaction of the Organization of American States and the UN.

907. Mezerik, A. G., ed. INVASION AND OCCUPATION OF CZECHO-SLOVAKIA AND THE UN. New York: International Review Service, 1968. 128 p.

A factual, chronological account of the Soviet invasion of Czechoslovakia in 1968 and the response in the UN.

908. Leiss, Amelia C., ed. APARTHEID AND UNITED NATIONS COLLECTIVE MEASURES: AN ANALYSIS. New York: Carnegie Endowment, 1965. 178 p.

An examination of South African policy and world reactions to it. Analyzes the difficulties this case has caused the UN and the diplomatic, military, and economic efforts undertaken to alter the situation.

4. Border Disputes and Territorial Change

909. Luard, Evan, ed. THE INTERNATIONAL REGULATION OF FRONTIER DISPUTES. New York: Praeger, 1970. 247 p.

An examination of the techniques and procedures used by the League and the UN in dispute regulation. Studies the relative merits of mediation, arbitration, and judicial settlement.

910. Mance, Brigadier General Sir Osborne. FRONTIERS, PEACE TREATIES

AND INTERNATIONAL ORGANIZATIONS. London: Oxford University Press, 1946. 196 p. (For the Royal Institute of International Affairs.)

> A comprehensive analysis of the frontier problems from 1919-39, including the issues revolving around transportation and communication.

911. Bloomfield, Lincoln P. EVOLUTION OR REVOLUTION? THE U.N. AND THE PROBLEMS OF PEACEFUL TERRITORIAL CHANGE. Cambridge, Mass.: Harvard University Press, 1957. 220 p.

> An analysis of the role of the UN in the process of effecting a peaceful change in the international status of territories. A review of the record of both the League and the UN, focusing attention on the legal aspects.

5. Internal Wars

(See also Chapter 9.E.3. c and d, and 904.)

912. Luard, Evan, ed. INTERNATIONAL REGULATION OF CIVIL WARS. New York: New York University Press, 1972. 240 p.

> Ten authors show nature, purposes, and effectiveness of intervention, surveying the main efforts of international bodies to resolve civil wars.

913. Kelly, George A., and Miller, Linda B. INTERNAL WAR AND INTERNATIONAL SYSTEMS: PERSPECTIVES ON METHOD. Cambridge, Mass.: Harvard University, Center for International Affairs, 1969. 40 p.

> Brief analysis of how to look at internal wars from an international perspective.

6. The United Nations and Vietnam

914. Mezerik, A. G., ed. VIET NAM AND THE UN--1967. New York: International Review Service, 1967. 191 p. Paperbound.

> Factual outline of the action--or inaction--of the UN during the early years of the Viet Nam conflict.

915. Bloomfield, Lincoln P. THE U.N. AND VIET NAM. New York: Carnegie Endowment, 1968. 44 p. Paperbound..

> Brief outline of the role of the UN in the Viet Nam war.

7. Techniques

916. Shore, William T. FACT-FINDING IN THE MAINTENANCE OF INTERNATIONAL PEACE. New York: Oceana, 1970. 183 p.

> An Historic survey, weighted on the technical side, of the procedures and machinery used since 1899. Shows how fact-finding is often blocked and hampered but still sees it as useful. Concludes that the technique should be refined and further applied.

917. Young, Oran R. THE INTERMEDIARIES: THIRD PARTIES IN INTERNATIONAL CRISES. Princeton, N.J.: Princeton University Press, 1967. 427 p.

> A sophisticated and theoretical effort to explore the possibilities of third party intervention. Studies and analyzes the relevant variables in developing strategies, especially in situations which bring the United States and Soviet Union into direct conflict.

918. _____. THE POLITICS OF FORCE: BARGAINING DURING INTERNATIONAL CRISES. Princeton, N.J.: Princeton University Press, 1969. 436 p. (For the Center of International Studies.)

> An excellent analysis of bargaining under international crisis conditions. Conceptually relies heavily on Thomas Schelling. Studies the meaning of crises, basis of bargaining, effects of the political context, tactics of bargaining, and the role of coercion and violence.

918a. Bar-Yaacov, Nissim. THE HANDLING OF INTERNATIONAL DISPUTES BY MEANS OF INQUIRY. New York and London: Oxford University Press, 1975. 370 p. (For the Royal Institute of International Affairs.)

> The author covers a wide range of historical cases limiting himself to the pure factual determination approach of those commissions operating under the Hague Conventions. Compares these with the UN experience and finds the two quite different.

E. PEACEKEEPING: PREVENTIVE DIPLOMACY

1. General

(See also 102, 205, 662, 663, 742, 801.)

919. Wainhouse, David W., ed. INTERNATIONAL PEACE OBSERVATION: A HISTORY AND FORECAST. Baltimore, Md.: The Johns Hopkins University Press, 1965. 663 p. (For the American Society of International Law.)

> A solid and comprehensive study of past experiences and pos-

sible future role of "peace observation" based on case studies drawn from the League, Inter-American, and UN experience. Concerned with methods and procedures which have been used to prevent and limit conflict.

920. _____ et al. INTERNATIONAL PEACEKEEPING AT THE CROSSROADS: NATIONAL SUPPORT--EXPERIENCE AND PROSPECTS. Baltimore, Md.: The Johns Hopkins University Press, 1974. 634 p.

Focuses on political, financial, and logistical aspects of international peacekeeping operations with details on the ways in which states, international organizations, and local authorities have dealt with technical problems of providing transportation, communications, manpower, and facilities. Details the organizational structures for international peacekeeping. Case studies used.

921. Higgins, Rosalyn. UNITED NATIONS PEACEKEEPING 1946-1967: DOCUMENTS AND COMMENTARY. Vol. 1: THE MIDDLE EAST. Vol. 2: ASIA. New York: Oxford University Press. Vol. 1, 1969. 688 p. Vol. 2, 1970. 504 p. (For the Royal Institute of International Affairs.)

Invaluable reference work, the result of exhaustive research, containing just about every salient and relevant fact in the fields of history, diplomacy, and politics. The commentaries are exhaustive and judicious.

921a. Rikhye, Indar Jit, et al. THE THIN BLUE LINE: INTERNATIONAL PEACEKEEPING AND ITS FUTURE. New Haven, Conn.: Yale University Press, 1974. 369 p.

An excellent review of the successes and failures, and the political and legal capabilities of the UN and regional organizations for effective third-party control of conflict. Considers how a more efficient system could be developed. Suggests developing a conflict control team, a computer-supported conflict monitoring apparatus, and a satellite telecommunications network.

922. Legault, Albert, ed. RESEARCH ON PEACE-KEEPING OPERATIONS: CURRENT STATUS AND FUTURE NEEDS. Paris, France: International Information Center on Peace-keeping Operations, 1967. 57 p. Paperbound.

A description of research undertaken in the peacekeeping field with indications of future needs.

923. Calvocoressi, Peter. WORLD ORDER AND NEW STATES--PROBLEMS OF KEEPING THE PEACE. London: Chatto and Windus, 1962. 121 p. (For the Institute of Strategic Studies.)

A lucid analysis of the problems of keeping the peace in areas of the world where neither of the two great powers is accepted as paramount.

924. Citrin, Jack. UNITED NATIONS PEACEKEEPING ACTIVITIES: A CASE

STUDY IN ORGANIZATIONAL TASK EXPANSION. Denver, Colo.: University of Denver Press, 1965. 85 p. Paperbound. (For the Social Science Foundation and Graduate School of International Studies.)

> A study of the need for expansion in the organization as it has taken on responsibilities in the peacekeeping areas.

925. Frydenberg, P., ed. PEACE-KEEPING: EXPERIENCE AND EVOLUTION: THE OSLO PAPERS. Oslo, Norway: Norwegian Institute of International Affairs, 1964. 339 p.

> Comprehensive treatment of the evolution of international techniques for peacekeeping with an evaluation of their effectiveness and the possibilities for future expansion of their use.

926. Cox, Arthur M. PROSPECTS FOR PEACEKEEPING. Washington, D.C.: Brookings, 1967. 170 p.

> A readable and well-organized treatment which takes the U.S. position. The author supports collective peacekeeping as essential. Considers Canada's past and future role in the process.

927. Landy E[rnest]. A[dolph]. THE EFFECTIVENESS OF INTERNATIONAL SUPERVISION: THREE DECADES OF I.L.O. EXPERIENCE. Dobbs Ferry, N.Y.: Oceana, 1966. 281 p.

928. James, Frederick Alan. THE POLITICS OF PEACE-KEEPING. New York: Praeger, 1969. 452 p. (For the Institute for Strategic Studies.)

> An excellent history of the UN's peacekeeping activities. Factual and analytic. Puts UN actions into the context of world politics and especially great power conflicts.

929. Rikye, I[ndar]. J[it]. UNITED NATIONS PEACE-KEEPING OPERATIONS: HIGHER CONDUCT. Paris, France: International Information Center on Peacekeeping Operations, 1967. 16 p. Paperbound.

> Brief description of the role of the UN.

2. International Forces

(See also 771.)

930. Russell, Ruth B. UNITED NATIONS EXPERIENCE WITH MILITARY FORCES: POLITICAL AND LEGAL ASPECTS. Washington, D.C.: Institute for Defense Analysis, International Studies Division, 1963. 196 p.

> A competent study of the major issues faced in setting up military forces in both national and international law.

931. Burns, Arthur Lee, and Heathcote, Nina. PEACE-KEEPING BY U.N. FORCES FROM SUEZ TO THE CONGO. Princeton Studies in World Politics. Princeton, N.J.: Princeton University Press, 1963. 256 p.

(For Princeton University, the Center of International Studies.)
A provocative and closely argued book on UN military operations with special emphasis on the Congo. Also includes the Suez, Jordan, and Lebanon. Studies the scope and authority of the Secretary-General's Office, the legal authority of the forces in the host country, and the effectiveness of ad hoc organizations for the forces. Makes concrete suggestions for future uses of forces.

932. Boyd, James M. UNITED NATIONS PEACE-KEEPING OPERATIONS: A MILITARY AND POLITICAL APPRAISAL. Praeger Special Study in International Politics and Public Affairs. New York: Praeger, 1971. 278 p.

Concentrates primarily on the UN Military Staff Committee, comparing its work and effectiveness in the Middle East, Congo, and Cyprus. Deals pragmatically with military operations: problems of force creation, composition and organization, logistics, command, and control. Gives detailed analysis of the impact of the international power struggle on international endeavors.

933. Williams, Walter L., Jr. INTERGOVERNMENTAL MILITARY FORCES AND WORLD PUBLIC ORDER. Dobbs Ferry, N.Y.: Oceana, 1972. 718 p.

A compendium of concepts and facts concerning multinational and supranational military forces used primarily in peace-keeping operations. Concludes that voluntary international law will not work in the area of conflict unless it is backed by some form of force. Discusses both theory and practice.

934. Bloomfield, Lincoln P., ed. INTERNATIONAL MILITARY FORCES: THE QUESTION OF PEACEKEEPING IN AN ARMED AND DISARMING WORLD. Boston, Mass.: Little, Brown and Co., 1964. 307 p.

The author gives a general theory and experience of international forces. Studies the use of forces in the Suez and Congo, showing conditions likely to affect the efficiency of such operations. Studies topics such as logistics and conflicts of loyalties.

935. Skern, L. M. K. MILITARY STAFFING AT UN HEADQUARTERS FOR PEACE-KEEPING OPERATIONS: A PROPOSAL. Paris, France: International Information Center on Peacekeeping Operations, 1967. 14 p.

Based on analysis of the difficulties of past experiences, the author suggests ways to make the functioning of headquarters more effective through improved staffing arrangements.

936. Fabian, Larry L. SOLDIERS WITHOUT ENEMIES: PREPARING THE UNITED NATIONS FOR PEACEKEEPING. Washington, D.C.: Brookings, 1971. 323 p.

Well-researched and informative evaluation of UN peacekeeping potential. Using case studies, the author explores the historical background and problems involved and the institution-building of the forces. Emphasizes political and military preparedness and concludes his analysis with some practical suggestions for the future.

937. Wilson, A. J. SOME PRINCIPLES FOR PEACE-KEEPING OPERATIONS: A GUIDE FOR SENIOR OFFICERS. Paris, France: International Information Center on Peacekeeping Operations, 1967. 12 p.

A brief outline of the principles which have led to successful action in the field.

938. Taborn, P., and Putignano, A. RECORDS OF THE HEADQUARTERS, UNITED NATIONS COMMAND. Preliminary Inventories and Papers. Washington, D.C.: Government Printing Office, 1960. 7 p. Mimeographed.

An inventory of the records of the UN Command and subordinate agencies from 1950 to 1957 including correspondence, reports, transcripts of meetings, agreements, and journals.

939. Legault, Albert. THE AUTHORIZATION OF PEACE-KEEPING OPERATIONS IN TERMS OF THE NATURE OF THE CONFLICT. Monograph no. 8. Paris, France: International Center on Peacekeeping Operations, June 1968. 62 p. Paperbound.

Brief but informative account of the procedures for "legalizing" international action.

940. Bowett, D. W. UNITED NATIONS FORCES: A LEGAL STUDY. New York: Praeger, 1964. 603 p.

A review of the experience of the UN with attention to constitutional, functional, and administrative problems. Outlines steps necessary to create a permanent force including legal, logistical, and administrative prerequisites. The author spent two years in the Secretariat.

941. Seyersted, Finn. UNITED NATIONS FORCES IN THE LAW OF PEACE AND WAR. Leiden, Netherlands: Sijthoff, 1966. 447 p.

An illuminating account of the problems created by the use of the UN force with special attention to the legal aspects. Sees need for the UN to accede to relevant conventions, for example, the Geneva Convention.

942. Johnsen, Julia E. INTERNATIONAL POLICE FORCE. New York: Wilson, 1944. 253 p.

Study of the use of international forces before World War II.

943. Thomas, Bryan W. AN INTERNATIONAL POLICE FORCE. London: Allenson, 1936. 172 p.

944. Hindsmarsh, Albert E. FORCE IN PEACE: FORCE SHORT OF WAR IN INTERNATIONAL RELATIONS. Cambridge, Mass.: Harvard University Press, 1933. 256 p.

945. Stenquist, Nils. THE SWEDISH U.N. STAND-BY FORCE AND EXPERIENCE. Paris, France: International Information Center on Peacekeeping Operations, 1967. 18 p. Paperbound.

   A brief study of the steps and arrangements of Sweden to keep a force prepared for peacekeeping operations.

946. Frye, William R. A UNITED NATIONS PEACE FORCE. London: Federal Union, 1957. 239 p.

   A study of the peace forces used and appraisal of whether some such instrument might be made available to the UN on a permanent basis to prevent or contain small wars. The author has been UN correspondent for the CHRISTIAN SCIENCE MONITOR.

947. Ennals, David. A UNITED NATIONS POLICE FORCE? London: Fabian International, 1959. 24 p.

   A brief analysis of the needs and potentialities for creating a permanent force to be used by the UN.

948. Fradkin, Elvira K. A WORLD AIRLIFT: THE UNITED NATIONS AIR POLICE PATROL. New York: Funk and Wagnalls, 1950. 216 p.

949. Von Horn, C. SOLDIERING FOR PEACE. New York: McKay, 1967. 402 p.

   The author traces his career as Chief of UN Peacekeeping forces in the Middle East and Congo. Discusses the Arab-Israeli border clashes of 1950-60 and describes the 1960 Congo uprising. Stresses the political pressures exerted on the command and the problems of finance and personnel.

950. Harbottle, M. THE IMPARTIAL SOLDIER. New York: Oxford University Press, 1970. 210 p.

   A valuable account by a UN "peace soldier" of his experiences in the field, where he was Chief of Staff from 1966-68. Concentrates on collective attitudes and personalities of leaders and on military engagements. Shows how well and effectively a multinational force of soldiers and civilians from countries with divergent ideologies and social systems can work together.

951. _____. THE BLUE BERETS. Harrisburg, Pa.: Stackpole, 1972. 157 p.

Further account of the force in the Middle East with special attention to the soldiers themselves, their responsibilities, and the way they have carried them out.

952. Gyani, P. S. CHARACTERISTICS AND SOME ASPECTS OF LAUNCHING U.N. PEACE-KEEPING FORCES. Paris, France: International Information Center on Peacekeeping Operations, 1968. 13 p.

Brief analysis of the bringing into being of UN forces.

3. Case Studies

a. PEACEKEEPING IN THE ARAB WORLD

953. Brock, David. PREFACE TO PEACE: THE UNITED NATIONS AND THE ARAB-ISRAEL ARMISTICE SYSTEM. Washington, D.C.: Public Affairs Press, 1964. 151 p.

An analysis of the role of the UN in managing the armistice with attention to the political and organizational aspects. Gives historical background, evolution, and the erosion of the usefulness of the observers.

954. Burns, Lt. Gen. E. L. M. BETWEEN ARAB AND ISRAELI. New York: Obolensky, 1963. 336 p.

An excellent account of the author's experiences as Chief of Staff of the UN Truce Supervisory Organization in 1954-56 and his efforts to maintain peace in the difficult situation he faced.

955. Forsythe, David P. UNITED NATIONS PEACEKEEPING: THE CONCILIATION COMMISSION FOR PALESTINE. Baltimore, Md.: The Johns Hopkins University Press, 1972. 218 p.

A detailed history of the work of the commission in 1949 with an assessment of the various roles, functions, successes, and failures. Useful chronology compares work of commission with other similar organs. The author attempts to merge a substantive review of the commission with theoretical speculation and generalizations about UN peacemaking.

956. Hamzeh, F. S. INTERNATIONAL CONCILIATION WITH SPECIAL REFERENCE TO THE WORTH OF THE UNITED NATIONS CONCILIA-

The Struggle for Peace and Security

TION COMMISSION FOR PALESTINE. The Hague, Netherlands: Pasmans, 1963. 177 p.

An assessment of the usefulness of the commission in the search for peace in the Palestine situation.

957. Hutchison, Elmo H. VIOLENT TRUCE: A MILITARY OBSERVER LOOKS AT THE ARAB-ISRAELI CONFLICT 1951-1955. New York: Devin-Adair, 1956. 225 p.

A first-hand account by one of the observers as he carried out his responsibilities for the UN.

958. Lall, Arthur. THE UN AND THE MIDDLE EAST CRISIS, 1967. New York: Columbia University Press, 1968. 332 p.

A detailed account from the time of the withdrawal of UNEF in May 1967 to the establishment of the Jarring mission six months later. The author was Permanent Representative of India to the UN and a member of the Advisory Committee to the UNEF. Examines major proposals in the Security Council and General Assembly, background and argumentation, and the results of these initiatives.

959. Robinson, Jacob. PALESTINE AND THE UNITED NATIONS: PRELUDE TO SOLUTION. Washington, D.C.: Public Affairs Press, 1947. 276 p.

An able piece of reportage covering the emergence of the Palestine issue on the agenda and the debates leading up to the establishment of the UN Special Committee on Palestine. Objective and thorough.

960. Halderman, J. W. THE MIDDLE EAST CRISIS: TEST OF INTERNATIONAL LAW. Dobbs Ferry, N.Y.: Oceana, 1969. 200 p.

An account with legal analysis of the crisis and the issues involved.

961. Wright, Quincy. THE MIDDLE EAST: PROSPECTS FOR PEACE. Hammarskjold Forum Series, no. 13. Dobbs Ferry, N.Y.: Oceana, 1969. 113 p. (For the Association of the Bar of the City of New York.)

Contains working paper, summary of discussion, and bibliography. An outline of the issues relating to the Arab-Israeli conflict by representatives of the major participants in that conflict.

962. Gabbay, Rony. A POLITICAL STUDY OF THE ARAB-JEWISH CONFLICT. Geneva, Switzerland: Droz, 1959. 611 p.

963. Nathan, Robert R., et al. PALESTINE: PROMISE AND PROBLEM.

Washington, D.C.: American Council on Public Affairs, 1946. 685 p.

964. Zasloff, Joseph J. GREAT BRITAIN AND PALESTINE: A STUDY OF THE PROBLEMS BEFORE THE UNITED NATIONS. Munich, Germany: Verlagshaus der Americanischen Hochkommission, 1952. 198 p.

965. Mezerik, A. G., ed. THE ARAB-ISRAELI CONFLICT IN THE UN. New York: International Review Service, 1969. 234 p.

> Objective, chronological account in detail of the major events in the Arab-Israeli situation down to 1969. Includes major policy statements by combatants and great powers.

966. Lauterpacht, Elihu, ed. THE SUEZ CANAL SETTLEMENT. New York: Praeger, 1960. 82 p. (For the British Institute of International and Comparative Law.)

> A selection of documents on developments from October 1956 till March 1959.

967. Barker, A. J. SUEZ: THE SEVEN DAY WAR. New York: Praeger, 1965. 223 p.

968. Rosner, Gabriella. THE UNITED NATIONS EMERGENCY FORCE. New York: Columbia University Press, 1963. 316 p.

> A comprehensive account of the creation, organization, functions, status, and operations of the force covering the political, legal, and practical aspects. The author sees the force as a symbol of the growing community interest in a peaceful and settled world. A useful selection of documents.

969. Mezerik, A. G., ed. THE UNITED NATIONS EMERGENCY FORCE (UNEF), 1956-1967; CREATION, EVOLUTION, END OF MISSION. New York: International Review Service, 1969. 182 p.

> Chronological account of the UNEF from inception to disbanding. Gives arguments for and against its dismantling.

970. Lauterpacht, Elihu, ed. THE UNITED NATIONS EMERGENCY FORCE (BASIC DOCUMENTS). New York: Praeger, 1960. 48 p.

> Collection of the principal documents bearing on the legal aspects of the establishment, operation, and status of the UNEF in Egypt during and after 1956. Includes relevant resolutions of the General Assembly and letters of the Secretary-General.

The Struggle for Peace and Security

b. KASHMIR

(See also 768, 769.)

971. Korbel, Josef. DANGER IN KASHMIR. Princeton, N.J.: Princeton University Press, 1954. 367 p.

   Good research into the UN Commission, its powers, actions, and effects.

972. Khan, Rahmatullan. KASHMIR AND THE UNITED NATIONS. Delhi, India: Vikas, 1969. 206 p.

   A critical evaluation of the actions of the UN from an Indian position.

973. Brecher, Michael. THE STRUGGLE FOR KASHMIR. New York: Oxford University Press, 1953. 223 p.

   General account of the conflict indicating the role of the UN.

c. THE CONGO

(See also 697, 722.)

974. Lefever, Ernest W. UNCERTAIN MANDATE: POLICIES OF THE U.N. CONGO OPERATION. Baltimore, Md.: The Johns Hopkins University Press, 1967. 270 p. (For the American Society of International Law.)

   A good account of the objectives of the various governments associated with the effort. Gives military and political aspects of UN involvement. Defends and supports the policy of the organization.

975. _____. CRISIS IN THE CONGO: A UNITED NATIONS FORCE IN ACTION. Washington, D.C.: Brookings, 1965. 227 p.

   A detailed review and analysis of the UN peacekeeping effort, especially clear on the relationship between UN forces and those of the Armee Nationale Congolaise and on the operational problems which arose. Based to a large extent on interviews.

976. Lefever, Ernest W., and Joshua, Wynfred. UNITED NATIONS PEACE-KEEPING IN THE CONGO, 1960-64: ANALYSIS OF POLITICAL, EXECUTIVE AND MILITARY CONTROL. 4 vols. Washington, D.C.: United States Arms Control and Disarmament Agency, 1966.

An exhaustive description and analysis of the totality of the Congo operation.

977. Gordon, King. UN IN THE CONGO: A QUEST FOR PEACE. New York: Carnegie Endowment, 1962. 184 p.

A thorough account of UN operations in the Congo from July 1960 until September 1962, based largely on UN documents and the author's own personal observations in the Congo where he served as the UN's Chief Information Officer.

978. Hoskyns, Catherine. THE CONGO SINCE INDEPENDENCE, JANUARY 1960-DECEMBER 1961. London: Oxford University Press, 1965. 518 p. (For the Royal Institute of International Affairs.)

A thorough study giving the background to UN intervention and the diplomacy leading up to it. Shows the slow evolution of UN policy, especially towards Katanga.

979. Legum, Colin. CONGO DISASTER. Baltimore, Md.: Penguin, 1961. 174 p. Paperbound.

Good account by a South African of the development of the problem of the Congo and the response of internal and external forces--including the UN--to it.

980. Franck, Thomas M., and Carey, John, eds. THE ROLE OF THE UNITED NATIONS IN THE CONGO. The Hammarskjold Forum Series, no. 2. Dobbs Ferry, N.Y.: Oceana, 1963-64. 100 p. Pamphlet. (For the Association of the Bar of the City of New York.)

A good analysis of the involvement of the organization in the situation. Working paper and summary of discussion.

981. Martelli, George. EXPERIMENT IN WORLD GOVERNMENT: AN ACCOUNT OF THE UNITED NATIONS OPERATION IN THE CONGO, 1960-64. London: Johnson, 1966. 244 p.

A detailed account of the peacekeeping operation giving some historical background to the secession movement. Sees this operation as the first experiment in world government and recommends that the UN confine itself to operations not involving the use of force.

982. Merian, Alan P. CONGO: BACKGROUND OF CONFLICT. Evanston, Ill.: Northwestern University Press, 1961. 368 p.

Primarily concerned with the history and political developments preceding UN involvement in the situation.

983. Hempstone, Smith. REBELS, MERCENARIES AND DISSIDENTS: THE KATANGA STORY. New York: Praeger, 1962. 256 p.

> Eyewitness account of the fighting of December 1961 along with critical discussion of UN involvement, which the author judges to be illegal.

984. Valahu, Mugur. THE KATANGA CIRCUS: A DETAILED ACCOUNT OF THREE UN WARS. New York: Speller, 1964. 364 p.

> An impassioned advocate of Katanga's separatism castigates the UN for its actions.

985. Centre de Recherche et d'Information Socio-Politiques. CONGO 196- . Brussels, Belgium, yearly during the 1960's.

> A yearly account from a Belgian perspective of events as they evolved in the Congo.

986. Okumu, Washington. LUMUMBA'S CONGO: ROOTS OF CONFLICT. New York: Obolensky, 1963. 250 p.

987. Schuyler, Philippa. WHO KILLED THE CONGO? Chicago, Ill.: Regnery, 1961. 240 p.

988. O'Brien, Conor Cruise. TO KATANGA AND BACK: A U.N. CASE HISTORY. New York: Simon and Schuster, 1963. 370 p.

> An embattled former UN official gives his version of his mission in Katanga which resulted in his ouster in 1961. Especially bitter about U.S. pressure exerted on the Secretariat. The author accuses the British of sabotaging UN action in Katanga. Also attacks British, French, and United States newspapers for distortion of the news.

989. Tondel, Lyman M., Jr., ed. THE LEGAL ASPECTS OF THE UNITED NATIONS ACTION IN THE CONGO. Hammarskjold Forum. Dobbs Ferry, N.Y.: Oceana, 1963. 137 p. (For the Association of the Bar of the City of New York.)

> The text of the working paper on the role of the UN in the Congo along with a summary of the discussion.

990. Simmonds, R. LEGAL PROBLEMS ARISING FROM UN MILITARY OPERATIONS IN THE CONGO. The Hague, Netherlands: Nijhoff, 1968. 372 p.

991. Hoskyns, Catherine. THE CONGO: A CHRONOLOGY OF EVENTS, JANUARY 1960-DECEMBER 1961. London: Oxford University Press, 1962. 42 p. Pamphlet. (For the Royal Institute of International Affairs.)

A useful and complete chronology.

992. United Nations Review. SUMMARY CHRONOLOGY OF UN ACTIVITY RELATING TO THE CONGO, 30 JUNE 1960-30 JUNE 1964. New York, 1965. 198 p.

d. CYPRUS

993. Stegenga, James A. THE UNITED NATIONS FORCE IN CYPRUS. Columbus, Ohio: Ohio State University Press, 1968. 241 p.

> The events before and after the outbreak are carefully examined. Studies UNFYCP in operation and concludes it has been a model of efficiency and economy, and has made many useful contributions to restoring order on Cyprus. The author argues that a UN force has a limited capacity to mitigate civil conflict and is no substitute for traditional political settlement procedures. Studies administrative arrangements, control mechanisms, command, deployment, and effect.

994. Miller, Linda B. CYPRUS: THE LAW AND POLITICS OF CIVIL STRIFE. Cambridge, Mass.: Harvard Center for International Affairs, 1968. 97 p.

> A study of the origins and evolution of the conflict, focusing on the role of legal norms, international institutions, and foreign governments. Gives the resolutions of 1964-67. Includes a statistical profile of UN forces.

995. Xydis, Stephen G. CYPRUS: CONFLICT AND CONCILIATION. Columbus, Ohio: Ohio State University Press, 1967. 722 p.

> A detailed, well-documented account of events from 1954 to 1958. Makes use of the private papers of the Greek government and includes a good account of Greek politics. Shows much of the behind-the-scenes negotiating which went on. The point of view is definitely Greek.

F. ARBITRATION AND ADJUDICATION

(See also Chapter 7.F and 416, 646-48, 1372, 1380, 1381.)

996. Ralston, Jackson H. INTERNATIONAL ARBITRATION FROM ATHENS TO LOCARNO. Stanford, Calif.: Stanford University Press, 1929. 417 p.

997. Cory, Helen M. COMPULSORY ARBITRATION OF INTERNATIONAL

DISPUTES. New York: Columbia University Press, 1932. 294 p.

Analysis of selected conferences between 1820 and 1932.

998. Simpson, J. L., and Fox, Hazel. INTERNATIONAL ARBITRATION: LAW AND PRACTICE. New York: Praeger, 1959. 350 p.

A comprehensive guide to the procedures of international tribunals, with emphasis on the International Court of Justice, analyzing their doctrinal and practical aspects.

999. Carlston, Kenneth S. THE PROCESS OF INTERNATIONAL ARBITRATION. New York: Columbia University Press, 1946. 318 p.

A competent study of the organization and procedures of international arbitration. The author studies five courts: Central American Court of Justice, Permanent Court of International Justice, International Court of Justice, Court of the European Community, and European Court of Human Rights.

1000. Darby, William Evans. INTERNATIONAL ARBITRATION: INTERNATIONAL TRIBUNALS. London: Dent, 1904. 524 p.

Discusses the schemes for arbitral tribunals suggested and the experiences of these during the nineteenth century.

1001. Morris, Robert C. INTERNATIONAL ARBITRATION AND PROCEDURE. New Haven, Conn.: Yale University Press, 1911. 250 p.

1002. Ralston, Jackson H. INTERNATIONAL ARBITRAL LAW AND PROCEDURE, BEING A RESUME OF THE PROCEDURES AND PRACTICE OF INTERNATIONAL COMMISSIONS, AND INCLUDING THE VIEWS OF ARBITRATORS UPON QUESTIONS ARISING UNDER THE LAW OF NATIONS. Boston, Mass.: Ginn, 1910. 372 p.

1003. Stuyt, Alexander M. SURVEY OF INTERNATIONAL ARBITRATIONS, 1795-1970. New York: Oceana, 1973. 587 p.

Good overview of the use and usefulness of arbitration.

1004. Foster, John W. ARBITRATION AND THE HAGUE COURT. Boston, Mass.: Houghton Mifflin Co., 1904. 147 p.

1005. Domke, Martin. COMMERCIAL ARBITRATION. Mundelein, Ill.: Callahan, 1968. 469 p.

A concise survey of the various types of commercial arbitration examining practice and law.

1006. Lissitzyn, Oliver James. THE INTERNATIONAL COURT OF JUSTICE: ITS ROLE IN THE MAINTENANCE OF INTERNATIONAL PEACE AND SECURITY. New York: Carnegie Endowment, 1951. 134 p.

    A careful analysis of the working of the court with reflections on the judicial process in world affairs. A detailed examination of the judgments and advisory opinions in relation to international law.

1007. Anand, Ram Prakash. STUDIES IN INTERNATIONAL ADJUDICATION. Delhi, India: Vikas, 1969. 218 p.

    The author surveys the relationship of various nations and groups to the international court. Describes its workings and the way it develops international law. Includes discussion of the role of individuals and dissenting opinions. Analyzes execution of judicial awards since 1945.

1008. Grieves, Forest L. SUPRANATIONALISM AND INTERNATIONAL ADJUDICATION. Urbana, Ill.: University of Illinois Press, 1969. 281 p.

    A study of the international judicial process with emphasis on its jurisdiction. Relates to theories and concepts of supranationalism.

1009. Jenks, C[larence]. Wilfred. THE PROSPECTS OF INTERNATIONAL ADJUDICATION. Dobbs Ferry, N.Y.: Oceana, 1964. 805 p.

    A massive exploration of the prospects for further advances in international adjudication with respect especially to increasing the effectiveness of the International Court of Justice as an instrument for effecting the rule of law in international relations.

1010. Keith, Kenneth James. THE EXTENT OF THE ADVISORY JURISDICTION OF THE INTERNATIONAL COURT OF JUSTICE. Leiden, Netherlands: Sijthoff, 1971. 254 p.

    A well-written, well-argued, and well-documented book on the advisory competence of both the Permanent Court and the present International Court of Justice and analysis of the role which the advisory opinions can and do play in the peaceful settlement of international disputes. Concludes that the reasons for the non-use of the court are to be found in political realities rather than in lack of its constitutional competence.

1011. Chung, Il Yung. LEGAL PROBLEMS INVOLVED IN THE CORFU CHANNEL INCIDENT. Geneva, Switzerland: Droz, 1959. 287 p.

    A scholarly study showing the depolititization of an international situation by recourse to judicial settlement.

1012. Nantwi, E. K. THE ENFORCEMENT OF INTERNATIONAL JUDICIAL DECISIONS AND ARBITRAL AWARDS IN PUBLIC INTERNATIONAL LAW. Leiden, Netherlands: Sijthoff, 1966. 224 p.

   A survey of the history of decisions drawing from the general principles of law.

Chapter 10

PROMOTING CROSS-NATIONAL TRANSACTIONS

Chapter 10
PROMOTING CROSS-NATIONAL TRANSACTIONS

International organizations have been important in developing laws, regulations, and policies affecting cross-national transactions. Although the execution of these ultimately relies on state action, organizations have been effective in promoting compliance. The topics from a purely legal perspective are covered in most international law texts and many monographs. Books in this section describe and analyze the nature and extent of international organization involvement and effectiveness.

A. REGULATING COMMUNICATIONS

1. General

1013. Alexandrowicz, Charles Henry. THE LAW OF GLOBAL COMMUNICATIONS. New York: Columbia University Press, 1971. 204 p.

    The author analyzes the international legal provisions governing postal communications, radio transmission, civil aviation, satellite communications, and maritime transport. He describes the structures and modes of working of the various international organizations set up to regulate communications. Examines the mixed public-private agencies.

1014. McWhinney, Edward, ed. THE INTERNATIONAL LAW OF COMMUNICATION. Dobbs Ferry, N.Y.: Oceana, 1971. 172 p.

    A collection of essays from a colloquium on the new international law of communications. Shows the role of international organizations in the promotion of the development of this law with special attention to East-West cooperation in space telecommunications.

1015. Mance, Brigadier General Sir [Harry] Osborne. INTERNATIONAL ROAD, TRANSPORT, POSTAL, ELECTRICITY AND MISCELLANEOUS QUESTIONS. New York: Oxford University Press, 1947. 265 p.

    Good historical survey of the development of regulations stressing the significance of international conferences and the League's organs in this development.

1016. Clark, George Norman. UNIFYING THE WORLD. London: Swarthmore, 1920. 116 p.

A short essay on international regulation of communications.

2. International Telecommunications:
The International Telecommunications Union (ITU)

(See also 157, 630.)

1017. Codding, George A., Jr. THE INTERNATIONAL TELECOMMUNICATIONS UNION: AN EXPERIMENT IN INTERNATIONAL COOPERATION. Leiden, Netherlands: Brill, 1952. 505 p.

A good description of the development of machinery for international collaboration in telecommunications from the time of the inception of the International Telegraphic Union of 1865. Analyzes the evolutionary, structural, and functional aspects of international procedures showing how problems with international implications arise and how international organizations have developed techniques to solve these problems.

1018. Fischer, H. INTERNATIONAL COMMUNICATIONS: MEDIA, CHANNELS, FUNCTIONS. New York: Communications Arts Books, Hastings House, 1971. 508 p.

Description of the problems, responses, and effectiveness of international cooperation in the field of communications.

1019. Leive, David M. INTERNATIONAL TELECOMMUNICATIONS AND INTERNATIONAL LAW: THE REGULATION OF THE RADIOSPECTRUM. Dobbs Ferry, N.Y.: Oceana, 1970. 400 p.

Essentially a study of the ITU in which the author analyzes the present ITU regime, singles out inadequacies and recommends modifications. Outlines the powers and procedures of the various bodies in the organization and describes conference structure and organization.

1020. Smith, Delbert D. INTERNATIONAL TELECOMMUNICATION CONTROL: INTERNATIONAL LAW AND THE ORDERING OF SATELLITE AND OTHER FORMS OF INTERNATIONAL BROADCASTING. Leiden, Netherlands: Sijthoff, 1969. 247 p.

An analysis of the legal, political, economic, and technical aspects of telecommunication control. The role of international institutions in the development and supervision of regulations is examined.

1021. Tomlinson, John D. THE INTERNATIONAL CONTROL OF RADIOCOMMUNICATIONS. Ann Arbor, Mich.: Edwards, 1945. 314 p.

> A scholarly monograph on the history and legal problems of radiocommunications. Concerned mainly with administrative questions.

1022. Twentieth Century Fund. GLOBAL COMMUNICATIONS IN THE SPACE AGE: TOWARD A NEW ITU. New York, 1972. 73 p. Pamphlet.

> Presents the organization, purposes, and possible future role of the ITU.

1023. Leive, David M. THE FUTURE OF THE INTERNATIONAL TELECOMMUNICATIONS UNION: A REPORT FOR THE 1973 PLENIPOTENTIARY CONFERENCE. Washington, D.C.: American Society of International Law, 1972. 50 p.

1024. Mance, Brigadier General Sir [Harry] Osborne. INTERNATIONAL TELECOMMUNICATIONS. New York: Oxford University Press, 1944. 102 p.

> Brief outline of the development of regulations and the role and significance of international organizations, especially the International Telecommunications Union.

3. International Civil Aviation: The International Civil Aviation Organization (ICAO)

(See also 206, 298, 880.)

1025. Buergenthal, Thomas. LAW-MAKING IN THE INTERNATIONAL CIVIL AVIATION ORGANIZATION. Procedural Aspects of International Law Series, vol. 7. Syracuse, N.Y.: Syracuse University Press, 1969. 250 p.

> A scholarly and solid treatment of law and practice in the areas of membership, legislation, settlement of disputes, and amendatory procedures. The author explores the extent to which law affects the ICAO's decision-making process. Examines the nature of the law and how it is developed.

1026. Cheng, Bin. THE LAW OF INTERNATIONAL AIR TRANSPORT. Dobbs Ferry, N.Y.: Oceana, 1962. 768 p.

> A comprehensive treatment of the international aspects of the law of air transport. Description of ICAO's rights, functions,

and operations.

1027. Chuang, Richard V. THE INTERNATIONAL AIR TRANSPORT ASSOCIATION: A CASE STUDY OF A QUASI-GOVERNMENTAL ORGANIZATION. Leiden, Netherlands: Sijthoff, 1972. 203 p.

An account of the organization, powers, procedures, and functions of the ICAO.

1028. International Civil Aviation Organization. Public Information Office. MEMORANDUM ON ICAO: THE STORY OF THE INTERNATIONAL CIVIL AVIATION ORGANIZATION. Montreal, Canada, May 1953. 56 p.

A description of the structure and operations of the organization.

1029. Kihl, Young W. CONFLICT ISSUES AND INTERNATIONAL CIVIL AVIATION DECISIONS: THREE CASE STUDIES. Social Science Foundation, Monograph Series in World Affairs, vol. 8, monograph no. 11. Denver, Colo.: University of Denver Press, 1971. 107 p.

An investigation of three cases of conflict of interest and the role of the ICAO in the settlement of each. Shows the institutional setting of the ICAO and the concepts and methods employed as an analytic framework in the study.

1030. McWhinney, Edward, and Bradley, Martin A., eds. THE FREEDOM OF THE AIR. Dobbs Ferry, N.Y.: Oceana, 1968. 259 p.

Seventeen papers survey the conditions and problems of international aviation. A number are concerned with the activities of the ICAO and IATA.

1031. Schenkman, Captain Jacob. INTERNATIONAL CIVIL AVIATION ORGANIZATION. Geneva, Switzerland: Droz, 1955. 422 p.

A factual account giving the history, structure, and activities of the organization. Detailed account of the ICAO's work in technical, economic, and legal fields.

1032. Straszheim, Mahlon T. THE INTERNATIONAL AIRLINE INDUSTRY. Washington, D.C.: Brookings Institution, Transport Research Program, 1969. 297 p.

A study of measures of efficiency in international aviation, with an assessment of the effects on public aviation both national and international.

1033. Mance, Brigadier General Sir H[arry]. Osborne. INTERNATIONAL AIR TRANSPORT. New York: Oxford University Press, 1944. 126 p.

Brief survey of the current law of air transport and the role organizations have played in its development.

1034. Wassenbergh, H. A. POST-WAR INTERNATIONAL AVIATION POLICY AND THE LAW OF THE AIR. 2nd rev. ed. The Hague, Netherlands: Nijhoff, 1962. 209 p.

Traces the development of law and policy with special reference to the International Civil Aviation Organization.

1035. Colegrove, Kenneth W. INTERNATIONAL CONTROL OF AVIATION. Boston, Mass.: World Peace Foundation, 1930. 234 p.

4. The Sea and Waterways

(See also 297.)

1036. Alexander, Lewis H., ed. THE LAW OF THE SEA: INTERNATIONAL RULES AND ORGANIZATION FOR THE SEA: PROCEEDINGS OF THE THIRD ANNUAL CONFERENCE OF THE LAW OF THE SEA INSTITUTE, JUNE 24-27, 1969. Columbus, Ohio: Ohio State University Press, 1969. 469 p.

Papers analyzing the development and functioning of the law of the sea, some of which show the role of international organizations in the process. Future developments are projected.

1037. Baxter, R. R. THE LAW OF INTERNATIONAL WATERWAYS. Cambridge, Mass.: Harvard University Press, 1964. 371 p.

Well-documented study of the existing law covering straits, canals, and rivers and describing the various organizations administering them. The author analyzes the obstacles to further international administration.

1038. Gullion, Edmund A. USES OF THE SEAS. Englewood Cliffs, N.J.: Prentice-Hall, 1968. 221 p.

An examination of the problems and potential of developing international legislation, including a consideration of organizations and institutions.

1039. McDougal, Myres S., and Burke, William T. THE PUBLIC ORDER OF THE OCEANS: A CONTEMPORARY INTERNATIONAL LAW OF THE SEA. New Haven, Conn.: Yale University Press, 1962. 1226 p.

A scholarly and detailed study of the seas, including the past and future role of international agencies in developing and administering law.

1040. Mance, Brigadier General Sir H[arry]. Osborne. INTERNATIONAL SEA TRANSPORT. New York: Oxford University Press, 1945. 210 p.

Good outline of the development of regulations for sea transport showing the role played by international organizations.

1041. Neild, Robert R., ed. TOWARDS A BETTER USE OF THE OCEANS: A STUDY AND PROGNOSIS. Stockholm, Sweden: International Institute for Peace and Conflict Resolution, 1968. 322 p.

A careful analysis of the problems and conflicts involved in the future development of the seas. Contains suggestions for the promotion of cooperation and regulation.

1042. Oda, Shigeru. THE INTERNATIONAL LAW OF THE OCEAN DEVELOPMENT: BASIC DOCUMENTS. Leiden, Netherlands: Sijthoff, 1972. 519 p.

Documentary and source material on the law of the sea; includes conventions, resolutions of the General Assembly, and ECOSOC drafts.

1043. Padelford, Norman J., comp. PUBLIC POLICY FOR THE SEAS. 2nd ed. Cambridge, Mass.: The M.I.T. Press, 1970. 338 p.

A careful analysis of the legal problems involved in the use of the sea and the laws and organizations concerned with these problems.

1044. Mance, Brigadier General Sir H[arry]. Osborne. INTERNATIONAL RIVER AND CANAL TRANSPORT. New York: Oxford University Press, 1945. 123 p.

Good outline of the development and current state of law and regulation covering rivers and canals. Shows the usefulness of international conferences and administrations.

1045. Chamberlain, Joseph P. THE REGIME OF INTERNATIONAL RIVERS: DANUBE AND RHINE. New York: Columbia University Press, 1923. 234 p.

5. Space

(See also 105, 206, 297.)

1046. White, Irvin L. DECISION-MAKING FOR SPACE: LAW AND POLITICS IN AIR, SEA AND OUTER SPACE. West Lafayette, Ind.: Purdue University Studies, 1970. 270 p.

> An examination of the variety of factors influencing decision-making in the General Assembly. Use of quantitative methods and statistical analysis to identify the relationship between votes cast and supportive dialogue.

1047. Evans, F. T., and Howard, H. D. OUTLOOK ON SPACE. New York: Hillary House, 1966. 179 p.

> A nontechnical introduction to the growing relationship between space research and international organizations.

1048. Fawcett, James E. S. OUTER SPACE AND INTERNATIONAL ORDER. London: The David Davies Memorial Institute of International Studies, 1964. 14 p. Pamphlet.

> A brief look at the challenge of space with consideration of the potential for cooperation and regulation.

1049. Galloway, E., ed. INTERNATIONAL COOPERATION IN OUTER SPACE: A SYMPOSIUM. Washington, D.C.: Government Printing Office, 1971. 732 p.

> A collection of papers on the evolution of cooperative activities in space. Indicates the role of international organizations in this development and points out prospects for the future.

1050. Kash, Don E. THE POLITICS OF SPACE COOPERATION. Lafayette, Ind.: Purdue University Press, 1969. 137 p.

> A study of the foreign policy implications of U.S. participation in international space programs beginning with the launching of Sputnik in 1957. Analyzes the goals of international cooperative programs and the organization and structure of existing programs.

1051. McWhinney, Edward, and Bradley, Martin A. NEW FRONTIERS IN SPACE LAW. Leiden, Netherlands: Sijthoff, 1969. 134 p.

> A careful and scholarly analysis of the problems and potential of space cooperation.

1052. Mezerik, A. G., ed. OUTER SPACE: UN, US, USSR. New York: International Review Service, 1960. 52 p. Pamphlet.

> A short outline of activities of the United States and Soviet Union in and concerning space exploration. Describes the role

of the UN in attempts at treatymaking and shows the involvement of the various committees.

1053. Schwartz, Leonard E. INTERNATIONAL ORGANIZATIONS AND SPACE COOPERATION. Durham, N.C.: Duke University, World Law Center, 1963. 108 p.

A good reference piece giving details on all bodies playing a substantial role in space cooperation; outlining past achievements and future plans. Includes both governmental and non-governmental organizations.

1054. United Nations. SPACE ACTIVITIES AND RESOURCES: REVIEW OF UNITED NATIONS, NATIONAL AND INTERNATIONAL PROGRAMS. New York, 1965. 172 p.

An overall view of the developments in the use of space for peace and the benefit of man. Goes into the activities of specialized agencies and international groups aiding the UN.

1055. _____. SPACE ACTIVITIES AND RESOURCES: A REVIEW OF THE ACTIVITIES AND RESOURCES OF THE UNITED NATIONS, OF ITS SPECIALIZED AGENCIES AND OF OTHER COMPETENT INTERNATIONAL BODIES RELATING TO THE PEACEFUL USES OF OUTER SPACE. New York, 1972. 204 p.

Updates above entry.

1056. Lachs, Manfred. THE LAW OF OUTER SPACE: AN EXPERIENCE IN CONTEMPORARY LAW-MAKING. Leiden, Netherlands: Sijthoff, 1972. 204 p.

A founding member of the UN Committee for The Peaceful Uses of Outer Space reviews the record of the international lawmaking process for outer space. Shows how the UN has worked to secure not only world agreements, but has also promoted narrow accords, especially between the United States and the Soviet Union. A good description of how the committee sought to secure consensus at every step of its process.

1057. Miles, Edward. INTERNATIONAL ADMINISTRATION OF SPACE EXPLORATION AND EXPLOITATION. Monograph Series in World Affairs, vol. 8, no. 4. Denver, Colo.: University of Denver Press, 1971. 51 p.

1058. Taubenfeld, Howard J., ed. SPACE AND SOCIETY: STUDIES FOR THE SEMINAR ON PROBLEMS OF OUTER SPACE. Dobbs Ferry, N.Y.: Oceana, 1964. 190 p.

6. Postal Relations: The Universal Postal Union (UPU)

(See also 160.)

1059. Codding, George A., Jr. THE UNIVERSAL POSTAL UNION: COORDINATOR OF THE INTERNATIONAL MAIL. New York: New York University Press, 1964. 296 p.

>A comprehensive study of the origins, development, constitution, organs, and bureau of the UPU including an analysis of economic, political, and technical forces operating.

7. Rail Transport

1060. Wedgwood, Sir Ralph L., and Wheeler, J. E. INTERNATIONAL RAIL TRANSPORT. New York: Oxford University Press, 1946. 174 p. (For the Royal Institute of International Affairs.)

>A comprehensive study of the development of regulations for rail transport. Stresses the significance of conferences in developing and implementing these.

B. REGULATING INTERNATIONAL TRADE

1. General

1061. Metzger, Stanley D. INTERNATIONAL LAW, TRADE AND FINANCE: REALITIES AND PROSPECTS. Dobbs Ferry, N.Y.: Oceana, 1962. 184 p.

>A well-documented study of the steps by which "international tranquility" has been achieved through international agreements in the expanding field of commercial and economic transactions.

1062. Kravis, Irving B. DOMESTIC INTERESTS AND INTERNATIONAL TRADE ORGANIZATIONS. Philadelphia, Pa.: University of Pennsylvania Press, 1964. 448 p.

1063. Wilcox, Clair. A CHARTER FOR WORLD TRADE. New York: Macmillan, 1949. 350 p.

>The vice-chairman of the U.S. delegation to the Havana Conference comments on the articles of the abortive Draft Charter.

2. General Agreement on Tariffs and Trade (GATT)

(See also 73, 84, 156, 284, 630, 880.)

1064. White, Eric Wyndham. GATT AS AN INTERNATIONAL TRADE ORGANIZATION: SOME STRUCTURAL PROBLEMS OF INTERNATIONAL TRADE. Geneva, Switzerland: General Agreement on Tariffs and Trade, Secretariat, 1961. 29 p. Mimeographed.

   A good short introduction to international trade and how GATT conceives and exercises its role.

1065. Dam, Kenneth W. THE GATT: LAW AND INTERNATIONAL ECONOMIC ORGANIZATION. Chicago, Ill.: University of Chicago Press, 1970. 480 p.

   A full account of the activity and problems of the organization. Challenges some of the basic assumptions of the authors of GATT and analyzes the consequences flowing from them.

1066. Curzon, Gerard. MULTILATERAL COMMERCIAL DIPLOMACY: THE GENERAL AGREEMENT ON TARIFFS AND TRADE AND ITS IMPACT ON NATIONAL AND COMMERCIAL POLICIES AND TECHNIQUES. New York: Praeger, 1966. 367 p.

   A good account of the impact of the organization on the policies of states.

1067. Koch, Karin. INTERNATIONAL TRADE POLICY AND THE GATT, 1947-1967. Stockholm, Sweden: Almqvist, 1969. 334 p.

   A good account of how GATT really works, showing the complexity of the relations of GATT and its members and of GATT and other international bodies. Analyzes differences of American and British approaches to trade policy. Discusses rules and laws and how these can be circumvented or ignored.

1068. Jackson, John H. WORLD TRADE AND THE LAW OF GATT. New York: Bobbs-Merrill, 1969. 988 p.

   An orderly, historical treatment of the evolution of the organization and its policies. Shows how consensus on arrangements is created and preserved. Goes into all important articles of the agreement. Emphasizes legal and institutional questions.

1069. Gupta, K. R. A STUDY OF THE GENERAL AGREEMENT ON TARIFFS AND TRADE. New Delhi, India: Chand, 1967. 239 p.

   An analysis of the various provisions of GATT with an examination of their working in actual practice. Points out weaknesses and shortcomings, and suggests ways to make provisions more effective. Written from the perspective of the developing countries.

1070. Evans, John W. THE KENNEDY ROUND IN AMERICAN TRADE POLICY: THE TWILIGHT OF GATT? Cambridge, Mass.: Harvard University Press, 1971. 383 p. (For the Center for International Affairs.)

A participant in the negotiations gives an authoritative and comprehensive account of the legal and economic development of the main issues relevant to the talks. Appraises the results of the Kennedy Round and assesses prospects for the future. Questions whether the Kennedy Round in effect represents the beginning of a new international trade system.

1071. Flory, Thiebaut. LE GATT. Paris, France: Librairie generale de droit et de jurisprudence, 1968. 316 p.

A definitive treatment of GATT. Shows GATT in movement, its goals and the obstacles with which it has had to deal. Shows how the organization has extended its technique of multilateral trade negotiation and assumed a useful arbitral role.

1072. Brown, William Adams, Jr. THE UNITED STATES AND THE RESTORATION OF WORLD TRADE: AN ANALYSIS AND APPRAISAL OF THE ITO CHARTER AND THE GENERAL AGREEMENT ON TARIFFS AND TRADE. Washington, D.C.: Brookings, 1950. 586 p.

1073. Fletcher School of Law and Diplomacy. AN ANALYSIS AND APPRAISAL OF THE GENERAL AGREEMENT ON TARIFFS AND TRADE. Boston, Mass.: 1955. 104 p. (For the United States Council of the International Chamber of Commerce.)

3. International Commodity Agreements and Cartels

1074. Mason, Edward S. CONTROLLING WORLD TRADE: CARTELS AND COMMODITY AGREEMENTS. New York: McGraw-Hill, 1946. 289 p.

An account of the development of commodity agreements and cartels and their roles in the world trading system.

1075. Marx, Daniel. INTERNATIONAL SHIPPING CARTELS. Princeton, N.J.: Princeton University Press, 1953. 336 p.

Good analysis of cartels and their relation to national policies and international trade.

1076. Edwards, Corwin D., ed. A CARTEL POLICY FOR THE UNITED NATIONS. New York: Columbia University Press, 1946. 130 p.

   Exposition of the background of the development of cartels. The author pleads for more concern on the part of the UN and outlines a possible policy.

1077. Baranyai, L., and Mills, J. C. INTERNATIONAL COMMODITY AGREEMENTS. Mexico City, Mexico: Centro de Estudios Monetarios Latinoamericanos, 1963. 190 p.

   A critical look at the effects of commodity agreements especially in the Latin American area.

C. THE INTERNATIONAL MONETARY SYSTEM: POLICIES AND REGULATION

1. General

(See also 111 and 1122.)

1078. Shuster, Milan R. THE PUBLIC INTERNATIONAL LAW OF MONEY. London: Oxford University Press, 1973. 369 p.

   An analysis of the world monetary system and the techniques of regulation.

1079. Kindleberger, C. POWER AND MONEY: THE ECONOMICS OF INTERNATIONAL POLITICS AND THE POLITICS OF INTERNATIONAL ECONOMICS. New York: Basic Books, 1971. 246 p.

   A good analysis of the interaction of economic and political forces.

1080. Cohen, Stephen D. INTERNATIONAL MONETARY REFORM, 1964-1969: THE POLITICAL DIMENSION. New York: Praeger, 1970. 221 p.

   An incisive analysis of the political aspects of international monetary reform. Examines the negotiations preceding the creation of Special Drawing Rights.

1081. Bosman, H. W. J., and Alting, Gevsau. THE FUTURE OF THE INTERNATIONAL MONETARY SYSTEM. Boston, Mass.: Heath, 1970. 180 p.

   The author examines the present problems in the system and the reasons for suspecting an inherent instability. Describes multilateral surveillance, consultation, and adjustment processes.

1082. Krause, Lawrence B. SEQUEL TO BRETTON WOODS: A PROPOSAL FOR REFORM OF THE WORLD MONETARY SYSTEM. Washington, D.C.: Brookings, 1971. 58 p.

1083. Triffin, Robert. OUR INTERNATIONAL MONETARY SYSTEM: YESTERDAY, TODAY AND TOMORROW. New York: Random House, 1968. 206 p.

> A participant in the Morgenthau debate on international monetary reform, the author looks at the history of the system as it has evolved and makes projections for the future.

1084. _____. THE EVOLUTION OF THE INTERNATIONAL MONETARY SYSTEM: HISTORICAL REAPPRAISAL AND FUTURE PERSPECTIVES. Princeton Studies in International Finance, no. 12. Princeton, N.J.: Princeton University, Department of Economics, International Finance Section, 1964. 87 p. Pamphlet.

> Brief outline of the development of the international system with prospects for the future.

1085. Grubel, Herbert G. THE INTERNATIONAL MONETARY SYSTEM; EFFICIENCY AND PRACTICAL ALTERNATIVES. Harmondsworth: Penguin, 1969. 208 p.

> A good introduction to the system in all its aspects.

1086. Jacobson, Per. INTERNATIONAL MONETARY PROBLEMS 1957-1963: SELECTED SPEECHES OF PER JACOBSON. Washington, D.C.: International Monetary Fund, 1964. 368 p.

> A compilation of the author's major speeches made while he was Managing Director of the IMF. Touches on many problems as well as on the work of the World Bank and IMF.

1087. Harrod, Roy F. REFORMING THE WORLD'S MONEY. New York: St. Martin's Press, 1965. 189 p.

> The author stresses the need for an increase in liquidity and shows how this could be obtained through the IMF.

1088. Machlup, Fritz. PLANS FOR REFORM OF THE INTERNATIONAL SYSTEM. Princeton, N.J.: Princeton University Press, 1964. 93 p. Pamphlet.

> Brief look at the ways international agencies could be used to improve the international system.

1089. Hawkins, Robert G., and Rolfe, Sidney E. A CRITICAL SURVEY OF PLANS FOR INTERNATIONAL MONETARY REFORM. New York: New York University, Graduate School of Business Administration, 1965. 80 p. Pamphlet.

1090. Schammell, William M. INTERNATIONAL MONETARY POLICY. 2nd ed. London: Macmillan; New York: St. Martin's, 1961. 428 p.

1091. Tew, Brian. INTERNATIONAL MONETARY CO-OPERATION, 1945-63. London: Hutchinson's University Library, 1963. 199 p.

1092. Halm, George N. INTERNATIONAL MONETARY COOPERATION. Chapel Hill, N.C.: University of North Carolina Press, 1945. 363 p.

> Presents experiences under the gold standard and during years between wars. Outlines the principal features of IMF and the World Bank. Written before adoption of Bretton Woods.

1093. Morgan, Carlyle. BRETTON WOODS: CLUES TO A MONETARY MYSTERY. Boston, Mass.: World Peace Foundation, 1945. 143 p.

1094. Giersch, Herbert, ed. INTEGRATION THROUGH MONETARY UNION? SYMPOSIUM, JUNE 1970. Tuebingen, Germany: Mohr, 1971. 178 p.

> A collection of papers considering the impact of monetary union on political integration.

2. The International Monetary Fund (IMF)

(See also 74, 285, 630, 1117.)

1095a. Horsefield, J. Keith, ed. THE INTERNATIONAL MONETARY FUND 1945-1965: TWENTY YEARS OF INTERNATIONAL MONETARY CO-OPERATION. Vols. 1 and 3. Washington, D.C.: International Monetary Fund, 1969. Vol. 1, 663 p; vol. 3, 549 p.

1095b. DeVries, Margaret G., et al. THE INTERNATIONAL MONETARY FUND 1945-1965: TWENTY YEARS OF INTERNATIONAL MONETARY CO-OPERATION. Vol. 2. Washington, D.C.: International Monetary Fund, 1969. 621 p.

> This three-volume study provides a comprehensive description and analysis of the Fund. Volume 1 covers the historical development; volume 2 is an analysis of the experience and policies of the organization; and volume 3 contains a comprehensive collection of major documents, including some which were not previously published. Excellent reference work. Covers legal, economic, and administrative aspects.

1096. Gold, Joseph. VOTING AND DECISIONS IN THE INTERNATIONAL MONETARY FUND: AN ESSAY ON THE LAW AND PRACTICE OF THE FUND. Washington, D.C.: International Monetary Fund, 1972. 380 p.

1097. _____. THE REFORM OF THE FUND. Washington, D.C.: International Monetary Fund, 1969. 64 p. Mimeographed.

    A brief exposition of the problems of the Fund and the response to these in the form of changes in its policy.

1098. _____. THE FUND AND NON-MEMBER STATES: SOME LEGAL EFFECTS. Washington, D.C.: The International Monetary Fund, 1966. 55 p. Mimeographed.

    Explanation of the effects of the Fund's policies on nonmember states.

1099. _____. THE INTERNATIONAL MONETARY FUND AND PRIVATE BUSINESS TRANSACTIONS: SOME LEGAL EFFECTS OF THE ARTICLES OF AGREEMENT. Washington, D.C.: The International Monetary Fund, 1965. 26 p. Mimeographed.

    Brief analysis of the legal effects of the policies and actions of the Fund on the private sector.

1100. _____. THE INTERNATIONAL MONETARY FUND AND INTERNATIONAL LAW: AN INTRODUCTION. Washington, D.C.: The International Monetary Fund, 1965. 26 p. Mimeographed.

    Brief exposition of the relationship between the powers and rights of the Fund and general international law.

1101. Aufricht, Hans. THE INTERNATIONAL MONETARY FUND: LEGAL ASPECTS, STRUCTURE, FUNCTIONS, 1945-63. New York: Praeger, 1964. 150 p.

    Contains basic data concerning the organization and functioning of the Fund. Difficult technical issues are treated in a clear manner.

1102. _____. THE FUND AGREEMENT: LIVING LAW AND EMERGING PRACTICE. Princeton, N.J.: Princeton University Press, International Finance Section, 1969. 96 p.

1103. Horie, Shigeo. THE INTERNATIONAL MONETARY FUND: RETROSPECT AND PROSPECT. New York: St. Martin's, 1964. 208 p.

    A one-time president of the Bank of Tokyo explores the past and present of the Fund and projects the future of the international monetary system.

1103a. Payer, Cheryl. THE DEBT TRAP: THE INTERNATIONAL MONETARY FUND AND THE THIRD WORLD. New York: Monthly Review Press, 1975. 251 p.

    Shows the difficulty the debtor countries are in using case studies from a number of countries. Concerned with the kinds of conditions imposed on countries in their bilateral arrangements and through the IMF.

Chapter 11
PROMOTING ECONOMIC COOPERATION AND WELFARE

Chapter 11
PROMOTING ECONOMIC COOPERATION AND WELFARE

A. GENERAL

(See also Chapter 12.A and 100, 503, 796, 1241, 1251.)

1. Economic Organization and the League

a. GENERAL

1104. Hill, Martin. THE ECONOMIC AND FINANCIAL ORGANIZATION OF THE LEAGUE OF NATIONS: A SURVEY OF TWENTY-FIVE YEARS' EXPERIENCE. Washington, D.C.: Carnegie Endowment for International Peace, 1945. 162 p.

   A compact and useful description of the work of the League in financial and economic matters.

1105. McClure, Wallace M. WORLD PROSPERITY AS SOUGHT THROUGH ECONOMIC WORK OF THE LEAGUE OF NATIONS. New York: Macmillan, 1933. 613 p.

   An excellent account of the economic activities of the League covering such topics as economic jurisprudence, provisions in the covenant, world economic conferences, reconstruction of the European financial system, and world banking.

1106. Saiter, James A. THE ECONOMIC CONSEQUENCES OF THE LEAGUE: THE WORLD ECONOMIC CONFERENCE. London: Europa, 1927. 244 p.

b. BANK FOR INTERNATIONAL SETTLEMENTS

1107. Dulles, Eleanor L. THE BANK FOR INTERNATIONAL SETTLEMENTS

AT WORK. New York: Macmillan, 1932. 631 p.

1108. Einzig, Paul. THE BANK FOR INTERNATIONAL SETTLEMENTS. New York: Macmillan, 1930. 179 p.

1109. Papi, Guiseppe Ugo. THE FIRST TWENTY YEARS OF THE BANK FOR INTERNATIONAL SETTLEMENTS: WITH A BIBLIOGRAPHICAL APPENDIX ON THE BANK AND COGNATE SUBJECTS COMPILED ON THE BASIS OF INFORMATION SUPPLIED BY THE BIS. Rome, Italy: Boncaria, 1951. 270 p.

1110. Schloss, Henry H. THE BANK FOR INTERNATIONAL SETTLEMENTS. Amsterdam, Netherlands: North-Holland, 1958. 195 p.

2. Economic Organization in the Modern World

1111. Hawtrey, R. S. BRETTON WOODS: FOR BETTER OR WORSE. London: Longmans, Green, 1946. 142 p.

> An analysis made at the time of the arrangements for international economic cooperation concluded at Bretton Woods.

1112. Jessup, Philip C., et al. INTERNATIONAL REGULATION OF ECONOMIC AND SOCIAL QUESTIONS. New York: Carnegie Endowment, 1955. 180 p.

> A survey of the changes in the international scene which have resulted from the existence and operation of international organizations.

1113. Jordan, B. S., ed. MULTINATIONAL COOPERATION: ECONOMIC, SOCIAL AND SCIENTIFIC DEVELOPMENT. New York: Oxford University Press, 1972. 392 p.

> A collection of studies by experts showing the purposes, practices, and accomplishments of UN agencies. An examination of economic cooperation among nations in the form of free trade areas and trading agreements. Reviews current and future multinational exchanges of science and technology.

1114. Cox, Robert W., ed. THE POLITICS OF INTERNATIONAL ORGANIZATIONS: STUDIES IN MULTILATERAL SOCIAL AND ECONOMIC AGENCIES. New York: Praeger, 1970. 319 p.

> A high-level symposium on social and economic agencies and the advances these have made towards multilateral integration. Analyzes the role of agencies in the political development of

new nations and in formulating international monetary and trade politics. Encourages increased use of scientific methods in the study of development and the potential role of international organizations.

1115. Gardner, Richard N., and Millikan, Max F., eds. THE GLOBAL PARTNERSHIP: INTERNATIONAL AGENCIES AND ECONOMIC DEVELOPMENT. New York: Praeger, 1968. 505 p.

A symposium dealing with problems of international agencies and economic development critically examining potentialities and limitations. Sees need for increased use of international agencies.

1116. Van Meerhaeghe, M. A. G. INTERNATIONAL ECONOMIC INSTITUTIONS. New York: Wiley, 1967. 404 p.

A description and analysis of the organization and work of the IMF, World Bank and its subsidiaries, GATT, and commodity agreements.

1117. Alexandrowicz, Charles Henry. WORLD ECONOMIC AGENCIES: LAW AND PRACTICE. London: Stevens, 1962. 327 p.

The historical development of international economic cooperation since World War I. Analyzes organized economic cooperation from economic and legal points of view. Looks at UPU, ITU, ILO, FAO, WHO, ICAO, IMCO, World Bank, IMF, GATT, commodity agreements, and ECOSOC. The author emphasizes the regulatory and legislative roles of organizations and shows the techniques whereby these have become internationally responsive.

1118. Lary, Hal B. THE INSTITUTIONAL STRUCTURE OF THE FREE WORLD ECONOMY. Washington, D.C.: Industrial College of the Armed Forces, 1963-64. 28 p.

1119. Spaull, Hebe. THE AGENCIES OF THE U.N.: A SURVEY OF ECONOMIC AND SOCIAL ACHIEVEMENTS. London: Allen & Unwin, 1967. 133 p.

A brief description of the organization, purposes, and achievements of the specialized agencies and other UN related organizations active in the economic and social fields.

1120. Mangone, Gerard J., ed. UN ADMINISTRATION OF ECONOMIC AND SOCIAL PROGRAMS. New York: Columbia University Press, 1966. 313 p.

Six specialists wrote chapters on the organization, coordination, and field administration of UN social and economic programs, showing the problems which have arisen and the attempts made

Promoting Economic Cooperation and Welfare

to resolve them.

1121. Sharp, Walter R. FIELD ADMINISTRATION IN THE UNITED NATIONS SYSTEM: THE CONDUCT OF INTERNATIONAL ECONOMIC AND SOCIAL PROGRAMMES. London: Stevens, 1961. 570 p.

   The first study of the entire process of UN management of overseas field operations and programs. Primarily concerned with administrative aspects. Discusses role of resident representatives, staffing problems, headquarters-field relations, and issues such as centralization-decentralization.

1122. Meier, Gerald M. A WORLD MONETARY ORDER. Fairlawn, N.J.: Oxford University Press, 1974. 318 p.

1123. United Nations. Economic Commission for Europe. FIFTEEN YEARS OF ACTIVITY OF THE ECONOMIC COMMISSION FOR EUROPE, 1947-1962. New York, 1964. 177 p.

   Descriptive account of the work of the commission and its organization and structure.

1124. Wightman, David. ECONOMIC CO-OPERATION IN EUROPE: A STUDY OF THE UNITED NATIONS ECONOMIC COMMISSION FOR EUROPE. New York: Praeger, 1956. 299 p. (For Carnegie Endowment for International Peace.)

B. AID THROUGH UNIVERSAL ORGANIZATIONS

The literature on development and aid is voluminous. The works included here emphasize the role international agencies have played in this process.

1. United Nations Relief and Rehabilitation Administration (UNRRA)

1125. Woodbridge, George, ed. UNRRA: THE HISTORY OF THE UNITED NATIONS RELIEF AND REHABILITATION ADMINISTRATION. 3 vols. New York: Columbia University Press, 1950. 1698 p.

   An official history of the work of UNRRA. Two volumes are devoted to description, commentary, and analysis of the work of the agency; the third consists principally of essential documents. Includes data concerning the establishment, internal organization, financing, scope of functions, and working methods. Critical and forthright regarding the difficulties encountered.

1126. United Nations Relief and Rehabilitation Administration. THE STORY OF U.N.R.R.A. Washington, D.C., 1948. 47 p. Pamphlet.

    Brief description of the agency and its aims and accomplishments.

1127. Klemme, Marvin. THE INSIDE STORY OF UNRRA, AN EXPERIENCE IN INTERNATIONALISM; A FIRST HAND REPORT ON THE DISPLACED PEOPLE OF EUROPE. New York: Lifetime Editions, 1949. 307 p.

2. Development: Problems and International Strategies

1128. Higgins, Benjamin. ECONOMIC DEVELOPMENT: PRINCIPLES, PROBLEMS AND POLICIES. New York: Norton, 1968. 918 p.

    A comprehensive overview of the whole problem of development with an analysis of the role of international agencies and agreements.

1129. Commission on International Development. PARTNERS IN DEVELOPMENT (PEARSON REPORT). New York: Praeger, 1969. 415 p. Paperbound.

    Clear and illuminating analysis of past trends and current problems. Summarizes projected difficulties and proposes a future strategy for concerted action. Concludes that only slight progress has been made and that the pace of development has been much slower than expected.

1130. Pearson, Lester B. CRISES OF DEVELOPMENT. New York: Praeger, 1970. 117 p. (For the Council on Foreign Relations.)

    A strong case for renewed and improved assistance is set forth. A broad analysis of the total development picture: trade, technical assistance, overpopulation, debt levels, private investment, nationalization, government instability, and internal social tensions.

1131. Hirschman, Albert O. THE STRATEGY OF ECONOMIC DEVELOPMENT. New Haven, Conn.: Yale University Press, 1958. 230 p.

    An analysis of the various strategies being used by national governments and international organizations.

1132. Robock, S. H., and Soloman L. M., eds. INTERNATIONAL DEVELOPMENT 1965. New York: Oceana, 1966. 197 p.

    Description and analysis of the state of development and projection for future action. Concerned with foreign aid, population growth, adult literacy, and public and private planning in relation to economic growth.

3. Aid through Universal Multilateral Channels

(See also 849, 1181.)

1133. Friedmann, Wolfgang G., et al. INTERNATIONAL FINANCIAL AID. New York: Columbia University Press, 1966. 512 p.

>A comprehensive description of the major issues in aid theory and administration. Goes into the magnitude, characteristics, methods, and policies of donors. Includes both multilateral and bilateral programs.

1134. Jackson, Sir Robert G. A., ed. A STUDY OF THE CAPACITY OF THE UNITED NATIONS DEVELOPMENT SYSTEM. 2 vols. Geneva, Switzerland: United Nations, 1969. (United Nations Document DP/5.)

>Excellent analysis of problems, sources, and effectiveness of aid distributed by multilateral agencies.

1135. Sen, Sudhir. UNITED NATIONS IN ECONOMIC DEVELOPMENT: NEED FOR A NEW STRATEGY. Dobbs Ferry, N.Y.: Oceana, 1969. 365 p.

>A practical and constructive analysis of the achievements of UN development efforts, surveying some thirty agencies. Focuses on practical problems arising out of the deficiencies in the organization. Analyzes methods, programs, and procedures which have impeded the performance of programs. The author spent ten years with development programs in various administrative capacities.

1136. Ducksworth-Barker, V. BREAKTHROUGH TO TOMORROW: THE STORY OF INTERNATIONAL COOPERATION FOR DEVELOPMENT THROUGH THE UNITED NATIONS. New York: United Nations, 1970. 72 p.

>Brief survey of the programs and policies of the UN.

1137. Kirdar, Uner. THE STRUCTURE OF UNITED NATIONS ECONOMIC AID TO UNDERDEVELOPED COUNTRIES. The Hague, Netherlands: Nijhoff, 1966. 385 p.

>A detailed study of various forms of financial and technical assistance with emphasis on aid programs mediated and administered by the UN and other international bodies. Includes a large number of statistics. Gives history, constitutions, and legal analysis of financing techniques of the various organi-

zations.

1138. Keenleyside, Hugh L. INTERNATIONAL AID: A SUMMARY WITH SPECIAL REFERENCE TO THE PROGRAMMES OF THE UNITED NATIONS. New York: Heineman, 1966. 343 p.

> The author, a former Director-General of Technical Assistance of the UN, gives a comprehensive and clear summary of what aid is, how it has been given, and its effectiveness.

1139. Little, J. M. D., and Clifford, J. M. INTERNATIONAL AID. London: Allen & Unwin, 1965. 360 p.

> Comprehensive account of the principles and effectiveness of various forms of foreign aid--bilateral and multilateral.

1140. Basch, Antonin. FINANCING ECONOMIC DEVELOPMENT. New York: Macmillan, 1964. 334 p.

> A long-time official of the World Bank sets forth the accomplishments and problems connected with the three main sources of aid: private, governmental, and multilateral.

1141. Jackson, [Sir] Robert G.A. THE CASE FOR AN INTERNATIONAL DEVELOPMENT AUTHORITY. Syracuse, N.Y.: Syracuse University Press, 1959. 70 p.

> Brief analysis of the needs for development, setting forth the case for increased international involvement and direction. Calls for new approaches and organizations with different operating principles and practices.

1142. McLaughlin, Kathleen. THE WORLD'S WAR ON WANT. Dobbs Ferry, N.Y.: Oceana, 1961. 80 p.

1143. Shonfield, Andrew. THE ATTACK ON WORLD POVERTY. New York: Random House, 1960. 269 p.

1144. Hoffmann, Paul G. WORLD WITHOUT WANT. New York: Harper and Row, 1962. 144 p.

> A concise informed picture of poverty and the steps that may be taken to increase the pace of development.

1145. Maury, Marian. THE GOOD WAR: THE UN'S WORLD-WIDE FIGHT AGAINST POVERTY, DISEASE AND IGNORANCE. New York: Macfadden-Bartell, 1965. 191 p.

1146. Leonard, W. UNITED NATIONS DEVELOPMENT AID: CRITERIA AND

METHODS OF EVALUATION. New York: Arno, n.d. 135 p.

Overview of UN programs and policies with emphasis on means of evaluating effectiveness.

1147. Mezerik, A. G. INDUSTRIALIZATION OF UNDERDEVELOPED COUNTRIES. New York: International Review Service, 1968. 88 p.

Focuses on the UN's role in helping national industrialization. Discusses the functions, structure, and programs of UN Industrial Development Organization. Examines the nature of the problem and the kinds of action needed to avert disaster.

1148. Elder, Robert E., and Murden, F. D. ECONOMIC COOPERATION: SPECIAL UNITED NATIONS FUND FOR ECONOMIC DEVELOPMENT. New York: Woodrow Wilson Foundation, 1954. 27 p. Pamphlet.

Brief defense of increasing commitments to development through the UN and related agencies.

1149. United Nations. Economic and Social Council. CATALOGUE OF ECONOMIC AND SOCIAL PROJECTS OF THE UNITED NATIONS AND THE SPECIALIZED AGENCIES. New York, March 1949- . Irregular.

Descriptive catalog arranged under the various departments and divisions of the UN and specialized agencies. Explains projects currently represented in the work programs. Comprehensive index.

1150. Mezerik, A. G., ed. FINANCIAL ASSISTANCE FOR ECONOMIC DEVELOPMENT. New York: International Review Service, 1959. 71 p.

Chronology of worldwide financial assistance since the 1950's including UNRRA from 1943-59. An analysis of the policies and developments in international financial relations.

1151. Rubin, Seymour J., ed. FOREIGN DEVELOPMENT LENDING: LEGAL ASPECTS. Dobbs Ferry, N.Y.: Oceana, 1971. 352 p. (For the American Society of International Law.)

The proceedings of a conference of legal advisers of national and international institutions on the legal problems of foreign lending and assistance.

1152. Sewell, James Patrick. FUNCTIONALISM AND WORLD POLITICS: A STUDY BASED ON UNITED NATIONS PROGRAMS FINANCING ECONOMIC DEVELOPMENT. Princeton, N.J.: Princeton University Press, 1966. 373 p.

A history of the development of the World Bank and its affiliates and other UN agencies involved in financing economic development. The chief interest of the author is to find out whether international cooperation on limited tasks is likely to follow a certain course and produce particular kinds of results.

1153. Fontaine, Pierre-Michel. FUNCTIONALISM AND REGIONALISM IN THE UNITED NATIONS: THE ECONOMIC COMMISSION FOR LATIN AMERICA. Lexington, Mass.: Heath, 1974. 320 p.

Examines the commission not only in terms of its contribution to Latin American economic development but also as a political factor in the inter-American subsystem. Analysis of the commission's supportive role vis-a-vis regional and subregional programs in the area.

1154. Montgomery, John D. FOREIGN AID IN INTERNATIONAL POLITICS. Englewood Cliffs, N.J.: Prentice-Hall, 1967. 118 p.

Thoughtful analysis of all forms of aid given by the United States including that given through the UN and other multilateral agencies.

1155. McKitterick, Nathaniel. U.S. DIPLOMACY IN THE DEVELOPMENT AGENCIES OF THE UNITED NATIONS. Planning Pamphlet, no. 122. Washington, D.C.: National Planning Association, 1965. 67 p.

Brief outline of the aims and policies of the United States in UN agencies.

4. United Nations Conference on Trade and Development (UNCTAD)

(See also 880.)

1156. Hagras, Kamal. UNITED NATIONS CONFERENCE ON TRADE AND DEVELOPMENT: A CASE STUDY OF UN DIPLOMACY. New York: Praeger, 1965. 184 p.

A straightforward account by an official of the United Arab Republic of the machinery, procedures, institutionalization, and findings of the first conference. In parts dull and superficial.

1157. Gosovic, Branislav. UNCTAD: CONFLICT AND COMPROMISE. THE THIRD WORLD'S QUEST FOR AN EQUITABLE WORLD ECONOMIC ORDER THROUGH THE UNITED NATIONS. Leiden, Netherlands: Sijthoff, 1972. 363 p.

An exceptionally thorough analysis of the UNCTAD up to 1970. Surveys activities of international organizations created to help and modify the world trading system and the global division of labor. Analyzes origins, substantive endeavors, and the emergence of cohesion within the peculiar group system. Evaluates the work of the Secretariat. Stresses the evolving procedures for resolving conflicts among the members.

1158. Cordovez, Diego. UNCTAD AND DEVELOPMENT DIPLOMACY: FROM CONVENTION TO STRATEGY. Middlesex, England: Journal of World Trade Law, n.d. 167 p.

   A good account of the evolution of the UNCTAD idea and organization.

1159. Friedeberg, Alfred S. THE UNITED NATIONS CONFERENCE ON TRADE AND DEVELOPMENT OF 1964: THE THEORY OF PERIPHERAL ECONOMY AND THE CENTER OF INTERNATIONAL POLITICAL DISCUSSION. Rotterdam, Netherlands: University Press, 1968. 266 p.

5. Development Decades: How Useful Are They?

1160. Thant, U. THE UNITED NATIONS DEVELOPMENT DECADE: PROPOSALS FOR ACTION. New York: United Nations, 1962. 125 p.

   Brief history of international, financial, and technical cooperation with a clear, concise, and useful survey of the needs ahead. Proposes UN sponsored worldwide promotion of social and economic growth.

1161. Legum, Colin, ed. THE FIRST U.N. DEVELOPMENT DECADE AND ITS LESSONS FOR THE 1970'S. New York: Praeger (in cooperation with the Vienna Institute for Development), 1970. 340 p.

   Papers and summaries by a group of people from developing and developed countries of a wide political spectrum held under the auspices of the Vienna Institute for Development.

1162. Joyce, J[ames]. Avery. WORLD OF PROMISE: A GUIDE TO THE UNITED NATIONS DECADE OF DEVELOPMENT. Dobbs Ferry, N.Y.: Oceana, 1965. 175 p.

   An outline of the objectives and goals of the Development Decade.

1163. Broekmeijer, M. W. J. M. FICTION AND TRUTH ABOUT THE 'DECADE OF DEVELOPMENT.' Leiden, Netherlands: Sijthoff, 1966. 151 p.

   General assessment of the Development Decade with emphasis on the nature of obligations undertaken by the developed world.

6. Coordination

1164. Hoffman, Michael L. AID COORDINATION. Washington, D.C.: International Bank for Reconstruction and Development, 1966. 28 p.

    An overview of the problems of coordination and an assessment of achievements.

1165. Esman, Milton J., and Cheever, Daniel S. THE COMMON AID EFFORT: THE DEVELOPMENT ASSISTANCE ACTIVITIES OF THE ORGANIZATION FOR ECONOMIC CO-OPERATION AND DEVELOPMENT. Columbus, Ohio: Ohio State University Press, 1967. 435 p.

    An analysis of the activities in the Development Assistance Committee (DAC) leading towards more coordinated giving. Delineates the strategic elements in international politics that argue against a common aid effort to developing areas. Analyzes multifarious complexities encountered when several national and international agencies conduct uncoordinated aid programs.

1166. Rubin, Seymour J. THE CONSCIENCE OF THE RICH NATIONS: THE DEVELOPMENT ASSISTANCE COMMITTEE AND THE COMMON AID EFFORT. New York: Harper and Row, 1966. 175 p. (For the Council on Foreign Relations.)

    A clearly organized and lucidly written review of the doctrines and procedures of the DAC showing how involvement has been a learning experience for many of the participants. Stresses coordination activities.

1167. White, John. PLEDGED TO DEVELOPMENT: A STUDY OF INTERNATIONAL CONSORTIA AND THE STRATEGY OF AID. London: Overseas Development Institute, 1967. 235 p.

    A systematic analysis of the usefulness of consortia in the development process. Makes use of case studies.

7. Case Studies

1168. Schaaf, C. Hart, and Fifield, Russell H. THE LOWER MAKING: CHALLENGE TO COOPERATION IN SOUTHEAST ASIA. Princeton, N.J.: Van Nostrand, 1963. 136 p.

    Description of the development of the Lower Mekong involving many national and international agencies and the techniques for coordination and cooperation which have been devised.

1169. Wightman, David. TOWARD ECONOMIC COOPERATION IN ASIA: THE UNITED NATIONS ECONOMIC COMMISSION FOR ASIA AND THE FAR EAST. New Haven, Conn.: Yale University Press, 1963. 400 p.

> A case study of one of the commissions to show the extent to which it has been able to encourage cooperative development endeavors and to coordinate external donors.

8. Technical Cooperation

1170. Domergue, Maurice. TECHNICAL ASSISTANCE: THEORY, PRACTICE AND POLICIES. New York: Praeger, 1968. 196 p.

> A practical guide based on the experiences of an official of the Organization for Economic Cooperation and Development.

1171. Evans, George. UNITED NATION'S MUTUAL AID: AN INTRODUCTION TO THE UNITED NATIONS PROGRAMME OF TECHNICAL AND ECONOMIC ASSISTANCE. London: United Nations Association, 1951. 56 p.

> A good popular introduction to the work of the UN and its organization and policies in the field of technical assistance.

1172. Sufrin, Sidney C. TECHNICAL ASSISTANCE: THEORY AND GUIDE LINES. Syracuse, N.Y.: Syracuse University Press, 1966. 160 p.

> An analysis of a selection of projects and their execution.

1173. Tickner, Fred. TECHNICAL COOPERATION. New York: Praeger, 1966. 206 p.

> A description of the development of technical cooperation by the UN, specialized agencies, and cooperative arrangements such as the Columbo Plan. The author carefully analyzes typical projects and their problems.

1174. United Nations. Department of Public Information. TECHNICAL ASSISTANCE FOR ECONOMIC DEVELOPMENT. Washington, D.C., 1948. 106 p.

> A comprehensive view of the beginnings of technical assistance, showing the types and varieties of projects undertaken and the machinery set up.

1175. Von Goeckingk, Johanna. UNITED NATIONS TECHNICAL ASSISTANCE BOARD: A CASE STUDY IN INTERNATIONAL ADMINISTRATION. New York: Woodrow Wilson Foundation, 1955. 40 p. Pamphlet.

A brief account of the composition, functions, and activities of the board.

1176. Teaf, Howard M., Jr., and Franck, Peter G., eds. HANDS ACROSS FRONTIERS: CASE STUDIES IN TECHNICAL COOPERATION. Ithaca, N.Y.: Cornell University Press, 1955. 579 p.

Case studies showing the development of projects, their execution, and an evaluation of their effects on the development of the country.

1177. Alexander, Yonah. INTERNATIONAL TECHNICAL ASSISTANCE EXPERTS: A CASE STUDY OF U.N. EXPERIENCE. New York: Praeger, 1966. 233 p.

A study of the selection, training, and effectiveness of experts sent into the field by the UN.

1178. Sharp, Walter R. INTERNATIONAL TECHNICAL ASSISTANCE. Chicago, Ill.: Public Administration Service, 1952. 146 p.

A survey of the programs set up under Point Four and those of the UN. Looks at administrative difficulties encountered in the early years and at the tangled network of activities which soon emerged.

1179. Espy, W. R. BOLD NEW PROGRAM. New York: Funk and Wagnalls, 1950. 273 p.

1180. Shippen, Katherine Binney. THE POOL OF KNOWLEDGE: HOW THE UNITED NATIONS SHARE THEIR SKILLS. 2nd ed. New York: Harper, 1965. 113 p.

Primarily a study of the exchange of technical ideas through the UN Technical Assistance Program. Uses many examples. For popular consumption.

9. Fighting Hunger: Food and Agriculture Organization (FAO)

(See also 82, 83, 154, 1307.)

1181. Hambidge, Gove. THE STORY OF FAO. Princeton, N.J.: Van Nostrand, 1955. 303 p.

The Director of Information of FAO gives a vivid and interesting account of the purposes and objectives of the organization and outlines the various projects undertaken.

Promoting Economic Cooperation and Welfare

1182. Yates, P. Lamartine. SO BOLD AN AIM: TEN YEARS OF INTERNATIONAL CO-OPERATION TOWARD FREEDOM FROM WANT. Rome, Italy: Food and Agriculture Organization, 1955. 174 p.

   Examines the ideas and events which brought about the creation of the FAO. Describes policies and projects.

1183. Harrar, Jocob G., ed. STRATEGY TOWARD THE CONQUEST OF HUNGER: SELECTED PAPERS. New York: Rockefeller Foundation, 1967. 321 p.

   Account of national and international projects and programs with emphasis on the role of the FAO.

1184. Schultz, Theodore W., ed. FOOD FOR THE WORLD. Chicago, Ill.: University of Chicago Press, 1945. 353 p.

1185. United States Department of State. FOOD AND AGRICULTURE ORGANIZATION OF THE UNITED NATIONS. Department of State Publication 2826; United States-United Nations Report Series 16. Washington, D.C.: Government Printing Office, 1947. 26 p.

   Brief description of the organization and the role of the United States in its development and programs.

1186. Stanley, Robert G. FOOD FOR PEACE. New York: Gorden, 1973. 368 p.

1187. Griffin, Keith. THE POLITICAL ECONOMY OF AGRARIAN CHANGE: AN ESSAY ON THE GREEN REVOLUTION. Cambridge, Mass.: Harvard University Press, 1974. 264 p.

   Focuses on agrarian change in Asia and Latin America and the role FAO has had in these developments.

C. THE WORLD BANK GROUP

(See Chapter 11.B.3 and 285, 1082, 1083, 1086, 1088, 1092, 1093.)

1188. Reid, Escott. STRENGTHENING THE WORLD BANK. Chicago, Ill.: Adlai Stevenson Institute, 1973. 289 p.

   Outlines many recommendations including decentralization, more money for poor countries, better ways of attacking unemployment and poverty, and a stronger voice and vote in the UN for the developing countries.

1189. Mason, Edward S., and Asher, Robert E. THE WORLD BANK SINCE BRETTON WOODS. Washington, D.C.: Brookings, 1973. 550 p.

   A history of the World Bank and IFC, IDA, and the International Centre for Settlement of Investment Disputes. Shows their origins, institutional evolution, and functions. Also a major repository of information on the problems and progress of some ninety less developed member countries.

1190. King, John [Kerry]. ECONOMIC DEVELOPMENT PROJECTS AND THEIR APPRAISAL: CASES AND PRINCIPLES FROM THE EXPERIENCE OF THE WORLD BANK. Baltimore, Md.: The Johns Hopkins University Press, 1967. 571 p.

1191. Ordoobadi, Abbas. THE LOAN POLICY OF THE WORLD BANK GROUP: IBRD, IFC AND IDA. New York: Praeger, 1966. 200 p.

An analysis of the countries and projects to which loans have been made showing the criteria used by the Bank and its affiliates.

1192. Reid, Escott. THE FUTURE OF THE WORLD BANK: AN ESSAY. Washington, D.C.: International Bank for Reconstruction and Development, 1965. 71 p.

An analysis of the changing policies and role of the Bank.

1193. Morris, James. THE WORLD BANK: A PROSPECT. London: Faber and Faber, 1953. 195 p.

A layman's look at the Bank. The author vividly describes its history, function, and policies.

1194. International Bank for Reconstruction and Development. THE INTERNATIONAL BANK FOR RECONSTRUCTION AND DEVELOPMENT, 1946-1953. Baltimore, Md.: The Johns Hopkins University Press, 1954. 273 p.

Based primarily on the Bank's records and publications, the book assesses the Bank's activities and policies during its first years.

1195. Cairncross, Alexander K. THE INTERNATIONAL BANK FOR RECONSTRUCTION AND DEVELOPMENT. Essays on International Finance, no. 33. Princeton, N.J.: Princeton University, Department of Economics and Sociology, International Finance Section, 1959. 36 p. Pamphlet.

Brief explanation of the functions and role of the Bank and description of its lending policies.

1196. Broches, Aron. "International Legal Aspects of the Operations of the World Bank." Tome 98, vol. 3 in RECUEIL DES COURSE, ACADEMIE DE DROIT INTERNATIONAL, pp. 297-409. Hague, Netherlands:

Academie de droit international, 1959.

1197. International Bank for Reconstruction and Development. POLICIES AND OPERATIONS OF THE WORLD BANK, IFC AND IDA. Washington, D.C., 1963. 113 p.

1198. Morris, James. THE ROAD TO HUDDERSFIELD: A JOURNEY TO FIVE CONTINENTS. New York: Pantheon, 1963. 235 p.

1199. Heilbroner, Robert L. THIS GROWING WORLD: ECONOMIC DEVELOPMENT AND THE WORLD BANK GROUP. 2nd ed. New York: Public Affairs Committee, 1966. 20 p.

1200. Baker, James C. THE INTERNATIONAL FINANCE CORPORATION: ORIGIN, OPERATIONS AND EVALUATION. New York: Praeger, 1968. 294 p.

> A good account of the functioning and policies of the IFC and its relations with the other international organizations involved in lending.

1201. Matecki, Bronislaw Eugene. ESTABLISHMENT OF THE INTERNATIONAL FINANCE CORPORATION AND UNITED STATES POLICY. New York: Praeger, 1957. 194 p.

> A case study relating the policy of the Bank and the national policy of the United States. Indicates what influences have worked on the United States and how Bank officials have been able to modify U.S. positions.

1202. Weaver, James H. THE INTERNATIONAL DEVELOPMENT ASSOCIATION: A NEW APPROACH TO FOREIGN AID. New York: Praeger, 1965. 300 p.

> A history of the IDA with an examination of three major issues: soft loans, local currency, and bilateral versus multilateral aid. Good account of the practices of the association.

1203. International Bank for Reconstruction and Development. THE WORLD BANK GROUP IN ASIA. Washington, D.C., 1963. 90 p.

> An account of the World Bank and its affiliates which discusses in detail their efforts since 1950 to promote economic development in Asia. Gives the number and purposes of the loans made and describes projects.

Chapter 12
PROMOTING WORLD WELFARE

Chapter 12
PROMOTING WORLD WELFARE

A. SOCIAL WELFARE AND DEVELOPMENT

(See also Chapter 11.B.8 and 100, 1107, 1113-15, 1119-1121, 1125, 1127, 1130, 1134, 1138, 1149, 1160, 1164.)

1204. Asher, Robert E., et al. THE UNITED NATIONS AND THE PROMOTION OF THE GENERAL WELFARE. Washington, D.C.: Brookings, 1957. 1216 p. Parts II, III, and IV have been published separately as monographs: Asher, Robert E., et al. THE UNITED NATIONS AND ECONOMIC AND SOCIAL CO-OPERATION, 1957; Green, J. F. THE UNITED NATIONS AND HUMAN RIGHTS, 1956; Sayd, E. J. THE UNITED NATIONS AND DEPENDENT PEOPLE, 1956.

    A massive and comprehensive presentation of the major activities of the UN in the fields of social and economic cooperation and development, human rights, and concern for dependent peoples. The authors assess the roles, functions, successes, and failures of the UN and specialized agencies.

1205. Beckel, Graham. WORKSHOPS FOR THE WORLD: THE SPECIALIZED AGENCIES OF THE UNITED NATIONS. 2nd ed. New York: Abelard-Schuman, 1964. 285 p.

    A chapter is devoted to each agency and facts are given about the origin, activities, membership, and organization of the agency. Describes the formal and informal procedures for coordination and cooperation among the agencies and between agencies and the UN.

1206. Jones, Joseph Marion. THE UNITED NATIONS AT WORK: DEVELOPING LAND, FORESTS, OCEANS...AND PEOPLE. London: Pergamon, 1965. 240 p.

    A descriptive account of the work of the UN and specialized agencies in nonpolitical areas.

1207. Lewis, S. TOWARDS INTERNATIONAL COOPERATION. New York: Pergamon, 1966. 327 p.

    A textbook dealing with the areas of change and problems in international cooperation that must be resolved in order to unite diverse peoples. History of international cooperation and assessment of the possibilities for world government.

1208. Taylor, Paul. INTERNATIONAL CO-OPERATION TODAY: THE EUROPEAN AND UNIVERSAL PATTERN. London: Elek Books, 1971. 165 p.

    Concerned with the functional integration of states; giving ideas, concepts, and models.

1209. Lally, Dorothy. EXPANDING FRONTIERS IN SOCIAL WELFARE, 1935-1960: TWENTY-FIVE YEARS INTERNATIONAL COOPERATION--SOCIAL SECURITY. Washington, D.C.: United States Department of Health, Education and Welfare, Social Science Administration, 1960. 20 p. Pamphlet.

    Brief overview of the beginnings and development of international cooperation in the area of social security.

1210. Carnegie Endowment for International Peace. COORDINATION OF ECONOMIC AND SOCIAL ACTIVITIES. UN Studies, no. 2. New York, 1948. 109 p.

    An early outline of the institutional arrangements set up to handle the always difficult problems of coordination.

1211. League of Nations. Secretariat. Information Section. SOCIAL AND HUMAN WORK. Geneva, Switzerland, 1924. 47 p.

1212. Buchanan, G. S. INTERNATIONAL COOPERATION IN PUBLIC HEALTH: ITS ACHIEVEMENTS AND PROSPECTS. London: Lancet, 1934. 60 p.

B. SAFEGUARDING THE WORLD'S HEALTH: THE WORLD HEALTH ORGANIZATION (WHO)

1. General

(See also 55, 75, 90, 91, 161, 286, 287, 630, 786.)

1213. Berkov, Robert. THE WORLD HEALTH ORGANIZATION: A STUDY IN DECENTRALIZED INTERNATIONAL ADMINISTRATION. Paris,

France: Minard, 1957. 173 p.

> A detailed account of the administrative structure and functions of the organization with emphasis on the problems of decentralization versus centralization. Studies the history of regionalism in WHO.

1214. World Health Organization. THE FIRST TEN YEARS OF THE WORLD HEALTH ORGANIZATION. Geneva, Switzerland, 1958. 548 p.

> A clear, straightforward account of the structure, functions, and activities of the organization.

1215. Calder, Ritchie. TEN STEPS FORWARD: WORLD HEALTH 1948-58. Geneva, Switzerland: World Health Organization, 1958. 68 p. Illustrated pamphlet.

> An illustrated description of the first decade drawing examples from field programs.

1216. Carnegie Endowment for International Peace. "World Health Organization." INTERNATIONAL CONCILIATION 437(March 1948): 111-45.

> Good account of the administration of programs during the first years.

1217. Hobson, W. WORLD HEALTH AND HISTORY. Bristol, England: John Wright, 1963. 252 p.

> A history of international cooperation in the health field including the development of international agreements and organizations.

1218. Brockington, Colin F. WORLD HEALTH. Harmondsworth, England: Penguin, 1958. 405 p.

1219. Grant, Madeleine P. BIOLOGY AND WORLD HEALTH. New York: Abelard-Schuman, 1955. 202 p.

1220. Morgan, Murray. DOCTORS TO THE WORLD. New York: Viking, 1958. 286 p.

1221. Goodman, N. M. INTERNATIONAL HEALTH ORGANIZATIONS AND THEIR WORK. London: Churchill, 1952. 327 p.

2. A World System to Control Narcotics

1222. Renborg, Bertil A. INTERNATIONAL DRUG CONTROL: A STUDY OF INTERNATIONAL ORGANIZATION BY AND THROUGH THE LEAGUE OF NATIONS. Washington, D.C.: Carnegie Endowment, 1943. 316 p.

　　A former Chief of the Drug Control Service of the Secretariat of the League gives a complete, succinct account of the system as it gradually developed under the auspices of the League. A detailed description of the various aspects of the system as well as its work. Shows possible application of the principles to other problems requiring international regulation.

1223. Bailey, Stanley H. THE ANTI-DRUG CAMPAIGN. London: King, 1936. 263 p.

　　A history of international endeavors from 1902 with details of the League's system, organization, and operations.

1224. Eisenlohn, Louise E. S. INTERNATIONAL NARCOTICS CONTROL. London: Allen & Unwin, 1934. 295 p.

1225. World Peace Foundation. THE INTERNATIONAL OPIUM CONFERENCE. Boston, Mass, 1925. 194 p.

C. INTERNATIONALIZING LABOR STANDARDS

(See also 71, 85-87, 155, 202, 630.)

1. The Evolution of a System: The League and Before

(See also 1252, 1253.)

1226. Wilson, Francis Graham. LABOR IN THE LEAGUE SYSTEM. Stanford, Calif.: Stanford University Press, 1934. 384 p.

　　A scholarly work based on extended research and observation. Studies movement from the beginning of international labor activity to the establishment of the ILO. Analyzes structure, working, and accomplishments of the organization.

1227. Alcock. A. E. HISTORY OF THE INTERNATIONAL LABOR ORGANIZATION. New York: Octagon, 1971. 395 p.

　　A study of the origins and development of the ILO from 1919. Analysis of the importance of this development to general international organizations, showing the evolution of the system of standard-setting for sovereign states and enforcement procedures. Goes into the problems arising out of the cold war for the organization.

1228. Follows, John W. ANTECEDENTS OF THE INTERNATIONAL LABOUR ORGANIZATION. London: Oxford University Press, 1951. 244 p.

> A study of the origins of the idea and structure of the organization going back to early international labor conventions. Stops before the establishment of the ILO.

1229. Barnes, George N. HISTORY OF THE INTERNATIONAL LABOUR OFFICE. London: Williams and Norgate, 1926. 122 p.

1230. Beddington-Behrens, Edward. THE INTERNATIONAL LABOUR OFFICE: A SURVEY OF CERTAIN PROBLEMS OF INTERNATIONAL ADMINISTRATION. London: Parsons, 1924. 220 p.

1231. International Labour Office. ILO: THE FIRST DECADE. London: Allen & Unwin, 1931. 382 p.

1232. Johnston, George A. INTERNATIONAL SOCIAL PROGRESS: THE WORK OF THE INTERNATIONAL LABOUR ORGANIZATION OF THE LEAGUE OF NATIONS. New York: Macmillan, 1924. 263 p.

1233. Lowe, Boutelle Ellsworth. THE INTERNATIONAL PROTECTION OF LABOR: INTERNATIONAL LABOR ORGANIZATION, HISTORY AND LAW. New York: Macmillan, 1935. 594 p.

> A good, early account of the work of the organization, its structure and procedures. Careful analysis of the legal character of the standards it has developed and adopted.

1234. National Industrial Conference Board. THE WORK OF THE INTERNATIONAL LABOR ORGANIZATION. New York, 1928. 197 p.

1235. Perigord, Paul. THE INTERNATIONAL LABOR ORGANIZATION: A STUDY OF LABOR AND CAPITAL IN COOPERATION. New York: Appleton, 1926. 339 p.

1236. Solano, E. John, ed. LABOUR AS AN INTERNATIONAL PROBLEM: A SERIES OF ESSAYS COMPRISING A SHORT HISTORY OF THE INTERNATIONAL LABOUR ORGANIZATION AND A REVIEW OF GENERAL INDUSTRIAL PROBLEMS. London: Macmillan, 1920. 385 p.

2. The International Labor Organization (ILO) Today

(See also 786, 881, 1416, 1419, 1428.)

1237. International Labor Office. A NEW ERA: THE PHILADELPHIA CONFERENCE AND THE FUTURE OF THE I.L.O. Montreal, Canada, 1944. 145 p.

   Speeches of the delegates along with the final resolutions.

1238. Morse, David A. THE ORIGIN AND EVOLUTION OF THE I.L.O. AND ITS ROLE IN THE WORLD COMMUNITY. Ithaca, N.Y.: Cornell University, New York State School of Industrial Relations, 1969. 132 p.

   Three lectures by one of the Directors-General of the ILO giving the development and the changing nature of the organization. Shows how the ILO has responded to the rapidly changing world of the 50's and 60's. Projects future problems and suggests responses.

1239. Shotwell, James Thomas, ed. THE ORIGINS OF THE INTERNATIONAL LABOR ORGANIZATION. 2 vols. New York: Columbia University Press, 1934. 1133 p.

   The first volume covers the history of the development of international action on behalf of labor; the second is a collection of relevant documents.

1240. Landy, E[rnest]. A[dolf]. THE EFFECTIVENESS OF INTERNATIONAL SUPERVISION: THREE DECADES OF I.L.O. EXPERIENCE. Dobbs Ferry, N.Y.: Oceana, 1966. 281 p.

   A scholarly study of the supervisory machinery and activities of the organization by one with twenty years experience. Goes into both the formal (used only twice before 1967) and the less formal procedures. Shows that many states have changed their practices as a result of their exposure to the ILO. Indicates the relevance of the ILO method to other areas of international cooperation.

1241. Johnston, George A. THE INTERNATIONAL LABOUR ORGANIZATION: ITS WORK FOR SOCIAL AND ECONOMIC PROGRESS. London: Europa, 1970. 375 p.

   An excellent monograph on the history, structure, and activities of the organization. Shows the ILO trying to balance the socially desirable and economically possible. An analysis of the process of negotiation and discussion used to reach policies acceptable to labor, management, and government. Points up the importance of research and the collection of data. The author had long experience with the organization.

1242. Haas, Ernst B. BEYOND THE NATION-STATE: FUNCTIONALISM AND INTERNATIONAL ORGANIZATIONS. Stanford, Calif.: Stanford University Press, 1965. 485 p.

> The author poses the question as to how the normal aims and expectations of nations can be related to a process of growing international integration, and what kind of organization is necessary to maximize the process. Examines the ILO to show how functionalism works, indicating the shifts in policies and programs at various periods and the reasons for them.

1243. International Labor Organization. ILO AND THE UN: TWENTY-FIVE YEARS OF A PARTNERSHIP. Geneva, Switzerland, 1970. 54 p.

> A brief survey of the work of the organization showing changes in policies and emphasis over the years.

1244. Beguin, Bernard. "ILO and the Tripartite System." INTERNATIONAL CONCILIATION 523 (May 1959): 405-48.

> An excellent study of the origins, functioning, and problems of the tripartite system in the ILO.

1245. Price, John. THE INTERNATIONAL LABOUR MOVEMENT. New York: Oxford University Press, 1945. 273 p. (Issued under the auspices of the Royal Institute of International Affairs.)

> A history of the movement showing how it affected and was affected by the ILO.

3. Standard-Setting Internationally

1246. Jenks, C[larence]. Wilfred. THE INTERNATIONAL PROTECTION OF TRADE UNION FREEDOM. New York: Praeger, 1957. 592 p.

> Description of the development of international action for protecting freedom of association for trade unions, showing current law and practice governing arrangements for such protection. Analyzes the successes and limitations of the ILO procedures.

1247. _____. SOCIAL JUSTICE IN THE LAW OF NATIONS: THE I.L.O. IMPACT AFTER FIFTY YEARS. New York: Oxford University Press, 1970. 105 p. Paperbound. (For the Royal Institute of International Affairs.)

> An analysis of the unique structure and legislative procedures of the ILO with an assessment of the substantive achievements of the organization. Examines the pioneering experience of

the ILO in furthering social justice and in giving specific content to the general concept of social justice. Shows how the ILO has contributed to the development of world organizations in evolving international legislative procedures, international supervision, and compulsory jurisdiction.

1248. Dillon, Conley Hall. INTERNATIONAL LABOR CONVENTIONS. Chapel Hill, N.C.: University of North Carolina Press, 1942. 272 p.

   A scholarly study concentrating primarily on the interpretation and revision of conventions.

1249. Partan, Daniel G. THE DEVELOPMENT OF INTERNATIONAL LAW BY THE INTERNATIONAL LABOR ORGANIZATION. World Rule of Law Booklet Series, no. 37. Durham, N.C.: Duke University School of Law, Rule of Law Research Center, 1967. Reprint: Proceedings of the American Society of International Law. Vol. 59, 1965. Pp. 139-159.

   An examination of the legal character of the ILO code and conventions.

1250. Jenks, C[larence]. Wilfred. HUMAN RIGHTS AND INTERNATIONAL LABOUR STANDARDS. New York: Praeger, 1960. 175 p.

   An investigation of the contributions which the formulation of international labor standards by the ILO has made to the attainment of objectives in the Universal Declaration of Human Rights. The author examines the obligations and supervisory functions in a number of areas.

4. Development and the ILO

1251. Roberts, Richard S., Jr. ECONOMIC DEVELOPMENT, HUMAN SKILLS AND TECHNICAL ASSISTANCE: A STUDY OF I.L.O. IN THE FIELD OF PRODUCTIVITY AND MANAGEMENT DEVELOPMENT. Geneva, Switzerland: Droz, 1962. 157 p.

   An assessment of the effectiveness of ILO technical assistance projects, showing how they are selected and executed.

5. Albert Thomas: A Prototype

1252. Phelan, Edward Joseph. YES AND ALBERT THOMAS. London: Cresset, 1949. 186 p.

   A delightful account of the man, his work and the ILO. The author shows clearly how Albert Thomas exerted dynamic leadership in the operations of the organization and in reaching out to affect national policies.

1253. Schaper, B. W. ALBERT THOMAS. Assen, Netherlands: Van Gorcum, 1959. 394 p.

> A vivid picture of the early years of the ILO giving a good account of the political and social environment which was the background to the early evolution of the organization. Shows the effects on the organization of the development of socialist states.

6. Nations and the ILO

1254. Jenks, C[larence]. Wilfred. BRITAIN AND THE ILO. David Davies Memorial Lecture. London: David Davies Memorial Institute of International Studies, n.d. 30 p. Paperbound.

> Brief discussion of the role Britain has played in the evolution of the ILO administratively and substantively.

1255. Stewart, M. BRITAIN AND THE ILO: THE STORY OF FIFTY YEARS. London: Her Majesty's Stationery Office, 1969. 118 p.

> An analysis of the role of Britain in the creation of the ILO, the development of the International Labor Code, and the changes made after World War II.

1256. Tipton, John Bruce. PARTICIPATION OF THE UNITED STATES IN THE INTERNATIONAL LABOR ORGANIZATION. Urbana, Ill.: University of Illinois, Institute of Labor and Industrial Relations, 1959. 150 p.

> A good survey of U.S. participation in the organization, the problems of composing the delegations, and the difficulties resulting from the federal system.

1257. Windmuller, John P. AMERICAN LABOR AND THE INTERNATIONAL LABOR MOVEMENT, 1940-1953. Cornell International Industrial and Labor Reports, no. 2. Ithaca, N.Y.: Cornell University, Institute of International Industrial and Labor Relations, 1954. 259 p.

> A study of American labor and the ILO showing the interaction of the two.

1258. Fernbach, Alfred. SOVIET COEXISTENCE STRATEGY: A CASE STUDY OF EXPERIENCE IN THE INTERNATIONAL LABOR ORGANIZATION. Washington, D.C.: Public Affairs Press, 1960. 63 p.

1259. Shkunaev, V. G. THE INTERNATIONAL LABOR ORGANIZATION: PAST AND PRESENT. Moscow, USSR: International Relations Publishing House, 1969. 247 p.

> A former member of the Soviet Delegation to the ILO gives an historical survey of the development of the organization with emphasis on the role of the USSR.

1260. Hillery, Brian. IRELAND IN THE INTERNATIONAL LABOR ORGANIZATION. Dublin, Ireland: Department of Labor, 1969. 55 p.

1261. Kakkar, N. K. INDIA AND THE I.L.O.: THE STORY OF FIFTY YEARS. Delhi, India: Chand, 1970. 121 p.

> India's participation before her independence and in the early years of her nationhood is discussed.

1262. Bloss, Esther. LABOR LEGISLATION IN CZECHOSLOVAKIA WITH SPECIAL REFERENCE TO THE STANDARDS OF THE INTERNATIONAL LABOR ORGANIZATION. New York: AMS Press, 1968. 210 p.

> How a Communist state has worked out her relationship with the ILO and the extent to which her labor policies conform to international standards.

D. THE MINDS OF MEN: UNESCO'S MISSION

(See also 72, 88, 89, 158, 159, 630, 786.)

1263. Kolasa, Jan. INTERNATIONAL INTELLECTUAL COOPERATION: THE LEAGUE EXPERIENCE AND THE BEGINNINGS OF UNESCO. Warsaw, Poland: Polskiej Akademii Nauk, 1962. 208 p.

> A straightforward account of the efforts to bring intellectuals together and to create some sort of structure for cooperation.

1264. Ranasinghe, Alex. UNESCO'S CULTURAL MISSION. New York: Carlton, 1969. 160 p.

> A study of the origins, structure, aims, and achievements of the organization. The author examines attempts to formulate a philosophy. Shows how the organization has struggled to define its role in promoting education. Good analysis of the problems of participation of the American Catholics.

1265. Laves, Walter H. C., and Thomson, Charles A. UNESCO: PURPOSE, PROGRESS, PROSPECTS. Bloomington, Ind.: Indiana University Press, 1957. 492 p.

> A well-written, well-documented account of the founding, growth, and activities of UNESCO. Both authors were mem-

bers of the staff of the organization. Emphasizes the usefulness of the organization especially in promoting and lubricating contact and cooperation among learned societies. Critical of the negative U.S. attitude.

1265a. Sewell, James Patrick. UNESCO AND WORLD POLITICS. Princeton, N.J.: Princeton University Press, 1955. 376 p.

Using published and unpublished materials the author investigates the formation and evolution of UNESCO. Emphasis is placed on the role of political leaders.

1266. Besterman, Theodore A. UNESCO: PEACE IN THE MINDS OF MEN. New York: Praeger, 1951. 132 p.

A short survey by a senior officer in the Secretariat between 1946 and 1949 of the organization and its work, outlining aims and achievements. Shows the difficulties of resolving the problem of the philosophy for the organization and setting priorities for projects.

1267. Evans, Luther H. THE UNITED STATES AND UNESCO: A SUMMARY OF THE UNITED STATES DELEGATION MEETINGS OCTOBER-NOVEMBER, 1945. Dobbs Ferry, N.Y.: Oceana, 1971. 217 p.

A summary of the meetings which discussed the creation of the organization by an adviser to the delegation who subsequently became Director-General.

1268. Shuster, George N. UNESCO: ASSESSMENT AND PROMISE. New York: Harper and Row, 1963. 130 p. (For the Council on Foreign Relations.)

An objective and critical account of the organization by a former member of the Executive Board. Discusses purposes and achievements and the role of UNESCO in world affairs. Special attention is given to the implications for U.S. foreign policy.

1269. Thomas, Jean. U.N.E.S.C.O. Paris, France: Gallimard, 1962. 266 p.

The author served as Director of the Cultural Activities Department and Assistant Director-General. The account is objective and critical with emphasis on the field work.

1270. Tripp, Brenda M. H. "UNESCO in Perspective." INTERNATIONAL CONCILIATION 497 (March 1954): 323-83.

An account of the organization, its philosophical struggles, and work. Discusses the process of decision-making.

1271. Wilson, Howard E. "The Development of UNESCO." INTERNATIONAL CONCILIATION 431 (May 1947): 295-336.

Good discussion of the origins of the idea for the agency and

Promoting World Welfare

the constitutional provisions.

1272. Ascher, Charles S. PROGRAM-MAKING IN UNESCO 1946-51: A STUDY IN THE PROCESS OF INTERNATIONAL ADMINISTRATION. Chicago, Ill.: Chicago Public Administration Service, 1951. 90 p. Pamphlet. (For Public Administration Clearing House.)

    A lively and revealing account by an executive officer of UNESCO of the process of formulating and determining a plan of work for a conference. Shows the difficulties--often concerning trivia--which confront the conference planner.

1273. Pillsbury, Kent. UNESCO EDUCATION IN ACTION: A FIELD STUDY OF THE UNESCO DEPARTMENT OF EDUCATION. Columbus, Ohio: Ohio State University Press, 1963. 106 p.

1274. Sathyamurthy, T. V. THE POLITICS OF INTERNATIONAL COOPERATION: CONTRASTING CONCEPTIONS OF UNESCO. Geneva, Switzerland: Droz, 1964. 313 p.

    An attempt to describe and analyze the intellectual foundations of peace. A critique of the intellectual philosophies influencing the various programs. Discusses the influence of the Directors-General and of various influential delegates.

1275. Huxley, Julian S. UNESCO: ITS PURPOSE AND PHILOSOPHY. Washington, D.C.: Public Affairs Press, 1947. 62 p. Pamphlet.

    The first Director-General of the organization discusses the development of ideas, philosophy, programs, and difficulties experienced due to rival doctrines.

E. SCIENTISTS COOPERATE

(See also 92, 162, 1113.)

1276. Behrman, Daniel. WEB OF PROGRESS: UNESCO AT WORK IN SCIENCE AND TECHNOLOGY. Paris, France: United Nations Educational, Scientific and Cultural Organization, 1964. 106 p.

1. Restricting the Atom to Peaceful Purposes: The International Atomic Energy Agency (IAEA)

(See also 81, 630.)

1277. Caulfield, Daniel Webster. THE INTERNATIONAL ATOMIC ENERGY AGENCY AND ITS RELATIONSHIP TO THE UNITED STATES. Regensberg, Germany: Walhalla and Praetoria, 1959. 121 p.

    A discussion of the role the United States has taken in the creation and activity of the IAEA. Critical.

1278. McKnight, Allan D. ATOMIC SAFEGUARDS: A STUDY IN INTERNATIONAL VERIFICATION. New York: United Nations Institute for Training and Research, 1971. 323 p.

    A good discussion of the system evolved by the IAEA as a particular example of a system for international verification of treaty obligations. The author was Inspector-General of the agency from 1964-68. Goes into the political development of safeguards and internal workings of the Board of Governors. Discusses the administration of the safeguards.

1279. _____. NUCLEAR NON-PROLIFERATION: IAEA AND EURATOM. New York: Carnegie Endowment, 1970. 103 p.

    Good discussion of the work of the two agencies, showing their interrelationships and effectiveness in handling the problem.

1280. Szasz, Paul G. THE LAW AND PRACTICE OF THE INTERNATIONAL ATOMIC ENERGY AGENCY. Vienna, Austria: International Atomic Energy Agency, 1970. 1184 p.

    A massive text of the development, functions, and administration of the agency. Shows how the IAEA functions internally, also discusses its relations to other international organizations and to member states. The author spent eight years in the legal department of the agency. Gives exhaustive history and developmental background and a record of the agencies projects, the scope of its research, and its training activities.

1281. Hodgetts, J. E. ADMINISTERING THE ATOM FOR PEACE. International Political Science Association Series. New York: Atherton, 1964. 294 p.

    Descriptive account of the range of international efforts to confine the use of nuclear power to peaceful purposes.

1282. Kramish, Arnold. THE PEACEFUL ATOM IN FOREIGN POLICY. New York: Harper and Row, 1963. 287 p. (For the Council on Foreign Relations.)

    A study of the diplomacy and the actions of governments in

the endeavor to promote peaceful uses of the atom.

1283. Hydeman, Lee M., and Berman, William H. INTERNATIONAL CONTROL OF THE NUCLEAR MARITIME ACTIVITIES. Ann Arbor, Mich.: University of Michigan Law School, 1960. 384 p.

1284. Willrich, Mason, ed. INTERNATIONAL SAFEGUARDS AND NUCLEAR INDUSTRY. Baltimore, Md.: The Johns Hopkins University Press. 320 p. (For the American Society of International Law.)

> Experts--lawyers, scientists, and social scientists--examine the safeguards system developed by the IAEA to prevent disaster in the world. Contains chilling information and levelheaded, pragmatic analysis of where the greatest dangers are to be found.

1285. Brodie, B. THE OBSOLETE WEAPON: ATOMIC POWER AND WORLD ORDER. New York: Harcourt, 1946. 214 p.

> Focuses on the possible effects on international organizations of nuclear weapons and various types of international controls which should be instituted.

1286. International Atomic Energy Agency and the United Nations. PEACEFUL USES OF ATOMIC ENERGY, PROCEEDINGS OF THE FOURTH INTERNATIONAL CONFERENCE ON THE PEACEFUL USES OF ATOMIC ENERGY. 15 vols. Vienna, Austria, 1972. (Proceedings Series--ST/PUB/300.)

> Covers the papers of the conference and records of discussion. Indexed in fifteenth volume.

2. Ecological Crises: Cooperative Responses

1287. Kay, David A., and Skolnikoff, Eugene B., eds. WORLD ECO-CRISIS: INTERNATIONAL ORGANIZATIONS IN RESPONSE. Madison, Wis.: University of Wisconsin Press, 1972. 300 p.

> The publication in book form of the Spring 1972 INTERNATIONAL ORGANIZATION. A collection of essays surveying the ecological situation and responses from an organizational and policy perspective. Projections for the future.

1288. Commission to Study the Organization of Peace. THE UNITED NATIONS AND THE HUMAN ENVIRONMENT. 22nd Report. New York: Carnegie Endowment, 1972. 75 p.

> A lucid description of the situation with concrete suggestions for international cooperation and the expansion of the functions

of international organizations.

1289. Hargrove, John Lawrence, ed. LAW, INSTITUTIONS AND THE GLOBAL ENVIRONMENT. Dobbs Ferry, N.Y.: Oceana, 1972. 411 p.

> A collection of papers from a conference of legal advisers of international organizations and selected governments on the institutional and legal problems of the global environment with a summary of the discussions.

1290. Serwer, D. INTERNATIONAL COOPERATION FOR POLLUTION CONTROL. New York: United Nations Institute for Training and Research, 1972. 73 p. Pamphlet.

> A good account of the need for cooperation, showing the various ways pollution will affect people internationally. The author explains the types of control needed and the issues involved.

1291. Black, Cyril E., and Falk, Richard A., eds. THE FUTURE OF THE INTERNATIONAL LEGAL ORDER. The Structure of the International Environment, vol. 4. Princeton, N.J.: Princeton University, Center for International Studies, 1972.

> Seventeen lawyers and specialists in international affairs write on food distribution, population, ocean resources, and air and water pollution. Discusses the legal aspects of man in his environment and the international institutions, agencies, and movements that must be instituted to meet the changing needs of mankind.

1292. Utton, Albert E., and Henning, Daniel H., eds. ENVIRONMENTAL POLICY: CONCEPTS AND INTERNATIONAL IMPLICATIONS. Praeger Special Studies in International Economics and Development. New York: Praeger, 1973. 266 p.

> Discusses theory and application of domestic and international environmental policy and controls. Shows what international efforts have achieved some measure of success.

3. The International Geophysical Year

1293. Sullivan, Walter. ASSAULT ON THE UNKNOWN: THE INTERNATIONAL GEOPHYSICAL YEAR. New York: McGraw-Hill, 1961. 460 p.

> A comprehensive account of evolution, execution, and results.

1294. Ross, Frank Xavier. PARTNERS IN SCIENCE: THE STUDY OF THE INTERNATIONAL GEOPHYSICAL YEAR. New York: Lathrop, Lee and Shepard, 1961. 192 p.

4. Population and International Organizations

1295. Partan, Daniel G. POPULATION IN THE UNITED NATIONS SYSTEM: DEVELOPING THE LEGAL CAPACITY AND PROGRAMS OF UN AGENCIES. Leiden, Netherlands: Sijthoff, 1973. 240 p.

1296. Symonds, Richard, and Carder, Michael. THE UNITED NATIONS AND THE POPULATION QUESTION, 1945-70. London: Chatto and Windus, 1973. 236 p. (For the Sussex University Press.)
> Traces population debate throughout its stormy existence from early discussion at the League through the unsuccessful postwar attempts to involve UNESCO and the WHO. Analyzes factors in mid-sixties which led to involvement by UN agencies in action programs. Discusses how policies at UN agencies have evolved and what influences these policies have had on various national policies and actions.

1296a. United Nations Fund for Population Activities. THE UNITED NATIONS AND POPULATION: MAJOR RESOLUTIONS AND INSTRUMENTS. Dobbs Ferry, N.Y.: Oceana, 1974. 212 p.
> Brings together resolutions of last thirty years. Covers whole spectrum of problems confronting the individual from health, aging, housing, children, etc.

F. THE WORLD'S CHILDREN: AN INTERNATIONAL RESPONSIBILITY? UNITED NATIONS INTERNATIONAL CHILDREN'S EMERGENCY FUND (UNICEF)

1297. Keeny, Spurgeon Milton. HALF THE WORLD'S CHILDREN: A DIARY OF UNICEF AT WORK IN ASIA. New York: Association Press, 1957. 280 p.
> An informed report by the Director of the Asia Regional Office of UNICEF. General philosophy, programs, and projects are described with an evaluation of the impact of the organization within Asia.

1298. United Nations International Children's Emergency Fund. CHILDREN OF THE DEVELOPING COUNTRIES: A REPORT OF UNICEF. Cleveland, Ohio: World Publishing, 1963. 130 p.
> An assessment of the extent of the problem of children with a description of the action being undertaken by the organization to relieve this.

G. NONGOVERNMENTAL ORGANIZATIONS

(See also 351, 352, 1030-33, 1053, 1083, 1135, 1244, 1245.)

1299. White, Lyman Cromwell, and Zocca, Marie Ragonetti. INTERNATIONAL NON-GOVERNMENTAL ORGANIZATIONS: THEIR PURPOSE, METHODS AND ACCOMPLISHMENTS. New Brunswick, N.J.: Rutgers University Press, 1951. 336 p.

> The material for this book was gathered by visits to the headquarters of some 250 nongovernmental organizations. A survey, appraising and describing functions and accomplishments of the organizations from 1850-1950. Classified by twelve major fields of interest.

1300. Rodgers, Raymond Spencer. FACILITATION OF PROBLEMS OF INTERNATIONAL ASSOCIATION: THE LEGAL, FISCAL AND ADMINISTRATIVE FACILITIES OF INTERNATIONAL NON-GOVERNMENTAL ORGANIZATIONS. Documents for the Study of International Non-Governmental Relations, no. 9. Brussels, Belgium: Union of International Associations, 1960. 167 p.

> Concerned with practical and administrative problems and their resolution by various associations.

1301. Verniers, Louis. INTERNATIONAL COOPERATION AND YOU. Brussels, Belgium: Union of International Associations, 1962. 82 p.

> A brief survey and study of governmental and nongovernmental organizations by a nonspecialist.

1302. Lador-Lederer, J. J. INTERNATIONAL NON-GOVERNMENTAL ORGANIZATIONS AND ECONOMIC ENTITIES: A STUDY IN AUTONOMOUS ORGANIZATIONS AND "JUS GENTIUM." Dobbs Ferry, N.Y.: Oceana, 1962. 403 p.

> A study of nonstate organizations and their impact on international relations and law. Historical, political, legal, sociological, and economic aspects are considered.

1303. White, Lyman C[romwell]. THE STRUCTURE OF PRIVATE INTERNATIONAL ORGANIZATIONS. Philadelphia, Pa.: Ferguson, 1933. 326 p.

1304. Joyce, James Avery. RED CROSS INTERNATIONAL AND THE STRATEGY OF PEACE. Dobbs Ferry, N.Y.: Oceana, 1959. 270 p.

> A good account, goes back to the beginnings of the International Red Cross and shows how it has been able to promote conventions and provide services.

1305. Barton, Clara H. A STORY OF THE RED CROSS: GLIMPSES OF FIELD WORK. New York: Appleton, 1929. 207 p.

1306. Adams, Michael. VOLUNTARY SERVICE OVERSEAS: THE STORY OF THE FIRST TEN YEARS. London: Faber and Faber, 1968. 234 p.

> The history of the work done from 1958-68 by a young Englishman.

1307. Harrar, Jacob G. STRATEGY TOWARD THE CONQUEST OF HUNGER. New York: The Rockefeller Foundation, 1967. 321 p.

> The story of the efforts of the foundation to improve world food production. Includes the relations of the foundation to other organizations--private, public, international, and governmental.

1308. Pickard, Bertram. THE GREATER UNITED NATIONS: AN ESSAY CONCERNING THE PLACE AND SIGNIFICANCE OF INTERNATIONAL NON-GOVERNMENTAL ORGANIZATIONS. New York: Carnegie Endowment, 1956. 86 p. Paperbound.

1309. UNESCO. Social Science Clearing House. INTERNAIONAL ORGANIZATIONS IN THE SOCIAL SCIENCES: A SUMMARY DESCRIPTION OF THE STRUCTURE AND ACTIVITIES OF NON-GOVERNMENTAL ORGANIZATIONS IN CONSULTATIVE RELATIONSHIP WITH UNESCO AND SPECIALIZED AGENCIES IN THE SOCIAL SCIENCES. Rev. ed. Paris, France: United Nations Educational, Scientific and Cultural Organization, 1961. 145 p.

> Aims, activities, officers and committees, and record of conferences of eighteen selected bodies.

1310. Bock, Edwin A. REPRESENTATION OF NON-GOVERNMENTAL ORGANIZATIONS AT THE UNITED NATIONS. Chicago, Ill.: Public Administration Clearing House, 1955. 438 p.

> A study of the representation, participation, and effect of nongovernmental organizations.

1311. Myers, Denys F. NON-SOVEREIGN REPRESENTATION IN PUBLIC INTERNATIONAL ORGANS. Report presented to the second session of the World Congress of International Associations in Brussels, 1913. Brussels, Belgium: Union of International Associations, 1913. 63 p.

1312. Knott, James E. FREEDOM OF ASSOCIATION: A STUDY OF INTERNATIONAL NON-GOVERNMENTAL ORGANIZATION PROCESS OF EMERGING COUNTRIES. Brussels, Belgium: Union of International Associations, 1962. 93 p.

> Account of the kinds of work voluntary agencies are doing in developing areas and their relations with national governments and agencies and international governmental organizations.

1313. Hero, Alfred. VOLUNTARY ORGANIZATIONS IN WORLD AFFAIRS COMMUNICATION. Boston, Mass.: World Peace Foundation, 1960. 157 p.

1314. Harley, John E[ugene]. INTERNATIONAL UNDERSTANDING: AGENCIES EDUCATING FOR A NEW WORLD. Stanford, Calif.: Stanford University Press, 1931. 604 p.

1315. Feld, Werner J. NON-GOVERNMENTAL FORCES AND WORLD POLITICS: A STUDY OF BUSINESS, LABOR AND POLITICAL GROUPS. New York: Praeger, n.d. 306 p.

> An excellent survey of nongovernmental actors in the international arena, including world parties, guerrilla groups, student movements, the Vatican, and the Ford Foundation.

1316. Ridgeway, George Loveland. MERCHANTS OF PEACE: THE HISTORY OF THE INTERNATIONAL CHAMBER OF COMMERCE. Boston, Mass.: Little, Brown, 1959. 291 p.

> A study of the Chamber of Commerce with emphasis on the contributions made by industrial and commercial leaders to world peace.

1317. Kraus, Hertha. INTERNATIONAL RELIEF ACTION 1914-1943. Scottdale, Pa.: Herald, 1944. 256 p.

> Primarily a training book written to help those contemplating post-war relief work, the author uses a number of case studies of relief action.

1318. Best, Ethelwyn, and Pike, Bernard. INTERNATIONAL VOLUNTARY SERVICE FOR PEACE, 1920-46. London: Allen & Unwin, 1948. 163 p.

1319. Guenter, Hans, ed. TRANSNATIONAL INDUSTRIAL RELATIONS. London: Macmillan, n.d.

> A good analysis of the extent to which industrial and trade relations are pointed to transnational relationships.

1320. Rohn, Peter H. RELATIONS BETWEEN THE COUNCIL OF EUROPE AND INTERNATIONAL NON-GOVERNMENTAL ORGANIZATIONS. Document 6. Brussels, Belgium: Union of International Associations, 1957. 76 p.

> Survey and description of the activities of nongovernmental organizations and the Council of Europe.

Chapter 13
INTERNATIONAL ORGANIZATIONS AND PEOPLE

Chapter 13

INTERNATIONAL ORGANIZATIONS AND PEOPLE

A. INTERNATIONAL INVOLVEMENT IN THE PROCESS OF DECOLONIZATION

1. General Studies

(See also 106.)

1321. Chowdhuri, R. N. INTERNATIONAL MANDATES AND TRUSTEE SYSTEMS: A COMPARATIVE STUDY. The Hague, Netherlands: Nijhoff, 1955. 328 p.

> An analysis and comparison of the history, operation, and functioning of the two systems. Gives good examples of the problems facing the Trusteeship Council and the solutions proposed and implemented.

1322. Hall, H. Duncan. MANDATES, DEPENDENCIES AND TRUSTEESHIPS. New York: Carnegie Endowment, 1948. 429 p.

> A critical and analytical treatment of the problem of mandates and trusteeships, comparing the two. Examines the general characteristics, procedures, and powers of the various organs which have been involved and relates the general action on dependencies to power politics.

1323. Holcombe, Arthur N. DEPENDENT AREAS IN THE POST-WAR WORLD. Boston, Mass.: World Peace Foundation, 1941. 108 p.

2. The League Experience

a. THE MANDATE SYSTEM

1324. Umozurike, Umozurike Ojo. SELF-DETERMINATION IN INTERNATIONAL LAW. Hamden, Conn.: The Shoe String Press, Archon Books, 1972. 324 p.

Shows how the principle of self-determination developed during the period of the mandates as well as during the first years of the United Nations.

1325. Wright, Quincy. MANDATES UNDER THE LEAGUE OF NATIONS. Chicago, Ill.: University of Chicago Press, 1930. 642 p.

A careful and exhaustive study of the origins and development of the mandate system. Goes into the structure. Seeks to place the system within the framework of contemporary international law.

1326. Ankers, P. M. THE MANDATES SYSTEM: ORIGINS, PRINCIPLES, APPLICATION. Geneva, Switzerland: League of Nations, Secretariat, 1945. 120 p.

1327. Bentwick, Norman. THE MANDATE SYSTEM. London: Longmans, Green, 1930. 200 p.

1328. Macaulay, Neil. MANDATES: REASONS, RESULTS, REMEDIES. London: Methuen, 1937. 223 p.

A critical look at the mandate system suggesting that it be ended.

1329. Margalith, Aaron M. THE INTERNATIONAL MANDATES. Baltimore, Md.: The Johns Hopkins University Press, 1930. 251 p.

1330. Upthegrove, Campbell L. EMPIRE BY MANDATE: A HISTORY OF THE RELATIONS OF GREAT BRITAIN WITH THE PERMANENT MANDATES COMMISSION OF THE LEAGUE OF NATIONS. New York: Bookman, 1954. 240 p.

A sketch of the emergence of the mandate system and the establishment of the Permanent Mandate Commission. The author discusses the general problems affecting the mandate territories of Britain and Britain's role in the Commission.

b. INDIVIDUAL MANDATES EXAMINED

1331. Van Maanen-Helmer, Elizabeth. THE MANDATES SYSTEM IN RELATION TO AFRICA AND THE PACIFIC ISLANDS. London: P.S. King, 1929. 331 p.

1332. Logan, Rayford W. THE OPERATION OF THE MANDATES SYSTEM IN AFRICA, 1919-27. Washington, D.C.: Foundation Publications, 1942. 62 p.

1333. Hyamson, A. M. PALESTINE UNDER THE MANDATE 1920-1948. London: Methuen, 1950. 219 p.

International Organizations and People

The author, with a long career in the Palestine Mandate Administration, tells the story of thirty years of British stewardship of Palestine. Defends British policy and action.

1334. Stoyanovsky, J. THE MANDATE OF PALESTINE. New York: Longmans, Green, 1925. 275 p.

1335. Andrews, Fannie Fern. THE HOLY LAND UNDER MANDATE. 2 vols. Boston, Mass.: Houghton Mifflin Co., 1931.

1336. Longrigg, Stephan H. SYRIA AND LEBANON UNDER FRENCH MANDATE. London: Oxford University Press, 1958. 404 p.

1337. Yanaihara, Tadeo. PACIFIC ISLANDS UNDER JAPANESE MANDATE. New York: Institute of Pacific Relations, 1940. 312 p.

1338. Paulweis, Peter C. THE JAPANESE MANDATE ISLANDS. Bandung, Indonesia: Van Dorp, 1936. 157 p.

1339. Eggleston, Frederic. THE AUSTRALIAN MANDATE OF NEW GUINEA. Melbourne, Australia: Melbourne University Press, 1928. 149 p.

c. SPECIALLY ADMINISTERED AREAS

1340. Mason, John B. DANZIG DILEMMA: A STUDY OF PEACEMAKING BY COMPROMISE. London: Oxford University Press, 1946. 377 p.

1341. Russell, Frank M. THE INTERNATIONAL GOVERNMENT OF THE SAAR. Berkeley, Calif.: University of California Press, 1926. 249 p.

1342. Wambaugh, Sarah. THE SAAR PLEBISCITE WITH A COLLECTION OF OFFICIAL DOCUMENTS. Cambridge, Mass.: Harvard University Press, 1940. 487 p.

1343. Kaeckenbeeck, Georges. THE INTERNATIONAL EXPERIMENT OF UPPER SILESIA: A STUDY IN THE WORKING OF THE UPPER SILESIA SETTLEMENT, 1922-37. London: Oxford University Press, 1942. 867 p.

1344. Stuart, Graham H. THE INTERNATIONAL CITY OF TANGIER. 2nd ed. Stanford, Calif.: Stanford University Press, 1955. 285 p.

d. PLEBISCITES

1345. Wambaugh, Sarah. A MONOGRAPH ON PLEBISCITES WITH A COLLECTION OF DOCUMENTS AND A CHRONOLOGICAL LIST OF CASES OF CHANGE OF SOVEREIGNTY IN WHICH THE RIGHT OF SELF-DETERMINATION HAS BEEN RECOGNIZED. New York: Oxford University Press, 1929. 1088 p.

1346. _____. PLEBISCITES SINCE THE WAR: WITH A COLLECTION OF OFFICIAL DOCUMENTS. 2 vols. Washington, D.C.: Carnegie Endowment, 1933.

3. The UN and Dependent Peoples

(See also 756.)

a. THE TRUSTEESHIP SYSTEM

1347. Toussaint, Charmian Edward. THE TRUSTEESHIP SYSTEM OF THE UNITED NATIONS. London: Stevens, 1957. 302 p. (For the London Institute of World Affairs.)

> A careful and detailed analysis of the legal and institutional aspects of the system. Analyzes history, purposes, and actual functioning of the system. Describes administrative methods and supervisory machinery.

1348. Thullen, George. PROBLEMS OF THE TRUSTEESHIP SYSTEM: A STUDY OF POLITICAL BEHAVIOR IN THE UNITED NATIONS. Geneva, Switzerland: Droz, 1964. 217 p.

> The author is primarily concerned with showing the political climate after the war which affected the principles, organization, and structure of the system. Studies some special problems such as those of the Ewe, Togoland, and the Gold Coast.

1349. Murray, James N., Jr. THE UNITED NATIONS TRUSTEESHIP SYSTEM. Illinois Studies in the Social Sciences, vol. 40. Urbana, Ill.: University of Illinois Press, 1957. 290 p.

> A descriptive survey of the functions, operations, and growth of the system. The author tends to be preoccupied with procedural mechanics. Detailed account of international involvement in Somaliland.

1350. United Nations. Secretariat. Department of Public Information. THE INTERNATIONAL TRUSTEE SYSTEM AND THE TRUSTEESHIP COUNCIL. Reference Pamphlet, no. 3. Lake Success, N.Y., 1949. 60 p. (Sales no. 1949.I.24.)

> Brief description of the functions and organization of the system.

1351. Lakshminarayan, C. V. ANALYSIS OF THE PRINCIPLES AND SYSTEM OF INTERNATIONAL TRUSTEESHIP IN THE CHARTER. Geneva, Switzerland: Imprimeries Populaires, 1951. 205 p.

b. NON-SELF-GOVERNING TERRITORIES

1352. Von Albertini, Rudolf. DECOLONIZATION, THE ADMINISTRATION AND FUTURE OF THE COLONIES, 1919-1960. Garden City, N.Y.: Doubleday, 1971. 690 p.

> A comprehensive survey with analysis of the attitudes of European countries, especially Britain and France, towards colonies from 1919 to the beginning of 1970. Shows their responses to international action and supervision, and analyzes their participation in the international systems developed to promote the independence of colonial areas.

1353. Wainhouse, David W. REMNANTS OF EMPIRE: THE UNITED NATIONS AND THE END OF COLONIALISM. New York: Harper and Row, 1964. 156 p. (For the Council on Foreign Relations.)

> A close look at what remains of the process of decolonization surveying all the little places still under vestigial white authority. Pays particular attention to the role of the UN and the policy issues presented by these areas for U.S. foreign policy. The author has been an official of the State Department.

1354. El-Ayouty, Yassin. THE UNITED NATIONS AND DECOLONIZATION: THE ROLE OF AFRO-ASIA. The Hague, Netherlands: Nijhoff, 1971. 315 p.

> A detailed account of the long battle of Afro-Asians to change the UN system and get a more liberal interpretation of Article XI. Good account of the historical development of attitudes and outline of UN methods and procedures.

1355. Sady, Emil J. THE UNITED NATIONS AND DEPENDENT PEOPLE. Washington, D.C.: Brookings, 1956. 213 p.

> A competent analysis of Chapters XI, XII, and XIII of the

Charter. The account is fair to the aspirations of dependent peoples and cognizant of the difficulties of the administrating powers. Thoughtful suggestions for improving the system.

1356. Mezerik, A. G., ed. COLONIALISM AND THE UNITED NATIONS. New York: International Review Service, 1964. 105 p.

The work is concerned with the anti-colonialist provisions of the Charter and attempts to reconcile this with the fact that the UN during its early years seemed to favor the Great Powers.

c. THE UNITED NATIONS AND SELF-DETERMINATION

1357. Sureda, A. Rigo. THE EVOLUTION OF THE RIGHT OF SELF-DETERMINATION: A STUDY OF UNITED NATIONS PRACTICE. Leiden, Netherlands: Sijthoff, 1973. 397 p.

1358. Johnson, Harold S. SELF-DETERMINATION WITHIN THE COMMUNITY OF NATIONS. Leiden, Netherlands: Sijthoff, 1967. 232 p.

A well-researched, descriptive account of the use of plebescites in settling issues of self-determination. Goes back to the inter-war years and surveys early cases along with UN supervised ones.

1359. Shukri, M. A. THE CONCEPT OF SELF-DETERMINATION IN THE UNITED NATIONS. Damascus, Syria: Al Jadidah, 1965. 374 p.

A study of the development of the concept prior to, in, and since the Charter. Stresses the relation of self-determination to colonialism. Looks at the issue from economic, legal, and humanitarian angles.

4. Case Studies

(See 722, 735.)

a. CAMEROON

1360. Gardinier, David E. CAMEROON: UNITED NATIONS CHALLENGE TO FRENCH POLICY. New York: Oxford University Press, 1963. 142 p. (For the Institute of Race Relations.)

A study of the effects of the trusteeship system on the political relations between Cameroon and France. A penetrating analysis of the framework of UN supervision; sees the UN as an effective catalyst for change.

b. INDONESIA

1361. Taylor, Alastair. INDONESIAN INDEPENDENCE AND THE UNITED NATIONS. London: Stevens, 1960. 485 p.

> An excellent, detailed study of the role of the UN in the Indonesian struggle for independence. During the period covered, the author was an international civil servant with the Security Council's field machinery. Good historical review of the numerous attempts to achieve settlement and analysis of the complex interaction of postwar pressures, Asian opinion, and the UN agencies involved.

1362. Kahin, G. M. NATIONALISM AND REVOLUTION IN INDONESIA. Ithaca, N.Y.: Cornell University Press, 1970. 490 p.

> A comprehensive history of the area. Good account of UN intervention and the role the organization played in the eventual agreements reached.

1363. Henderson, William. PACIFIC SETTLEMENT OF DISPUTES: THE INDONESIAN QUESTION, 1946-49. New York: Woodrow Wilson Foundation, 1954. 89 p.

1364. Wehl, David. THE BIRTH OF INDONESIA. London: Allen & Unwin, 1949. 216 p.

1365. van der Kroef, Justus M. THE WEST NEW GUINEA DISPUTE. New York: Institute of Pacific Relations, 1958. 43 p.

c. ITALIAN COLONIES

1366. Pelt, Adrian. LIBYAN INDEPENDENCE AND THE UNITED NATIONS; A CASE OF PLANNED DECOLONIZATION. New Haven, Conn.: Yale University Press, 1970. 1044 p. (For the Carnegie Endowment for International Peace.)

> A comprehensive, scholarly, and well-documented presentation of the role of the UN between 1949 and 1951. Records the political, economic, and social problems inherent in state-building and the responses to these by the administering power. Goes into the long debates and protracted negotia-

tions which led to the agreement for the UN to take over. An excellent description of the complex machinery which was set up to implement the UN decision. The author was UN Commissioner in Libya.

1367. Finkelstein, Lawrence S. SOMALILAND UNDER ITALIAN ADMINISTRATION: A CASE STUDY IN UNITED NATIONS TRUSTEESHIP. New York: Woodrow Wilson Foundation, September 1955. 48 p. Pamphlet.

   A brief study of the effects of UN supervision on the administration of the area.

1368. Karp, Mark. THE ECONOMICS OF TRUSTEESHIP IN SOMALIA. Boston, Mass.: Boston University Press, 1960. 199 p.

   A discussion, with emphasis on economic questions and policies, of the administration of Somalia.

1369. Rivlin, Benjamin. UNITED NATIONS AND ITALIAN COLONIES. New York: Carnegie Endowment, 1950. 114 p.

   A guide through the debates and discussions in the UN on the administration and disposition of the former Italian colonies.

1370. Becker, George H. THE DISPOSITION OF ITALIAN COLONIES, 1941-51. Annemasse, France: Granchamp, 1952. 270 p.

d. NEW GUINEA

(See also 736, 737.)

1371. Bettison, D. G., et al. THE INDEPENDENCE OF PAPUA-NEW GUINEA: WHAT ARE THE PREREQUISITES? London: Angus and Robertson, 1963. 78 p. (For the Public Lectures Committee of the Australian University.)

   Lectures concerned with the level of development in the territory and how to prepare the peoples for independence.

1372. Mair, Lucy P. AUSTRALIA AND NEW GUINEA. London: Christophers, 1949. 238 p.

e. PORTUGUESE TERRITORIES

1373. Nagueira, Franco. THE UNITED NATIONS AND PORTUGAL: A

STUDY OF ANTI-COLONIALIAM. London: Sedgwick and Jackson, 1963. 188 p.

> A lucid exposition and defense of Portugal's attitude toward UN concern with her African territories by a leading Portuguese statesman.

1374. Blair, Patricia W. "Portuguese Territories and the United Nations." INTERNATIONAL CONCILIATION 545(1963): entire issue.

f. PACIFIC TRUSTS OF THE UNITED STATES

1375. Coulter, John Wesley. THE PACIFIC DEPENDENCIES OF THE UNITED STATES. New York: Macmillan, 1957. 388 p.

1376. Trumbell, Robert. PARADISE IN TRUST: A REPORT ON AMERICANS IN MICRONESIA, 1946-58. New York: Sloane, 1959. 204 p.

1377. McDonald, Alexander H., ed. TRUSTEESHIP IN THE PACIFIC. Sydney, Australia: Angus and Robertson, 1949. 181 p.

g. RHODESIA

1378. Marshall, C. B. CRISIS OVER RHODESIA: A SKEPTICAL VIEW. Baltimore, Md.: The Johns Hopkins University Press, 1967. 75 p.

> Brief outline of the problem of Rhodesia including the role and action of the UN.

h. SOUTH WEST AFRICA

1379. Slonim, S. SOUTH WEST AFRICA AND THE UNITED NATIONS: AN INTERNATIONAL MANDATE IN DISPUTE. Baltimore, Md.: The Johns Hopkins University Press, 1972. 352 p.

> The author traces the origins and developments in the UN dispute over the mandate. Describes South Africa's attempts to annex the area with UN approval. Examines international implications of racism, colonialism, and minority rule. Analyzes the ICJ decision of 1971. Meticulous regard for documentation.

1380. Dugard, John, ed. THE SOUTH WEST AFRICA/NAMIBIA DISPUTE: DOCUMENTS AND SCHOLARLY WRITINGS ON THE CONTROVERSY

BETWEEN SOUTH AFRICA AND THE UNITED NATIONS. Berkeley, Calif.: University of California Press, 1973. 604 p.

The evolution of the dispute is presented through contemporary documents. The primary focus is on the history of South West Africa and the judgments and advisory opinions of the International Court of Justice.

1381. Segal, Ronald, ed. SOUTH WEST AFRICA: TRAVESTY OF TRUST. London: Deutsch, 1967. 352 p.

An anthology of expert papers and findings of an international conference on South West Africa held in 1966. Studies cover the case for international action, the history of South Africa's trust, the situation in the territory, and the nature of South Africa's abuse of her responsibility. The papers are generally critical of the decision of the International Court of Justice.

1382. Carroll, Faye. SOUTH WEST AFRICA AND THE UNITED NATIONS. Lexington, Ky.: University of Kentucky Press, 1967. 130 p.

A good historical background of the situation. The author evaluates the effectiveness of UN action and considers the probable consequences of the dispute. Based mainly on official records and documents.

1383. Dale R. THE EVOLUTION OF SOUTH WEST AFRICA DISPUTE BEFORE THE UNITED NATIONS 1945-1950. Doctoral dissertation, Princeton University Press, 1962. 335 p.

The author studies the problem of authority--whether the UN has a right to supervise the administration of an emergent nation by its new government. Good analysis of the interaction between a nation-state and an international organization.

1384. Van Wyke, J. THE UNITED NATIONS, SOUTH WEST AFRICA AND THE LAW. Capetown, South Africa: University of Capetown Press, 1968. 30 p.

A defense of South Africa's position attempting to show the illegality of UN action.

i. TANGANYIKA

1385. Chidzero, B. T. G. TANGANYIKA AND INTERNATIONAL TRUSTEESHIP. New York: Oxford University Press, 1961. 296 p.

A descriptive analysis of the effects of the trusteeship system on developments in Tanganyika and her preparation for independence.

B. PROTECTING THE RIGHTS OF MINORITIES

1386. de Azcarate y Florez, Pablo. LEAGUE OF NATIONS AND NATIONAL MINORITIES: AN EXPERIMENT. Translated by Ellen E. Brooke. Washington, D.C.: Carnegie Endowment, 1945. 225 p.

   A study of the theory and practice of the League system. Examines the origin of the treaties, the development of procedures, and the manner in which the League exercised its duties. The author was head of the League's Minorities Section in the Secretariat.

1387. Macartney, C[arlile]. A[ylmer]. NATIONAL STATES AND NATIONAL MINORITIES. New York: Oxford University Press, 1934. 553 p.

   An analysis of the minority treaties and the procedures used before the League. Good on the actual workings of the system.

1388. Stone, Julius. INTERNATIONAL GUARANTEES OF MINORITY RIGHTS. New York: Oxford University Press, 1932. 288 p.

   A scholarly analysis of the legal aspects of the League system. Shows weaknesses and suggests possible remedies.

1389. Claude, Inis L., Jr. NATIONAL MINORITIES: AN INTERNATIONAL PROBLEM. Cambridge, Mass.: Harvard University Press, 1955. 260 p.

   A comprehensive and detailed analysis of the reasons for the failure of the League system. Surveys pre-World War I and the League experience and concludes that there is little hope for meaningful international protection.

1390. Mair, Lucy P. THE PROTECTION OF MINORITIES. London: Christophers, 1928. 244 p.

1391. Rovcek, Joseph S. THE WORKING OF THE MINORITIES SYSTEM UNDER THE LEAGUE OF NATIONS. Prague, Czechoslovakia: Orbis, 1929. 122 p.

1392. Modeen, Tore. INTERNATIONAL PROTECTION OF NATIONAL MINORITIES IN EUROPE. Abo, Finland: Abo Akademi, 1969. 182 p.

   A systematic survey primarily of UN efforts to assure the rights of minorities.

1393. Bogley, Tennent H. GENERAL PRINCIPLES AND PROBLEMS IN THE INTERNATIONAL PROTECTION OF MINORITIES. Geneva, Switzerland: Imprimeries Populaires, n.d. 229 p.

1394. Lador-Lederer, J. J. INTERNATIONAL GROUP PROTECTION: AIMS AND METHODS IN HUMAN RIGHTS. Leiden, Netherlands: Sijthoff, 1968. 481 p.

>   A comprehensive and well-documented analysis of the aims and methods used to protect groups. Surveys the legal norms which have been developed and the multinational organizations created to supervise arrangements.

1395. Werner, M. THE U.N. CONVENTION ON THE ELIMINATION OF ALL FORMS OF RACIAL DISCRIMINATION. New York: Humanities, 1971. 132 p.

>   An examination of the background and content of the convention showing the scope and significance of the provisions.

1396. Lerner, Natan. THE U.N. CONVENTION ON THE ELIMINATION OF ALL FORMS OF RACIAL DISCRIMINATION. Leiden, Netherlands: Sijthoff, 1970. 132 p.

>   Good exposition of the possible effects and legal obligations of the convention. Describes the development of the convention, showing the negotiations involved.

C. THE REFUGEE: AN INTERNATIONAL RESPONSIBILITY?

1397. Venant, Jacques. THE REFUGEE IN THE POST-WAR WORLD. London: Allen & Unwin, 1953. 843 p.

>   A comprehensive survey of the problem of refugees and an account of the developments of international organizations from the time of the League. Emphasis is on legal and administrative problems. Primarily concerned with European refugees.

1398. Stoessinger, John G. THE REFUGEE AND THE WORLD COMMUNITY. Minneapolis, Minn.: The University of Minnesota Press, 1956. 206 p.

>   An International Refugee Organization officer surveys the refugee problem of the twentieth century. The author evaluates the successes and failures of the various methods used by the world community to alleviate the problem. An analysis

of the role of international refugee agencies, describing their character and activities.

1399. Schectman, Joseph B. THE REFUGEE IN THE WORLD. New York: Barnes, 1963. 404 p.

> A comprehensive survey of the international attempts to resolve the refugee problem from 1945, including attempts in Asia, Africa, and Europe with an appendix devoted to the Cuban refugee. Goes into governmental, nongovernmental, and international organization activities.

1400. Steiner, H. A. THE U.N. AND REFUGEES: CHANGING CONCEPTS. New York: Carnegie Endowment, 1962. 64 p. Pamphlet.

> A brief study of the achievements and future of the UN High Commissioner for Refugees.

1401. Rees, Elfan. "Century of the Homeless Man." INTERNATIONAL CONCILIATION 515(November 1957): 193-254.

> An excellent account of the problems of the refugee and international efforts to resolve them.

1402. Collins, P. A MANDATE TO PROTECT AND ASSIST REFUGEES: TWENTY YEARS OF SERVICE IN THE CAUSE OF REFUGEES 1951-1971. Geneva, Switzerland: Office of the United Nations High Commissioner for Refugees, 1971. 135 p.

> A good survey of the organization and activities of the office.

1403. Chandler, Edgar H. S. THE HIGH TOWER OF REFUGE. New York: Praeger, 1962. 264 p.

> An account of the nature of the problem and the efforts which have been made to resolve it. Includes a consideration of the work of the major international refugee organizations active since World War II.

1404. Holborn, Louise W. THE INTERNATIONAL REFUGEE ORGANIZATION: A SPECIALIZED AGENCY OF THE UNITED NATIONS, ITS HISTORY AND WORK 1946-1952. London: Oxford University Press, 1956. 782 p. (Issued under the auspices of the Liquidation Board of the International Refugee Organization.)

> An official history which illuminates the numerous and difficult problems faced by the organization during its lifetime. Good description of the complexity of the machinery developed.

1405. Buehrig, Edward H. THE U.N. AND THE PALESTINIAN REFUGEES:

A STUDY IN NON-TERRITORIAL ADMINISTRATION. Bloomington, Ind.: Indiana University Press, 1971. 231 p.

A graphic description of the UN Relief and Works Administration, its political setting and problems. Examines the services performed, financing difficulties, and the importance of U.S. influence on the policies and operations of the agency. Good analysis of the problem of establishing the legal rights of the agency. Shows the conflicts with national and other agencies within the UN.

1406. Kennedy, Edgar S. MISSION TO KOREA. London: Verschoyle, 1952. 191 p.

Examines the immensity of the refugee problem and the efforts made to deal with it.

1407. Macartney, C[arlile]. A. REFUGEES: THE WORK OF THE LEAGUE. London: League of Nations Union, 1930. 127 p.

1408. Reynolds, Ernest E. NANSEN. London: Blis, 1932. 285 p.

Biography of the League High Commissioner.

D. PROTECTING INDIVIDUALS

(See also Chapter 12.C.3 and 104, 203, 204, 351, 1312.)

1. Human Rights and International Organizations

1409. Sohn, Louis B., and Buergenthal, Thomas. INTERNATIONAL PROTECTION OF HUMAN RIGHTS. Contemporary Legal Education Series. Indianapolis, Ind.: Bobbs-Merrill, 1973. 1402 p.

Covers the full sweep of human rights--historical and modern. Surveys League and UN activities. Uses writings of publicists, national and international judicial decisions, resolutions, debates and actions of international agencies, diplomatic correspondence, government pronouncements, treaties, and other agreements.

1410. _____. BASIC DOCUMENTS ON INTERNATIONAL PROTECTION OF HUMAN RIGHTS. Contemporary Legal Education Series. Indianapolis, Ind.: Bobbs-Merrill, 1973. 250 p.

Carries the texts of treaties, declarations, and protocols. Companion to INTERNATIONAL PROTECTION OF HUMAN

RIGHTS (see 1409).

1411. Eide, Asbjorn, and Schou, August, eds. INTERNATIONAL PROTECTION OF HUMAN RIGHTS. Nobel Symposium, no. 7. New York: Wiley, 1968. 300 p.

>Fourteen essays prepared under the auspices of the Norwegian Nobel Institute. Concerned primarily with problems and arrangements for implementation. Covers both world and regional organizations.

1412. Ganji, Manouchehr. INTERNATIONAL PROTECTION OF HUMAN RIGHTS. Geneva, Switzerland: Droz, 1962. 317 p.

>An accurate, factual, and useful reference book. Places current problems concerning enforcement in historical perspective. An interesting chapter on the evolution of international action on slavery.

1413. Gotlieb, Allan, ed. HUMAN RIGHTS, FEDERALISM AND MINORITIES. Toronto, Canada: Canadian Institute of International Affairs, 1970. 278 p.

>A good anthology stressing domestic factors which influence efforts to internationalize rights. Contributors are mainly Canadian.

1414. Cornell Law School. HUMAN RIGHTS: PROTECTION OF THE INDIVIDUAL UNDER INTERNATIONAL LAW. Proceedings of the Fifth Summer Conference on International Law, Cornell Law School, June 18-20, 1964. South Hackensack, N.J.: Rothman, 1970. 300 p.

>A collection of papers and discussions covering both substantive and procedural aspects of human rights.

1415. Lauterpacht, Hersch. INTERNATIONAL LAW AND HUMAN RIGHTS. New York: Praeger, 1950. 491 p.

>Especially concerned with the legal effects of the Charter provisions which the author puts in historical setting. Sets down changes he sees as necessary to make guarantees effective. The analysis is put into the framework of the author's own view of a future federated world.

1416. Luard, Evan, ed. THE INTERNATIONAL PROTECTION OF HUMAN RIGHTS. New York: Praeger, 1967. 384 p.

>Comprehensive survey from the League period down to 1967. Especially clear on the differences in the way the UN has handled the South African situation and general international rights. Includes sections on the European efforts and the ILO.

1417. Moskowitz, Moses. THE POLITICS AND DYNAMICS OF HUMAN RIGHTS. Dobbs Ferry, N.Y.: Oceana, 1968. 295 p.

   A study of the forces which shape the concept of human rights and survey of UN efforts to develop rights and guarantees. Author sees the collective ideas of the present as inimical to furthering individual rights and is, therefore, pessimistic about future developments.

1418. _____. HUMAN RIGHTS AND WORLD POLITICS. Dobbs Ferry, N.Y.: Oceana, 1958. 160 p.

   Shows the proceedings and actions of the UN directed toward the fulfillment of the Charter provisions dealing with the promotion of human rights. Particularily concerned with the inadequacies of the means of implementation.

1419. Schwelb, Egon. HUMAN RIGHTS AND THE INTERNATIONAL COMMUNITY. Chicago, Ill.: Quadrangle Books, 1964. 95 p.

   An examination of historical events leading to the UN Declaration of Human Rights. Examines the Declaration as a standard for the measurement of the international recognition of human rights. Discusses the penetration of the declaration into international law and its effect on national policy. Reviews UN resolutions regarding colonialism and various areas of international cooperation.

1420. Pollack, R. S. THE INDIVIDUAL'S RIGHTS AND INTERNATIONAL ORGANIZATION. Northampton, Mass.: Smith College Press, 1966. 122 p.

   Assesses the status of the individual in public international law by examining treaties, conventions, and covenants.

1421. Chakravarti, Raghubir. HUMAN RIGHTS AND THE UNITED NATIONS. Calcutta, India: Progressive Publishers, 1958. 234 p.

   A survey and analytical essay on the legal aspects of human rights showing the work of the UN in their development. A comprehensive account of the problems and difficulties involved in establishing any legal protection for individuals.

1422. Carey, John. UN PROTECTION OF CIVIL AND POLITICAL RIGHTS. Syracuse, N.Y.: Syracuse University Press, 1970. 214 p.

   A U.S. alternate on the Subcommission on the Protection of Minorities of the UN Human Rights Commission gives a concise, systematic, and realistic survey of the international means of protection of the individual. Describes the ways political and quasi-judicial instruments can or do work, or fail to work, and why. Concludes that investigation and publicity are more potent than coercion or adjudication.

1423. Green, James Frederick. THE UNITED NATIONS AND HUMAN RIGHTS. Washington, D.C.: Brookings, 1956. 171 p.

> The author was Deputy Director of the International Economic and Social Affairs section of the Department of State. Gives a good, factual survey of the efforts of the UN in the human rights area. Examines the impact of divergent ideologies and the political climate on the development of meaningful individual guarantees.

1424. del Russo, Alessandra Luini. INTERNATIONAL PROTECTION OF HUMAN RIGHTS. Washington, D.C.: Lerner Law Book, 1971. 372 p.

> Analyzes various global and regional arrangements. Primarily descriptive.

1425. Drost, Pieter N. HUMAN RIGHTS AS LEGAL RIGHTS. Leiden, Netherlands: Sijthoff, 1951. 272 p.

> A survey of international efforts since 1555 to internationalize rights and provide guarantees. Studies need for implementing machinery showing the inadequacies of existing means. The author was in the Division of Human Rights of the Secretariat.

1426. Eichelberger, Clark M., ed. THE UNITED NATIONS AND HUMAN RIGHTS. Dobbs Ferry, N.Y.: Oceana, 1968. 250 p. (For the Commission to Study the Organization of Peace.)

> Commission papers and discussion of major human rights issues with proposals for strengthening the system through the UN. Studies proposals for the creation of a High Commissioner. Includes considerations of such issues as computers and privacy, electronic devices, biochemistry, and eugenics.

1427. Holcombe, Arthur N. HUMAN RIGHTS IN THE MODERN WORLD. New York: New York University Press, 1948. 175 p.

> Five lectures rationalizing U.S. attitudes and positions inimical to the assumption of substantive international obligations.

1428. Haas, Ernst B. HUMAN RIGHTS AND INTERNATIONAL ACTION: THE CASE OF FREEDOM OF ASSOCIATION. Stanford, Calif.: Stanford University Press, 1970. 184 p.

> The author applies functional theory of incremental international unification to the workings of the International Labor

Office (ILO). He is concerned with the "transformation of values at the national level" and the responsiveness of states to reports of the ILO's Committee on Freedom of Association. Classifies states in terms of political structures and relates classification to a series of hypotheses about state behavior in this context as well as to statistical analyses of the types of reports produced by the ILO committee. His conclusion: defendants as a group have not improved their record in implementing adverse decision. This is a rigorous, empirical piece of research.

1429. Corbett, Percy E. THE INDIVIDUAL AND WORLD SOCIETY. Princeton, N.J.: Princeton University Press, 1953. 59 p. Paperbound.

A survey and analysis of the various types of attempts to guarantee individual rights.

1430. Kutner, Luis. THE HUMAN RIGHT TO INDIVIDUAL FREEDOM. Coral Gables, Fla.: University Of Miami Press, 1970. 249 p.

Showing man's need for freedom and the possibilities for its realization. A pragmatic analysis proposing specific changes in the law.

1431. Singh, Nagendra. HUMAN RIGHTS AND INTERNATIONAL COOPERATION. New Delhi, India: Chaud, 1969. 527 p.

1432. Clark, Roger Stenson. A UNITED NATIONS HIGH COMMISSIONER FOR HUMAN RIGHTS. The Hague, Netherlands: Nijhoff, 1972. 201 p.

An examination of the various proposals for a high commissioner and a review of comparable offices. Shows areas in which a high commissioner might be able to function, particularly in correcting the so-called "double-standard" whereby individual petitions from certain parts of the world receive careful attention while others do not. Outlines objections of opponents.

1433. Korey, William. "The Key to Human Rights Implementation." INTERNATIONAL CONCILIATION 570 (November 1968): 1-70.

A description of the abortive efforts to set up an international court of human rights as an international penal code. Examines the European experience.

1434. Lillich, Richard B., ed. HUMANITARIAN INTERVENTION AND THE UNITED NATIONS. Charlottesville, Va.: University Press of Virginia, Virginia Legal Studies and Procedural Aspects of International Law

Institute, 1973. 240 p.

First half consists of edited proceedings in which the participants consider the customary international law status of the doctrine of humane intervention, the impact of the UN Charter on the customary norms, and the present and prospective role of the UN in this area. Two overview essays make up the second half of the book. Concerned with the right of outsiders to interfere on behalf of peoples within a state.

1435. Van Dyke, Vernon. HUMAN RIGHTS, THE UNITED STATES AND WORLD COMMUNITY. New York: Oxford University Press, 1970. 292 p.

An incisive commentary on the range of rights subject to present international protective efforts. Discusses possibility of wider acceptance by the United States of international conventions.

2. Human Rights as Legal Rights: Documents and Commentaries

1436. Robinson, Nehemiah. HUMAN RIGHTS AND THE CHARTER. New York: Institute of Jewish Affairs, 1958. 163 p.

A scholarly analysis of the clauses in the Charter dealing with the rights of individuals and the competence of the organization to handle these.

1437. Robertson, A. H. HUMAN RIGHTS IN THE WORLD: BEING AN ACCOUNT OF THE UNITED NATIONS COVENANTS ON HUMAN RIGHTS, THE EUROPEAN CONVENTION, THE AMERICAN CONVENTION, THE PERMANENT ARAB COMMISSION, THE PROPOSED AFRICAN COMMISSION AND RECENT DEVELOPMENTS AFFECTING HUMANITARIAN LAW. Manchester, England: Manchester University Press, 1972. 280 p.

A comparison of regional systems with the UN system; special emphasis is placed on institutional arrangements.

1438. Van Asbeck, F. M., ed. THE UNIVERSAL DECLARATION OF HUMAN RIGHTS AND ITS PREDECESSORS (1679-1948). Leiden, Netherlands: Brill, 1949. 99 p.

Texts and some exposition of treaties, conventions, and covenants.

1439. Brownlie, Ian. BASIC DOCUMENTS ON HUMAN RIGHTS. Oxford, England: Clarendon, 1971. 543 p.

A collection of sixty basic documents, national and international, regional and world, from 1688-1969. Emphasis on lawmaking treaties and resolutions of the General Assembly. Good introductory notes.

1440. United Nations Educational, Scientific and Cultural Organization. HUMAN RIGHTS: COMMENTS AND INTERPRETATIONS. London: Wingate, 1949. 288 p.

An analysis of existing provisions for human rights including the effectiveness of procedures for implementation and guarantees.

3. The UN Tries to Intervene: South Africa

(See also 719, 908.)

1441. Lowenstein, Alan K. BRUTAL MANDATE. New York: Macmillan, 1962. 265 p.

A comprehensive analysis of South Africa's policies, of conditions within the area, and of the attempts of the UN to become more effectively involved.

1442. Taubenfeld, Howard J., and Taubenfeld, R. F. RACE, PEACE, LAW AND SOUTHERN AFRICA. Hammarskjold Forum Series. no. 10. Dobbs Ferry, N.Y.: Oceana, 1968. 128 p. (For the Association of the Bar of the City of New York.) Pamphlet.

Contains working paper, summary of discussions, and bibliography. Discussion of the underlying issues which the problems of Southern Africa raise for the international system.

Chapter 14
CREATING A NEW WORLD

Chapter 14

CREATING A NEW WORLD

Man, in his discouragement and frustration with the world he lives in, has always turned his thoughts and imagination to better worlds. Sometimes he seeks only to improve what exists, studying present organizations and arrangements, projecting ways to improve these. At other times he seeks to create an entirely new order. Institutionalizing patterns of relations through improving existing international organizations or creating new ones has figured in many of his proposals and plans. This chapter represents a selection of works in which international organizations play an important role in thinking about a changed world.

A. SHAPING POST-WAR WORLDS

1. World War I Proposals

(See also 892.)

1443. Bridgman, Raymond L. WORLD ORGANIZATION. Boston, Mass.: Ginn, 1905. 178 p.

1444. Moritzen, Julius. THE PEACE MOVEMENT IN AMERICA. New York: Putnam, 1912. 41 p.

1445. Faries, John C. THE RISE OF INTERNATIONALISM. New York: Gray, 1915. 207 p.

1446. Angell, Norman. AMERICA AND THE NEW WORLD STATE: A PLEA FOR AMERICAN LEADERSHIP IN INTERNATIONAL ORGANIZATION. New York: Putnam, 1915. 205 p.

1447. Bartlett, Ruhl J. THE LEAGUE TO ENFORCE PEACE. Chapel Hill, N.C.: University of North Carolina Press, 1944. 252 p.

1448. Brailsford, Henry N. A LEAGUE OF NATIONS. London: Headley, 1917. 332 p.

1449. Goldsmith, Robert. A LEAGUE TO ENFORCE PEACE. New York: Macmillan, 1917. 331 p.

1450. Hobson, J[ohn]. A. TOWARDS INTERNATIONAL GOVERNMENT. New York: Macmillan, 1915. 216 p.

1451. Lawrence, Thomas J. THE SOCIETY OF NATIONS: ITS PAST, PRESENT AND POSSIBLE FUTURE. New York: Oxford University Press, 1919. 194 p.

1452. Pollard, Albert F. THE LEAGUE OF NATIONS: AN HISTORICAL ARGUMENT. Oxford, England: Clarendon, 1918. 68 p.

2. World War II Proposals

1453. Hoover, Herbert E., and Gibson, Hugh. THE PROBLEMS OF LASTING PEACE. Garden City, N.Y.: Doubleday, Doran, 1942. 295 p.

1454. Johnsen, Julia E. RECONSTITUTING THE LEAGUE OF NATIONS. New York: Wilson, 1943. 304 p.

1455. _____. WORLD PEACE PLANS. New York: Wilson, 1943. 304 p.

1456. Lorwin, Lewis L. POSTWAR PLANS OF THE UNITED NATIONS. New York: Twentieth Century Fund, 1943. 307 p.

1457. Nearing, Scott. UNITED WORLD: THE ROAD TO INTERNATIONAL PEACE. New York: Island Press, 1945. 265 p.

1458. Peaslee, Amos J. A PERMANENT UNITED NATIONS. New York: Putnam, 1942. 146 p.

1459. Perry, Ralph B. ONE WORLD IN THE MAKING. New York: Wyn, 1945. 275 p.

1460. Ralston, Jackson H. QUEST FOR INTERNATIONAL ORDER. Washington, D.C.: Byrne, 1941. 205 p.

1461. Shotwell, James T. THE GREAT DECISION. New York: Macmillan, 1944. 268 p.

1462. Heyman, Hans. PLAN FOR A PERMANENT PEACE. New York: Harper, 1941. 315 p.

B. THE INEFFECTIVE LEAGUE: NEW APPROACHES

The inability of the League system to create the peace and security desired gave rise to proposals for improvements and changes.

(See also 521, 522.)

1463. Phillmore, Lord. SCHEMES FOR MAINTAINING GENERAL PEACE. London: His Majesty's Stationery Office, 1920. 71 p.

1464. Allen, Devere. THE FIGHT FOR PEACE. New York: Macmillan, 1930. 740 p.

1465. Curti, Merle Eugene. THE AMERICAN PEACE CRUSADE. Durham, N.C.: Duke University Press, 1929. 229 p.

1466. Newfang, Oscar. THE ROAD TO WORLD PEACE: A FEDERATION OF NATIONS. New York: Putnam, 1924. 372 p.

1467. Scott, James Brown, ed. JAMES MADISON'S NOTES OF DEBATES IN THE FEDERAL CONVENTION OF 1787 AND THEIR RELATION TO A MORE PERFECT SOCIETY OF NATIONS. New York: Oxford University Press, 1918. 149 p.

1468. Streit, Clarence K. UNION NOW. New York: Harper, 1939. 315 p.

1469. Wilson, Archibald Duncan, and Elizabeth. FEDERALISM AND WORLD ORDER. London: T.S. Nelson, 1939. 198 p.

1470. Newfang, Oscar. WORLD FEDERATION. Translated by P. Gault. New York: Barnes and Noble, 1939. 133 p.

C. PROPOSALS FOR TOMORROW

(See also Chapter 3.C.7.)

Creating a New World

1. Changing the United Nations System

a. CHARTER REVISION

(See also 496.)

1471. Wilcox, Francis O., and Marcy, Carl M. PROPOSALS FOR CHANGES IN THE UNITED NATIONS. Washington, D.C.: Brookings, 1955. 537 p.

>Studies various means for Charter review and the history of the movement; discusses changes which have taken place with respect to basic purposes and practices of the UN. Presents official and unofficial proposals. Both authors were involved in developing U.S. policy towards the UN during the early years.

1472. Clark, Grenville, and Sohn, Louis B. WORLD PEACE THROUGH WORLD LAW. 4th rev. ed. Cambridge, Mass.: Harvard University Press, 1973. 391 p.

>A comprehensive proposal for strengthening the UN through revision of the Charter. The work is divided into three parts: the first is an analytic introduction and overall evaluation; the second a set of specific proposals article by article; and the third consists of proposals in detail for auxiliary instruments and procedures. Particularly concerned with making the UN an effective agency for supervising and monitoring inspected disarmament.

1473. Zacklin, Ralph. THE AMENDMENT OF THE CONSTITUTIVE INSTRUMENTS OF THE U.N. AND SPECIALIZED AGENCIES. Leiden, Netherlands: Sijthoff, 1968. 220 p.

>A careful, scholarly analysis. Discusses the various efforts at revisions of the Charter, examining informal changes brought about through practice and nonpractice.

1474. Jacob, Philip E., ed. "The Future of the United Nations, Issues of Charter Revision." ANNALS (American Academy of Political and Social Science) 296(November 1954): entire issue.

1475. Schwarzenberger, George, et al. REPORT ON THE REVIEW OF THE CHARTER OF THE UNITED NATIONS. London, 1956. 122 p.

>Report to the Conference of the International Law Association at Dubrovnik, 1956.

1476. Indian Council of World Affairs. REVISION OF THE UNITED NATIONS CHARTER: A SYMPOSIUM. London: Oxford University Press, 1956. 145 p.

> Short critique of the Charter showing how it could be changed to make it a more potent instrument.

1477. Brown, Benjamin H., ed. THE U.S. STAKE IN THE UN: PROBLEMS OF CHARTER REVIEW. New York: Columbia University, Graduate School of Business, American Assembly, 1954. 139 p.

1478. Kopal, V., and Mrozek, I. PROBLEMS OF THE REVISION OF THE UN CHARTER. Prague, Czechoslovakia: Czechoslovakian Academy of Science, 1957. 242 p.

1479. De Rusett, Alan. STRENGTHENING THE FRAMEWORK OF PEACE: A STUDY OF CURRENT PROPOSALS FOR AMENDING, DEVELOPING, OR REPLACING PRESENT INTERNATIONAL INSTITUTIONS FOR THE MAINTENANCE OF PEACE. London: Royal Institute of International Affairs, 1950. 238 p.

> A useful bringing together of the main contemporary proposals for adjustments of existing arrangements, the creation of international forces, world federation, and the unification of Europe.

1480. United States 83rd Congress, 2nd Session. Senate. Committee on Foreign Relations. Subcommittee on the U.N. Charter. REVIEW OF THE UNITED NATIONS CHARTER. HEARINGS...ON PROPOSALS TO AMEND OR OTHERWISE MODIFY EXISTING INTERNATIONAL PEACE AND SECURITY ORGANIZATIONS, INCLUDING THE UNITED NATIONS. Washington, D.C.: Government Printing Office, 1954-55. 14 parts, 2,065 p.

1481. United States Congress. Senate. Committee on Foreign Relations. Subcommittee on the United Nations Charter. REVIEW OF THE UNITED NATIONS CHARTER: A COLLECTION OF DOCUMENTS. Washington, D.C.: Government Printing Office, 1954. 908 p. (Senate Document 87.)

> Contains important documents and texts of basic international instruments related to the adoption of the Charter. Gives documentary history since 1943. Illustrative selection of official studies and acts.

1482. United States 81st Congress, 2nd Session. Senate. Committee on Foreign Relations. REVISION OF THE UNITED NATIONS CHARTER. Washington, D.C.: Government Printing Office, 1950. 808 p.

> Testimony is grouped according to the various resolutions in

the Senate on revisions of the Charter. Most of the central problems of international organizations come in for attention.

b. IMPROVING THE SYSTEM

(See also 1288.)

1483. Holcombe, Arthur N., ed. A STRATEGY OF PEACE IN A CHANGING WORLD. Cambridge, Mass.: Harvard University Press, 1967. 332 p.

 A collection of essays on the problems and possibilities of the UN with suggestions for changes which would enable it to serve as a world governmental body to end the cold war and keep peace. An essay on the role of politics in the General Assembly which contains valuable methodological tools for the analysis of voting patterns in that body.

1484. _____. PEACEFUL COEXISTENCE: A NEW CHALLENGE TO THE UNITED NATIONS. 12th Report of the Commission to Study the Organization of Peace. New York: Harper, 1960. 47 p. Paperbound.

 An outline of the issues with suggestions for ways the UN could be used as an effective agent to minimize the effects of the cold war.

1485. _____. STRENGTHENING THE UNITED NATIONS. Report of the Commission to Study the Organization of Peace. New York: Harper, 1957. 288 p.

 A survey of the record and appraisal of proposals and recommendations for reinforcing world organization. Gives innovative suggestions for modifications of existing practices in UN structure and functions.

1486. Sohn, Louis B., ed. THE UNITED NATIONS: THE NEXT TWENTY-FIVE YEARS. Report of the Commission to Study the Organization of Peace. Dobbs Ferry, N.Y.: Oceana, 1970. 269 p. Paperbound.

 Based on the experiences of the past and acute analysis, the contributors indicate how the UN should be changed and strengthened to provide solutions for the problems of the 1970's. The authors use behavioral and systems approaches to analyze the decision-making process.

1487. Jenks, C[larence]. Wilfred. THE WORLD BEYOND THE CHARTER: A TENTATIVE SYNTHESIS OF FOUR STAGES OF WORLD ORGANIZATIONS. New York: Humanities Press, 1969. 199 p.

Based on the impact of international organizations on international politics from pre-League days, the author stresses the need for expanding existing organizations, especially in the functional areas.

1488. Nef, John. TOWARDS WORLD COMMUNITY. World Academy of Art and Science, vol. 5. The Hague, Netherlands: Jink, 1968. 165 p.

Various looks at the extent of international cooperation and conclusions to be drawn from the past as regards movement towards genuine community.

1489. Corbett, Percy E. LAW AND SOCIETY IN THE RELATIONS OF STATES. New York: Harcourt, Brace, 1951. 247 p.

The author begins with the study of the law from which the principal theories of international law originated. In looking into the patterns in international practice, the author concludes that the future of international law is bound up with the future of international organizations.

1490. Head, Ivan L., ed. THIS FIRE-PROOF HOUSE: CANADIANS SPEAK OUT ABOUT LAW AND ORDER IN THE INTERNATIONAL COMMUNITY. Dobbs Ferry, N.Y.: Oceana, 1967. 176 p.

A lively and interesting set of papers showing the potential for the expansion of international law and processes of peaceful settlement and adjudication.

1491. Keohane, Robert O[wen]., and Nye, Joseph S., Jr., eds. TRANSNATIONAL RELATIONS AND WORLD POLITICS. Cambridge, Mass.: Harvard University Press, 1971. 428 p. (Also published as INTERNATIONAL ORGANIZATION 25 [Summer 1971]).

A collection of essays indicating progress and evolution toward transnational relations, organizations, and coalitions in various areas.

2. New Ways

(See also 117.)

1492. Pearson, Lester B. PEACE IN THE FAMILY OF MAN. London: British Broadcasting Corp., 1969. 104 p.

Lectures on the current state of the world with an examination of the means to increase economic and political cooperation. Discusses the potential role of the UN and prospects for achieving disarmament.

1493. Rochester, J. Martin. INTERNATIONAL INSTITUTIONS AND WORLD ORDER: THE INTERNATIONAL SYSTEM AS A PRISMATIC POLITY. A Sage Professional Paper in International Studies. Beverly Hills, Calif.: Sage, 1972. 71 p.

Examines the progress which has been and will be made toward world order using the records, biases, and effectiveness of international institutions.

1494. Appadorai, Angadipuram. THE USES OF FORCE IN INTERNATIONAL RELATIONS. Bombay, India: Asia Publishing House, 1958. 124 p.

A proposal for nations to give up sovereignty and surrender the right to use force to the UN. The author stresses the importance of increasing international efforts to speed development.

1495. Malik, Charles. MAN IN THE STRUGGLE FOR PEACE. New York: Harper and Row, 1963. 242 p.

A mixture of philosophical reflection and political reminiscences by the former foreign minister of Lebanon and a former President of the General Assembly. Among themes discussed are: peace, the future role of the UN, and the cold war.

1496. Woodward, E. L., et al. FOUNDATIONS FOR WORLD ORDER. Denver, Colo.: University of Denver Press, 1949. 174 p.

An analysis of the political foundations necessary for institutionalizing order.

1497. Stone, Julius. QUEST FOR SURVIVAL. Cambridge, Mass.: Harvard University Press, 1961. 104 p.

An examination of the problems of the future with suggestions as to how man must respond in order to maintain life.

1498. van Slyck, Philip. PEACE: THE CONTROL OF NATIONAL POWER: A GUIDE FOR THE CONCERNED CITIZEN ON PROBLEMS OF DISARMAMENT AND STRENGTHENING THE UNITED NATIONS. Boston, Mass.: Beacon, 1963. 186 p.

An analysis of the major issues of world affairs and proposals for restructuring the present world. Issues include the control of force, financing peace, problems of world authority, the role of the UN, and problems of and proposals for arms control.

1499. Wright, Quincy, et al, eds. PREVENTING WORLD WAR III: SOME PROPOSALS. New York: Simon and Schuster, 1962. 460 p.

>The authors examine three areas: first, how to stop the arms race, considering inspection, arbitration, an international force, and economic development needed to decrease tensions; second, reducing international tension, to which six papers are devoted examining multilateral and bilateral variations; and finally, how to build a world society with suggestions for national governments and international agencies which can hasten improvements in the climate, communications, and more integration.

1500. Cordier, Andrew W. PATHS TO WORLD ORDER. New York: Columbia University Press, 1967. 161 p.

>The author discusses diverse topics, analyzing progress which has been made and problems remaining in the path of a well-ordered international society.

1501. Bowett, D. W. THE SEARCH FOR PEACE. Boston, Mass.: Rutledge and Kegan Paul, 1972. 236 p.

>A collection of documents and source materials including extracts from political leaders on peacekeeping, disarmament, and the future of international society.

1502. Brackett, R. D. PATHWAYS TO PEACE. Minneapolis, Minn.: Denison, 1965. 387 p.

>The author discusses avenues by which motivated citizens can assume a participatory role in educational and religious activities leading to international peace and cooperation.

1503. Waterlow, Charlotte. SUPERPOWERS AND VICTIMS: THE OUTLOOK FOR WORLD COMMUNITY. Englewood Cliffs, N.J.: Prentice-Hall, 1974. 181 p.

>Explores many international social problems summarizing arguments for international cooperation to resolve them. Examines a new "religion" of world community as a necessity for the survival of the planet.

1504. Gray, Richard B. INTERNATIONAL SECURITY SYSTEMS: CONCEPTS AND MODELS OF WORLD ORDER. Itasca, Ill.: Peacock. 1969. 227 p.

>Studies attempts of the international security system to cope with the central problems in international policies--those of conflict resolution. Examines processes, concepts, institutions, and models--past, present, and future.

1505. Luard, Evan. NATIONALITY AND WEALTH: A STUDY IN WORLD GOVERNMENT. New York: Oxford University Press, 1963. 370 p.

> The author examines the inadequacy of the nation-state in its present international setting. Shows increasing actions on an international scale with emphasis on economic activities, which may reduce rather than exacerbate the inequalities existing between nations.

1506. Singh, Harnam, ed. STUDIES IN WORLD ORDER. Delhi, India: Kitab Mahal, 1972. 448 p.

1507. Burton, John W. WORLD SOCIETY. Cambridge, England: Cambridge University Press, 1972. 180 p.

> Explains what world society means and how to study it. Rather simplistic in the prescriptions it proposes.

1508. Hoffmann, Stanley, ed. CONDITIONS OF WORLD ORDER. Boston, Mass.: Houghton Mifflin, 1968. 397 p.

1509. Wright, Quincy, ed. THE WORLD COMMUNITY. Chicago, Ill.: University of Chicago Press, 1948. 323 p.

1510. Regala, Roberto. WORLD ORDER AND DIPLOMACY. Dobbs Ferry, N.Y.: Oceana, 1969. 105 p.

1511. Bell, Wendell, and Mau, James A. THE SOCIOLOGY OF THE FUTURE. New York: Russell Sage Foundation, 1971. 464 p.

> A rationale for normative future studies, an interesting model of social change, and a good annotated bibliography on the futures literature.

1512. Schuman, F. L. THE COMMONWEALTH OF MAN. New York: Knopf, 1952. 494 p.

> Examines the work of political philosophers and social scientists and applies findings to anarchy and order in the world community. Examines the social forces making for conflict and harmony in human and social relations. Warns against trying to establish world government by force. Approach is federalist rather than functional.

1513. Hollins, Elizabeth J., ed. PEACE IS POSSIBLE. New York: Grossman, 1966. 339 p. Paperbound.

> Anthology of future-oriented and strongly value-centered articles; includes consideration of problems of war, population, and development.

1514. Bogardus, Emory S. TOWARD A WORLD COMMUNITY. Los Angeles, Calif.: University of Southern California Press, 1964. 101 p.

Prerequisites and possible steps for moving in the direction of a meaningful world community.

a. THE FEDERALIST WAY

(See also 1415, 1469.)

1515. Bowie, Robert R., and Friederich, Carl J., eds. STUDIES IN FEDERALISM. Boston, Mass.: Little, Brown and Co., 1954. 927 p.

1516. Center for the Study of Democratic Institutions. A CONSTITUTION FOR THE WORLD. Santa Barbara, Calif., 1965. 111 p.

1517. Eaton, Howard O., ed. FEDERATION: THE COMING STRUCTURE OF WORLD GOVERNMENT. Norman, Okla.: University of Oklahoma Press, 1944. 234 p.

1518. Gill, Charles A. WORLD REPUBLIC. Philadelphia, Pa.: Dorrance, 1943. 119 p.

1519. Greaves, Harold Richard Goring. FEDERAL UNION IN PRACTICE. London: Allen & Unwin, 1940. 136 p.

1520. Johnsen, Julia E., comp. FEDERAL WORLD GOVERNMENT. New York: Wilson, 1948. 280 p.

1521. Millard, Everett L. FREEDOM IN A FEDERAL WORLD: HOW WE CAN LEARN TO LIVE IN PEACE AND LIBERTY BY MEANS OF WORLD LAW. Dobbs Ferry, N.Y.: Oceana, 1959. 224 p.

1522. Wynner, Edith. WORLD FEDERAL GOVERNMENT. Afton, N.Y.: Federal Press, 1954. 84 p.

b. WORLD GOVERNMENT

(See also 116, 389, 504, 981.)

1523. Committee to Frame a World Constitution. PRELIMINARY DRAFT OF A WORLD CONSTITUTION. Chicago, Ill.: University of Chicago Press, 1948. 91 p.

1524. Cornell, Julien. NEW WORLD PRIMER. New York: New Directions, 1947. 147 p.

1525. Ewing, Alfred. THE INDIVIDUAL, THE STATE AND WORLD GOVERNMENT. New York: Macmillan, 1947. 322 p.

1526. Kohn, Hans. WORLD ORDER IN HISTORICAL PERSPECTIVE. Cambridge, Mass.: Harvard University Press, 1942. 352 p.

1527. Madariaga, Salvador de. THE WORLD'S DESIGN. London: Allen & Unwin, 1938. 311 p.

1528. Mendlovitz, Saul H., ed. ON THE CREATION OF A JUST WORLD ORDER. PREFERRED WORLDS FOR THE 1990'S. New York: The Free Press, 1975. 302 p.

Scholars from seven countries--including the Soviet Union and China--present their models for obtaining peace, social justice, and the elimination of poverty, as well as offering solutions to ecological problems.

1529. Soloman, Jack. COMPLETE HANDBOOK ON WORLD GOVERNMENT. Chicago, Ill.: National Debate Research Co., 1960. 214 p.

1530. Niebuhr, Reinhold. THE ILLUSION OF WORLD GOVERNMENT. Whitestone, N.Y.: The Graphics Group, 1949. 31 p. Pamphlet.

A pessimistic view by a "realist" of the possibility of establishing world government.

c. OTHER ALTERNATIVES

1531. Groom, A. J. R., and Taylor, Paul, eds. FUNCTIONALISM: THEORY AND PRACTICE IN INTERNATIONAL RELATIONS. New York: Crane-Russak, 1975. 345 p.

A collection of original essays attempting to assess the state of contemporary functionalist theory and practice. Evaluates the successes and failures of functionalism within the contexts of the League, specialized agencies, international nongovernmental organizations, etc.

1532. Falk, Richard A. A STUDY OF FUTURE WORLDS. New York: The Free Press, 1975. 506 p.

A part of the "World Order Models Project." Comprehensive and thoughtful in its presentation of materials on issues as varied as war, ecology, human rights, economic development, and personal alienation.

INDEXES

AUTHOR INDEX

In addition to authors, this index includes all editors and compilers cited in the text. Numbers refer to entry numbers.

A

Academie de Droit International de la Hage 207
Adams, Michael 1306
Ahluwalia, Kuljit 549
Ahmad, Mushtaq 769
Akehurst, Michael Barton 650
Akzin, Benjamin 714
Alcock, A.E. 1227
Alexander, Lewis H. 1036
Alexander, Patricia S. 239
Alexander, Yonah 1177
Alexandrowicz, Charles Henry 1013, 1117
Alger, Chadwick F. 498-99
Alker, Hayward R., Jr. 702
Allen, Devere 1464
Alting, Gevsau 1081
Alwan, Mohamed 735
American Association for the United Nations 61, 437
American Society of International Law 163, 211
Ames, Herbert B. 899
Anand, Ram Prakash 689, 1007
Andemicael, Berhanykun 905
Andrews, Fannie Fern 1335
Androit, John L. 136
Angell, Norman 1446
Ankers, P.M. 1326
Appadorai, Angadipuram 1494

Appleton, Sheldon 618
Armstrong, Hamilton F. 35
Arne, Sigrid 435
Asamoah, O.V. 576
Ascher, Charles S. 1204, 1272
Ash, Lee 313
Asher, Robert E. 1189, 1204
Association of the Bar of the City of New York 327
Ataov, Turkkaya 777
Atherton, Alexine L. 377
Atlee, Clement R. 468
Aufricht, Hans 52, 56, 1101-2
Aulen, Gustaf 678
Australian Association of International Law 212
Avicenne, Paul 307
Azud, Jan 902

B

Baehr, Peter R. 710
Bailey, Stanley H. 1223
Bailey, Sydney D. 439, 586, 619, 626-27, 641, 882
Bains, J.S. 759
Baker, James C. 1200
Baker, William Gedney 734
Balassa, Bela 513
Ball, J.H. 841
Baranyai, L. 1077
Barker, A.J. 967

Author Index

Barkun, Michael 40, 493
Barnes, George N. 1229
Barros, James 489, 665, 719, 894-96
Bartlett, Ruhl J. 1447
Barton, Clara H. 1305
Bar-Yaacov, Nissim 918a
Basak, Adam 688
Basch, Antonin 1140
Baxter, R.R. 1037
Bechhoefer, Bernhard G. 858
Beckel, Graham 1205
Becker, Benjamin M. 463
Becker, George H. 1370
Beddington-Behrens, Edward 1230
Bedi, Mohinder S. 758
Bedjaoui, Mohammed 644
Beer, Max 423
Beguin, Bernard 1244
Behanon, Kavoor Thomas 652
Behrman, Daniel 1276
Beichman, Arnold 811
Beitz, Charles R. 352
Belin, Jacqueline 773
Bell, Wendell 1511
Bentwick, Norman 434, 530, 1327
Berkes, Ross N. 758
Berkov, Robert 1213
Berman, William H. 1283
Best, Ethelwyn 1318
Best, Gary 703
Besterman, Theodore A. 24, 26, 1266
Bettison, D.G. 1371
Bhutoo, A.Z. 901
Bilgrami, Jafar R. 756
Bingham, June 679
Black, Cyril E. 877, 1291
Blair, Patricia W. 611, 1374
Blaisdell, Donald C. 379
Blanks, Hazel Janet 249
Bloomfield, Lincoln P. 474, 728, 794, 879, 911, 915, 934
Bloss, Esther 1262
Bock, Edwin A. 1310
Bodnar, James S. 870
Bogardus, Emory S. 1514
Boggs, George T. 495
Bogley, Tennent H. 1393
Boland, Gertrude C. 754

Bosman, H.W.J. 1081
Bourquin, Maurice 842
Bowett, D.W. 559, 940, 1501
Bowie, Robert R. 1515
Boyd, Andrew 449, 588
Boyd, Anne Morris 232
Boyd, James M. 932
Brackett, R.D. 1502
Bradley, Martin A. 1030, 1051
Brailsford, Henry N. 1448
Brecher, Michael 973
Brett, Oliver 579
Breycha-Vauthier, Arthur Carl von 57
Bridgman, Raymond L. 1443
Brierly, James L. 526
Briggs, Herbert W. 601
Brimmer, Brenda 247
Brinton, Clarence Crane 504
Broches, Aron 1196
Brock, David 615, 953
Brockington, Colin F. 1218
Brodie, B. 1285
Brody, H. 484
Broekmeijer, M.W.J.M. 1163
Broms, Bengt 557
Brown, Benjamin H. 621, 1477
Brown, William Adams, Jr. 1072
Brown-John, C. Lloyd 853a
Brownlie, Ian 833, 1439
Bryson, Lyman 406
Buchanan, G.S. 1212
Buchanan, William 510
Buehrig, Edward H. 1405
Buell, Raymond L. 871
Buergenthal, Thomas 1025, 1409-10
Bunting, G.R. 405
Burke, William T. 1039
Burns, Arthur Lee 931
Burns, Lt. Gen. E.L.M. 954
Burton, John W. 1507
Burton, Margaret Ernestine 578
Butler, Harold B. 424

C

Cairncross, Alexander K. 1195
Calder, Ritchie 1215
Calogeropoulos-Stratis, S. 751
Calvocoressi, Peter 923
Campion, Eleanor Este 130

Author Index

Carder, Michael 1296
Cardozo, Michael H. 711
Carey, John 980, 1422
Carlston, Kenneth S. 396, 999
Carnegie Endowment for International Peace 320-21, 328, 1210, 1216
Carpozi, George J., Jr. 658
Carrigue, Katherine C. 345
Carroll, Faye 1382
Carroll, Marie Juliette 58
Castaneda, Jorge 565, 767
Caulfield, Daniel Webster 1277
Center for the Study of Democratic Institutions 1516
Center for War/Peace Studies 329
Centre de Recherche et d'Information Socio-Politiques 985
Chadwick, Gerald W. St. J. 391
Chai, F.Y. 590
Chakravarti, Raghubir 1421
Chamberlain, Joseph P. 380, 1045
Chamberlin, Waldo 8, 248, 563
Chandler, Edgar H.S. 1403
Chase, Eugene Parker 456
Cheever, Daniel S. 375, 1165
Chen, Lung-Chu 617
Chen, Samuel Shih-Tsai 292, 397
Cheng, Bin 1026
Chidzero, B.T.G. 1385
Childs, James Bennett 237
China Institute of International Affairs 744
Chinese Society of International Law 215
Chiu, Hungdah 573
Choate, J.H. 372
Chowdhuri, R.N. 1321
Chuang, Richard V. 1027
Chung, Il Young 1011
Citrin, Jack 924
Clark, George Norman 1016
Clark, Grenville 1472
Clark, Roger Stenson 1432
Claude, Inis L., Jr. 376, 457, 832, 837, 1389
Clausen, Peter 585
Cleaver, Harry 1187
Clifford, J.M. 664, 1139
Codding, George A., Jr. 1017, 1059

Cohen, Benjamin 448
Cohen, Stephen D. 1080
Colegrove, Kenneth W. 1035
Collart, Yves 65, 108
Collins, P. 1402
Colt, Jean-Pierre 880
Commission on International Development 1129
Commission to Study the Organization of Peace 336, 1288
Committee to Frame a World Constitution 1523
Congalton, A.A. 511
Conover, Helen F. 106, 116
Consortium on Peace Research, Education and Development 330
Conwell-Evans, Thomas P. 580
Cook, Blanche W. 118
Corbett, Percy E. 1429, 1489
Cordier, Andrew W. 401, 667, 675, 1500
Cordovez, Diego 1158
Cormack, M. 64
Cornell, Julien 1524
Cornell Law School 1414
Corwin, Edward S. 814
Cory, Helen M. 997
Cosgrove, C.A. 701
Coulter, John Wesley 1375
Council on Foreign Relations 35, 70, 331
Courlander, Harold M. 694
Cox, Arthur M. 926
Cox, Robert W. 630, 1114
Coyle, Benjamin V. 438
Crosswell, C.M. 548
Curti, Merle Eugene 1465
Curzon, Gerard 1066

D

Dale, Doris C. 604
Dale, R. 1383
Dallin, Alexander 781, 785
Dam, Kenneth W. 1065
Darby, William Evans 1000
Davis, Calvin de A. 373
Davis, Edward P. 138
Davis, Harriet Ide (Eager) 430
Davis, Kathryn W. 787

Author Index

Dayal, Shiv 755
Dean, Arthur H. 864
Deardoff, John 255, 257
de Azcarate, y Florez, Pablo 1386
de Grazia, Alfred 39
de Guinzbourg, Victor 482
del Russo, Alessandra Luini 1424
De Rusett, Alan 1479
Detter, Ingrid 571
Deutsch, Karl 505-7
Deutsche Gesellschaft fuer die Vereinten Nationen 824
de Vree, Johan K. 514
DeVries, Margaret G. 1095b
DeWitt, William 469
Dexter, Byron V. 36, 415
Diaz, Albert James 128
Dib, George Moussa 724
Dickinson, Thomas H. 819
Dillon, Conley Hall 1248
Dimitrov, Th. D. 238
Djonovich, Susan J. 270
Domergue, Maurice 1170
Domke, Martin 1005
Donelan, M.D. 886, 888
Douma, J. 95, 98
Downs, Robert B. 314-15
Doxey, Margaret P. 853
Droege, Heinz 823
Drost, Pieter N. 1425
Ducksworth-Barker, V. 1136
Dugard, John 1380
Duggan, Stephen P. 425
Dulles, Eleanor L. 1107
Dunn, Frederick S. 369
Dunner, Joseph 19
Dupuy, R.J. 208
Dupuy, Trevor Nevitt, Associates 862
Dutch Inter-University Institute for International Law 217

E

Eagleton, Clyde 388
Eastin, Roy B. 235
Eastman, Samuel Mack 743
Eaton, Howard O. 1517
Edmead, Frank 878
Edwards, Corwin D. 1076
Edwards, David V. 891

Edwards, John B.S. 535
Egger, Rowland 639
Eggleston, Frederic 1339
Ehni, Reinhart 772
Eichelberger, Clark M. 475, 1426
Eide, Asbjorn 1411
Einzig, Paul 1108
Eisenlohn, Louise E.S. 1224
El-Ayouty, Yassin 1354
Elder, Robert E. 1148
El-Hadi Affi, Mohamed 723
Elmandrjra, M. 466
Engel, Salo 521
Ennals, David 947
Esman, Milton J. 1165
Espy, W.R. 1179
Etzioni, Amitai 508
Etzioni, Minerva H. 906
Evans, F.T. 1047
Evans, George 1171
Evans, John W. 1070
Evans, Luther H. 1267
Evatt, Herbert V. 442
Ewing, Alfred 1525

F

Fabian, Larry L. 936
Fachiri, Alexander P. 684
Fakher, Hassein 558
Falk, Richard A. 398, 491, 574, 826, 877, 1291, 1532
Faries, John C. 1445
Fawcett, James E.S. 408, 1048
Fehrenbach, T.R. 460, 848
Feld, Werner J. 1315
Feller, A.H. 695
Fernbach, Alfred 1258
Field, Norman S. 144
Fifield, Russell H. 1168
Finer, Herman 597
Finke, Blythe F. 746
Finkelstein, Lawrence S. 802, 836, 1367
Finkelstein, Marina S. 836
Fischer, H. 1018
Fleming, Denna Frank 817-18
Fletcher School of Law and Diplomacy 1073
Flory, Thiebaut 1071
Flynn, Alice H. 62

Author Index

Follows, John W. 1228
Fontaine, Pierre-Michel 1153
Food and Agriculture Organization (FAO) 82, 83
Foote, Wilder 401, 675-76
Foreign Policy Association 332
Forgac, A. 699
Forsythe, David P. 955
Fosdick, Raymond B. 413, 431
Foster, John W. 1004
Fox, Hazel 998
Fradkin, Elvira K. 948
Franck, Peter G. 1176
Franck, Thomas M. 980
Freeman, Harrop A. 542
Friedeberg, Alfred S. 1159
Friedmann, Wolfgang G. 1133
Friedrich, Carl J. 1515
Friends Committee on National Legislation 111
Frydenberg, P. 925
Frye, William R. 946
Fuller, C. 38

G

Gabbay, Rony 962
Galloway, E. 1049
Galt, T.F. 444
Ganji, Manouchehr 1412
Gardinier, David E. 1360
Gardner, Richard N. 797-99, 1115
General Agreement on Tariffs and Trade (GATT) 73, 84, 284
Ghebali, Catherine 243
Ghebali, Victor Yves 243
Gibson, Hugh 1453
Giersch, Herbert 1094
Gill, Charles A. 1518
Ginsburg, G. 820
Gold, Joseph 1096-1100
Goldsmith, Robert 1449
Gonlubol, Mehmet 775, 777
Goodall, Merrill R. 754
Goodman, N.M. 1221
Goodrich, Leland M. 403, 453, 492, 529, 830, 845
Goodspeed, Stephen S. 374
Goodwin, Geoffrey L. 500, 779
Gordenker, Leon 490, 660, 846
Gordon, King 977

Gosovic, Branislav 1157
Gotlieb, Allan 1413
Gould, Wesley L. 40
Graham, Malbone W. 609
Grant, Madeleine P. 1219
Graves, E.C. 131
Gray, Richard B. 1504
Greaves, Harold Richard Goring 581, 1519
Green, James Frederick 1423
Green, Leslie C. 613
Greene, Fred 621
Gregg, Robert W. 493
Gregory, Winifred 132, 220, 241
Grieve, M.J. 888
Grieves, Forest L. 1008
Griffin, G. Edward 465
Griffin, Keith 1187
Groom, A.J.R. 1531
Gross, Ernest A. 441
Gross, Franz B. 804
Grotius Society 210
Grubel, Herbert G. 1085
Grzybowski, Kozimierz 784
Guenter, Hans 1319
Guetzkow, Harold 657
Guggenheim, Paul 773
Gullion, Edmund A. 1038
Gupta, K.R. 1069
Gutteridge, Joyce A.C. 458
Gyani, P.S. 952

H

Haagerup, Niels J. 749
Haas, Ernst B. 792-93, 838, 1242, 1428
Haas, Michael 47
Hadwen, John G. 629
Hagras, Kamal 1156
Halderman, J.W. 534, 960
Hall, H. Duncan 1322
Halm, George N. 1092
Hambidge, Gove 1181
Hambro, Eduard 277
Hammarskjold, Dag 645, 677
Hamzel, F.S. 956
Han, Henry H. 570
Hanreider, Wolfram P. 398
Harbottle, M. 950-51
Hargrove, John Lawrence 1289

Author Index

Harley, John Eugene 293, 1314
Harman, R.B. 46
Harper, Norman 736
Harrar, Jacob G. 1183, 1307
Harrod, Roy F. 1087
Hasan, K. Sarwar 768
Haviland, Henry Field, Jr. 375, 706, 800
Hawkins, Robert G. 1089
Hawtrey, R.S. 1111
Hazzard, Shirley 464
Head, Ivan L. 1490
Headicar, B.M. 38
Heathcote, Nina 931
Heilbroner, Robert L. 1199
Hempstone, Smith 983
Henderson, James L. 674
Henderson, William 1363
Henkin, Louis 859
Henning, Daniel H. 1292
Hero, Alfred 1313
Hertzberg, Hazel W. 447
Hertzberg, Sidney 447
Heyman, Hans 1462
Hicks, Frederick Charles 99
Higgins, Benjamin 796, 1128
Higgins, Rosalyn 408, 564, 778, 921
Hill, Martin 553, 1104
Hill, Norman Llewellyn 370, 390, 636
Hillery, Brian 1260
Hindsmarsh, Albert E. 944
Hingorani, R.C. 577
Hippolyte, Mirlande 722
Hirschman, Albert O. 1131
Hiscocks, Richard 591
Hobson, John A. 1450
Hobson, W. 1217
Hodgetts, J.E. 1281
Hoffman, Michael L. 1164
Hoffmann, Paul G. 1144
Hoffmann, Stanley 1508
Hogan, Willard N. 383, 454, 839
Holborn, Louise W. 1404
Holcombe, Arthur N. 1323, 1427, 1483-85
Holler, Frederick L. 48a
Hollins, Elizabeth J. 1513
Hoover, Herbert E. 1453

Horie, Shigeo 1103
Horsefield, J. Keith 1095a
Hoskyns, Catherine 978, 991
Houston, John A. 725
Hovet, Thomas Jr. 705, 720
Hovey, J.A. 606
Howard, H.D. 1047
Howard-Ellis, C. 412
Hsia, Chi-Feng 747
Hudson, Manley Ottmer 276, 303, 416, 681-83
Hudson, W.J. 737
Hunt, Ronald 353
Huss, P.J. 658
Hutchison, Elmo H. 957
Huxley, Julian S. 1275
Hyamson, A.M. 1333
Hyde, L.K., Jr. 788
Hydeman, Lee M. 1283

I

Ichihashi, Yamato 872
Indian Council on World Affairs 753, 1476
Indian Society of International Law 164
Institut de Droit International 209
Institute for Annual Review of United Nations Affairs 149
Institute of International Relations of the Faculty of Political Sciences, University of Ankara 776
Institute of Public Administration 780
International Atomic Energy Agency 81, 1286
International Bank and Monetary Fund 285
International Bank for Reconstruction and Development 1194, 1197, 1203
International Civil Aviation Organization 1028
International Committee for Social Sciences Documentation 311, 322
International Court of Justice 96-97, 280, 281
International Institute for the Unification of Private International Law 544

International Labour Office 85, 87, 1231, 1237
International Labour Office. Library 71, 86
International Labour Organization 1243
International Law Association, Canadian Branch 214
International Monetary Fund 285

J

Jacks, Lawrence P. 418
Jackson, Elmore 883
Jackson, John H. 1068
Jackson, Sir Robert G.A. 1134, 1141
Jacob, Philip E. 377, 1474
Jacobson, Harold Karon 48, 630, 782
Jacobson, Per 1086
James, Alan 404
James, Frederick Alan 928
Jenks, Clarence Wilfred 550, 552, 560, 1009, 1246, 1247, 1250, 1254, 1487
Jessup, Philip C. 545, 1112
Jimenez de Arechage, Eduardo 625
Johnsen, Julia E. 942, 1454-55, 1520
Johnson, Carol A. 113
Johnson, Grace Allen 899
Johnson, Harold S. 1358
Johnston, George A. 1232, 1241
Jones, H.D. 72
Jones, Joseph Marion 1206
Jones, Samuel S. 730
Jordan, B.S. 1113
Jordan, Robert S. 637
Joshua, Wynfred 976
Joyce, James Avery 461, 1162, 1304

K

Kaeckenbeeck, Georges 1343
Kahin, G.M. 1362
Kahng, Tae Sin 592
Kakkar, N.K. 1261
Kapungu, Leonard T. 852
Karp, Mark 1368

Kash, Don E. 1050
Kasluck, Paul 593
Kaufmann, Johan 629
Kay, David A. 403, 487, 713, 1287
Keen, Frank N. 522
Keenleyside, Hugh L. 1138
Keeny, Spurgeon Milton 1297
Keith, Kenneth James 1010
Kelchner, Warren H. 727
Kelen, Emery 673
Kelly, George A. 913
Kelsen, Hans 531-32, 567
Kennedy, Edgar S. 1406
Kenworth, Leonard S. 350
Keohane, Robert Owen 117, 704, 1491
Kertesz, Stephen D. 890
Khan, Rahmatullan 972
Kihl, Young W. 1029
Kindleberger, C. 1079
King, John Kerry 554, 648, 1190
Kirdar, Uner 1137
Kitton, M. 511
Klemme, Marvin 1127
Kluyver, Mrs. C.A. 246
Knott, James E. 1312
Knudson, J.I. 410
Koch, Karin 1067
Koh, Byung Charles 646
Kohn, Hans 1526
Kolosa, Jan 1263
Koo, Wellington, Jr. 622
Kopal, V. 1478
Korbel, Josef 971
Korey, William 1433
Kramer, John Francis 516
Kramish, Arnold 1282
Kraus, Hertha 1317
Krause, Lawrence B. 1082
Kravis, Irving B. 1062
Kruzas, Anthony T. 310
Kuehl, Warren F. 816
Kutner, Luis 1430

L

Lachs, Manfred 1056
Lador-Lederer, J.J. 1302, 1394
La Foy, Margaret 900
Lakshminarayan, C.V. 1351
Lall, Arthur 589, 958

Author Index

Lally, Dorothy 1209
Landy, Ernest Adolph 1240
Langer, Elisabeth M. 583
Langer, William W. 135
Langrod, Georges 642
Larus, Joel 399
Lary, Hal B. 1118
Lash, Joseph D. 669
Lasswell, Harold C. 617
Lauterpacht, Elihu 966, 970
Lauterpacht, Hersch 690, 1415
Laves, Walter H.C. 407, 1265
Lawrence, Thomas J. 1451
League of Nations 1, 59, 112, 265-66, 301, 344, 420, 432, 584
League of Nations Library 54, 60
League of Nations Health Organization 55
League of Nations Secretariat 419
League of Nations Secretariat. Information Section 6, 14, 1211
Lee, Marc J. 405, 697
Lefever, Ernest W. 974-76
Legault, Albert 102, 922, 939
Legum, Colin 979, 1161
Leidy, W. Phillip 233
Leiss, Amelia C. 908
Leive, David M. 1019, 1023
Leonard, Leonard Larry 296, 298-99, 381
Leonard, W. 1146
Lerner, Natan 1396
Levi, Werner 240, 382
Lewis, Marianna O. 326
Lewis, Peter R. 42
Lewis, S. 1207
Leyden Rijksuniversiteit 294
Liacouras, Peter J. 687
Lie, Trygve 666
Lillich, Richard B. 1434
Lindemann, Beate 825
Liska, George 509
Lissitzyn, Oliver James 1006
Little, J.M.D. 1139
Loftus, Martin L. 74
Logan, Rayford W. 1332
Longrigg, Stephen H. 1336
Lorenz, Denis 313
Lorwin, Lewis L. 1456
Loveday, A. 634
Lowe, Boutelle Ellsworth 1233

Lowenstein, Alan K. 1441
Luard, Evan 387, 827, 909, 912, 1415, 1505
Lyon, Peter 443
Lyons, Gene M. 849

M

Macartney, Carlile Aylmer 1387, 1407
Macaulay, Neil 1328
McClelland, Charles A. 459
McClure, Wallace M. 806, 1105
McConaughy, John Bothwell 249
McDonald, Alexander H. 1377
McDougal, Myres S. 1039
Machlup, Fritz 1088
McInnis, Edgar 741
MacIver, Robert M. 712
McKitterick, Nathaniel 1155
McKnight, Allan D. 1278-79
McLaughlin, Kathleen 1142
MacLaurin, John (pseud.) 700
McVitty, Marion H. 865-66
McWhinney, Edward 1014, 1030, 1051
Madariaga, Salvador de 1527
Mair, Lucy P. 1372, 1390
Malik, Charles 1495
Mance, Brigadier General Sir Harry Osborne 910, 1015, 1024, 1033, 1040, 1044
Mander, Linden A. 392
Mangone, Gerard J. 365, 389, 1120
Manly, Chesley 473
Manning, C.A. 733
Marburg, T. 411
Marcy, Carl M. 1471
Margalith, Aaron M. 1329
Marshall, C.B. 1378
Martelli, George 981
Martin, Andrew 530, 535, 835
Marx, Daniel 1075
Mason, Edward S. 1074, 1189
Mason, John B. 1340
Masters, Ruth D. 4
Matecki, Bronislaw Eugene 1201
Matsushita, Masatos 766
Mau, James A. 1511
Maury, Marian 1145
Meier, Gerald M. 1122
Meigs, Cornelia 445

Author Index

Melman, Seymour 869
Mendlovitz, Saul H. 400, 491, 826, 1528
Menon, V.K. Krishna 757
Merian, Alan P. 982
Merillat, H.C.L. 603
Merrill, John C. 221
Metzger, Stanley D. 1061
Meyriat, Jean 236
Mezerik, A.G. 9, 620, 907, 914, 965, 969, 1052, 1147, 1150, 1356
Michaels, David B. 551, 656
Michigan. University of. Law School 541
Miles, Edward 1057
Millard, Everett L. 1521
Miller, David C. 353
Miller, David Hunter 518, 523
Miller, Linda B. 904, 913, 994
Miller, Lynn 386
Miller, Richard Irwin 672
Miller, T.B. 731
Millikan, Max F. 1115
Mills, J.C. 1077
Mitrany, David 855
Modeen, Tore 1392
Montgomery, John D. 1154
Moor, Carol Carter 248
Moore, Bernard 471
Moore, Raymond A. 497
Morgan, Carlyle 1093
Morgan, Murray 1220
Morgenthau, Hans T. 828
Moritzen, Julius 1444
Morley, Felix 366
Morozov, G.I. 395
Morris, James 1193, 1198
Morris, Robert C. 1001
Morse, David A. 1238
Moscowitz, Harry 110
Moskowitz, Moses 1417-18
Moss, Alfred G. 297
Mrozek, I. 1478
Munro, Sir Leslie 696
Munves, James 481
Murden, F.D. 1148
Murray, Gilbert 433
Murray, James N., Jr. 1349
Muther, Jeanette E. 527
Myers, Denys Peter 2, 873, 1311

N

Nagueira, Franco 1373
Nantwi, E.K. 1012
Nathan, Robert R. 963
National Industrial Conference Board 1234
Nearing, Scott 1457
Nef, John 1488
Neild, Robert R. 1041
Netherlands International Law Review 217
Newfang, Oscar 1466, 1470
Nicholas, H.G. 440
Nichols, Calvin J. 633
Niebuhr, Reinhold 1530
Nigerian Society of International Law 216
Noel-Baker, Philip J. 524, 874
Northedge, F.S. 886
Nye, Joseph S., Jr. 117, 1491

O

O'Brien, Conor Cruise 462, 988
Oda, Shigera 1042
Okumu, Washington 986
Olton, Roy 18
Olynyk, Stephen D. 614
Ordoobadi, Abbas 1191
Osakwe, Chris 786

P

Padleford, Norman J. 492, 596, 628, 1043
Papi, Guiseppe Ugo 1109
Parry, Clive 300
Partan, Daniel G. 1249, 1295
Pastuhov, Vladimir D. 608, 662
Patch, William 250
Paulweis, Peter C. 1338
Paxman, John M. 495
Payer, Cheryl 1103a
Peace Research Society, The 333
Pearson, Lester B. 467, 1130, 1492
Peaslee, Amos J. 517, 1458
Pechota, Vratislav 889
Pelt, Adrian 1366
Perigord, Paul 1235

Author Index

Permanent Court of International
  Justice 98, 263, 279
Perry, Ralph B. 1459
Phelan, Edward Joseph 1252
Phillmore, Lord 1463
Pickard, Bertram 1308
Pickus, Robert 114
Pike, Bernard 1318
Pillsbury, Kent 1273
Plano, Jack C. 18, 378
Plischke, E. 515
Pollack, R.S. 1420
Pollard, Albert F. 1452
Pollock, Frederick 426
Pomerance, Michla 692
Potter, Pitman B. 384
Price, John 1245
Price, Peter 732
Prosser, Michael H. 483
Public Affairs Information Service 141
Purves, Chester 653
Putignano, A. 938

Q

Quan, Lau King 748
Quester, George H. 863

R

Rahmatullah, K. 555
Rajan, M.S. 556
Ralston, Jackson H. 996, 1002, 1460
Ram, V. Shiva 762
Ranasinghe, Alex 1264
Randle, Robert F. 892
Randolph, Lillian L. 885
Ranshoften-Wertheimer, Egan Ferdinand 635
Rapoport, Jacques 715
Rappard, William E. 427
Reddy, T. Ramakrishna 752
Rees, Elfan 1401
Regala, Roberto 1510
Reid, Escott 1188, 1192
Reinsch, Paul Samuel 368
Renborg, Bertil A. 1222
Reno, Edward A., Jr. 244

Reuter, Paul 385
Reynolds, C.V., Jr. 616
Reynolds, Ernest E. 428, 1408
Rhodes, James Robert 651
Riches, Cromwell Adams 623-24
Ridgeway, George Loveland 1316
Riggs, Robert E. 378, 708, 795
Rijksuniversiteit, Leiden 294
Rikhye, Indar Jit 921a, 929
Rivlin, Benjamin 1369
Roberts, Henry L. 35
Roberts, Jack 110
Roberts, Richard S., Jr. 1251
Robertson, A.H. 729, 1437
Robinson, J. William 295
Robinson, Jacob 49, 959
Robinson, James A. 498
Robinson, Nehemiah 1436
Robock, S.H. 1132
Rochester, J. Martin 1493
Rodgers, Raymond Spencer 1300
Roepke, Wilhelm 512
Rogers, W.C. 101
Rohn, Peter H. 303a, 303b, 348, 1320
Rolfe, Sidney E. 1089
Roosevelt, Eleanor 469
Ropke, Wilheim 512
Rosenne, Shabtai 582, 685-86
Rosner, Gabriella 968
Ross, Alf 536, 698
Ross, Frank Xavier 1294
Ross, Mary Bucher 359
Rothman, Marie H. 363
Rovcek, Joseph S. 1391
Rovine, Arthur 659
Royal Institute of International Affairs 213, 260, 638, 856
Rubin, Seymour J. 1151, 1166
Rubinstein, Alvin Z. 783, 820
Rudzinski, A. 51
Russell, Frank M. 1341
Russell, Ruth B. 527, 585, 801, 930
Russell, Sara S. 113
Russett, Bruce M. 702

S

Sady, Emil J. 355
Saiter, James A. 1106

Author Index

Salter, L. 834
Salvin, Marina 867
Sanders, R.F. 770
Sathyamurthy, T.V. 1274
Savage, Katharine 446
Savord, Ruth 325
Sayre, Francis B. 640
Schaaf, C. Hart 1168
Schaaf, R.W. 242
Schachter, Oscar 568
Schammell, William M. 1090
Schaper, B.W. 1253
Schechter, Alan H. 647
Schectman, Joseph B. 1399
Schenkman, Captain Jacob 1031
Schermers, Henry G. 561
Scheuner, Ulrich 825
Schiffer, Walter 367
Schleicher, Charles P. 759
Schloss, Henry H. 1110
Schmeckebier, Laurence Frederick 235, 815
Schnapper, M.D. 261
Schneider, J.W. 572
Schou, August 1411
Schultz, Theodore W. 1184
Schuman, F.L. 1512
Schuyler, Philippa 987
Schwartz, Leonard E. 1053
Schwarzenberger, George 414, 1475
Schwebel, Stephen M. 566, 661
Schwegmann, George A., Jr. 222-23
Schwelb, Egon 1419
Sclar, Deanna 360
Scott, James Brown 275, 371, 1467
Scott, William A. 812
Segal, Ronald 851, 1381
Sen, Sudhir 1135
Serwer, D. 1290
Setalvad, Motilal C. 829
Sewell, James Patrick 1152, 1265a
Seyersted, Finn 562, 941
Sharma, Brij Mohan 762
Sharma, D.N. 718
Sharp, Walter R. 595, 654, 1121, 1178
Shepard, M. 63
Shippen, Katherine Binney 1180
Shkunaev, V.G. 1259
Shonfield, Andrew 1143

Shore, William T. 916
Shotwell, James Thomson 867, 1239, 1461
Shukri, M.A. 1359
Shuster, George N. 1268
Shuster, Milan R. 1078
Sills, David L. 22
Silverstein, Harvey B. 707
Simmonds, R. 990
Simons, Anne Patricia 791, 830
Simpson, J.L. 998
Singer, David J. 632
Singh, Hdrnam 1506
Singh, Nagendra 393, 612, 760, 1431
Sissons, David 736
Skern, L.M.K. 935
Skolnikoff, Eugene B. 1287
Slonim, S. 1379
Sly, John F. 1059
Smith, Delbert D. 1020
Sohn, Louis B. 289-91, 1409-10, 1472, 1486
Solano, E. John 1236
Soloman, Jack 1529
Soloman, L.M. 1132
Sorensen, Max 749
Soviet Association of International Law 218
Soward, F.H. 741
Spaull, Hebe 1119
Speeckaert, G.P. 50
Srivastava, Padma 663
Stanley Foundation, The 334
Stanley, Robert G. 1186
Stegenga, James A. 993
Stein, E. 610
Steiner, H.A. 1400
Stenquist, Nils 945
Stevenson, Adlai E. 480
Stewart M. 1255
Stinebower, Leroy D. 598
Stockholm International Peace Research Institute (SIPRI) 205, 338
Stoessinger, John G. 631, 821, 1398
Stone, Julius 691, 844, 893, 1388, 1497
Stone, Ralph 421
Stoyanovsky, J. 1334
Strange, Susan 500
Strasser, Wolfgang 738

Author Index

Straszheim, Mahlon R. 1032
Streit, Clarence K. 1468
Stromberg, R.N. 840
Stuart, Graham H. 1344
Study Group of the Egyptian Society of International Law 750
Study Group of the Institut Royal des Relations Internationales of Brussels 739
Study Group of the Italian Society for International Organization 764
Study Group of the Japanese Association of International Law 765
Study Group of the Swedish Institute of International Affairs 771
Study Group on the Peaceful Settlement of International Disputes 884
Study Group Set Up by the Hebrew University of Jerusalem 763
Stuyt, Alexander M. 1003
Sufrin, Sidney C. 1172
Sullivan, Walter 1293
Summers, Robert Edward 805
Sureda, A. Rigo 1357
Sweetser, Arthur 429
Syatauw, J.J.G. 278
Symonds, Richard 1296
Szalai, Alexander 486
Szapiro, Jerry 485
Szasz, Paul G. 1280

T

Taborn, P. 938
Taubenfeld, Howard J. 1058, 1442
Taubenfeld, R.F. 1442
Tavaras de Sa, Hernane 478
Taylor, Alastair 742, 1361
Taylor, Paul 1208, 1531
Teaf, Howard M., Jr. 1176
Teng, Catherine G. 831
Tetlow, Edwin 476
Tew, Brian 1091
Thant, U 680, 1160
Theimer, Walter 21
Thomas, Bryan W. 943
Thomas, Jean 1269
Thompson, Elizabeth M. 349
Thompson, Margaret C. 503

Thomson, Charles A. 1265
Thorne, Christopher 898
Thullen, George 1348
Tickner, Fred 1173
Tipton, John Bruce 1256
Tiwari, S.C. 789
Tobiassen, L.K. 546
Tokyo Japan Branch of the International Law Association 219
Tomlinson, John D. 1021
Tompkins, E.B. 496
Tondel, Lyman M., Jr. 989
Topolski, Felix 462
Torre, Mottram 649
Toussaint, Charmian Edward 1347
Townley, Ralph 479
Trager, Frank N. 740
Triffin, Robert 1083-84
Tripp, Brenda M.H. 1270
Trumbell, Robert 1376
Tung, William L. 455
Turabian, Kate L. 361
Turbull, Laura S. 583
Turner, Robert K. 239
Twentieth Century Fund 1022
Twitchett, Kenneth J. 494, 701

U

Uhl, Alexander 803
Umozurike, Umozurike Ojo 1324
Unidroit. See International Institute for the Unification of Private International Law
Union of International Associations 53, 343, 607
United Nations 94, 105, 251, 267, 302, 304-5, 356, 602, 605, 861, 1054-55, 1286
United Nations Association of the United States of America 61, 148, 231, 335, 337, 903
United Nations Department of Public Information 1174
United Nations Economic and Social Council (ECOSOC) 78, 104, 273, 599, 1149
United Nations Economic Commission for Europe (ECE) 1123
United Nations Educational, Scientific and Cultural Organization

Author Index

(UNESCO) 27, 70, 88-89, 134, 137, 273, 306, 323, 356, 599, 1309, 1440
United Nations Fund for Population Activities 1296a
United Nations General Assembly 271, 587
United Nations Institute for Training and Research (UNITAR) 93
United Nations International Children's Emergency Fund (UNICEF) 1298
United Nations Library 66, 252-54, 256, 258-59, 317
United Nations Library (Dag Hammarskjold) 67, 364
United Nations Library (Geneva) 318
United Nations Library (New York) 68, 319
United Nations Office of Legal Affairs 262, 283
United Nations Office of Public Information 5, 351, 450-51, 528, 721, 726, 860, 1174
United Nations Relief and Rehabilitation Administration 1126
United Nations Review 992
United Nations Secretariat 107, 533
United Nations Secretariat. Department of Public Information 7, 77, 452, 1350
United Nations Secretariat. Office of Public Information for Human Welfare 80
United Nations Secretariat. Protocol and Liason Section 341
United Nations Security Council 272, 594
United Nations Trusteeship Council 274
United States Citizens in World Affairs 345
United States Congress. House Committee on Foreign Affairs 854
United States Congress. Senate 1480-82
United States Congress. Senate Committee on Foreign Relations 17
United States Delegation to the United Nations Conference on International Organization 537
United States Department of State 268, 282, 436, 790, 808-9, 1185
United States Department of State. Bureau of United Nations Affairs 347
United States Department of State. Division of International Conferences 807
United States Department of State. Division of International Organization Affairs 810
United States Department of State. Library 143
United States Department of the Army 109
United States Library of Congress 31-34, 133, 225, 230, 309, 316, 358
United States Office of Education 69
United World Federalists 115
Upthegrove, Campell L. 1330
Urquhart, Brian 670
Uruguayan Institute of International Law 822
Utton, Albert E. 1292

V

Valahu, Mugur 984
Van Asbeck, F.M. 1438
Vandenbosch, Amry 383, 454
Van der Kroef, Justus M. 1365
Van der Molen, Gezina Hermina 543
Van Dusen, Henry P. 671
Van Dyke, Vernon 1435
Van Maanen-Helmer, Elizabeth 1331
Van Meerhaeghe, M.A.G. 1116
van Panhuys, H.F. 288
Van Slyck, Philip 1498
Van Wagenen, Richard W. 501, 813
Van Wyk, J. 1384
Vatcher, William H., Jr. 850
Venant, Jacques 1397
Verma, D.N. 761
Verniers, Louis 1301
Viet, J. 100
Vincent, Jack E. 3, 717
Von Albertini, Rudolf 1352
Von Goeckingk, Johanna 1175
Von Horn, C. 949

Author Index

W

Wadsworth, James J. 477
Wainhouse, David W. 868, 919-20, 1353
Waldock, Humphry 887
Walford, Arthur J. 41
Wallenstein, Arthur 377
Walp, Paul K. 538
Walters, F.P. 409
Walton, Ann D. 326
Wambaugh, Sarah 1342, 1345-46
Wassenbergh, H.A. 1034
Wasson, Donald 325
Waterlow, Charlotte 1503
Waters, Maurice 488
Watkins, James T. 295
Watts, V. Orva 470
Weaver, James H. 1202
Wedgwood, Sir Ralph L. 1060
Wehl, David 1364
Weiler, Lawrence D. 791
Weissberg, Guenter 547
Weitz, Harold 575
Wells, Herbert G. 422
Weng, Byron S.J. 745
Werner, M. 1395
Werners, S.E. 600
Wheeler, J.E. 1060
Wheeler-Bennett, John W. 875-76
White, Carl M. 43
White, Eric Wyndham 1064
White, Gilliam N. 693
White, Irvin L. 1046
White, John 1167
White, Lyman Cromwell 1299, 1303
White, Wilbur W. 20
Wightman, David 1124, 1169
Wilcox, Clair 1063
Wilcox, Francis O. 716, 800, 1471
Wild, Payson S. 857
Wilkie, Lloyd 346
Williams, Sir John Fischer 519, 525, 539
Williams, Stillman P. 103
Williams, Walter L., Jr. 933
Willoughby, W.W. 897
Willrich, Mason 1284
Wilson, A.J. 937
Wilson, Archibald 1469
Wilson, Duncan 1469
Wilson, Elizabeth 1469
Wilson, Florence 520
Wilson, Francis Graham 1226
Wilson, Howard E. 1271
Winchell, Constance M. 44
Windmuller, John P. 1257
Winton, Harry N. 76
Withey, Stephen B. 812
Witt, William D. 469
Woetzel, Robert K. 691
Woito, Robert 114
Wolbert, Robert G. 35
Wood, Robert S. 402
Woodbridge, George 1125
Woodward, E.L. 1496
Woolf, Leonard Sidney 394
World Health Organization 75, 90-91, 286-87, 1214
World Law Fund 339
World Meterological Organization. Secretariat 92
World Peace Foundation 146, 340, 1225
Wortley, B.A. 472
Wriggins, Howard 655
Wright, Quincy 540, 843, 961, 1325, 1499, 1509
Wynar, L.R. 45
Wynner, Edith 1522

X

Xydis, Stephen G. 995

Y

Yanaihara, Tadeo 1337
Yates, P. Lamartine 1182
Yemin, Edward 569
Yoo, Tae-Ho 847
Young, Harold C. 310
Young, Margaret Labash 310
Young, Oran R. 881, 917-18
Young, Tien-Chen 643

Z

Zacher, Mark W. 668
Zacklin, Ralph 1473
Zasloff, Joseph J. 964
Zehnder, Alfred 774
Zeydel, Walter H. 563
Zimmern, A.E. 417
Zocca, Marie Ragonetti 1299

TITLE INDEX

This index includes all titles of books, published reports, and theses which are cited in the text. In some cases the titles have been shortened. Journals, titles of articles, and chapter titles are not included. Numbers refer to entry numbers.

A

ABC Pol Sci 145
Activities of Gatt (year), The 156
Acts and Documents concerning the Organization of the Court (ICJ) 280
Acts and Documents concerning the Organization of the Court (PCIJ) 279
Administering the Atom for Peace 1281
Administration of India's Foreign Policy through the United Nations, The 759
Administration of International Organizations, The 639
Administration of the United Kingdom's Foreign Policy through the United Nations, The 778
Advisory Function of the International Court in the League and UN Eras, The 692
Africa and the United Nations 720
African States and the United Nations Versus Apartheid 719
Afro-Asian Group in the United Nations, The 718
Agencies of the United Nations, The 1119

Aggression and World Order 844
Aid Coordination 1164
Aland Island Question, The 895
Albert Thomas 1253
Algeria before the United Nations 735
Amendment of the Constitutive Instruments of the United Nations and Specialized Agencies, The 1473
America and the New World State 1446
American Agencies Interested in International Affairs 325
American Journal of International Law, The 163
American Labor and the International Labor Movement 1257
American Library Resources 314
American Newspapers 1821-1936 220
American Peace Crusade, The 1465
American Political Science Review, The 166
American Security Policy and the United Nations 801
Analysis and Appraisal for the General Agreement on Tariffs and Trade, An 1073
Analysis and Prediction in International Mediation 878

Title Index

Analysis of the Principles and System of International Trusteeship in the Charter 1351
Anatomy of Influence, The 630
Annals of the Chinese Society of International Law, The 215
Annotated Bibliography on Disarmament and Military Questions 112
Annuaire, Institut de Droit International 209
Annual Register of Grant Support 360
Annual Register of World Events, The 10
Annual Report of the Permanent Control of International Justice 200
Annual Reports (PICJ) 279
Annual Review of United Nations Affairs 149
Antecedents of the International Labour Organization 1228
Anti-Drug Campaign, The 1223
Apartheid and the United Nations Collective Measures 908
Approach to the Analysis of Resolutions of the Economic and Social Council, An 502
Approach to the Analysis of Resolutions of the Security Council, An 575
Arab Bloc in the United Nations, The 724
Arab-Israel Conflict in the UN, The 965
Arabs and the United Nations, The 723
Arbitration and the Hague Court 1004
Area and International Document Service 296
Arms Control Agreements 868
Arms Control and Disarmament 127
Articles and Studies on the World Health Organization 75
Assault on the Unknown, The 1293
Assembly of the League of Nations, The 578
Associations, 150
Atomic Safeguards 1278
Attack on World Poverty, The 1143
Australia and New Guinea 1372

Australia and the Colonial Question at the United Nations 737
Australia and the United Nations 736
Australian Mandate of New Guinea, The 1339
Australian Yearbook of International Law 212
Authority of the United Nations over Non-Members, The 574
Authorization of Peace-Keeping Operations in Terms of the Nature of the Conflict, The 939

B

Background 167
Bank for International Settlements, The (Einzig) 1108
Bank for International Settlements, The (Schloss) 1110
Bank for International Settlements at Work, The 1107
Bases of International Order, The 404
Basic Courses in International Organization 348
Basic Documents (WHO) 287
Basic Documents of International Organizations 292
Basic Documents of the United Nations 289
Basic Documents on Human Rights 1439
Basic Documents on International Protection of Human Rights 1410
Basic Facts about the United Nations 5
Basic Instruments and Selected Documents Series (GATT) 284
Basic Problems of Disarmament 861
La Belgique et les Nations Unies 739
Betrayal from Within 665
Better League of Nations, A 522
Between Arab and Israeli 954
Beyond the Nation-State 1242
Bibliographical List of Official and Unofficial Publications (ICJ) 98
Bibliographical Services throughout the World 307
Bibliographical Style Manual 94, 364

Title Index

Bibliographic Index, The 25
Bibliography of the Charter of the United Nations, A 66, 94
Bibliography of the International Court of Justice 96
Bibliography of the International Court of Justice, Including the Permanent Court, 1918-64 95
Bibliography of the International Labor Organization 71
Bibliography of the Publications of the United Nations and Specialized Agencies in the Social Welfare Field 78
Bibliography of the Technical Work of the Health Organization of the League 55
Bibliography on Peace Research in History 118
Bibliography on the Economics of Disarmament 111
Bibliography on the International Labour Organization 71
Bibliography on the Protection of Human Rights 104
Biology and World Health 1219
Birth of Indonesia, The 1364
Bloc Politics in the United Nations 705
Blue Berets, The 951
Blueprint for Peace 799
Bold New Program 1179
Books on the Work of the League of Nations 54
Breakthrough to Tomorrow 1136
Bretton Woods 1093
Bretton Woods: For Better or Worse 1111
Brief Guide to the League of Nations Publications 60
Britain and the I.L.O. 1254
Britain and the I.L.O.: The Story of Fifty Years 1255
Britain and the United Nations 779
British Yearbook of International Law 213
Brutal Mandate 1441
Bulletin of Peace Proposals 178
Bulletin of the Public Affairs Information Service 141

Burma's Role in the United Nations 740

C

Cameroon: United Nations Challenge to French Policy 1360
Canada and the United Nations 741
Canada at Geneva 743
Canadian Yearbook of International Law, The 214
Capacity of International Organizations to Conclude Treaties, The 573
Cartel Policy for the United Nations, A 1076
Case for an International Development Authority, The 1141
Case of China and Japan before the League of Nations, The 899
Case Law of the International Court, The 277
Cases on United Nations Law 291
Catalog of Books Represented by Library of Congress Printed Cards, A 31
Catalog of Publications in English of the International Labour Office, 1919-1950 85
Catalogue of Economic and Social Projects of the United Nations and the Specialized Agencies 1149
Catalogue of Publications: Meteorology and Related Fields (WHO) 92
Catalogue of Publications, 1945-1972 (FAO) 82
Catalogue of Publications, 1920-1935 (League) 59
Catalogue of the Publications of the International Court of Justice 97
Caucusing Groups of the United Nations, The 717
Century of the Homeless Man, The 1401
Ceres: FAO Review 154
Chaco Dispute and the League of Nations, The 900
Changing Charter, The 535
Changing United Nations, The 457
Changing World 148

Title Index

Chapters on Current International Law and the League of Nations 539
Characteristics and Some Aspects of Launching U.N. Peace-Keeping Forces 952
Character of International Sanctions and Their Application, The 856
Charter for World Trade, A 1063
Charter of the United Nations: Commentary and Documents, The 529
Charter of the United Nations: Report to the President 537
Checklist of United Nations Documents 252
Children of the Developing Countries 1298
China and the League 747
China and the United Nations 744
China Joins the U.N. 746
China Representation in the U.N. 620
China's Role with the League of Nations 748
Chinese Representation 621
Chinese Representation in the Security Council and the General Assembly of the United Nations 619
Christian Science Monitor Index, The 226
Chronicle of United Nations Activities 15
Chronology and Fact Book of the United Nations, A 8
Chronology of International Events 11
Citations Rules and Forms of United Nations Documents and Publications 363
Collection of Advisory Opinions (PCIJ) 279
Collection of Judgments (PCIJ) 279
Collection of Judgments, Orders and Advisory Opinions (PCIJ) 279
Collections of Texts Governing the Jurisdiction of the Court 281
Collective Security 836
Collective Security: A Progress Report 835

Collective Security: A Record 842
Collective Security: The Why and How 841
Collective Security and American Foreign Policy from the League of Nations to NATO 840
Collective Security and the Future International System 838
Colonialism and the United Nations 1356
Columbia Journal of Transnational Law 169
Commentary of the Charter of the United Nations, A 530
Commercial Arbitration 1005
Committees of the League of Nations, The 584
Common Aid Effort, The 1165
Commonwealth and the United Nations, The 731
Commonwealth of Man, The 1512
Comparison and Evaluation of Current Disarmament Proposals, A 865
Complementary Structures of Third Party Settlement of International Disputes 889
Complete Handbook on World Government 1529
Compulsory Arbitration of International Disputes 997
Computer Simulation of Audience Exposure in a Mass Media System, A 516
Concept of Self-Determination in the United Nations, The 1359
Conditions of World Order 1508
Conference on the United Nations of the Next Decade Reports 334
Conflict and Peace in the Modern International System 827
Conflict Issues and International Civil Aviation Decisions 1029
Conflict Management 877
Congo: A Chronology of Events, The 991
Congo: Background of Conflict 982
Congo Disaster 979
Congo 196-. 985
Congo Since Independence, The 978
Conscience of the Rich Nations, The 1166

Title Index

Consolidated List of Depository Libraries and Sales Agents 317
Consolidated Treaty Series, The 300
Constitutional Developments of the League of Nations 538
Constitutionalism of the United Nations System 297
Constitution and World Organization, The 814
Constitution for the World 1516
Constitutions of the United Nations 536
Consultation and Consensus in the Security Council 590
Controlling World Trade 1074
Cooperation and Conflict 179
Co-operation or Coercion? 418
Coordination of Economic and Social Activities 1210
Corfu Incident of 1923, The 894
Covenant and the Charter, The 526
Creating a New World Politics 891
Crisis in the Congo 975
Crisis of Development 1130
Crisis over Rhodesia 1378
Critical Evaluation of the UN, A 467
Critical Survey of Plans for International Monetary Reform, A 1089
Cumulative Book Index, The 28
Current Issues 67, 94
Current National Bibliographies 34
Current Research in International Affairs 321
Current Thought on Peace and War 119
Cyprus: Conflict and Conciliation 995
Cyprus: The Law and Politics of Civil Strife 994

D

Dag Hammarskjold (Public Papers) 675
Dag Hammarskjold: A Biographical Interpretation of "Markings" 671
Dag Hammarskjold: Custodian of the Brushfire Peace 669
Dag Hammarskjold and Crisis Diplomacy 672

Dag Hammarskjold's United Nations 668
Dag Hammarskjold's White Book 678
Danger in Kashmir 971
Danzig Dilemma 1340
Day in the Life of the United Nations, A 481
DEA News 355
Debt Trap, The 1103a
Decision-Making for Space 1046
Decisions of the International Court of Justice 278
Decisions óf the United Nations Organs in the Judgments and Opinions of the International Court of Justice 688
Decolonization, the Administration and Future of the Colonies 1352
Defeat of an Ideal 464
Delegations to the United Nations 341
Denmark and the United Nations 749
Dependent Areas in the Post-War World 1323
Development of International Law by the International Court, The 690
Development of International Law by the International Labor Organization, The 1249
Development of International Law through the Political Organs of the United Nations, The 564
Development of the League of Nations Idea, The 411
Development of UNESCO, The 1271
Dictionary of Political Science 19
Digest of Legal Activities of International Organizations and Other Institutions 544
Diplomacy of Indian Foreign Policy in the United Nations, The 758
Diplomats in International Cooperation 711
Directory of Information Resources in the United States, A 309
Directory of Non-Governmental Organizations, A 345
Directory of Periodicals Published by International Organizations 53, 139

Title Index

Directory of Publishing Opportunities 359
Directory of Special Libraries and Information Centers 310
Disarmament (Hammarskjold Forum) 859
Disarmament (Noel-Baker) 874
Disarmament: A Bibliographic Record 109
Disarmament: A Select Bibliography 94, 107
Disarmament: A Selected Chronology 17
Disarmament; A Study Guide and Bibliography on the Efforts of the United Nations 65, 108
Disarmament and Arms Control: An International Quarterly Journal 165
Disarmament and Security Since Locarno 875
Disarmament Deadlock, The 876
Disposition of Italian Colonies, The 1370
Dissertation Abstracts 122
Doctoral Dissertations Accepted by American Universities 123
Doctors to the World 1220
Doctrine of Equality of States as Applied in International Organizations, The 557
Documentary History of Arms Control and Disarmament 862
Documentary Textbook on the United Nations 293
Documents of International Meetings 242
Documents of International Organizations: A Bibliographic Handbook 238
Documents of International Organizations: A Selected Bibliography 239
Documents of the League of Nations 246
Documents Relating to International Organizations 240
Domestic Interests and International Trade Organizations 1062
Drafting of the Covenant, The 518

Dynamics of International Organization, The 377

E

Economic and Financial Organization of the League of Nations, The 1104
Economic and Social Council, The 598
Economic Consequences of the League 1106
Economic Cooperation in Europe 1124
Economic Development: Principles, Problems and Policies 1128
Economic Development: Special UN Fund for Economic Development 1148
Economic Development, Human Skills and Technical Assistance 1251
Economic Development Projects and Their Appraisal 1190
Economic Sanctions and International Enforcement 853
Economics of Trusteeship in Somalia, The 1368
Educational Film Catalog 357
Educational Film Guide 357
Effectiveness of International Decisions, The 566
Effectiveness of International Supervision, The 1240
Egypt and the United Nations 750
Elections in the United Nations General Assembly 628
Empire by Mandate 1330
Enabling Instruments of Members of the United Nations 563
Encyclopedia of Modern World Politics, An 21
Enforcement of International Judicial Decisions and Arbitral Awards in Public International Law, The 1012
Environmental Policy 1292
Essential Facts about the League of Nations 6
Establishment of the International Finance Corporation and United States Policy 1201
Les Etats de Group de Brazaville aux Nations Unies 722

Title Index

Eternal Machiavelli in the United Nations World, The 482
Eternal Triangle, The 618
Everyman's United Nations: A Complete Handbook . . . 1945-1965 450
Everyman's United Nations: A Summary of the Activities . . . 1966-1970 451
Evolution of International Organizations, The 387
Evolution of the International Monetary System, The 1084
Evolution of the Right of Self-Determination, The 1357
Evolution of the South West Africa Dispute before the United Nations, The 1383
Evolution of the United Nations, The 405
Evolution or Revolution 911
Evolving United Nations, The 494
Expanding Frontiers in Social Welfare 1209
Experiment in World Government 981
Experiments in International Administration 640
Extent of the Advisory Jurisdiction of the International Court of Justice, The 1010

F

Facilitation of Problems of International Association 1300
Fact Finding in the Maintenance of International Peace 916
Facts on File 12
FAO Books in Print 83
Fearful Master, The 465
Federalism and World Order 1469
Federal Republic of Germany and the United Nations, The 823
Federal Union in Practice 1519
Federal World Government 1520
Federation: The Coming Structure 1517
Fiction and Truth about the "Decade of Development" 1163
Field Administration in the United Nations System 1121

Fifteen Men on a Powder Keg 588
Fifteen Years of Activity of the Economic Commission for Europe 1123
Fight for Peace, The 1464
Financial Assistance for Economic Development 1150
Financing Economic Development 1140
Financing International Organizations 632
Financing the UN 633
Financing the United Nations System 631
First Assembly, The (League) 579
First Fifty Years: The Secretary-General in World Politics, The 659
First Ten Years of the World Health Organization, The 1214
First Twenty Years of the Bank for International Settlements, The 1109
First U.N. Development Decade and Its Lessons for the 1970's, The 1161
Food and Agricultural Organization of the United Nations 1185
Food for Peace 1186
Food for the World 1184
Force in Peace 944
Foreign Affairs 170, 331
Foreign Affairs Bibliography 35
Foreign Affairs 50-Year Bibliography, The 36
Foreign Aid in International Politics 1154
Foreign Development Lending 1151
Foreign Press, The 221
Foreign Relations of the United States, 1946 790
Forging World Order 378
Formosa, China and the United Nations 617
Foundation Directory, The 326
Foundation of a More Stable World Order, The 407
Foundations for World Order 1496
Foundations of Modern Society 392
Foundations of World Organization 406

Title Index

Frederick May's London Press Dictionary 224
Freedom in a Federal World 1521
Freedom of Association 1312
Freedom of the Air, The 1030
From Collective Security to Preventive Diplomacy 399
From Geneva to San Francisco 434
From Many, One 504
From the League to U.N. 433
Frontiers, Peace Treaties and International Organizations 910
Functionalism: Theory and Practice in International Relations 1531
Functionalism and Regionalism in the United Nations 1153
Functionalism and World Politics 152
Fund Agreement, The 1102
Fundamentals of World Organization 382
Fund and Non-Member States, The 1098
Future of the International Legal Order, The 877, 1291
Future of the International Monetary System, The 1081
Future of the International Telecommunications Union, The 1023
Future of the United Nations, The 468
Future of the United Nations: Issues of Charter Revisions, The 1474
Future of the World Bank, The 1192
Futurist, The 185

G

LE GATT 1071
GATT--Law and International Economic Organization, The 1065
GATT: Publications 84
GATT Activities in (year) 156
GATT as an International Trade Organization 1064
GATT Bibliography 73
General Assembly: Patterns, Problems, Prospects, The 585
General Assembly of the United Nations: A Study of Procedure and Practice, The 586
General Bibliography of International Organization and Post-War Reconstruction 52
General Catalog of UNESCO Publications and UNESCO Sponsored Publications 89
General Indexes (PCIJ) 263, 279
General International Organization: A Source Book 295
General Principles and Problems in the International Protection of Minorities 1393
Genesis of the United Nations 789
Genesis of the Universal Postal Union, The 1059
Geneva Protocol, The 523
Geneva Protocol for the Pacific Settlement of International Disputes, The 524
Geneva Protocol of 1924, The 525
Glass House, The 477
Global Communications in the Space Age 1022
Global Partnership, The 1115
Good War, The 1145
Government Document Bibliography in the United States and Elsewhere 237
Government Publications and Their Use 235
Graduate Level Survey of Future Studies, A 353
Great Britain and Palestine 964
Great Decision, The 1461
Great Design, The 445
Greater United Nations, The 1308
La Grece et Les Nations Unies 751
Grotius Society Transactions 210
Guide to League of Nations Publications 56
Guide to Microforms in Print 128
Guide to National Bibliographic Information Centers 306
Guide to Reference Material 41
Guide to Reference Materials in Political Science 45
Guide to Reference Works 44
Guide to the Charter of the United Nations 528
Guide to the Practice of International Conferences, A 608
Guide to the Use of United Nations Documents, A 247

Title Index

Guide to United States Government Serials and Periodicals 136
Guide to United States Publications 136

H

Hague Academy of International Law. Jubilee Book, The 208
Hague Court Reports, The 275
Half the World's Children 1297
Hammarskjold (Kelen) 673
Hammarskjold (Urquhart) 670
Hammarskjold: Servant of a World Unborn 674
Hammarskjold Forums 327
Handbook of International Organizations 1
Handbook of International Organizations in the Americas 4
Handbook of Resolutions and Decisions (WHO) 286
Handbook of the League of Nations 2
Handbook of the United Nations, A 3
Handling of International Disputes by Means of Inquiry 918a
Hands across Frontiers 1176
Headline Series 332
Headquarters of International Institutions 550
High Tower of Refuge, The 1403
History of the International Labor Organization 1227
History of the International Labour Office 1229
History of the League of Nations, A (Knudson) 410
History of the League of Nations, A (Walters) 409
History of the United Nations Charter, A 527
Holy Land under Mandate, The 1335
How the United Nations Works 444
How to Plan and Conduct Model UN Meetings 356
How to Use United Nations Documents 248
How United Nations Decisions Are Made 629

Humanitarian Intervention and the United Nations 1434
Human Rights: Comments and Interpretations 1440
Human Rights: Federalism and Minorities 1413
Human Rights: Protection of the Individual under International Law 1414
Human Rights and International Action 1428
Human Rights and International Cooperation 1431
Human Rights and International Labour Standards 1250
Human Rights and the Charter 1436
Human Rights and the International Community 1419
Human Rights and the United Nations 1421
Human Rights and World Politics 1418
Human Rights as Legal Rights 1425
Human Rights in the Modern World 1427
Human Rights in the World 1437
Human Rights, the United States and World Community 1435
Human Right to Individual Freedom 1430

I

Idea and Practice of World Government, The 389
Idea of a League of Nations, The 422
Illusion of World Government, The 1530
ILO Publications 87
Immunities and Privileges of International Officials 553
Impartial Soldier, The 950
Implications of Expanding Membership for United Nations Administration and Budget 654
Implied Powers of the United Nations 555
Independence of Papua-New Guinea, The 1371
Index Bibliographicus 26

321

Title Index

Index to Microfilm of UN Documents in English 94
Index to Documents of the Trusteeship Council 258
Index to Proceedings of the Economic and Social Council 256
Index to Proceedings of the General Assembly 253
Index to Proceedings of the Security Council 254
Index to the Times (London) 228
India and International Law 760
India and the I.L.O. 1261
India and the League of Nations (Ram and Sharma) 762
India and the League of Nations (Verma) 761
India and the United Nations 753
Indian Journal of International Law 164
India's Role in the Korean Question 755
India's Role in the U.N. 756
India's Role in the United Nations 752
Individual and World Society, The 1429
Individual's Rights and International Organization, The 1420
Individual, the State and World Government, The 1525
Indonesian Independence and the United Nations 1361
Industrialization of Underdeveloped Countries 1147
In Pursuit of World Order 998
Inside Story of UNNRA, The 1127
Inspection for Disarmament 869
Institute of International Affairs 320
Institutional Structure of the Free World Economy, The 1118
Integration through Monetary Union? 1094
Interdependent, The 231, 335
Intergovernmental Military Forces and World Public Order 933
Intermediaries, The 917
Internal War and International Systems 913
In the Cause of Peace 666
ILO: The First Decade 1231

ILO and the Tripartite System 1244
ILO and the UN 1243
International Administration 636
International Administration: A Bibliography 101
International Administration: Its Evolution and Contemporary Applications 637
International Administration: The United Nations and Specialized Agencies 63
International Administration of an International Secretariat, The 653
International Administration of Space Exploration and Exploitation 1057
International Administrative Jurisdiction 648
International Affairs (de Grazia) 39
International Affairs (Royal Institute of International Affairs) 171
International Agencies in Which the United States Participates 810
International Aid 1139
International Aid: A Summary with Special Reference to the Programmes of the United Nations 1138
International Airline Industry, The 1032
International Air Transport 1033
International Air Transport Association, The 1027
International and Comparative Law Quarterly, The 172
International Arbitral Law and Procedure 1002
International Arbitration 998
International Arbitration: International Tribunals 1000
International Arbitration and Procedure 1001
International Arbitration from Athens to Locarno 996
International Associations 150
International Atomic Energy Agency and Its Relationship to the United Nations, The 1277
International Atomic Energy Agency Publications 81
International Bank for Reconstruction and Development, The 1195

Title Index

International Bank for Reconstruction and Development, 1946-1953, The 1194
International Bibliography of Political Science 37
International City of Tangier, The 1334
International Civil Aviation Organization, The 1031
International Civil Servant in Law and in Fact, The 645
International Civil Service, The (Bedjaoui) 644
International Civil Service, The (Langrod) 642
International Civil Service, The (Young) 643
International Commodity Agreements 1077
International Communications 1018
International Conciliation (Carnegie Endowment) 147, 328
International Conciliation (Colt) 880
International Conciliation (with special reference to the worth of the United Nations Conciliation Commission for Palestine) 956
International Conflict and Collective Security 839
International Congresses and Conferences, 1840-1937 241
International Congress Organization 607
International Control of Aviation 1035
International Control of Radio and Communications 1021
International Control of the Nuclear Maritime Activities 1283
International Cooperation and Programmes of Economic and Social Development 100
International Cooperation and You 1301
International Cooperation for Pollution Control 1290
International Cooperation in Outer Space 1049
International Cooperation in Public Health 1212

International Cooperation Today 1208
International Court of Justice, The 687
International Court of Justice: An Essay in Political and Legal Theory, The 686
International Court of Justice: Its Role in the Maintenance of International Peace and Security, The 1006
International Court of Justice: Selected Documents, The 282
International Court of Justice and Impartiality Between Nations, The 689
International Development 1132
International Development Association, The 1202
International Disputes: Case Histories 888
International Disputes: The Legal Aspects 887
International Disputes: The Political Aspects 886
International Drug Control 1222
International Economic Institutions 1116
International Encyclopedia of the Social Sciences 22
International Equilibrium 509
International Experiment of Upper Silesia, The 1343
International Finance Corporation, The 1200
International Financial Aid 1133
International Government (Eagleton) 388
International Government (Woolf) 394
International Governmental Organizations: Constitutional Documents 517
International Government of the Saar, The 1341
International Group Protection 1394
International Guarantees of Minority Rights 1388
International Health Organizations and Their Work 1221
International Immunities 552
International Index to Periodicals 140

Title Index

International Institutional Law 561
International Institutions 385
International Institutions and World Order 1493
International Intellectual Cooperation 1263
International Journal 173
International Labor Conventions 1248
International Labor Organization, The 1235
International Labor Organization: Past and Present 1259
International Labour Movement, The 1245
International Labour Office, The 1230
International Labour Organization: Its Work for Social and Economic Progress 1241
International Labour Organization Yearbook 202
International Labour Review 155
International Law and Human Rights 1415
International Law and Organization: An Introductory Reader 398
International Law and Organization: General Sources of Information 49
International Law and the United Nations (University of Michigan Law School) 541
International Law and the United Nations (Wright) 540
International Law and the Use of Force by States 833
International Law Commission, The 601
International Law of Communications, The 1014
International Law of the Ocean Development, The 1042
International Law through the United Nations 577
International Law, Trade and Finance 1061
International Legal Aspects of the Operations of the World Bank, 1196
International Legislation 303

International Legislation by the United Nations 570
International Library Directory 312
International Mandates, The 1329
International Mandates and Trustee Systems 1321
International Military Forces 934
International Monetary Cooperation 1092
International Monetary Co-operation, 1945-63 1091
International Monetary Fund: A Selected Bibliography, The 74
International Monetary Fund: Legal Aspects, Structure, Functions, The 1101
International Monetary Fund: Retrospect and Prospect, The 1103
International Monetary Fund and International Law, The 1100
International Monetary Fund and Private Business Transactions, The 1099
International Monetary Fund, 1945-1965, The 1095a, 1095b
International Monetary Policy 1090
International Monetary Problems 1086
International Monetary Reform 1080
International Monetary System, The 1085
International Narcotic Controls 1224
International Non-Governmental Organizations 1299
International Non-Governmental Organizations and Economic Entities 1302
International Opium Conference, The 1225
International Order and Economic Integration 512
International Organization (Blaisdell) 379
International Organization (Chamberlain) 380
International Organization (Hill) 390
International Organization (Leonard) 381
International Organization (World Peace Foundation) 146, 340

Title Index

International Organization: A Classified Bibliography 48
International Organization: An Interdisciplinary Bibliography 47
International Organization: A Select Bibliography 50
International Organization: Law in Movement 408
International Organization and Integration 288
International Organizations (Chadwick) 391
International Organizations: Some Theoretical Problems 395
International Organizations and Space Cooperation 1053
International Organizations from the Soviet Point of View 784
International Organizations in the Social Sciences 1309
International Organizations in Which the United States Participates 815
International Organizations in Which the United States Participates, 1949 347
International Organization under the United Nations System 455
International Peace/Disarmament Directory 346
International Peace Force and Public Opinion, An 510
International Peacekeeping at the Crossroads 920
International Peace Observation 919
International Peace Research Newsletter 180
International Personality of Intergovernmental Organizations 562
International Police Force, An 943
International Police Force 942
International Political Science Abstracts 120
International Politics: A Selective Monthly 143
International Privileges and Immunities 551
International Protection of Human Rights, The (Del Russo) 1424
International Protection of Human Rights, The (Eide) 1411
International Protection of Human Rights, The (Ganji) 1412
International Protection of Human Rights, The (Luard) 1416
International Protection of Human Rights, The (Sohn and Buergenthal) 1409
International Protection of Labor, The 1273
International Protection of National Minorities in Europe 1392
International Protection of Trade Union Freedom, The 1246
International Rail Transport 1060
International Refugee Organization, The 1404
International Register of Current Team Research in the Social Sciences, The 323
International Regulation of Civil Wars 912
International Regulation of Economic and Social Questions 1112
International Regulation of Frontier Disputes 909
International Regulations and Organizations: Comparative and Area Studies 48a
International Relations Dictionary, The 18
International Relations Digest of Periodical Literature 135
International Relief Action 1317
International Repertory of Institutions for Peace and Conflict Research 324
International Repertory of Social Science Documentation Centers 311, 322
International Review Service 9
International River and Canal Transport 1044
International Road, Transport, Postal, Electricity and Miscellaneous Questions 1015
International Safeguards and Nuclear Industry 1284
International Sea Transport 1040
International Secretariat, The 635
International Secretariat of the Future, The 645

Title Index

International Security Systems 1504
International Shipping Cartels 1075
International Social Progress 1232
International Social Science Bulletin 70
International Space Bibliography 105
International Status of the United Nations, The 547
International Technical Assistance 1178
International Technical Assistance Experts 1177
International Telecommunication Control 1020
International Telecommunications 1024
International Telecommunications and International Law 1019
International Telecommunications Union, The 1017
International Trade Policy and GATT 1067
International Tribunals Past and Future 681
International Trusteeship System and the Trusteeship Council, The 1350
International Understanding 1314
International Voluntary Service for Peace 1318
International Yearbook and Statesmen's Who's Who, The 190
Interpretation of Ambiguous Documents by International Administrative Tribunals 647
In the Cause of Peace 666
Introduction to the Study of International Organizations, An 384
Invasion and Occupation of Czechoslovakia and the UN 907
Ireland in the International Organization 1260
Irreconcilables, The 421
Israel and the United Nations 763
Israel Yearbook on Human Rights 204
Issues before the (number) General Assembly 709
Issues before the U.N. 27th General Assembly 299
Is the United Nations Dead? 463
Italy and the United Nations 764

J

James Madison's Notes of Debate in the Federal Convention 1467
Japan and the League of Nations 766
Japan and the United Nations 765
Japanese Annual of International Law, The 219
Japanese Mandate Islands, The 1338
Journal of Conflict Resolution, The 174
Journal of International Affairs 175
Journal of Peace Research 181
Journal of Politics, The 176

K

Kashmir 757
Kashmir and the United Nations 972
Katanga Circus, The 984
Keesing's Contemporary Archives 13
Kennedy Round in American Trade Policy, The 1070
Key to Human Rights Implementation, The 1433
Key to League of Nations Documents Placed on Public Sale 58
Korea: A Study of U.S. Policy in the United Nations 845
Korean War and the United Nations, The 847

L

Labor as an International Problem 1236
Labor in the League System 1226
Labor Legislation in Czechoslovakia 1262
Latin America in the United Nations 725
Latin American Relations with the League of Nations 727
Law and Organization in World Society 396
Law and Practice of the International Atomic Energy Agency, The 1280
Law and Society in the Relations of States 1489

Title Index

Nature and Function of International Organizations, The 374
Netherlands Yearbook of International Law 217
Neutrality and Collective Security 843
New Diplomacy and the United Nations 699
New Era, A 1237
New Frontiers in Space Law 1051
New International Actors, The 701
New International Atomic Energy Agency Publications 81
New Nations in the United Nations, The 713
New Publications in the United Nations Headquarters Library 319
New Serial Titles 133
Newspaper Man's United Nations, The 485
Newspapers Currently Received and Permanently Retained in the Library of Congress 225
Newspapers in Microform: United States, 1948-72 230
Newspapers on Microfilm 230
Newspapers on Microfilm for Foreign Countries, 1948-72 223
Newspapers on Microfilm for the United States, 1948-72 222
Newspapers Received Currently in the Library of Congress 225
New States and International Organizations 714
New World Primer 1524
New York Times Index, The 227
New York University Journal of International Law and Politics 168
1,978 International Organizations Founded Since the Congress of Vienna, The 343
Non-Governmental Forces and World Politics 1315
Non-Self-Governing Areas 106
Non-Sovereign Representation in Public International Organs 1311
Nuclear Diplomacy 863
Nuclear Non-Proliferation 1279

O

Obsolete Weapon, The 1285
Occasional Papers 334
Oesterreich un die Vereinten Nationen 738
Official Journal (League) 265
Official Publications of European Governments 234
Official Records (ECOSOC) 273
Official Records (GA) 271
Official Records (SC) 272
Official Records (TC) 274
One World in the Making 1459
On the Creation of a Just World Order 1528
Operation of the Mandates System in Africa, The 1332
Organizing for Peace 375
Organizing Mankind 386
Organizing the United Nations 436
Origin and Evolution of the I.L.O. and Its Role in the World Community, The 1238
Origins of Peace 892
Origins of the International Labor Organization, The 1239
Origins of the League Covenant, The 520
Origin, Structure and Working of the League of Nations, The 412
Other State Department, The 811
Our International Monetary System 1083
Outer Space 1052
Outer Space and International Order 1048
Outlook on Space 1047

P

Pacific Dependencies of the United States, The 1375
Pacific Islands under Japanese Mandate 1337
Pacific Settlement of Disputes 1363
Pakistan and the United Nations 768
Palestine: Promise and Problem 963
Palestine and the United Nations: Prelude to Solution 959

Title Index

Palestine under the Mandate 1333
Panmunjom 850
Paradise in Trust 1376
Parliamentary Diplomacy 545
Participation of the Soviet Union in Universal International Organizations 786
Participation of the United States Government in International Conferences 807
Participation of the United States in the International Labor Organization 1256
Partners in Development 1129
Partners in Science 1294
Path from Violence to International Order, The 834
Paths to World Order 1500
Pathways to Peace 1502
Peace: The Control of National Power 1498
Peaceful Atom in Foreign Policy, The 1282
Peaceful Coexistence 1484
Peaceful Settlement among African States 905
Peaceful Settlement of Disputes 882
Peaceful Settlement of Disputes and the United Nations, The 902
Peaceful Uses of Atomic Energy 1286
Peace in the Family of Man 1492
Peace is Possible 1513
Peace-Keeping: Experience and Evolution 925
Peacekeeping: International Challenge and Canadian Response 742
Peace-Keeping by the United Nations 901
Peace-Keeping by U.N. Forces 931
Peace-Keeping Operations: A Bibliography 102
Peace Movement in America, The 1444
Peace Research 182
Peace Research Abstracts Journal 121
Peace Research Society Papers 333
Peace Research Reviews 183
Peace, Security and the United Nations 828
Peace Studies: College Courses 352

Peking's UN Policy 745
Penguin Political Dictionary 21
Periodicals of International Organizations 138
Permanent Court of International Justice, The 683
Permanent Court of International Justice: Its Constitution, Procedure and Work, The 684
Permanent Missions and Delegations to the United Nations 341
Permanent United Nations, A 1458
Perspective 126
Pioneers in World Order 430
Plan for a Permanent Peace 1462
Plans for Reform of the International Monetary System 1088
Play within the Play, The 478
Pleadings, Oral Statements and Documents (PCIJ) 279
Pleadings, Oral Arguments, Documents (ICJ) 280
Plebiscites Since the War 1346
Pledged to Development 1167
Policies and Operations of the World Bank, IFC and IDA 1197
Policies of the British Dominions in the League of Nations, The 733
Policy Panel Reports 337
Political Community and the North Atlantic Area 507
Political Community at the International Level 506
Political Economy of Agrarian Change, The 1187
Political Integration: A Survey of Theories 503
Political Integration: The Formation of Theory 514
Political Role of the General Assembly, The 706
Political Science: A Bibliographic Guide to the Literature 46
Political Study of the Arab-Jewish Conflict, A 962
Political Unification 508
Politics and Dynamics of Human Rights 1417
Politics and the Future of ECOSOC 596
Politics in the United Nations 708

Title Index

Politics of Force, The 918
Politics of International Cooperation, The 1274
Politics of International Organizational Studies in Multilateral Economic Agencies, The 1114
Politics of International Organization, The 403
Politics of Peace-Keeping, The 928
Politics of Space Cooperation, The 1050
Pool of Knowledge, The 1180
Popular Guide to Government Publications, A 233
Population in the United Nations System 1295
Portuguese Territories and the United Nations 1374
Postwar International Aviation Policy and the Law of the Air 1034
Postwar Negotiation for Arms Control 858
Postwar Plans of the United Nations 1456
Power and International Relations 837
Power and Law 732
Power and Money 1079
Power to Keep the Peace, The 879
Practice and Procedure of International Conferences, The 369
Preface to Disarmament 866
Preface to Peace 953
Preliminary Draft of a World Constitution 1523
Presiding Officers in the United Nations, The 600
Preventing World War III 1499
Privileges and Immunities of the International Civil Servant 656
Privileges and Immunities of the Personnel of International Organizations, The 554
Problem of International Sanctions, The 855
Problems of Lasting Peace, The 1453
Problems of the Revision of the UN Charter 1478
Problems of the Trusteeship System 1348

Proceedings (American Society of International Law) 211
Proceedings (Nigerian Society of International Law) 216
Process of International Arbitration, The 999
Process of International Organizations, The 402
Program-Making in UNESCO 1272
Progress in International Organization 416
Proper Law of International Organizations, The 560
Proposals for Changes in the United Nations 1471
Prospects for Peacekeeping 926
Prospects of International Adjudication, The 1009
Protection of International Personnel Abroad 548
Protection of Minorities, The 1390
Provisional Rules of Procedure of the Security Council 594
Publications of the International Court of Justice 280
Publications of the Permanent Court of International Justice 279
Publications of the United Nations System 76
Publications of the World Health Organization, 1947-57 90
Publications of the World Health Organization, 1968-1972 91
Public International Conference, The 370
Public International Law of Money 1078
Public International Unions 368
Public Opinion and the United Nations 511
Public Order of the Oceans, The 1039
Public Papers of the Secretaries-General of the United Nations, 667, 675
Public Policy for the Seas 1043
Publishers' Trade List Annual: Books In Print 29
Publisher's Trade List Annual: Subject Guide 30

Title Index

Q

Quaker Service Bulletin 184
Quest for International Order, The 1460
Quest for Peace, The 401
Quest for Peace Since the World War, The 427
Quest for Peace through Diplomacy, The 890
Quest for Survival 1497
Quiet, Approach, The 662

R

Race, Peace, Law and Southern Africa 1442
Readers' Guide to Periodical Literature 142
Read Your Way to World Understanding 61
Realities and Make-Believe 652
Rebels, Mercenaries and Dissidents 983
Recent Trends in the Development of International Law 393
Recent Trends in the Law of the United Nations 532
Reconstituting the League of Nations 1454
Records (League) 266
Records of the Headquarters, United Nations Command 938
Recueil des Cours 207
Red Cross International and the Strategy of Peace 1304
Red Spies in the UN 658
Reflection on International Administration 634
Reforming the World's Money 1087
Reform of the Fund, The 1097
Refugee and the World Community, The 1398
Refugee in the Post-War World, The 1397
Refugee in the World, The 1399
Refugees: The Work of the League 1407
Regime of International Rivers, The 1045
Relations between the Council of Europe and International Non-Governmental Organizations 1320
Relations between the Council of Europe and the United Nations 729
Relationship among the Principal Organs of the United Nations, The 558
Reluctant Door, The 546
Remnants of Empire 1353
Repertoire of Serial Documents, 1919-47, A 243
Repertory of Practice of United Nations Organs 533
Report of a Study Group on the Peaceful Settlement of International Disputes 884
Report of the Commission 336
Report on the Debate in the United Nations Disarmament Commission 870
Report on the Review of the United Nations Charter 1475
Report on the Work of the League during the War 420
Reports of Judgments, Advisory Opinions and Others (ICJ) 280
Reports of the Hague Conferences, The 371
Representation of Non-Governmental Organizations at the United Nations 1310
Research in the International Organization Field 501
Research on International Organization 500
Research on Peace-Keeping Operations 922
Resolutions of the General Assembly 270
Resources for Teaching about the United Nations 349
Resources of Canadian Academic and Research Libraries 315
Review of the United Nations Charter 1482
Review of the United Nations Charter: A Collection of Documents 1481
Review of the United Nations Charter: Hearings 1480
Revision of the United Nations Charter 1476

Title Index

Revolution on East River 461
Rise of Internationalism, The 1445
Road to Huddersfield, The 1198
Road to World Peace, The 1466
Role of a National Delegation in the General Assembly, The 710
Role of the United Nations in the Congo, The 980
Role of the United Nations in the Maintenance of World Peace, The 829
Rules of Procedure of the Functional Commissions of the Economic and Social Council 599
Rules of Procedure of the General Assembly 587

S

Saar Publications, The 1342
Sanctions against South Africa 851
Sanctions and Treaty Enforcement 857
Sanctions as an Instrumentality of the United Nations 854
Scandanavian States and the League of Nations 730
Schemes for Maintaining General Peace 1463
Die Schweiz und die Vereinten Nationen 774
Die Schweiz und die Vereinten Nationen von 1944-47 772
Search for Peace 1501
Second Lesson: Seven Years at the United Nations, The 471
Secretariat of the United Nations, The 641
Secretary-General of the United Nations, The 661
Security Council, The 591
Security Council in a Universal UN, The 589
Seeking World Order 816
Selected Bibliography of Specialized Agencies Related to the United Nations 68, 94
Selected Bibliography on International Organization 51
Selected Inventory of Periodical Publications, A 134

Selected Pamphlets on the United Nations and International Relations 64
Selection of Personnel for International Service, The 649
Self-Determination in International Law 1324
Self-Determination within the Community of Nations 1358
Sequel to Bretton Woods 1082
Serial Titles Newly Received 133
Servant of Peace 676
Shaping Our Times 694
Short History of International Organizations, A 365
Sino-Japanese Controversy and the League of Nations, The 897
SIPRI Yearbook of World Armaments and Disarmament 205, 338
Skyjacking and Terrorism 298
Small States and Territories 715
So Bold an Aim 1182
Social and Human Work 1211
Social Justice in the Law of Nations 1247
Social Science Literature: A Bibliography for International Law 40
Society of Nations: Its Organization and Constitutional Development, The 366
Society of Nations: Its Past, Present and Possible Future, The 1451
Sociology of the Future, The 1511
Soldiering for Peace 949
Soldiers without Enemies 936
Solidarity in the General Assembly 754
Somaliland under Italian Administration 1367
Some Aspects of the Covenant of the League of Nations 519
Some Implications of Expanding UN Membership 610
Some Principles for Peace-Keeping Operations 937
Some Views of American Defense Officials about the United Nations 813
Sources of Information 57
Sources of Information in the Social Sciences 43

Title Index

South West Africa: Travesty or Trust 1381
South West Africa and the United Nations 1382
South West Africa and the United Nations: An International Mandate 1379
South West Africa/Namibia Dispute, The 1380
Soviet and American Policies in the United Nations 820
Soviet at Geneva, The 787
Soviet Coexistence Strategy 1258
Soviets in International Organizations, The 783
Soviet Union at the United Nations, The 781
Soviet View of the United Nations, The 785
Soviet Yearbook of International Law 218
Sow the Wind, Reap the Whirlwind 483
Space Activities and Resources (1965) 1054
Space Activities and Resources (1972) 1055
Spain and the United Nations 770
Staffing the United Nations Secretariat 651
Statesman's Year Book 191
Status and the United Nations Secretariat, The 655
Story of FAO, The 1181
Story of the Red Cross, The 1305
Story of the United Nations, The 446
Story of U.N.N.R.A., The 1126
Strategy for Peace, The 334
Strategy of Economic Development, The 1131
Strategy of Peace in a Changing World, The 1483
Strategy of World Order, The 491, 896
Strategy toward the Conquest of Hunger 1183, 1307
Strengthening the Framework of Peace 1479
Strengthening the United Nations 1485

Strengthening the World Bank 1188
Structure 561
Structure of Private International Organizations, The 1303
Structure of the International Environment, The 1291
Structure of the United Nations, The 452
Structure of United Nations Economic Aid to Underdeveloped Countries, The 1137
Struggle for Kashmir, The 903
Student's Guide to United Nations Documents and Their Use, A 249
Studies in Federalism 1515
Studies in International Adjudication 1007
Studies in World Order 1506
Study Guide on the Work of the Economic and Social Council, A 80
Study Guide to the General Agreement on Tariffs and Trade, A 1069
Study of Current Bibliographies of National Official Publications, A 236
Study of the Capacity of the United Nations Development System, A 1134
Subject Collections 313
Subject Guide to Microforms in Print 129
Subject Guide to Publications of the International Labour Office 86
Suez 967
Suez Canal Settlement, The 966
La Swisse et les Nations Unies 773
Summary Chronology of UN Activity Relating to the Congo 992
Superparliaments, The 606
Superpowers and Victims 1503
Supranationalism and International Adjudication 1008
Survey of International Arbitrations 1003
Sweden and the United Nations 771
Swedish U.N. Stand-By Force and Experience, The 945
Swords into Plowshares 376
Synopsis of United Nations Cases in the Field of Peace and Security 831

Title Index

Syria and Lebanon under French Mandate 1336
Systems of Integrating the International Community 515

T

Tanganyika and International Trusteeship 1385
Tangle of Hopes 792
Teaching Human Rights 351
Teaching Political Science 354
Technical Assistance: Theory and Guidelines 1172
Technical Assistance: Theory, Practice and Policies 1170
Technical Assistance for Economic Development 1174
Technical Cooperation 1173
Telecommunications Journal 157
Telling the UN Story 350
Ten Steps Forward 1215
Ten Years of World Co-operation 419
Termination of Membership in International Organizations 612
Test Ban and Disarmament 864
Theory and Practice of International Organization, The 397
Theory of Economic Integration, The 513
Thin Blue Line, The 921a
Third Party Settlement of Disputes in Theory and Practice 885
Thirty-Eighth Floor, The 664
This Fireproof House 1490
This Growing World 1199
This Kind of Peace 848
To End War 114
To Katanga and Back 988
Toward a Feasible International Court 691
Toward a Genuine World Security System 103
Toward a Theory of World Preservation 826
Toward a World Community 1514
Toward Economic Cooperation in Asia 1169
Towards a Better Use of the Oceans 1041
Towards a World Community 1488

Towards International Cooperation 1207
Towards International Government 1450
Toward Wider Acceptance of UN Treaties 568
Toward World Order 383
Toward World Peace 680
Transaction 186
Transactions (Problems of War) 210
Transnational Industrial Relations 1319
Transnational Relations and World Politics 1491
Treaty-Making Power of International Organizations 572
Treaty Profiles 303b
Treaty Series (League) 301
Treaty Series (UN) 302
Trends in International Peacemaking 881
Trusteeship in the Pacific 1377
Trusteeship System, The 1347
Trygve Lie (Public Papers) 667
Turkey and the United Nations 776
Turkey in the United Nations 777
Turkish Participation in the United Nations 775
22nd United Nations General Assembly, The 707
Two Hague Conferences, The 372

U

Ulrich's Periodicals Directory 131
UN: Today and Tomorrow, The 469
UN Administration of Economic and Social Programs 1120
UN and China Dilemma, The 615
UN and Nonaligned Nations 716
U.N. and Peaceful Co-existence 663
U.N. and Refugees, The 1400
U.N. and the Middle East Crisis, The 958
U.N. and the Palestinian Refugees, The 1405
U.N. and Vietnam, The 915
Unanimity Rule and the League of Nations, The 623
Uncertain Mandate 974
U.N. Convention on the Elimination of All Forms of Racial Discrimination, The (Lerner) 1396

Title Index

U.N. Convention on the Elimination of All Forms of Racial Discrimination, The (Werner) 1395
UNCTAD: Conflict and Compromise 1157
UNCTAD and Development Diplomacy 1158
UNDEX: United Nations Documents Index 252
U.N. Diary 484
U.N.E.S.C.O. 1269
UNESCO: A Selected List of References 72
UNESCO: Assessment and Promise 1268
UNESCO: Its Purpose and Philosophy 1275
UNESCO: Peace in the Minds of Men 1266
UNESCO: Purpose, Progress, Prospects 1265
UNESCO and World Politics 1265a
UNESCO Bulletin 158
UNESCO Bulletin for Libraries 27
UNESCO Chronicle 158
UNESCO Courier 159
UNESCO Education in Action 1273
UNESCO General Catalogue 89
UNESCO in Perspective 1270
UNESCO Newsletter 158
UNESCO Publications 88
UNESCO's Cultural Mission 1264
Uniform System of Citation, A 362
Unifying the World 1016
U.N. in Action, The 443
UN in the Age of Change, The 447
UN in the Congo: A Quest for Peace, The 977
Union List of Microfilms 130
Union List of Serials 132
Union Now 1468
Union Postale 160
UNITAR Publications 93
United Kingdom Administration and International Organization 780
United Nations, The (Evatt) 442
United Nations, The (Falk and Mendlovitz) 491
United Nations, The (Goodrich) 453
United Nations: A Reassessment, Sanctions, Peacekeeping and Humanitarian Assistance, The 495
United Nations: A Short Political Guide, The 439
United Nations: A View from Within, The 479
United Nations: Background, Organization, Functions, Activities, The 454
United Nations: Constitutional Developments, Growth and Possibilities 448
United Nations: International Organization and Administration, The 488
United Nations: Past, Present, and Future, The 489
United Nations: Peace and Progress, The 698
United Nations: Piety, Myth and Truth 449
United Nations: Planned Tyranny, The 470
United Nations: Sacred Drama, The 462
United Nations: Structure for Peace, The 441
United Nations: Ten Years' Legal Progress, The (Kelsen) 567
United Nations: Ten Years' Legal Progress, The (Van der Molen) 543
United Nations: The Continuing Debate, The 459
United Nations: The First Ten Years, The 472
United Nations: The First Twenty-Five Years, The (Eichelberger) 475
United Nations: The First Twenty-Five Years, The (Tetlow) 476
United Nations: The Next Twenty-Five Years, The 1486
United Nations Administrative Tribunal, The 646
United Nations Agreements 261
United Nations and Africa, The 721
United Nations and Decolonization, The 1354
United Nations and Dependent People, The 1355

Title Index

United Nations and Disarmament, The 860
United Nations and Domestic Jurisdiction 556
United Nations and Economic Sanctions against Rhodesia, The 852
United Nations and How it Works, The 1438
United Nations and Human Rights, The (Eichelberger) 1426
United Nations and Human Rights, The (Green) 1423
United Nations and Italian Colonies 1369
United Nations and Latin America, The 726
United Nations and Pakistan, The 769
United Nations and Population, The 1296a
United Nations and Portugal, The 1373
United Nations and Power Politics, The 700
United Nations and Related Organizations, The 69
United Nations and the Human Environment, The 1288
United Nations and the Maintenance of International Peace and Security, The 830
United Nations and the News Media, The 486
United Nations and the Peaceful Unification of Korea, The 846
United Nations and the Population Question, The 1296
United Nations and the Promotion of the General Welfare, The 1204
United Nations and the Rule of Law, The 534
United Nations and the Superpowers, The 821
United Nations and the Use of Force, The 832
United Nations and United States Foreign Economic Policy, The 796
United Nations and U.S. Foreign Policy, The 794
United Nations and World Community 695
United Nations and World Realities, The 697
United Nations as a Political Institution, The 440
United Nations at Twenty and After, The 474
United Nations at Work, The 1206
United Nations Bibliographic Series 94
United Nations Bulletin 151
United Nations Chronology 7
United Nations Conference on International Organization, San Francisco, 1945 267
United Nations Conference on International Organization: Selected Documents 268
United Nations Conference on Trade and Development, The 1156
United Nations Conference on Trade and Development of 1964 1159
United Nations Development Aid 1146
United Nations Development Decade, The 1160
United Nations Documents Index 252
United Nations Documents, 1941-45 260
United Nations Economic and Social Council, The (Finer) 597
United Nations Economic and Social Council (Sharp) 595
United Nations Economic and Social Council: Index to Documents, 1946-65 257
United Nations Emergency Force, The (Basic Documents) 970
United Nations Emergency Force, The (Mezerik) 969
United Nations Emergency Force, The (Rosner) 968
United Nations Experience with Military Forces 930
United Nations Force in Cyprus, The 993
United Nations Forces: A Legal Study 940
United Nations Forces in the Law of Peace and War 941
United Nations High Commissioner for Human Rights, A 1432

Title Index

United Nations Hope for a Divided World 696
United Nations in a Changing World, The 458
United Nations in Action, The 456
United Nations in Action: Ten Cases, The 290
United Nations in Economic Development 1135
United Nations in International Politics, The 490
United Nations in Perspective, The 496
United Nations International School, The 605
United Nations in the Balance, The 492
United Nations in the Making, The 269
United Nations in War and Peace, The 460
United Nations Juridical Yearbook 199
United Nations Library, The 604
United Nations Monetary and Financial Conference 285
United Nations Mutual Aid 1171
United Nations News, The 16
United Nations Newsletter 152
United Nations Official Records, 1948-62 251
United Nations Organization and International Law, The 542
United Nations Peace Force, A 946
United Nations Peace Force?, A 947
United Nations Peacekeeping Activities 924
United Nations Peacekeeping in the Congo 976
United Nations Peacekeeping, 1946-1967 Documents and Commentary. Volume I: The Middle East 921
United Nations Peacekeeping, 1946-1967 Documents and Commentary. Volume II: Asia 921
United Nations Peace-Keeping Operations: A Military and Political Appraisal 932
United Nations Peace-Keeping Operations--Higher Conduct 929

United Nations Peacemaking: The Conciliation Commission for Palestine 955
United Nations Political System, The 487
United Nations Primer 435
United Nations Publications 77
United Nations Publications: Check List 79
United Nations Reconsidered, The 497
United Nations Reporter 152
United Nations Review 151
United Nations Security Council 255
United Nations, South West Africa and the Law, The 1384
United Nations System, The 466
United Nations System and Its Functions, The 493
United Nations Technical Assistance Board 1175
United Nations Textbook 294
United Nations Trusteeship System, The 1349
United Nations Weekly Bulletin 153
United States--United Nations 808
United States and International Organization 802
United States and International Organizations, The 805
United States and the First Hague Peace Conference of 1899, The 373
United States and the League, The 819
United States and the Restoration of World Trade, The 1072
United States and the United Nations, The (Gross) 804
United States and the United Nations, The (Weiler and Simons) 791
United States and the United Nations, The (Wilcox and Haviland) 800
United States and the United Nations: Can We Do Better?, The 797
United States and the United Nations: Promoting the Public Welfare, The 768
United States and the United Nations: Report by the President 809

Title Index

United States and the United Nations: The Public View, The 812
United States and the World Court, The 817
United States and UNESCO, The 1267
United States and World Organization, The 816
United States Publications 232
United States Security, Arms Control and Disarmament 110
United World 1457
United World Federalism 115
Universal Declaration of Human Rights and Its Predecessors, The 1438
Universal Postal Union, The 1058
Universal Reference System 39
UN Monthly Chronicle 151
UN Protection of Civil and Political Rights 1422
UN Record: Ten Fateful Years for America, The 473
UNRRA: The History of the United Nations Relief and Rehabilitation Administration 1125
UN Secretary General and the Maintenance of Peace, The 660
Uruguay and the United Nations 822
U.S. Diplomacy in the Development Agencies of the United Nations 1155
Use of Experts by International Tribunals, The 693
Use of United Nations Documents, The 250
Uses of Force in International Relations 1494
Uses of the Seas 1038
USSR and the UN's Economic and Social Activities, The 782
U.S. Stake in the UN 1477
U.S./U.N.: Partners for Peace 803
U.S./U.N. Foreign Policy and International Organization 795
U Thant of Burma 679

V

Vantage Conference Reports 334

Viet Nam and the UN 914
Violent Truce 957
Vista 148, 335
Voluntary Organizations in World Affairs 1313
Voluntary Service Overseas 1306
Voting and Decisions in the International Monetary Fund 1096
Voting and Handling of Disputes in the Security Council 625
Voting in the Security Council 626
Voting Procedures in International Political Organizations 622

W

Wall Street Journal Index, The 229
War/Peace Report 187, 329
Washington Conference, The 871
Washington Conference and After, The 872
Web of Interdependence, The 793
Web of Progress 1276
Western Europe and the United Nations 728
West New Guinea Dispute, The 1365
We, The People 437
White's Political Dictionary 20
WHO Chronicle 161
Who Killed the Congo? 987
Who's Who in the United Nations 342
Why Not Admit Red China to the United Nations? 616
Willing's Press Guide 224
WMO Bulletin 162
Working of the Minorities System under the League of Nations, The 1391
Work of the International Labor Organization, The 1234
Work of the International Law Commission, The 602
Workshop of Security 593
Workshops for the World 1205
World Airlift, A 948
World Bank: A Prospect, The 1193
World Bank Group in Asia, The 1203
World Bank Since Bretton Woods, The 1189
World beyond the Charter, The 1487
World Bibliography of Bibliographies, A 24

Title Index

World Community, The 1509
World Court, The 682
World Court: What It Is and How It Works, The 685
World Court Reports 276
World Disarmament 873
World Eco-Crisis 1287
World Economic Agencies 1117
World Federal Government 1522
World Federalist 188
World Federation 1470
World Government: A List of Selected References 116
World Guide to Libraries 308
World Health 1218
World Health and History 1217
World Health Organization, The 1216
World Health Organization: A Study in Decentralized International Administration 1213
World Justice 189
World Legal Order 806
World List of Social Science Periodicals 137
Worldmark Encyclopedia of the Nations 23
World Monetary Order, A 1122
World of Promise 1162
World Order and Diplomacy 1510
World Order and Local Disorder 904
World Order and New States 923
World Order Book Series 339
World Order in Historical Perspective 1526
World Organization 1443
World Peace Plans 1455
World Peace through World Law 1472
World Politics 177
World Politics in the General Assembly 702
World Politics in the General Assembly 702
World Polity 193
World Prosperity as Sought through Economic Work of the League of Nations 1105
World Republic 1518
World's Design, The 1527
World Society 1507
World's War on Want, The 1142
World Trade and the Law of GATT 1068
World Treaty Index 303a
World Understanding: A Selected Bibliography 62
World Without Want 1144

Y

Yearbook (ICJ) 280
Yearbook of Air and Space Law 206
Yearbook of International Congress Proceedings 194
Yearbook of International Organizations 192
Yearbook of the International Court of Justice 201
Yearbook of the International Law Commission 198
Yearbook of the League of Nations 196
Yearbook of the United Nations 197
Yearbook on Human Rights 203
Years of Opportunity 415
Yes and Albert Thomas 1252

Z

Zehn Jahre Vereinte Nationen von 1945-1955 824

SUBJECT INDEX

A

Abstracts
 dissertations 122
 peace research 119, 121
 political science 120
Academie de Droit International de la Hage 207
Access practices 546
Africa
 international relations bibliography 113
 mandate system and 1331-32
 UN and 719-22, 734
 See also Afro-Asian bloc, UN and; Algeria, UN and; Arab bloc, UN and; Egypt, UN and
African unity 905
Afro-Asian bloc, UN and 718. See also Africa, UN and
Aggression, committee to define 297
Aid. See Economic Aid
Air and space law, yearbook 206
Aland Island Question 895
Algeria, UN and 735. See also Arab bloc, UN and
American Association of University Women Educational Foundation 360
American Philosophical Society 360
American Political Science Association, fellowship 360
American Society of International Law 211
Apartheid 219, 908
Arab bloc, UN and 723-24. See also Africa, UN and; Algeria, UN and; Egypt, UN and; Middle East, peacekeeping in
Arbitration. See International arbitration
Asia
 agrarian change in 1187
 economic cooperation in 1169
 peacekeeping in 921
 World Bank and 1203
Australia, UN and 736-37
Australian Association of International Law 212
Austria, UN and 738
Avenol, Joseph 665

B

Bank for Economic Settlements 1107-10
Bargaining, during international crises 918
Belgian Congo. See Congo
Belgium, UN and 739
Berlin airlift, UN role in 446
Bibliographies
 general
  international 24-26
  national 28-34
  periodical 27, 126, 127
 international organizations 47-53
 international relations 35-40
 social and political sciences 41-46
Border disputes 909-11
Bretton Woods 1093, 1111
Budgets, UN 631-33, 654
Burma, UN and 740

Subject Index

Business and Professional Women's Foundation 360

C

Cameroon, trusteeship system and 1360
Canada, UN and 741-43
Carnegie Endowment for International Peace 147, 328
  fellowship 360
Cartels 1074-76
Center for Advanced Study in Behavioral Sciences, fellowship 360
Center for War/Peace Studies 187, 329
Chaco dispute 900
China
  League of Nations and 747-48
  membership in UN 612, 615-21, 722, 744-46
Chinese Society of International Law 215
Chronologies
  League of Nations 14
  UN 7-9, 15, 16
Civil aviation 1032-35. See also International Civil Aviation Organization
Civil wars, international regulation of 912-13
Collective security 835-44
Colonialism. See Non-Self-Governing Territories
Columbo Plan 1173
Commission to Study the Organization of Peace 336
Commodity agreements 1074, 1077, 1116-17
Commonwealth
  League of Nations and 733
  UN and 731-32
  See also United Kingdom, UN and; Canada, UN and
Communications, regulation 1013-16
Congo
  history 982, 985-87
  UN role in 697, 722, 931, 934, 949, 974-81, 983-84, 988-92
Consortium on Peace Research 330
Corfu Channel incident 894, 1011
Council of Europe, international nongovernmental organizations and 1320
Council of Nations 729
Council on Foreign Relations 170, 331
Cyprus, UN and 993-95
Czechoslovakia
  ILO and 1262
  UN and 907

D

The Danforth Foundation 360
Danzig, mandate and 1340
Decade of Development. See Development decades
Decision-making, in Security Council 589-90
Decision-making process
  general 630
  UN 629
Decolonization 1352-54
Denmark, UN and 749. See also Scandanavia, UN and
Development Assistance Committee 1165-66
Development decades 1160-63
Dictionary
  international relations 18
  political science 19
  politics 20, 21
Diplomacy, UN and 487, 699, 703. See also Mediation; Peacekeeping; UN, role in settling disputes; League of Nations, role in settling disputes
Diplomats 710-11. See also UN, personnel; International organizations, personnel
Disarmament 17, 94
  arms control and 858-76
  bibliography 107-12
  directory 346
  periodical 127, 165
  yearbook 205
Dissertations
  general 122, 123
  political science 124
  UN 125
Domestic jurisdiction, UN and 556
Dominican Republic, sanctions against 853a

Subject Index

Drug control. See International drug control
Dutch Inter-University Institute for International law 217

E

Economic aid
 coordination of 1164-67
 international organizations and 1133-55
Ecological crisis. See Environmental policy
Economic and Social Council (ECOSOC) 502, 595-99, 1117
 guide to publications 80
Economic development, role of international organizations in 128-32
Economic integration 503, 512-13
Economic organizations
 BIS and 1107-10
 League of Nations and 1104-6
 in modern world 1111-24
ECOSOC. See Economic and Social Council
Egypt, UN and 750. See also Africa, UN and; Arab bloc, UN and
Encyclopedias
 social sciences 22
 international relationships 23
Environmental policy, international organizations and 1287-92
Espionage, at the UN 658
Euratom 1279
European Economic Community, UN and 701

F

FAO. See Food and Agriculture Organization
Far East, economic cooperation in 1169
Federalism 1515-22
Fellowships. See Grants and fellowships.
Food and Agriculture Organization (FAO) 1117, 1181-87
 guides to publications 82-83
 periodical 154

Foreign affairs
 bibliographies 35, 36
 periodical 170
Foreign Policy Association 332
Fulbright-Hays Grants 360
Functionalism 1242, 1531
The Fund for Peace, fellowships 360
Future studies, teaching aids 353
Futurism 1532
 journals 185-86

G

GATT. See General Agreement on Tariffs and Trade
General Agreements on Tariffs and Trade (GATT) 1064-73, 1116-17
 bibliography 73
 guides to publications 84
 See also International trade
General Assembly. See United Nations General Assembly
Geneva Disarmament Conference 787, 875
Government publications and documents
 European 234
 general 233, 235, 236-37
 international organizations
  general 238-42, 283-87, 296
  League of Nations 243-46, 264-66
  UN 247-62, 267-74, 288-95, 297-99
  World Court 263, 275-82
  in microform 296-99
 United States 232
Grants and fellowships 360
Great Britain
 ILO and 1254-55
 mandate system and 1330
 UN and 778-80
Greece, UN and 751
Greek-Bulgarian incident 896
Grotius Society 210
Guggenheim Foundation. See John Simon Guggenheim Memorial Foundation

H

Hague Academy of International Law 208

Subject Index

Hague Court 1004
Hague Peace Conferences 371-73
Hammarskjold, Dag 668-78
Handbooks
  international organizations, general 1, 4
  League of Nations 2, 6
  UN 3, 5
Headquarters of international institutions 550
Human rights
  bibliography 104
  international organizations and 1409-42
  labor and 1250
  teaching handbook 351
  UN and 1204
  yearbooks 203-4
  See also Minorities, national
Hunger. See Food and Agriculture Organization

I

IAEA. See International Atomic Energy Agency
IBRD. See International Bank for Reconstruction and Development
ICAO. See International Civil Aviation Organization
ICJ. See International Court of Justice
IDA. See International Development Association
IFC. See International Finance Corporation
IGY. See International Geophysical Year
ILC. See International Law Commission
ILO. See International Labor Organization
IMCO. See International Maritime Consultative Organization
IMF. See International Monetary Fund
India
  ILO and 1261
  League of Nations and 761-62
  UN and 752-60
Indonesia, trusteeship system and 1361-65

Institut de Droit International 209
Intergovernmental Maritime Consultative Organization (IMCO) 1117
International administration bibliography 101
International administration tribunals 648. See also United Nations Administration Tribunal
International affairs
  bibliography 39
  journal 175
  research institutions 320-21, 325
International arbitration 996-1012. See also International Court of Justice; Permanent Court of International Justice.
International Atomic Energy Agency (IAEA) 1277-86
  guides to publications 81
International Bank and Monetary Fund, documents 285
International Bank for Reconstruction and Development (IBRD) 1191, 1194-95, 1197
International Centre for Settlement of Investment Disputes 1189
International Chamber of Commerce 1316
International Civil Aviation Organization (ICAO) 1025-31, 1117. See also Civil Aviation
International Civil Service 642-45
International conferences
  history and structure 369-70, 606
  organization 607-8
  See also Hague Peace Conference
International cooperation 1207-10
  bibliography 99, 100
International Court of Justice (ICJ) 543, 685-93, 998-99, 1006, 1010
  bibliography 95-97
  documents 277, 278, 280-82
  yearbook 201
International Development Association (IDA) 1189, 1191, 1202
International disputes
  role of law in 327
  UN and 534
International drug control 1222-25
International Finance Corporation (IFC) 1189, 1191, 1200-1

Subject Index

International Geophysical Year (IGY) 1293-94
Internationalism 1445
International Labour Organization (ILO) 1117
  bibliography 71
  development and 1251
  guides to publications 85-87
  nations and 1254-62
  periodical 155
  today 1237-45
  under League and before 1226-36
  unions and 1246-50
  yearbook 202
  See also Thomas, Albert
International law 393, 396, 408
  environment and 1298, 1291
  human rights and 1414-15
  IMF and 1100-102
  India and 760
  international labor and 1249
  international organizations and 559-84
  League of Nations and 538-39
  periodicals 163, 164, 168, 169, 172
  self-determination and 1324
  telecommunications and 1019-20
  UN and 540-45
  UN charter and 530
  use of force and 833
  yearbook 193
International Law Association, Canadian Branch 214
International law associations, yearbooks 207-19
International Law Commission (ILC) 543, 601-2
  yearbook 198
International Monetary Fund (IMF) 1086-87, 1092, 1095a-103, 1116-17
  bibliography 74
  See also International monetary system
International monetary system 1078-94
International nongovernmental organizations 1299-1320
International organizations
  addresses pp. 72-73
  bibliographies 47-53
  documents 238-99, 517
  economic aid and 1133-55
  history 365-70
  lists 343-47
  organizational aspects 374-97
  personnel 341-42, 553-54, 649-52
  readers 398-408
  research and 498-516
  research institutions 328-40
  teaching aids 348-58
  yearbooks 192-206
International Political Science Association 120
International politics, economics and 1079
International Research and Exchanges Board, fellowships 360
International Studies Association 167
International Telecommunications Union (ITU) 1017-24, 1117
  periodical 157
International trade
  agreements regulating 1016, 1063
  organizations 1062
  See also General Agreement on Tariffs and Trade
International tribunals 681. See also International Court of Justice; Permanent Court of International Justice
Ireland
  ILO and 1260
Israel, UN and 763. See also Middle East, peacekeeping in
Italian colonies, trusteeship system and 1366-70
Italy
  sanctions against 853a
  UN and 764
ITU. See International Telecommunications Union

J

Japan
  League of Nations and 766
  UN and 765
John Simon Guggenheim Memorial Foundation 360
Jordan, UN military force and 931

K

Kashmir, UN and 971-73

Subject Index

Korean War, India's role in 755, 845-50

L

Labor. See Trade unions. See also International Labor Organization
Latin America
 agrarian change in 1187
 League of Nations and 727
 UN and 725-26
League of Nations
 Assembly 578-79
 bibliography 54-55
 chronology 14
 committees 581-84
 Council 580
 covenant 518-26, 538
 documents 243-46, 264-66
 economic organizations and 1104-6
 guide to publications 56-60
 handbooks 1, 2, 6
 history 409-34
 international law and 539
 mandate system under 1324-46
 membership 609, 611
 proposals for future 1447-52
 proposals for peacekeeping 1463-70
 role in settling disputes 894-900
 yearbooks 195-96
Lebanon
 mandate and 1336
 UN military force in 931
Legal advisers, UN and 603
Libraries, guides to 306-19
Libya, trusteeship system and 1366
Lie, Trygve 666-67

M

Manchurian crisis 898
Mandate system and trusteeships
 general 1321-23
 League of Nations 1324-46
 UN 1347-85
Mediation 877-93. See also Diplomacy, Peacekeeping; UN, role in settling disputes; League of Nations, role in settling disputes.
MeKong Delta, development 1168
Methodology, international organizations and 498-516

Mexico, UN and 767. See also Latin America, UN and
Microforms, guides 128-30
Middle East, peacekeeping in 921, 949, 951, 953-70
Military forces
 international 933-34, 937, 939, 942-44
 UN 930-32, 935-36, 938, 940-41, 945-52
 See also Peacekeeping
Minorities, national 1386-96. See also Human rights
Monetary system. See International monetary system.
Mussolini, Corfu incident and 894

N

Narcotics control. See International drug control
National delegations, role in UN 710
National Education Association, fellowships 360
National Fellowships Fund 360
Nationalism 505
National jurisdiction, limits to 297
National Science Foundation, fellowships 360
Nations
 blocs 717
 general 712
 new nations 713-16
 See also under name of nation or bloc
Netherlands International Law Review 217
Neutrality 773, 843
New Guinea
 mandate and 1339
 trusteeship system and 1371-72
Newspapers
 directories 220-25
 indexes to 226-29
 on microfilm 222-23, 230-31
Nigerian Society of International Law 216
Non-Self-Governing Territories 1352-56
 bibliography 106

Subject Index

O

OAS. See Organization of American States
Office of Education, fellowships 360
Organization of American States (OAS), UN and 906

P

Pacific Islands, mandate system and 1331, 1337-38
Pakistan, UN and 768-69
Palestine 955-56, 959, 963-64
  mandate and 1333-35
  See also Middle East
PCIJ. See Permanent Court of International Justice
Peace. See World peace
Peace and Conflict, research institutions 324
Peaceful coexistence 1484
  UN and 663
  See also World peace
Peacekeeping 918a-20, 922-23, 925-28
  in Arab world 953-70
  bibliography 102-3
  readers on 399, 401
  UN and 487, 492, 495, 901-8, 921, 924, 929
  See also Diplomacy; Mediation; World peace
Peace Research Society 333
Peace studies, teaching aids 352
Periodicals
  guides to
    general 131-33
    international relations 134, 135
    social science 137
    international organizations 138-39
  indexes to
    general 142
    political science 140, 143-45
    public affairs 141
  international organizations
    FAO 154
    ILO 155
    GATT 156
    general 146-50, 163-77
    ITU 157
    UN 151-53
    UNESCO 158, 159
    UPU 160
    WHO 161
    WMO 162
Permanent Court of Arbitration, documents 275
Permanent Court of International Justice (PCIJ) 682-84, 999, 1010
  bibliography 95, 98
  documents 263, 276-77, 279
  yearbook 200
Plebiscites 1345-46
Political integration 503-15
Political science
  bibliography 37, 45, 46
  teaching aids 354-55
Politics. See World politics
Population, international organizations and 1295-96a
Portuguese territories, trusteeship system and 1373-74
Post-war reconstruction 52
Power politics, UN and 700
Privileges and immunities 548-49, 551-54, 656
Public health 1212
Publishing directory 359

R

Rail transport 1060
Red Cross 1304-5. See also international nongovernmental organizations
Refugees 1397-1408
Research institutions
  foundations 326
  international affairs 320-21, 325, 327
  international organizations 328-40
  peace and conflict 324
  social science 322-23
Rhodesia
  sanctions against 852, 853a, 854
  trusteeship system and 1378
Rockefeller Brothers Fund 360
The Rotary Foundation, fellowships 360
Royal Institute of International Affairs 213

Subject Index

S

Saar, mandate 1341-42
Sanctions, international organizations and 851-57
UN and 495
San Francisco Conference 537
Scandanavia, UN and 730. See also Denmark, UN and; Sweden, UN and
Sea, international law of 1036, 1038-43, 1046
Sea bed, peaceful uses, documents 297
Secretariats, administration 634-41, 653, 655
Secretary-General 659-64. See also Lie, Trygve; Hammarskjold, Dag; Thant, U
Security Council. See United Nations Security Council
Self-determination, UN and 1357-59
Sino-Japanese controversy 897, 899
Skyjacking 298
Social justice 1247
Social Science Research Council, fellowships 360
Social sciences
 bibliography 38, 40, 42, 43
 research institutions 322-23
 survey 42, 43
Social welfare
 UN and 1204-6
 general 1207-12
Society for the Psychological Study of Social Issues, fellowships 360
Somaliland, trusteeship system and 1367-68
South Africa
 sanctions against 851
 UN intervention in 1441-42
Southern Fellowship Fund, The 360
South West Africa, trusteeship system and 1379-84
Soviet Association of International Law 218
Space
 bibliography 105
 international cooperation in 1048-55
 international law of 1046, 1056-58
 peaceful uses of 297
 research 1047

Spain, UN and 770
Stanley Foundation 334
Stevenson, Adlai 480
Stockholm International Peach Research Institute 338
Style manuals 361-64
Suez Canal 966-67
 UN military force in 931, 934
Supranationalism 1008
Sweden
 military force 945
 UN and 771
 See also Scandanavia, UN and
Switzerland
 League and 722, 774
 UN and 773
Syria, mandate and 1336

T

Tanganyika, trusteeship system and 1385
Tangier, mandate and 1344
Teaching aids, international organizations 348-58
Technical cooperation 1170-80
Telecommunications, space 1014. See also International Telecommunications Union
Terrorism 298
Test Ban Treaty (of 1963) 864
Thant, U 679-80
Third-party intervention 917
Third world, IMF and 1103
Thomas, Albert 1252-53
Tokyo Japan Branch of the International Law Association 219
Trade. See International trade
Trade unions, international protection of 1246-50
Transnationalism 117
Transnational law 169
Treaties 572-73
 UN 568
Treaty collections 300-305
Trusteeships. See Mandate system and trusteeships
Turkey, UN and 775-77

U

UNCTAD. See United Nations Con-

348

Subject Index

ference on Trade and Development
UNESCO. See United Nations Educational, Scientific and Cultural Organization
UNICEF. See United Nations International Children's Emergency Fund
UNITAR. See United Nations Institute for Training and Development
UNRRA. See United Nations Relief and Rehabilitation Administration
United Kingdon. See Great Britain
United Nations
 agreements entered 547
 analysis of 457-76
 bibliographies 61-75, 94
 budgets 631-33, 654
 charter 448, 458, 463, 496, 526-37
  bibliography 66, 94
  revision 1471-82
 chronology 7, 8, 9, 15, 16
 documents 247-62, 267-74, 288-95, 297-99, 482, 488
 economic achievements 1119-21
 economic aid and 1134-38, 1145-50, 1152-55 (See also International organizations, economic aid and)
 development decade 1160-63
 environment and 1288
 evolution 405
 guides to publications 76-93
 handbook 3, 5
 history 432-37, 453-54, 456
 human rights and 1409, 1415-19, 1421-23, 1426, 1432, 1434, 1436-37, 1440-42
 implied powers 555
 international law and 540-45, 563-77
 membership 610-14, 654 (See also China, membership in UN)
 libraries 317-19, 604
 news media and 585-86
 organizational aspects 438-52, 455, 481
 peacekeeping role 727-34, 901-8, 953-95
 personal accounts 477-80
 personnel 341-42

presiding officers 600 (See also Hammarskjold, Dag; Lie, Trygve; Secretary-General; Thant, U
proposals for changing world 1471-91
readers 487-97
social welfare and 1204-6
speeches by heads of state 483
teaching aids 349-50, 356
technical cooperation 1171, 1173-75, 1177-78, 1180
trusteeship system and 1347-85
world politics and 694-709
yearbooks 197, 199
United Nations Administrative Tribunal 646-47
United Nations Association of the United States of America 148, 231, 335, 337
United Nations Conference on Trade and Development (UNCTAD) 1156-59
United Nations Declaration of Human Rights 1419, 1438
United Nations Economic Commission for Europe (UNECE) 1123-24
United Nations Educational, Scientific and Cultural Organization (UNESCO) 1263-76
 bibliography 72
 guides to publications 88, 89
 periodicals 27, 158-59
United Nations Emergency Force 968-70
United Nations General Assembly 585-87
 world politics in 702, 704, 706-9
United Nations Institute for Training and Development (UNITAR)
 guides to publications 93
United Nations International Children's Emergency Fund (UNICEF) 1297-98
United Nations International School 605
United Nations Military Staff Committee 932
United Nations Relief and Rehabilitation Administration (UNRRA) 1125-27
United Nations Security Council 588-94

Subject Index

United Nations Technical Assistance Program 1180
United States
 economic aid and 1154-55
 FAO and 1185
 human rights and 1427, 1435
 IAEA and 1277
 IFC and 1201
 ILO and 1256-57
 international organization and 792-93, 798-99, 802, 805, 807, 810, 814-17
 leadership in international organizations 1446
 League of Nations and 819
 territories, Pacific trusteeship system and 1375-77
 UN and 708, 734, 788-91, 794-97, 800-801, 803-4, 806, 808-9, 811-13, 820-21
 UNESCO and 1267-68
 World Court and 817-18
Universal Postal Union (UPU) 1059, 1117
 periodical 160
University Consortium for World Order Studies, fellowship 360
Upper Silesia, mandate and 1343
UPU. See Universal Postal Union
Uruguay, UN and 822
USSR
 ILO and 1258-59
 UN and 781-87

V

Viet Nam, UN and 914-15
Voting procedures
 general 622, 624
 League of Nations 622-23
 UN 622, 624-28

W

War Prevention 826. See also Peace-keeping
Washington Conference 871-72
Waterways, law of 1036-45
Western Europe, UN and 728-29. See also Austria, UN and; Belgium, UN and; The Commonwealth, UN and; Denmark, UN and; Greece, UN and; Italy, UN and; Scandanavia, UN and; Spain, UN and; Sweden, UN and; Switzerland, UN and; United Kingdom, UN and; West Germany, UN and
West Germany, UN and 823-24
White House Conference on International Cooperation 799
WHO. See World Health Organization
WMO. See World Meteorological Organization
Woodrow Wilson International Center for Scholars, fellowships 360
World Bank 1086, 1092, 1116-17, 1188-203. See also International monetary system
World Court. See International Court of Justice; Permanent Court of International Justice
World government 1523-30
World Law Fund 339
World Health Organization (WHO) 1117
 bibliography 75
 documents 286
 guides to publications 90, 91
 history 1213-21
 periodicals 161-62
World Meteorological Organization (WMO), guides to publications 92
World peace 1444, 1447, 1449, 1453, 1455, 1457, 1460, 1462, 1492-1514
 bibliography 114-18
 factfinding to maintain 916
 journal 174, 178-84, 187-89
 UN role 827-34
 See also Collective security; Peacekeeping; War prevention
World Peace Foundation 340
World politics
 journals 176-77
 UN and 694-709
 UNESCO and 1265a

Y

Yearbooks
 general 190-91
 international law 193, 207-19
 international organizations 192-206

Ref
Z
6464
I6
A74